Critical Citizens for an Intercultural World

Languages for Intercultural Communication and Education
Editors: Michael Byram, *University of Durham, UK* and Alison Phipps, *University of Glasgow, UK*

The overall aim of this series is to publish books which will ultimately inform learning and teaching, but whose primary focus is on the analysis of intercultural relationships, whether in textual form or in people's experience. There will also be books which deal directly with pedagogy, with the relationships between language learning and cultural learning, between processes inside the classroom and beyond. They will all have in common a concern with the relationship between language and culture, and the development of intercultural communicative competence.

Other Books in the Series
Developing Intercultural Competence in Practice
  Michael Byram, Adam Nichols and David Stevens (eds)
Intercultural Experience and Education
  Geof Alred, Michael Byram and Mike Fleming (eds)

Other Books of Interest
Foreign Language and Culture Learning from a Dialogic Perspective
  Carol Morgan and Albane Cain
The Good Language Learner
  N. Naiman, M. Fröhlich, H.H. Stern and A. Todesco
Language, Culture and Communication in Contemporary Europe
  Charlotte Hoffman (ed.)
Language Learners as Ethnographers
  Celia Roberts, Michael Byram, Ana Barro, Shirley Jordan and Brian Street
Language Teachers, Politics and Cultures
  Michael Byram and Karen Risager
Motivating Language Learners
  Gary N. Chambers
New Perspectives on Teaching and Learning Modern Languages
  Simon Green (ed.)
Teaching and Assessing Intercultural Communicative Competence
  Michael Byram

**Please contact us for the latest book information:
Multilingual Matters, Frankfurt Lodge, Clevedon Hall,
Victoria Road, Clevedon, BS21 7HH, England
http://www.multilingual-matters.com**

LANGUAGES FOR INTERCULTURAL COMMUNICATION
AND EDUCATION 3
Series Editors: **Michael Byram and Alison Phipps**

Critical Citizens for an Intercultural World
Foreign Language Education as Cultural Politics

Manuela Guilherme

MULTILINGUAL MATTERS LTD
Clevedon • Buffalo • Toronto • Sydney

This book is dedicated to my sons,
Miguel and João

Library of Congress Cataloging in Publication Data
Guilherme, Manuela
Critical Citizens for an Intercultural World: Foreign Language Education as Cultural Politics/Manuela Guilherme.
Languages for Intercultural Communication and Education: 3.
Includes bibliographical references and index.
1. Critical pedagogy. 2. Multicultural education. 3. Languages, Modern–Study and teaching. I. Title. Series.
LC196.G85 2002
418'.0071–dc21   2002026343

British Library Cataloguing in Publication Data
A catalogue entry for this book is available from the British Library.

ISBN 1-85359-610-8 (hbk)
ISBN 1-85359-609-4 (pbk)

Multilingual Matters Ltd
UK: Frankfurt Lodge, Clevedon Hall, Victoria Road, Clevedon BS21 7HH.
USA: UTP, 2250 Military Road, Tonawanda, NY 14150, USA.
Canada: UTP, 5201 Dufferin Street, North York, Ontario M3H 5T8, Canada.
Australia: Footprint Books, PO Box 418, Church Point, NSW 2103, Australia.

Copyright © 2002 Manuela Guilherme.

All rights reserved. No part of this work may be reproduced in any form or by any means without permission in writing from the publisher.

Contents

Series Editors' Preface vii
Preface ix
Acknowledgements xiii

    Introduction 1
        Meeting Change: An Educational Challenge 1
        Educational Counterpoints to Critical Pedagogy 5

1 Critical Pedagogy as Cultural Politics 17
    Critical Pedagogy as Cultural Politics 20
    The Roots of Critical Pedagogy 22
    Critical Pedagogy: A Language of Critique and
        Possibility 34
    The Critique of Critical Pedagogy 57
    Conclusion 61

2 Philosophical Foundations for Critical Cultural Awareness 63
    Critical Theory 63
    Postmodernism 90
    Conclusion 118

3 The Critical Dimension in Foreign Culture Education 121
    Principles Suggested for Foreign Culture Education 121
    The 'Intercultural Speaker' and the Question of
        Cultural Identity 124
    The Critical Dimension in Models for Intercultural
        Communicative Competence 132
    The Critical Dimension in Reference Documents 146
    The Political Dimension of Foreign Language/Culture
        Education 154
    Conclusion 167

4 Teachers' Voices: Critical Cultural Awareness in EFL
   Classes in Portugal 170
      Methodology 172
      Teaching Culture Critically in Foreign Language
         Classes 174
      Defining a Critical Approach to Foreign Cultures 177
      Educating Critical Citizens 190
      Conclusion 202

5 Preparing Critical Citizens and Educators for an
   Intercultural World 206
      A Multiple-Perspective Approach 207
      An Interdisciplinary Approach 208
      A Critical Approach 219
      The Agenda for Foreign Language/Culture Education 224

Bibliography 227

Appendix 1 Questionnaire 253
Appendix 2 *Questionário* A 265
Appendix 3 *Questionário* B 274
Appendix 4 Statistical Results of the Questionnaires A and B 284
Appendix 5 Interview Guide for Focus-Group 291
Appendix 6 Questions for American Teacher Trainers 293

Index 294

Series Editors' Preface

It has become a commonplace to describe the world as a village, to call for better cross-cultural communication and greater social harmony and tolerance. The authors of the UNESCO report *Learning: The Treasure Within* called for more emphasis on 'learning to live together', as well as on 'learning to know', the traditional purpose of education. Learning to live together involves the ability to understand each other, to communicate, to interact with others. Language and intercultural education has a significant role to play, and a key purpose of this series is to encourage the study of languages and cultures in ways which can ultimately enrich practice.

This book is, in our view, an important contribution to the field of critical cultural awareness in Languages, Intercultural Communication and Education. It argues powerfully and with impressive theoretical and empirical rigour for the placing of critical and political cultural issues at the heart of learning and teaching. Guilherme's work is not content with functionalist views of language teaching or with serving the needs of dominant ideologies. In imaginative ways she carves out a space for resistance and for creative practice in the work of educating others and ourselves to learn to live together, to know and to be.

This book is one of a series which includes books that describe and analyse successful practice within and beyond the walls of the conventional classroom, and which also includes books that develop new theory, critique existing models and explore new combinations of disciplines. There are many different and innovative ways of contributing to the field of Languages, Intercultural Communication and Education. Consequently, both monographs and edited volumes of conceptual theorising and/or empirical studies are within our scope. It is essential that education and the variegated academic fields of modern languages and cultures respond to and provoke change in an imaginative way, and Multilingual

Matters has provided us and our contributors with an opportunity to explore linguistic and cultural experience and education from many different angles.

Alison Phipps and Michael Byram

Preface

It is difficult to think of a time in history when education was viewed as a more significant enabling social, political and cultural force than at the end of the twentieth and the dawning of the twenty-first century. In this time period, education has become the key platform issue for politicians at the local, national and international level, and has become the promise of tomorrow for those who continue to pursue the dream of global justice and responsible social action. Political slogans such as 'education for critical consciousness' (Freire, 1973), 'education as cultural politics' (Giroux), and more pertinent to the thesis of this work, 'language teachers, politics and cultures' (Byram & Risager, 1999) started to surface prior to and during the Civil Rights movement in the United States, and led to education being referred to today as the 'Civil Rights issue of our times'. Perhaps even more relevant, is the fact that within the field of education, a new paradigm for practice has evolved that focuses on culturally responsive teaching and challenges mainstream ethnocentrism and hegemony. Within this paradigm shift in education a heightened awareness of the roles of language, communication and critical cultural awareness has emerged as important issues in the foreign language curriculum. The relationship between language, culture and politics also has called the attention of all educators, but particularly foreign language and culture educators, who must define and redefine their practices within this new educational landscape.

The hypothesis set forth in this publication that critical cultural awareness is a most desirable goal for foreign language education, and that the foreign language curriculum needs to take on a more critical dimension in both its content and instruction practices, challenges every language and culture educator to play a much more pro-active role in the creation of a critically aware and reflective citizenry for the future. This work successfully argues and illustrates with both empirical data and qualitative examples, how the language and culture curriculum, if developed and taught from a critical cultural perspective, is perhaps the most suitable area of the curriculum to develop citizens who are critically and socially responsible inhabitants of the planet. By exploring the main philosophical, political, literary and social movements (Critical Theory, Postmodernism, neo-Marxism, Cultural Studies, etc.) and their manifestation on educational theories, the author investigates the context in which education, but more specifically, foreign language and culture education, has been operating during this same period of time in ways that have not been explored before. More importantly, this work also outlines a course of action for realising the vision in international discourse for at least the past three decades, of having education play the role of 'transformative agent' and bringing about the desirable political, social, educational and cultural outcomes of a more democratic word society. Calling on language and culture educators to take the lead in this effort, the author makes a compelling argument for these educators to view themselves as the political and cultural workers that they are, and to make this notion an explicit element of their mission and practices. Drawing on the established belief that 'schools can make a change' (Fullan, 1993) and that 'teachers are cultural workers' (Freire, 1998), the author proposes numerous educational initiatives ranging from curriculum development, to teacher preparation and continuous professional development for practising educators. In every case, she advocates for placing students, teachers and social and political issues at the centre of this developmental process in order to create dynamic educational contexts that both relate to and address students' and educators' diverse realities. Furthermore, the author successfully analyses the link between the teaching of language and culture and the political and social contexts in which they are taught. She argues that the language and culture curriculum needs to provide many more opportunities for critical social analysis and that the foreign language classroom might be a more suitable learning context to broach and discuss such issues as nationalism, racism, sexism, etc. Additionally, the concept of personal, social, political and linguistic identities is suggested as a relevant and indispensable topic of study and discussion for the foreign language and culture classroom and the use of a multicultural framework for framing and analysing the issues in question.

    The author further challenges language educators to introduce complex and increasingly sophisticated forms of analysis into their course syllabi, and to consider pedagogical practices that develop higher levels of critical understanding on the part of students and provide the basis for a foreign language curriculum that is active, political and transformative in nature. The author skilfully juxtaposes earlier concepts of critical theory with more contemporary intellectual arguments and begs for the development and inclusion of postmodernist and postcolonial discourse in the curriculum that address social relations of schooling, power, and the dominant canons of knowledge. In other words, the entire text calls upon language educators to argue for the foreign language curriculum to assume a much more prominent role, if not take centre stage, in the general school curriculum when it comes to discussing and improving racial and social relations and helping all students to acquire the knowledge, attitudes and critical social skills indispensable to successfully interact in inter-cultural situations and to take personal, social, and political action that will help make the world more democratic and just. Arguing that in the past an underlying set of assumptions or paradigms grounded in traditional Marxist and neo-Marxist thought dominated most areas of the curriculum, including foreign language, the author illustrates how students and teachers have been both subjected to and subjects of what we call education, or more specifically, foreign language and culture education. A compelling argument is made by the author to have educators, theorists and educational reformists re-examine their own assumptions and allow this 'generative process' become the basis of their professional practices.

This work is likely to provoke much discussion in the language teaching community, and as such, provide a fertile context for exploring further the role of critical cultural awareness in the overall foreign language curriculum. As such this book will have multiple levels of application. It is likely to become a fundamental reference for researchers in this area for it links a number of theories and ideas that had not been explicitly connected in this area up to this point. Several of the chapters, especially Chapters 4 and 5, will prove extremely beneficial for curriculum planners and policy makers in both establishing the goals and purposes of foreign language in the general curriculum, and in promoting general schooling goals such as developing culturally responsible and critically responsive citizens. Moreover, this publication has a definite key role in teacher education programs and in post-graduate courses for language educators and students of language and culture in general. And as a general academic contribution to the fields of critical pedagogy, critical reflection, and critical education in general, it offers numerous possibilities to those who toil in education with the goal of transforming current curriculum development and teaching practices in the area of foreign languages and cultures, and ultimately bring about the type of social and political reform that leads to a more democratic and just society for all.

Duarte M. Silva, Ed.D
Executive Director, California Foreign Language Project,
Stanford University School of Education, USA

Acknowledgements

First, I would like to express my deep gratitude to the editors who have made possible the publication of this book, especially to Dr Alison Phipps for her comments, suggestions and constant encouragement and availability. To Professor Michael Byram, University of Durham, the supervisor of my doctoral thesis that was the basis for this book, I am profoundly grateful for the attentiveness and thoroughness of his readings and corrections of my work. His advice has been invaluable and always available to me. His vision and calm reassurance will continue to play a significant role in my professional career. He has also provided me with the opportunity to take part in useful discussions with him and with other specialists and fellow researchers from all over the world, all of which has enriched my understanding of current theories in the field of foreign language/culture education. I also wish to thank all the staff at the School of Education at the University of Durham for their kind hospitality and helpfulness and, in particular, to Dr Keith Morrison for proof-reading my text on Critical Theory.

I am deeply grateful to Dr Duarte Silva, Executive Director of the *California Foreign Language Project* at Stanford University, California, for first introducing me to Critical Pedagogy and for giving me access to specialists and fellow researchers, to important resources and materials. I also owe him gratitude for proof-reading some of my texts and instruments of research, as well as for discussing with me the preliminary results of my empirical study. I am greatly indebted to him for his support throughout my research, especially during my study visits to Stanford. His vision and incentive were a source of inspiration throughout the conceptualisation and composition of this book and his friendship a source of energy. I would also like to acknowledge the assistance of his colleague, Dr Hyekyung Sung with the statistics (factor analysis).

I wish to acknowledge the co-operation of the Portuguese Ministry of Education in allowing me a year's sabbatical. Funding from the *Fundação para a Ciência e a Tecnologia* permitted me to study in England full-time for one year and the *Fundação Luso-Americana para o Desenvolvimento* awarded me grants to travel to Stanford University in the interests of my research.

My colleagues in the Portuguese education system who took part in the group and individual interviews and answered the questionnaires provided me with extremely interesting opinions and experiences upon which my observations and conclusions are based. I am especially thankful to them for sharing their time and ideas with me and for their valuable lessons in professionalism which were a source of motivation to pursue this study. I also wish to acknowledge the American professors who were so generous as to share their experiences and thoughts with me.

I am very grateful to Dr Claire Williams, University of Liverpool, for proof-reading the whole book, checking and improving my English, and for her continuous support and good-humoured friendship, all of which were a source of great strength. I also wish to thank Dr Helena Barbas and her daughter for helping me with their computer expertise.

My family and friends have helped and encouraged me throughout my research either by being patient with the whole process or by coming up with solutions for everyday difficulties, both of which are crucial for the accomplishment of such a project. The fact that my sons joined me during my stay in England and that my parents put up with our long absence deserves special attention. To my sons, Miguel and João, I express my heartfelt appreciation for their company and inspiration throughout this journey.

Finally, the colleagues with whom I have worked along my career have contributed to my experience as a teacher (and learner) of foreign languages/cultures, as have all the students I have had the pleasure to teach.

Introduction

Nowadays, educators of foreign languages and cultures, at all levels, have great challenges to face. There has recently been a renewed interest in teaching/learning about culture in foreign language classes, but this enterprise has encountered in its path new cultural, social, and political circumstances that required more than the mere acquisition of factual information and/or the pure formal analysis of literary passages. Political, economic, and cultural globalisation have meant greater mobility of citizens pursuing more stimulating education or work opportunities and greater access to a wider range of contacts, information and experiences, which have resulted in more options and, therefore, more competitiveness. Furthermore, a postindustrial, service-based economy requires a flexible and insightful workforce. Increasing links between nations and the growth in more complex multicultural societies demand the preparation of critical and committed citizens, capable of establishing personal and professional relationships across cultures in the search for individual and collective improvement and empowerment, at different levels.

Meeting Change: An Educational Challenge

In the last decades there have been two major topics in the political discourse with regard to education that have been evident to the general public and, especially, to educational policy makers and educators themselves. First, the importance of education for the development and improvement of our communities, be it the professional group, the social community, the nation or the global world. Second, the need for change in our educational systems in order to meet the challenges of change that we are facing in every field of our individual and collective lives.

During the 1960s, youth emerged as a 'public entity', demanding a voice and some terrain in the political, economic and social arenas. All of a sudden, young people became the main characters of contemporary history. By the late 1970s, there was some evidence that 'schools can make a difference' (Fullan, 1993: 2). The 1980s can be considered as the decade of major educational reforms. For example, in 1988, some European countries like Great Britain and Portugal started implementing nationwide reforms with newly designed curricula, which granted more administrative autonomy to schools. Meanwhile, in the United States 'restructuring', as referred to by Smyth, was the keyword:

> Marc Tucker (who was responsible for the Carnegie Report *A Nation Prepared*) called it a 'cultural transformation'. He described the difficulties of radically changing people's roles and likened it to the then Soviet Union. Gorbachev is trying to mobilise masses of people who have never had much control of their lives and aren't sure how to handle it when given the opportunity. The same thing has to occur in our schools. They call it perestroika. We call it 'restructuring'. (Smyth, 1995: 29)

One common feature of these policies was their grand scope. However, the grandness of the enterprise and the fact that it was implemented from the top downwards hindered its success. The problem seems to be that reforms are usually imposed upon schools, and particularly teachers and students, not made in collaboration with them. And this seems to be the reason why neither teachers nor students have effectively been mobilised and, as a result, only superficial changes have taken place in classroom practice. In general, what actually happens in day-to-day classes has stayed pretty much the same. Although content themes, textbooks and some pedagogic rituals may have changed, the overall quality has not been greatly improved despite a new emphasis on marking and examining for both students and teachers. In most cases, the latter have become more and more laden with bureaucratic tasks, a tactic which enables administrators to claim that they have improved the quality of teaching. With regard to higher education, Bassnett calls this tendency 'evaluationism'. She writes that academic life is now 'about demonstrating accountability, about teams of inspectors, about paperwork and bureaucracy' (Bassnett, 2001: 67).

The 1990s brought the acknowledgement that, despite these efforts, education was not working yet. On the whole, educational reforms, despite being grand, have not been broad enough to be 'part of a larger project for reconstituting a public culture that is democratic and socially just' (Giroux, 1994a: 123). Besides, they had not been able to motivate the main agents of school change locally. There was the feeling that the main agents of educational reform – teachers, students, administrators – had not understood the nature and the meaning of these school reforms they were implementing. There was, by the end of the decade, a feeling that governments had to concentrate on education, education and education. Tony Blair called it his 'passion' and some other European leaders embraced his enthusiasm!

Students themselves embody the change, they need to be guided, stimulated and to be given the conditions to let it blossom and flourish. The role for policy makers and administrators is to facilitate this by providing system reforms appropriate to the process. The teacher should be the creative and proficient escort. The fact that the teacher's role as a conceptual agent of educational change has been neglected in favour of being considered as its executor may well be considered as a major cause for the frequent failure of educational reforms. More and more often we come to the conclusion that 'educational change depends on what teachers do and think – it's as simple and as complex as that' (Fullan, 1991: 117). Therefore, higher education, both at undergraduate and postgraduate level, has a great responsibility in the process of educational change.

Educational change is both enticing and intimidating for everyone involved, because once it has taken off it will really transform our society and our lives. This may be the reason why policy makers have been too cautious and ended up contributing towards the perpetuation of the status quo and that may also be the reason why teachers have not been brave enough to take the plunge. So, for real change to happen, Fullan claims a change of mentality is needed:

> We need a different formulation to get at the heart of the problem, a different hill, so to speak. We need, in short, a new mindset about educational change ... Without such a shift of mind the insurmountable basic problem is the juxtaposition of a continuous *change theme* with a continuous *conservative system*. (Fullan, 1993: 3, his emphasis)

A shift of mind is indeed something that does not seem to have reached our schools on the whole. The major challenges educational systems have to face are the dynamics of change itself and the interaction between the local and the global, that is, to confront both diversity and universality at an incredible speed. A multiplicity of options are already available through multiple channels of communication. What Adorno and Horkheimer called the 'culture industry' has turned into what McLaren calls a 'predatory culture'. This author argues:

> Life is lived in a 'fun' way through speed technology in anticipation of recurring accidents of identity and endless discursive collisions with otherness because in predatory culture it is virtually impossible to be cotemporal with what one both observes and desires. (McLaren, 1995: 2)

Essential notions such as time, space and identity are being challenged. Boundaries between nations, cultures, languages, social classes, races, working communities or disciplines are becoming more complex and overlapping. Therefore, 'just as there are multiple layers to everyone's identity, there are multiple discourses of identity and multiple discourses of recognition to be negotiated' (The New London Group, 1996: 71). Education, in general, will not be able to avoid this trend and foreign language and culture education will definitely not. First, the social and political context for foreign language/culture teachers/students should be broader than the closer environment if they are not to take an ethnocentric 'We-versus-They' approach towards the languages/cultures they are teaching/learning. Second, if they take the above-mentioned changes into consideration, they will experience a change both of content and of perspective in their day-to-day activities. Foreign language/culture education will then have an important role in preparing pupils to cross borders – linguistic, cultural, social, political, racial – because 'border crossers', in Giroux's terminology, will be gifted citizens more capable of being socially and economically successful (Giroux, 1992).

On the other hand, educational agents should not deal just with 'what it is' but also with 'what it can be'. The transformative potential of schools towards society is a new element that educational thought in the 1980s and 1990s has reintroduced into the arena. Either presented as 'resistance' (Aronowitz & Giroux, 1986; Giroux, 1983; Giroux & McLaren 1994; Kanpol, 1994; McLaren, 1995), as 'possibility' (Giroux, 1992, 1997b), as 'hope' (Freire, 1993), or as 'utopia' (Gadotti, 1996) it aims at promoting change rather than merely following it or adjusting to it.

As we shall see, some educational movements, such as Progressivism (Dewey) and Reconstructionism (Counts, Rugg and Brameld), tried early in the twentieth century to invigorate the notion of the school having a social and political purpose. However, the enlightenment models of schools that were supposed to mirror, assist and fit the structure of an existing class-based society have predominated. Although selection gradually evolved from being based almost exclusively on class lines to become more permissive in recognition of individual achievement, it still had to conform to established patterns according to class-based standards.

It is also fundamental that higher education and teacher development programmes aimed at foreign language/culture teachers explicitly relate their practices to philosophical and educational theoretical frameworks so that teachers become aware of which potential trends they may choose from to inspire their practices. Besides the pedagogical implications of their choices, these will also determine the social and political meanings of the educational process. Moreover, the teachers' awareness of the essence of their everyday teaching practices will not only legitimate these but it will also enable them to make more sense of the purposes of their own and their students' learning. Therefore, the study of the critical dimension in foreign language/culture education will here be put in context both in philosophical terms, within Critical Theory and Postmodernism, and in educational terms, within Critical Pedagogy.

Educational Counterpoints to Critical Pedagogy

Before introducing Critical Pedagogy and in order to outline a proposal for its definition, it seems useful to present some educational standpoints that may be viewed as opposing Critical Pedagogy. The model of the modern school portrays the main tendencies that have been dominant in educational theory, policy and practice, namely, (a) the conservative; (b) the liberal; (c) the humanistic; and (d) the radical. However different and even contradictory they may be, they also share certain features characteristic of the enlightenment project. This outcome is not unexpected since 'education is very much the dutiful child of the Enlightenment ...' (Usher & Edwards, 1994: 24). These tendencies thus have a positivist view of knowledge, that is, to a greater or lesser extent they do not question the ideal of objectivity, the transmission of grand texts, the instrumentality of knowledge to technological and industrial progress, or the standardisation of knowledge. The conservative, liberal and radical pedagogies venerate reason and emancipation through progress, while the humanistic ones put less emphasis on these aspects. The conservative, liberal and humanistic pedagogies promote individual freedom and uphold ideals of harmony and unity, while the radical ones accentuate the struggle among socio-economic classes. Knowledge, however, is viewed by all as a transcendental neutral vantage point, stripped of its critical possibilities.

Conservative pedagogies

Neoconservative images of education policies are linked to particular governments such as those of Thatcher/Major in Great Britain and

Reagan/Bush in the United States. The discourse of excellence has dominated neoconservative approaches to education, for schooling is used as an instrument for economic growth. It is nonetheless reproductive of existing social forms, as Giroux and McLaren point out:

> Within this view of excellence, learning is linked to acquiring 'the basics' and uncritically adopting values consistent with industrial discipline and social conformity. (Giroux & McLaren, 1989: xvii)

There is a canon of knowledge to be transmitted, which is considered as a form of textual authority, a kind of transhistorical truth, which is predefined and whose meanings are stable and unproblematic (Aronowitz & Giroux, 1991; Giroux, 1992). Culture tends to be uniform, eurocentric, according to a western tradition of high culture which constitutes 'cultural capital' that is the only one valued and reinforced by schools independent of the students' social and cultural background (Bourdieu & Passeron, 1977).

Teachers are supposed to be reliable and rigorous executors of preestablished hegemonic syllabi. This is 'the pedagogy of *coverage*. We have to *cover* this now. We have to *cover* that, next' (Wink, 1997: 151). Although the educational system is inclusive in that it allows everybody to attend school, it is still the school's job to select and exclude through testing and examining. The evaluation criteria are based on stereotypical and unified notions of intelligence, a common core of values, and there is a strong sense of 'deviance' when any sort of boundary is crossed (Gardner, 1983; Kanpol, 1994). Learning here is training rather than development.

The school is expected to fulfil economic, social and political roles, namely: (a) to select and prepare competent workers to take predetermined positions in a clearly divided and hierarchical labour structure; (b) to form individuals that will be guardians of the existing social order, moral authority and institutional organisations; (c) to train disciplined and obedient citizens. Neoconservative systems of education have not, however, put into doubt their mission of preparing free thinkers for a free democratic society. Nevertheless, this is understood to mean that citizens are prepared to integrate into it rather than transform it:

> It is important to remember that . . . democracy loses its once dynamic nature and is reduced to a set of inherited principles and institutional arrangements that teach students how to adapt to rather than question the basic precepts of society. (Aronowitz & Giroux, 1991: 187).

A critical spirit is, therefore, not within the scope of neoconservative pedagogies, or if it is considered, it should lead to the exclusion of whatever disrupts this reproductive process and consequently to the imposition of the dominant model.

Liberal pedagogies

Liberal pedagogies differ from neoconservative ones mainly in that they require the educational system to be more dynamic in the sense that it must adapt to the evolution of society and respond to the needs of economic growth. Schools exist to provide students with the prerequisites necessary for their performance in the labour market and for their social mobility. The educational system must be a *'social efficiency system*, a byproduct of a growing industrialized and bureaucratized society' (Kanpol, 1997: 6). According to this current of thought, schools are little more than sites for instruction.

The philosophical, social and political subject is the individual who is the source of all actions: a unified, stable and transparent subject. Knowledge is objective, value-free and depoliticised. Culture is consensual and the result of historical agreement. Schools are innocent transmitters of a body of technical knowledge and information (Giroux, 1994a; Giroux & McLaren, 1994). Teachers are required to master effective teaching techniques. Students are expected to be individual achievers.

Modern schools should, however, contribute to public as well as personal development. There is a commitment to individual emancipation and to communal improvement, to democracy, to scientific progress and to change. Justice is supposed to be ensured by the application of laws and accurate selection procedures guarantee the establishment of a meritocracy. Both the rights of the individual and of the society are protected and schools are institutions devoted to reinforcing democracy understood as social order (Choi, 1995; Kanpol, 1994).

Humanistic pedagogies

Unlike liberal pedagogies, humanistic reforms, of which the Summerhill[1] experience is a good example, aim at humanising schooling, not at promoting economic progress. Their action is situated at the micro level not at the macro level, thus social change is a goal to be obtained through individual self-fulfilment. Due to an emphasis on individual freedom there is more autonomy in the learning process, which becomes more reflective as a consequence. The school hierarchy is less rigid, so teacher–pupil interaction is more egalitarian and collaborative. Nevertheless, individual action is still the centre of the educational process, school is not politically involved, knowledge is based on a canon of high culture information and truth is there to be looked for (Choi, 1995; Giroux, 1992, 1994a).

Both the individual and knowledge are 'givens' and attention to the process of their construction and interaction is often neglected. Social and personal change happens as a natural consequence of the learning event. There is no collision or instability. The social order is accepted and perpetuated and the 'cultural capital' unconsciously reproduced. Usher and Edwards state the issue clearly:

> Yet to cling to the autonomous subject of humanistic discourse, to accept the constructed subject of this discourse as 'natural' rather than constructed, to refuse to question it by rejecting any alternative which suggests that the subject may be constructed from sources outside itself is to remain trapped within an agency/determination dualism and the futile choice between the two. (Usher & Edwards, 1994: 29)

Agency, as viewed by humanistic pedagogies, does not involve change but instead healing social wounds. The choice between agency and determination does not make sense here since the concept of agency is limited by that of determination. The context is constructed but not susceptible to deconstruction. Humanistic school discourse is also very much linked to multicultural education and to schools situated in areas of economic deterioration and as such it should be problematised. In these fields it connects with humanitarian concerns and attitudes of cultural tolerance. Despite the respectful and self-abnegating disposition of most professionals who deal with these school populations, there are still risks to be avoided. A humanistic discourse can turn into a patronising and colonising one if the Other – in terms of social class or ethnicity or both – is not seen as a social and cultural equal. Dialogue may turn into compassionate or 'middle-class narcissistic' monologue and tolerance may become a 'courteous, thoughtful way of accepting, of *tolerating*, . . . a civilised way of permitting a coexistence . . .' (Freire, 1998: ix, 42).

Radical pedagogies

Radical pedagogies are in some way or other related to neo-Marxist theories of education. Accordingly, the educational system is regarded through a macroanalysis of the influence of society on the school. Society is seen through an economic lens that determines all relationships in terms of socio-economic class and school is seen as reflecting this enveloping structure. This is a deterministic view of the schooling process, since school failure is to be solved through the transformation of the outside socio-economic organisation. Consequently, neo-Marxists are generally suspicious of educational reforms.

Radical pedagogies view schools mostly as institutions which inevitably reproduce the economic, social and cultural matrices of the capitalist societies and those matrices are seen as homogeneous and static (Aronowitz & Giroux, 1986). According to their belief, most school failure is explained by a lower socio-economic status since subordinated relationships are produced and reproduced at school, which is part of an unavoidable vicious circle of submission, poverty and misfortune.

Although neo-Marxist approaches to education underestimate the human capacity for counteragency inside schools, they have the merit of having focused on the political character of schooling. The notion of the 'hidden curriculum' put forth by Jackson (1968) and later expanded by Bowles and Gintis (1976) and also by Apple (1979) is important to the comprehension of the subtle but overwhelming pressure that society imposes on school life. The 'hidden curriculum' which consists of 'the norms and values that are implicitly, but effectively, taught in schools and that are not usually talked about in teachers' statements of ends or goals' (Apple, 1979: 84) is differently understood by the above-mentioned researchers. While Jackson introduced this idea having mostly social expectations in mind, Apple tried to reconcile a more cultural approach with Bowles and Gintis' political one:

> Now what that meant was that I had to support the antiliberal positions of people like Bowles and Gintis in *Schooling in Capitalist America* ... For them, if you understand the hidden curriculum, you understand schooling, and the only way to understand it is to actually compare children by class trajectories. While I was a bit uncomfortable with this because of its 'teacher bashing,' its unsubtle sense of culture, of the complexities of human experience, I wanted to support it because it seemed to me that it was at least an attempt at politicizing a tradition and destabilizing the more conservative and reformist liberal tradition. (Apple, 1993: 168)

The basic message of radical theories is that the school is consciously or unconsciously used for the reproduction of the socio-economic order of capitalist societies. Aronowitz and Giroux identified three dimensions of the reproduction model of schooling: (a) the economic-reproductive model; (b) the cultural-reproductive model; and (c) the hegemonic-state reproductive model (Aronowitz & Giroux, 1986).

The economic-reproductive model focuses on the link between economy and education or, more precisely, between the school and the workplace. According to this model the school reproduces and reinforces the technical and hierarchical division of labour and wealth. The cultural-reproductive model has been developed mostly by authors like Apple and Bourdieu who have come to think of culture and school as autonomous, despite its intrinsic relationship with social and economic power (Aronowitz & Giroux, 1986). Positions of domination and subordination in society generate specific subcultures which, overtly or covertly, reach a confrontation at school, through 'symbolic violence' (Bourdieu & Passeron, 1977) and the 'hidden curriculum' (Apple, 1979). Dominant 'cultural capital' plays an important role at school and relates with power in such a way that it perpetuates social inequality (Bourdieu & Passeron, 1977).

The hegemonic-state reproductive model is more concerned with the intervention of the state in the educational system. The state is not considered as a neutral institution standing above the struggles for domination in society and impartially administering education. It is recognised as being politically vitiated and permeated by sectarian dominant influences. These theories rely on the concept of 'hegemony', identified by Gramsci, that explains political life as an attempt to attain and keep power through a linear operation of persuasion, consensus and consent (Gramsci, 1971, 1974). This model takes a macrodimensional perspective on the relation between politics and education and explains the relation between the state and the school as an exercise of intellectual leadership indirectly put into action by the ruling classes.

Even though the reproductive theories of education have put the focus on different and very important aspects of the tensions that the school has to work with and despite the fact that these theories have evolved and become more and more sophisticated, there are some vital flaws in them. These may be summed up by Giroux's statement that they have theorised primarily *about* schools rather than *for* schools and, therefore, 'radical educators have abandoned the language of possibility for the language of critique' (Giroux & McLaren, 1989: 130). This means that they have missed the school's potential for democratic intervention, they have failed to develop a 'theory of ethics' that might justify such intervention and they have not attempted to redescribe the role teachers might play within such a public project.

Aronowitz and Giroux distinguished yet another model among radical theories of education that constitutes a significant advance on the reproductive models, which they 'generously call neo-Marxist theories of resistance' (Aronowitz & Giroux, 1986: 73). These theories accentuate culture and cultural production but they overemphasise the ideological aspect of this production. By politicising the notion of culture, by denouncing the ideological nature of the curriculum and by alerting teachers to the interests that underlie the contents and materials they are provided with, these theories have shown the connection between the political network and school routines. However, school life is characterised in absolute terms of ideological domination. Aronowitz and Giroux consider that, among other weaknesses, these theories do not pay enough attention to questions of gender and race or to the development of the individual personality under the conditions of cultural domination, in spite of their concern about cultural production. And they conclude:

> These models of critique are important in a twofold sense. First, they illustrate critical approaches to unraveling the relationship between schools and social control. Second, they constitute a starting point for recognizing the theoretical limitations that underlie this form of criticism and the need to move beyond it in the quest for a more comprehensive critical theory of pedagogy. (Aronowitz & Giroux, 1986: 149)

Each of the above-mentioned pedagogical theories have contributed significantly to the development of Critical Pedagogy since its theory and practice have emerged in education via constant debate, negotiation, and even confrontation with them. Although Critical Pedagogy is often in conflict with its predecessors, it would be impossible to define it without relating it to them.

The new sociology of education

The trend that is generally known as 'The New Sociology of Education' consists of the development of sociological studies on education focused at the micro level, that is, the school itself, mainly the school curricula and the teaching or educational practices. The British sociology of education was very much influenced in its beginnings by the work of the London School of Economics and the Centre for Contemporary Cultural Studies in Birmingham.[2] It is best known for the work of Young and Bernstein, especially the publication of *Knowledge and Control* in 1971. Their work was corroborated by Bourdieu's, in France, and Apple's, in the United States. In Great Britain, the expansion of this trend was taken over by colleges of education, with the primacy of the London Institute of Education and the Open University (Ball, 1995; Banks, 1982; Bates, 1980).

As far as the United States is concerned, the role of sociology in education has been constituted mostly by empirical–analytic and applied policy studies. In other words, there has been a lack of interpretative and critical approaches to curriculum, although there has been an increased level of interest in such types of studies. Most of the research has been concentrated on status issues related to social stratification and on classroom material, predominantly on the textbook (Apple, 1996b). Ethnographic and anthropological studies focusing on the performance of children from minority groups at school have proliferated in the last decades (Guilherme, 1994).

The New Sociology of Education has challenged the taken-for-granted premises of school knowledge and of school common practices. The sociological analysis of curricula contents and classroom procedures has been undertaken under the notion that reality and knowledge are socially constructed. However, the power of human agency may often have been overestimated due to an excessive emphasis on the microlevel dimension, although social agency within this scope has also been relevant.

Nevertheless, the sociology of education has continued to establish the link between knowledge and power. This also meant lessening the emphasis on technical rationality and on the notion of pedagogy as methodological refinement. Its main concerns have been the selection, stratification and evaluation of knowledge as well as the questions of status that also impregnate the social encounters in the classroom. Bernstein articulates his position in relation to Durkheim and Marx:

> Both Durkheim and Marx have shown that the structure of society's classifications and frames reveals both the distribution of power and the principles of social control. I hope to show, theoretically, that educational codes provide excellent opportunities for the study of classification and frames through which experience is given a distinctive form ... Irrespective of the question of the intrinsic logic of the various forms of public thought, the forms of their transmission, that is their classification and framing, are social facts. (Bernstein, 1971: 47, 49)

The focus of sociology of education lies on the interaction between teachers and students and the ways they articulate their different cultural backgrounds with the school curriculum and the construction of meaning within a network of power and control. Although these outside pressures are recognised, teachers and students play active roles. When the learning context is understood this way, school routines are not viewed as unproblematic, because there is an underlying conflict between being controlled and the need for agency, the limiting constraints and the urge for transformation. By undertaking such sociological, ethnographic and anthropological studies in schools which provide evidence of these forces at work in the classroom, the New Sociology of Education has played a role in education that is theoretical, practical and political as well. The results of these studies have yielded critical data to formulate new theories, inform pedagogical practices and establish effective policies.

Despite the lack of prescription for any broader political action, the New Sociology of Education aims at neutralising the forces of power inside the school environment through the transformation of educational practice (Bates, 1980). Young accounts for their urge:

> We are then led to ask questions about the context and definition of success and how they are legitimized. In other words, the methods of assessment, selection and organization of knowledge and the principles underlying them become our focus of study. The point is important because what is implied is that questions have to be raised about matters that have either not been considered important or have been tacitly accepted as 'given'. (Young, 1971: 25)

The political goal of sociology of education consists of questioning the status quo but within the limits of the school. By being aware that knowledge is not neutral by nature, that curriculum goals are not value-free and that assessment criteria are not self-evident, teachers and students may adopt a different attitude towards teaching and learning. To some extent, social relationships inside and outside the classroom are also taken into consideration and the significance of structural social inequalities is put into question in terms of who has access to the total benefits of education.

Critical Pedagogy shares most of the concerns of the New Sociology of Education and their perspectives on the micro levels of society, particularly those connected with the educational institutions, do overlap. Critical Pedagogy benefits from the questions set forth by the educational sociologists about the validation, selection and distribution of knowledge. Like the New Sociology of Education, Critical Pedagogy recognises the value of both the cognitive and social dimensions of schooling and it also emphasises the importance of analysing the political and cultural aspects of the curriculum. In sum, it can be stated that the above-mentioned precepts of the New Sociology of Education are also embraced by critical pedagogues. However, Critical Pedagogy reveals some differences in scope, in theory, and in practice, as we shall see in the next chapter.

It is by basing its focus on the premises of Critical Pedagogy that the present study approaches the development of 'critical cultural awareness' in foreign language and culture education, a term borrowed from Byram, Morgan et al. (1994). The concept may be applied to the study of foreign cultures in language and cultural studies courses, both in secondary and higher education. This book aims to define the meaning and purpose of critical cultural awareness and, ultimately, to identify the specific needs of prospective and practising teachers, as far as teacher education and professional development programmes in this area are concerned. It attempts to accomplish these aims through three stages: (a) by developing a theory of critical cultural awareness based on Critical Pedagogy, with close reference to both Critical Theory and Postmodernism; (b) by examining the critical dimension in some documents and models used worldwide as references for foreign language/culture education; and (c) by investigating what teachers' concepts of critical cultural awareness are, in a case study in Portugal where the English national syllabus for secondary school students suggests a critical interpretation of the cultural content without providing a definition for it.

Accordingly, Chapter 1 concentrates on Critical Pedagogy viewed as the educational backdrop for the promotion of critical cultural awareness in foreign language/culture education. A number of strategies recommended by Critical Pedagogy, namely reflection, dissent, difference, dialogue, empowerment, action, and hope, which may contribute decisively towards a critical approach to foreign cultures, are identified and discussed in this chapter. Nonetheless, Critical Pedagogy has undergone criticism and does involve risks that are pointed out in this chapter. There is also a brief description of its original sources: philosophical schools of thought, like Critical Theory and Postmodernism, educational movements like Progressivism, with special reference to Dewey, and Reconstructionism, as well as Cultural Studies. Paulo Freire is singled out for his important role as the founder of Critical Pedagogy and Henry Giroux is also abundantly quoted as one of the main post-Freirean theoreticians of Critical Pedagogy. Both philosophical reference-points for Critical Pedagogy, namely Critical Theory and Postmodernism, are the object of particular attention in Chapter 2. They are examined separately and, since neither of them is monolithic, different aspects within each of these philosophical schools of thought are itemised and explored in relation to critical cultural awareness. Critical Theory puts forward a distinctive type of rationality that is critical, intersubjective and understood as emancipatory. However, Horkheimer and Adorno place it within social tensions while Habermas emphasises communicative rationality that aims for consensus, a main topic of discussion in this chapter. In addition, critical theorists, mainly Horkheimer, Adorno and Marcuse, highlight the threat of the 'culture industry' produced by the media boom. This critique was expanded and radicalised by the so-called postmodernists, who also undertook the dismantling of the traditional epistemological canon, of scientific logic, of technological rationale and of the status quo in general. Notions like 'meta-narrative', *'différend'*, 'deconstruction', *'différance'*, 'simulation', 'technologies of power', and 'solidarity' are borrowed from acknowledged postmodernists and introduced to this study in relation to the adoption of a critical perspective on culture and on citizenship.

Chapter 3 applies the theoretical frameworks described in the previous chapters more specifically to foreign language/culture education. First, it provides a summary of the principles drawn from the above-mentioned theoretical backgrounds and discusses their application to issues of identity concerning the definition of the *critical* 'intercultural speaker' viewed as an ideal to be achieved through foreign language/culture education. Second, it examines the critical dimension, in the light of the principles previously set down, of widely used models for teaching/learning foreign languages/cultures formulated by authors like Kramsch, Byram, Pennycook, and others, in the *Common European Framework* by the Council of Europe, and in the *Standards for Foreign Language Learning* which is a national reference for teachers in the United States. Finally, the chapter argues for the political nature of foreign language/culture education and focuses on the relationship between this and citizenship education.

Chapter 4 then introduces a case study carried out among secondary school teachers of English in mainland Portugal. They are mandated by the national syllabus to undertake 'a critical interpretation' of cultural content. This chapter gives an account of the methods used for collecting data, namely questionnaires, focus-groups and a number of individual interviews. Finally, the organisation, validity, and reliability of the data collection and analysis are discussed. The results of the analysis of both quantitative and qualitative data are presented using an integrative approach. This description begins with an overview of the general attitude of participants towards the inclusion of culture in the foreign language curriculum and the implementation of a critical approach to it, continues with attempts at defining what a critical approach to foreign culture means, and implies and concludes by making a link between the promotion of critical cultural awareness and citizenship education.

Chapter 5 draws from the findings of this study and the tenets put forward in the previous chapters through the discussion of theories, models, and documents, and suggests some guidelines for the critical study of foreign cultures. First, a *multiple-perspective approach* integrates critical cultural awareness within a comprehensive framework of Human Rights Education and Education for Democratic Citizenship by referring to contradictory philosophical worldviews. This problematises essential and dominant concepts in the field. Second, in foreign language and/or culture education, an *interdisciplinary approach* refers to three main interdisciplinary areas, namely Cultural Studies, Intercultural Communication, and Critical Pedagogy, which are interactive and themselves contain various disciplinary and subdisciplinary fields. Third, a *critical approach* includes a set of 'operations' which work at and across different levels, more precisely, at the local, national and global levels as well as across different beliefs, values, and attitudes. These operations are to be defined and problematised with reference to the theoretical arguments introduced in the previous chapters.

Notes

1. The Summerhill School was founded in the United Kingdom in 1921. It is an international school since only a third of its students come from the United Kingdom, a third from Japan and the rest from all over the world. Lessons are optional and school's rules are agreed upon in weekly meetings where each pupil's vote is as powerful as a member of staff's. The school works like a community where harmony and freedom are the main goals.
2. The work of Raymond Williams and Stuart Hall, the leading theorists of the Birmingham School, will be referred to extensively throughout this book in recognition of the importance of their ideas in the domains of culture, identity, ethnicity, and intercultural relations.

Chapter 1
Critical Pedagogy as Cultural Politics

Critical Pedagogy provides the educational backdrop for the development of critical cultural awareness in foreign language/culture education. Although, according to Pennycook, 'critical approaches to TESOL should [not] be assumed to be critical pedagogy applied to TESOL' (Pennycook, 1999: 341), Critical Pedagogy presents important guidelines for an understanding of pedagogy as cultural politics. It therefore offers stimulating paths towards showing a possible cultural and political role of foreign language/culture education in contemporary societies both nationally and internationally. For this purpose, Critical Pedagogy supplies us with some pedagogical perspectives and processes, that will be expanded upon later, namely reflection, dissent, difference, dialogue, empowerment, action and hope, that are to be considered tools for a critical approach to foreign languages/cultures. These notions, when implemented within the scope of foreign language/culture education, acquire particular meanings that invest our tasks with definite cultural and political purposes.

The multiple, flexible and eclectic nature of Critical Pedagogy (CP) makes the often simple task of labelling, defining, or describing it very complex. First, it is defined as a pedagogy rather than a teaching method. It should not be considered as such because teaching has often been understood as transmission of knowledge, and method, in this case, as mastery of teaching techniques. The reason why the term pedagogy is adopted here is not, as implied by Apple with regard to CP, for 'linguistic elegance' or due to an attempt to change the general opinion that 'teaching is seen as a low-status occupation' (Apple, 1996b: 141, 142). Instead, CP is a pedagogy that includes teaching understood as part of the teaching/learning process viewed as the dialectical and dialogical reproduction and production of knowledge. It is a pedagogy since it 'refers to the process by which teachers and students negotiate and produce meaning' (McLaren, 1995: 34). Furthermore, pedagogy is a broader term that implies a project, one that takes place at school but that does not end within its physical limits. It consists of a reinterpretation of previous and ongoing experiences and it entails a vision for the present and for the future, that is, it has a political purpose for social transformation. The point where pedagogy detaches from teaching is well illuminated by Simon:

> To me 'pedagogy' is a more complex and extensive term than 'teaching,' referring to the integration in practice of particular curriculum content and design, classroom strategies and techniques, and evaluation, purpose, and methods ... Together they organize a view of how a teacher's work within an institutional context specifies a particular version of what knowledge is most worth, what it means to know something, and how we might construct representations of ourselves, others, and our physical and social environment. In other words, talk about pedagogy is simultaneously talk about the details of what students and others might do together and the cultural politics such practices support. (Quoted in McLaren, 1995: 34–5)

Viewed in this light, pedagogy informs teaching by giving it meaning and purpose. Pedagogy is about cultural and political engagement and transforms teaching and learning into a form of cultural politics since it provides the opportunity for both teachers and students to construct their views of themselves and of the world in a proactive attitude that reaches beyond the interpretative endeavour.

Second, CP is described here as a movement because of it being an 'ever-evolving critical pedagogy' (Giroux, 1997b: xii) and of not being a monolithic body of theory or practice. Moreover, besides applying a 'language of critique' it also engages with a 'language of possibility' that aims towards democratic education and social improvement (Giroux, 1992). It may be regarded as an attempt at educational and social reform that starts from within the school.

Most proponents of CP have not given it a specific definition and they even advise their readers to be cautious about doing so 'because there is no generic definition that can be applied to the term' (Giroux, 1994a: 131). Giroux refuses to give simple prescriptions for a practice that would not be context-specific. However, he recognises common insights that permeate CP discourse and practice, that may be summed up as a special concern with culture, ethics, politics and their interconnectedness.

Culture in CP is viewed as crossing disciplinary boundaries and the hierarchical division between high and popular culture. Moreover, difference is an ever-present notion that accounts for the heterogeneity of cultural production and that problematises the relationship between cultural production and reproduction in our societies that are growing ever more ethnically diverse and, hopefully, more politically aware. CP meets the challenge of dealing with culture by 'bringing the laws of cultural representation face to face with their founding assumptions, contradictions, and paradoxes' (Giroux & McLaren, 1994: 216). The past, present and future constructions of individual and collective identities are brought into discussion in a critical and visionary way. CP questions dominant cultural patterns and seeks the reasons which lead to them being blindly accepted and unquestioned.

CP is a way of life. It probes deeply into our roles as teachers, students, citizens, human beings. This is the reason why it is impossible to give simple prescriptions about how to *do* CP: 'I doubt I can teach someone how to *do* critical pedagogy. We do not *do* critical pedagogy; we *live* it' (Wink, 1997: 103). This characteristic provides for a strong link between CP and ethics. The notion of ethics here is both observant of universal human rights and attentive to particular stories located in specific contexts:

> Ethics must be seen as a central concern of critical pedagogy. This suggests that educators should attempt to understand more fully how different discourses offer students diverse ethical referents for structuring their relationship to the wider society. But it also suggests that educators should go beyond the postmodern notion of understanding how student experiences are shaped within different ethical discourses ... Thus ethics is taken up as a struggle against inequality and as a discourse for expanding basic human rights. (Giroux, 1992: 74)

In relation to ethics, questions of human suffering, dignity and emancipation are worries central to CP. Within this framework, CP is closely connected with multicultural democratic citizenship education. It has to do with individual improvement, social solidarity and public responsibility. This concern for the public and the democratic process leads us to another important feature which is also often associated with critical pedagogies, the political dimension.

In his introduction to Giroux's well-known work, *Teachers as Intellectuals*, Freire explained in his straightforward manner that education and, by extension, CP is a political act. He states:

> I believe that central to a realizable critical pedagogy is the need to view schools as democratic public spheres. This means regarding schools as democratic sites dedicated to forms of self and social

empowerment. In these terms, schools are public places where students learn the knowledge and skills necessary to live in an authentic democracy. (Giroux, 1988: xxxii)

Through the production of knowledge, the training of skills, self and social development, the ultimate goal of schools should be to prepare empowered citizens to live in authentic democracies. This is not a humanitarian effort to accommodate subordinate cultures nor a political strategy to replace political forces, but an authentic movement to make, in Giroux's terms, the pedagogical more political and the political more pedagogical.

Despite the diversity of practices, which is itself encouraged by the literature on CP, and the various theories with which CP connects without entirely coinciding, there is, nevertheless, a consistent corpus of research on CP that is acknowledged by 'outsider' educational specialists as having provided 'the most systematic commentary on and reformulation of the contemporary educational situation' (Usher & Edwards, 1994: 219).

Critical Pedagogy as Cultural Politics

Schools are not only sites where knowledge is transmitted but also knowledge producing agencies. In this instance, it is indispensable to use pupils' experiences of their more restricted cultural circles, of the larger society into which they integrate, and of other cultures they come into contact with. In order to be productively critical about what they are learning, students need to make it meaningful first and this happens through the relationship they establish between what they know and what they have just come to know about. This process involves 'relearning' and 'unlearning' before it reaches 'learning' which means reinterpreting or even discrediting previous knowledge before coming to another temporary and incomplete stage of knowing (Wink, 1997). From this perspective, knowledge is not only 'accumulated capital' (Giroux, 1992: 98) and schools are not 'banking systems' as Freire described the process of accumulating received knowledge. Therefore, learning is not only about 'reading the word' but also about 'reading the world', to use Freire's words again:

> The reading of the word, also a function of a search for text comprehension and thus of the objects contained therein, directs us now to a previous reading of the world. I must make it clear that this reading of the world, which is based on sensory experience, is not enough. But on the other hand, it must not be dismissed as inferior

to the reading of the abstract world of concepts that proceeds from generalization to the tangible. (Freire, 1998: 19)

Accordingly, the cultural content of knowledge acquired at school identifies with the closer and broader premises of the students' lived experiences, although it should not be limited by them. Therefore, schooling is not only about what goes on in school, and schools are both instructional and cultural agencies. Through reflecting upon and speculating about their everyday observations and their significant incidents or discoveries, students learn about the complexity of social relationships, find out about the difference between appearance and reality, look for underlying normative frameworks that impose meanings, values and beliefs and recognise asymmetrical relations of power that determine the structure they are becoming more aware of (Giroux, 1981: 81). Thus, they will be more prepared to face the unexperienced and to develop intellectual capacities and social skills that will enable them to shape or reshape future experiences, to integrate and envisage social change, in sum, to empower themselves both in an affirmative and transformative way.

CP also redefines the link between theory and practice. Theory is not simply considered as preparation for practice, theory proceeds from practice, interrelates with it, informs and reforms practice, and vice-versa. As a result, it intervenes with ways of knowing and ways of living thus being a cultural enterprise as well as an educational one. CP deals with the relationship between the self, the others and the world and by leading the pupils to critically examine these relationships it makes them believe that they can make a difference and, in so doing, the pedagogical and the cultural become political too.

As far as CP is concerned, the political element in pedagogy does not mean indoctrination, although it is ideological in the sense that it is understood as political and it implies taking a position.[1] Furthermore, due to the critical and dialogical qualities of CP, it does not tend to be hegemonical either. The political here acquires a broader meaning that includes the whole network of social interactions as informed by the power relations underlying the tensions people have to deal with but of which they are only partly aware. Giroux is clear on this issue:

> In effect, as a form of cultural production, critical pedagogy becomes a critical referent for understanding how various practices in the circuit of power inscribe institutions, texts, and lived cultures in particular forms of social and moral regulation which presuppose particular visions of the past, present and future. (Giroux, 1992: 160)

To engage in CP as a form of cultural politics is, in short, to be committed to the task of preparing our students for critical and participatory citizenship. This entails expanding individual capacities and social opportunities to fully develop cultural, social and political identities within the narrow scope of their closer relationships or the wider contexts of national or transnational communities. Equally important is enabling our students, and by extension our citizens, to make informed choices about their lives and, above all, to make them aware that they are entitled to a choice.

In general terms, CP is a culture of politics since it involves advancing a public discourse on democracy and social justice and giving voice to those histories that have been marginalised or even silenced. Furthermore, it entails establishing a vision for a just society and striving for its realisation.

As a result of all that has been discussed above, CP implies a reformulation of the teacher's role into an intellectual and transformative one. Teachers themselves must be conceptually and critically engaged in the mission of empowering their pupils by empowering themselves. This notion provides for an informed praxis, by relating theory to practice and vice versa, and deepens their own commitment to democratic principles. By negotiating between the relativity of their own and their students' perspectives and universals which ensure human rights, they forge civic courage, social and political initiative.

The Roots of Critical Pedagogy

The foundation of CP cannot be attributed to one single theory. It results from an impressive and effective blend of elements from several theoretical standpoints reflecting CP theorists' intellectual journeys. With regard to its philosophical foundations, CP mainly adopts Critical Theory and Postmodernism, and, despite their different and, to some extent, irreconcilable theories, CP views them as complementary with respect to the understanding of culture and the functioning of radical democracy. As far as education is concerned, CP made use of the most progressive educational theories of the twentieth century in order to design its own version of pedagogy. Besides the ones already mentioned (the New Sociology of Education and, originally, radical pedagogies), CP was also inspired by Dewey's progressivism, the reconstructionists' theoretical insights into citizenship education and, most particularly, Freire's theory of education. Although CP owes most of its theoretical foundations to 'western-centred' philosophical and educational schools of thought, its main feature is its openness to different cultural frames of mind. This is due to many factors. Among them is the influence of postmodernism, with French poststructuralism at its core, which responds to an era of postmodernity when all sorts of borders, institutionalised by what in contrast is identified as modernity, are disrupted and which accounts for the 'decentring' perspective of CP. Furthermore, as we shall see, the vital role that Freire's thought plays in CP, bearing in mind the Latin-American context where he based and developed his educational theory and practice, in spite of his adoption of some European and North American philosophical and educational theories, explains CP's non-Eurocentric stance. Similarly, the fact that CP has developed in the United States mostly within the scope of multicultural education (CABE, 1992), and under the influence of the post-1960s movements in favour of Third World cultures has provided it with a special sensitivity to cultural insights into the Third World. The combination of these influences has provided CP with a global stance, in the sense that it is inclusive and it values all cultural perspectives equally as long as they are themselves respectful of human rights and, reciprocally, of other cultures.

In sum, it may be stated that 'inclusiveness' as well as 'incompleteness' are essential features in the character of CP since it attempts to bring together several, some even apparently irreconcilable, cultural and, as previously mentioned, philosophical and educational frameworks. Besides, it is still in the process of being 'made', which fosters its dialogical and controversial nature.

Since it is impossible, within the scope or at this point of the study, to give a detailed account of the various theoretical contributions to CP, only some of the aspects believed to be most relevant to the intersection this study makes between CP and foreign culture education will be pointed out.

Critical theory: The concern for emancipation

Emancipation is a notion that CP borrows from Critical Theory in its quest for democratic education.[2] On the one hand, emancipation is a concept that Critical Theory tries to rescue from the original modernist ideals of human freedom and equality but, on the other hand, its pursuit of emancipation rejects the functionalist paradigms that were provided by positivist developments of modernity. Emancipation is, therefore, part of Critical Theory's paradoxical relationship with modernity which combines the love for the democratic ideals achieved through rationalisation and the contempt for instrumental reason.

As we shall see in the next chapter, the concern for emancipation underpins both Horkheimer and Adorno's critique of mass culture and Habermas' objectives while he was designing his Theory of Communicative Action. Horkheimer and Adorno, like Marcuse and also Gramsci, identified a new form of political and social domination through the ideological and hegemonical use of culture and the development of one-dimensional thought.[3] Horkheimer and Adorno's 'culture industry' argument is that the massification and commodification of culture makes society expect that 'every detail is so firmly stamped with sameness that nothing can appear which is not marked at birth, or does not meet with approval at first sight' (Horkheimer & Adorno, 1972: 128). Conformity to a culture that is not even produced by themselves prevents people from having an emancipatory attitude, that is, from exercising critical thinking. By politicising the whole concept of culture, critical theorists have illuminated the liberating role cultural institutions, such as schools, might play by using a language of critique, and have enabled critical pedagogues to look at schooling as a form of cultural politics.

Besides other aspects of his theory, which will be described later, Habermas' emphasis on the virtues of 'communicative rationality' shows his concerns for emancipation in a more optimistic way than Horkheimer and Adorno's. Habermas believes that by coupling thought and action it is possible to achieve mutual understanding and consensus in the form of universal values agreed upon by means of argumentation.

However, CP recommends a critical use of these theories. Giroux notes Horkheimer and Adorno's elitism in preserving the distinction between high and popular culture as well as Habermas' neglect of the possibility of conflicting positions and of the existence of contradictory ways in dealing with recurrent situations which may well prevent consensus. Nevertheless, Critical Theory provides educators with useful suggestions in order to link theory and practice, cross over disciplinary borders, and become committed to the democratic ideals of human emancipation and mutual understanding.

Postmodernism: Affirming difference

As we shall see in the next chapter, postmodernism develops out of concepts and perspectives initially proposed by French poststructuralists. These, in their turn, expanded, to some extent and in some cases inadvertently, on ideas put forward by the first generation of the Frankfurt philosophers, namely Horkheimer, Adorno, Marcuse *et al.*, despite their opposition to their successors, Habermas in particular. However, postmodernism, as we shall see, cannot be understood as a monolithic movement. On the contrary, it is represented by several divergent voices that have, nonetheless, cultivated a new interpretation of our postindustrial and postcolonial world. Postmodernist perspectives have had a great impact on cultural studies and provide a great potential for educational change in this area, as is discussed in the next chapter (Agger, 1992). Their attacks on foundationalism, essentialism and universalism reinforced by their plea for diversity, locality and contingency have allowed for interesting responses in several academic fields to the increasing transgressions of cultural, social and political boundaries that have been taking place in our postindustrial societies in the age of electronically mediated cultures (Aronowitz & Giroux, 1991).

The emphasis on difference from a philosophical point of view problematised notions that had previously seemed very stable, such as subjectivity and tradition. The concept of subjectivity is modified by the change in the concept of the subject itself, understood as hybrid and multilayered, resulting from the intersection of several discourses, and also variable. Furthermore, tradition is considered as 'a form of countermemory' achieved through the exclusion of many voices and the imposition of a comprehensive version of the dominant one (Giroux, 1992: 122).[4] These arguments have implications for the notions of culture and knowledge and, therefore, for foreign culture education. They account for the validity of marginal identities, for example those concerning ethnicity, race or gender, for the rejection of universal referents that have justified the hierarchical evaluation of others, and for the refusal to accept the lines drawn between high and popular cultures or between left- and right-wing politics.

Here again critical educators need to be cautious because, like Critical Theory, Postmodernism does not provide a complete pedagogical formulation. Postmodernist notions of identity and difference may become too reductionist in nature and may be pedagogically unsound, if they are not complemented with other points of view. Nevertheless, Postmodernism allows for a broader understanding of what is considered cultural content in foreign culture education and it provides a new perspective of it, as we shall see.

Some CP theorists also notice the absence of an explicit ethical and political project, which other authors find is implicit (Smyth, 1995), others find in some postmodernist movements such as postmodernist feminism (Giroux, 1992) and others still in 'critical' or 'resistance postmodernism' which they distinguish from 'ludic postmodernism' (Kanpol, 1997; McLaren, 1995). Critical pedagogues are thus advised to introduce both the ethical and political dimensions that supply a sense of solidarity which is required when dealing with difference. However, the innovative input that Postmodernism brings to the curriculum in general, and to cultural studies in particular, cannot be overlooked by teachers/learners since it gives them the opportunity to grasp the complexity and multiplicity of cultural meanings and subject positions.

Cultural studies: Transgressing boundaries

Cultural Studies is an interdisciplinary field of study which has brought serious academic attention to popular culture topics and, therefore, challenged the lines drawn between disciplines and between high and popular culture.[5] The Frankfurt aesthetic theory – which Agger considers, together with the Marxist sociology of culture, as comprising 'the prehistory of cultural studies' (Agger, 1992: 75) – reintroduced an interdisciplinary approach that had previously been common to human sciences' studies. The Frankfurt School theorists, namely Adorno and Marcuse, also focused their attention on mass culture. It was, however, the Centre for Contemporary Cultural Studies at the University of Birmingham that coined the name for this new field of research and that gave the new objects of study equal status in an effort to keep pace with the changing world beyond. Cultural Studies later experienced a boom in the US and then spread throughout the world in the form of work on ethnicity, feminism, postcolonialism, education, etc. Its focus has, therefore, expanded from class to race, gender and other areas.

Cultural Studies is a fundamental area of study for educators who believe that pedagogy is a form of cultural politics and, in particular, for critical pedagogues who teach/learn foreign culture. Both Cultural Studies and CP have ethical and political concerns since they both attribute great importance to everyday matters, human suffering and critical citizenship. Cultural workers, among whom are critical pedagogues, must be critically aware of the ever newer intersections between power, knowledge and culture that work at every level producing the tensions existing in our societies (Giroux, 1994b). Cultural Studies allow critical pedagogues to go beyond reductionist cultural analyses that either explain every cultural act or event as an unavoidable consequence of a wider ideological structure or give a romanticised view of culture where everything seems harmonious and peaceful. By combining a 'theory of subcultures' (Agger, 1992: 82) with a 'theory of contexts' (Grossberg, 1994: 5), Cultural Studies also attempts to give a balanced perspective of how society works by situating it between pluralism and holism. Although working at the microlevel of subcultures, Cultural Studies do not neglect the articulation of the way they themselves interrelate and develop while in interaction. The notion of context here is, therefore, very dynamic since it is constantly being reorganised through evolving relationships between its parts.

Moreover, interdisciplinarity does not necessarily mean a shallow analysis of the topics in hand. On the contrary, it is considerably deep because it means looking under the surface of events and trying to find as many explanations as possible to account for their multiple aspects. Interdisciplinarity also responds to new intellectual demands made by a changing society as well as creating new questions to be investigated. An interdisciplinary approach to culture entails a tendency towards more complex analyses and a problem-posing stance that characterise CP.

Both the transgression of disciplinary boundaries and the serious attention paid to everyday matters represent a real challenge to culture teachers' praxis. It involves changes both in content and in process since the object of learning is part of our everyday experience and the true purpose of the teaching/learning encounter is to have students reflect upon it and obtain greater meaning and knowledge from it. As Grossberg argues, 'the task is to win an already positioned, already invested individual or group to a different set of places, a different organization of the space of possibilities' (Grossberg, 1994: 19). The object of study is not distant, static or finished, it is there, it is part of our lived experience. Texts are not only printed, they are aural, visual or even alive. And their study is not only about 'textuality' or 'intertextuality' but also about 'subtextuality', that is, the 'hidden messages and values' that are transmitted through cultural artifacts, attitudes or images we confront from day to day (Agger, 1992: 90). This allows teachers/students to become aware of 'how power works through the popular and everyday to produce knowledge, social identities, and maps of desire' (Giroux, 1997b: 260), and eventually makes them ethically and democratically committed to a remapping of cultural politics.

Progressivism: Dewey's quest for democracy

All CP theorists acknowledge the importance of Dewey's legacy. His quest for democracy, the link he made between reflective thinking and experience, and between theory and practice, as well as the relevance he gave to a pedagogy of dialogue which changed the school culture have all become guidelines for critical pedagogues too. They disapprove, however, of the use of Dewey's ideas made by progressive educational reformists in the 1960s and 1970s who privileged experience, practice and problem-solving methodologies and neglected theory and reflective thinking. Education was, therefore, conceived as preparation for the job market and democracy taken as economic freedom (Aronowitz & Giroux, 1986; Giroux, 1997b; Kanpol, 1994). On the contrary, Dewey, as Freire later did too, emphasised personal growth over knowledge acquisition, personal perception over automatic skills, and 'knowing', an internal process, over disassociated 'knowledge', an external body of information (Dewey, 1956). Dewey also called for relevant knowledge that would relate to students' experiences through reflective thinking. This triangle – knowledge, experience, reflective thinking – would constitute the learning process. Reflective thinking, in this instance, is embedded in experience in that it is about a problem that arises and the search for its solution:

> ... reflective thinking, in distinction from other operations to which we apply the name of thought, involves (1) a state of doubt, hesitation, perplexity, mental difficulty, in which thinking originates, and (2) an act of searching, hunting, inquiring, to find material that will resolve the doubt, settle and dispose of the perplexity. (Dewey, 1933: 12)

In this way, Dewey saw the relationship between theory and practice as a web that is continuously made and remade. Furthermore, he saw the connection between experience and learning as part of a wider democratic project that linked education and society. The main goal of education was, in his opinion, to form citizens who would be able to integrate and make use of a democratic system (Dewey, 1956). This triangular mode of learning would provide young individuals with the attitudes and skills necessary for the reinforcement of a democratic way of life and would also empower them to take advantage of all the possibilities they have access to while living in a democratic society.

Dewey's preoccupation in linking education to democratic experience and reflective thinking is part of his ambiguous relationship with modernity (Biesta & Miedema, 1996). On the one hand, he refused to accept most of the educational legacies of the Enlightenment such as a distant and fixed canon of knowledge to be passively acquired and teachers as unquestionable conveyors of the Truth. On the other hand, he recovered and resurrected some of the basic concepts in modern thought such as democracy, freedom, and emancipation and claimed that 'the other side of an educative experience is an added power of subsequent direction or control' (Dewey, 1956: 90). Kanpol makes a direct connection between

Dewey and the Frankfurt School with respect to their common attempt to rescue the democratic ideals of the Enlightenment that the development of modernity had mismanaged and to their common enhancement of an 'active and critical citizenry' (Kanpol, 1994: 8).

However, for CP theorists Dewey did not go as far as they would have liked. Freire makes this statement in his Introduction to Giroux's *Teachers as Intellectuals*:

> This position owes a great deal to John Dewey's view on democracy, but it goes beyond his position in a number of ways, and these are worth mentioning ... As an ideal, the discourse of democracy suggests something more programmatic and radical. First, it points to the role that teachers and administrators might play as transformative intellectuals who develop counterhegemonic pedagogies that not only empower students by giving them the knowledge and social skills they will need to be able to function in the larger society as critical agents, but also educate them for transformative action ... This is very different from Dewey's view, because I see democracy as involving not only a pedagogical struggle but also a political and social struggle, ... (Giroux, 1988: xxxiii)

Although Dewey restored the importance of experience in the educational process and put an emphasis on the social purpose of schooling, he envisaged a change in the politics of classroom culture as a short-term goal, and eventually the refinement of democratic society. As a pragmatist, he rejected the project of an ideal society and concentrated instead on the improvement of the actual individuals and societies. As he himself states, 'we cannot set out of our heads, something we regard as an ideal society' and 'the aim set up must be an outgrowth of existing conditions' (Dewey, 1956: 96, 121). This is the point where CP moves away from Dewey. CP departs from the critical acknowledgement of the 'existing conditions' and sets transformative action as its goal. However, CP could not have aimed at transformative action without Dewey's first steps towards a creative democracy based on critical consciousness, dialogue and action and his establishment of a direct connection between the inner democratisation of schools and the democratisation of society as a whole.

Reconstructionism: Citizenship education as a goal

Reconstructionism developed in education during the 1930s and 1940s and its main theorists were Counts, Rugg and Brameld. In several aspects it establishes a bridge between Progressivism and CP, because it shares with both a concern for the political significance of education and also considers schooling as a form of citizenship education.

According to Giroux, Reconstructionism constituted an attempt to expand Dewey's work on the schools' role in a democratic society. Like Dewey, reconstructionists linked school life with the world outside and favoured a connection between the school curricula and the problems the students had to face in their everyday lives (Giroux, 1989). Some authors, like Giroux and Rorty, consider Dewey a reconstructionist, a somewhat exaggerated view since as a pragmatist his thought diverges from a reconstructionist perspective of education (Stanley, 1992). Dewey focuses more on the individual, has a more optimistic view of a free society, sees 'good' education as being impartial and underscores his 'problem-solving' methodology, while reconstructionists emphasise the social aspect of schooling, take into greater account the power pressures that permeate life in society and at school, acknowledge the ideological character of curricula and teaching and adopt a problem-posing attitude that has been expanded by CP.

In the middle of the twentieth century, Reconstructionism developed an educational philosophy which showed certain features that have been recovered and expanded by CP theorists (Giroux, 1989). These may be summed up in the importance of citizenship education as involving a discourse for ethics and radical democracy. Education is understood as integrating a wider social project towards the reinvigoration and radicalisation of original democratic principles. Schools are viewed as public spheres that take a leading role in this project for the transformation and 'reconstruction' of society. It is precisely this potential for transforming the wider social context that reconstructionists attribute to schools that means that they fill the gap between progressive educators and critical pedagogues. Reconstructionism also paved the way for CP in other aspects of citizenship education, such as the acknowledgement that schools are not politically innocent and curricula, as they are established by the state and as delivered by the teachers, are ideologically vitiated, although some reconstructionists, like Ruggs, still struggled for curriculum objectivity (Stanley, 1992: 23).

However, the main recurring similarity between Reconstructionism and CP, which marks a departure from Progressivism, is the importance of the role they assign to teachers, who are given the status of 'transformative intellectuals' within the project for democratic citizenship education. This role fits into an emancipatory view of citizenship education that enables teachers and students to become empowered citizens whose contribution to democracy is not simply the electoral vote or obeying the laws but also active and critical participation in community life and in building together a plan for the future. Although the ideal society is somewhat pervasive in Progressivism, Reconstructionism and CP, it is once again the emphasis on the future that makes the difference for both reconstructionists and critical pedagogues. And it is this future-planning that makes room for teachers to act as intellectuals, involved not in defending the existing order, but in exploring the potential for society's improvement.

Freire: A pedagogy of hope

Freire is widely recognised as the founder of CP. Giroux himself acknowledges that 'in some quarters his name has become synonymous with the very concept and practice of critical pedagogy' (Giroux, 1994a: 141). As a leading figure in education in the second half of this century, 'an icon in critical circles, the "John Dewey" of the present era', Freire has inspired a most consistent educational movement (Kanpol, 1997: 13). In fact, he does draw from Dewey's educational theory but builds upon his ideas with regard to the role of schools in the democratisation of public life. Therefore, Freire represents a later phase of the evolution of education in the twentieth century which culminates in the recognition of schools as main cultural and political agencies that act as a basis for the future of democratic societies. Indeed this is the belief that drives the CP movement.

Freire introduced some concepts which have traced the path of his theory of education, namely *'literacia'*, *'conscientização'*, and, in a later stage, the notion of teachers as 'cultural workers'. Literacy, as understood by Freire, is not merely the capacity to 'read the word' but it also entails the capacity of 'reading the world' *critically*. Freire uses the concept of literacy in a way that is complementary to the acquisition of utilitarian knowledge or of information *per se* or even the mere ability to read and write. Literacy, in Freire's terms, comprises a form of cultural politics, and being literate ultimately means being critically aware of one's own context. Freire himself puts it best in his *Letter to North-American Teachers* when he postulates that 'reading and writing words encompasses the reading of the world, that is, the critical understanding of politics in the world' (Freire, 1987: 212–13). Literacy thus leads to the next concept put forward by Freire, *'conscientização'*.

Both concepts, *'literacia'* and *'conscientização'*, are very much linked to the modernist ideal of emancipation. By becoming literate, the individual will be more prepared to perform her/his role in society, s/he will understand better what is happening around her/him and will be more conscious while acting. Moreover, *'conscientização'* is the process 'by means of which men, through a true praxis, leave behind the status of *objects* to assume the status of historical *Subjects'* (Freire, 1970: 158). In sum, Freire focuses on the process of cultural production rather than on the process of social reproduction, that is, by validating the process of cultural production in education based on everybody's experience and reflection, he disrupts the process of the social reproduction of classes. Moreover, he combines the modernist notions of rationalisation and education with postmodern concepts of power and culture by understanding power as not simply repressive but generative, and culture as not only reproduced but constantly recreated. He acknowledges the tensions resulting from class, race or gender relations, understands culture as being produced within this web of conflicts, and, furthermore, emphasises the potential of this source of energy. *'Conscientização'* is then the capability to comprehend the relationships between agents, the reasons behind their actions, and their position in relation to each other. Freire states it clearly:

> A person who has reached conscientization has a different understanding of history and of his or her role in it. He or she will refuse to become stagnant, but will move and mobilize to change the world. (Freire, 1996: 183)

Within this perspective, rationalisation, or reflective thought, is linked to action, thus resulting in praxis. Therefore, education is mostly transformative rather than simply reproductive. Freire recognises his own evolution on this issue, from the belief, shown in his first book *Educação como Prática da Liberdade*, that the very unveiling of reality would mean transforming it, to his later notion of *'conscientização'*, through which one becomes aware that 'knowing the reality' and 'transforming the reality' are not exactly the same thing, but rather 'two dialectic poles' (Freire, 1993: 103, translation mine).

Therefore, Freire combines a language of critique with a language of possiblity and introduces notions such as empowerment and voice that are very dear to critical pedagogues, as we shall see later. They stem from the above-mentioned concepts of *'literacia'* and *'conscientização'* since these enable students and teachers to validate their own personal stories, their own visions of the world and thus be able to intervene in the course of history. Such concerns led him to his view of teaching as a 'pedagogy of dialogue' and a 'pedagogy of hope'. However, by attributing to teachers the role of 'cultural workers', Freire appeals to them not to 'reduce teaching to merely a feel-good process' because that would devalue teaching 'which, by its very nature, involves rigorous intellectual pursuits' (Freire, 1998: 4). Freire claims that teachers cannot be neutral because they always provide their students with their own 'reading' of the word and the world, and he also states that it is fundamental that they acknowledge this fact, otherwise, they are just delivering somebody else's message. Furthermore, he also asserts that it is the teacher's duty to teach 'material relevant to the discipline' (Freire, 1987: 212). In doing so, he accentuates the professional nature of the task of being a teacher and rejects indoctrination, demagoguery, or the reduction of teaching to a 'parenting role' (Freire, 1998: 4).

From Giroux's point of view, Freire redefined the very notion of the intellectual. On the one hand, he adopts the concept of 'organic intellectual' put forward by Gramsci and expands this notion by searching out the intellectual in each one of us, in the sense that we each produce a particular vision of the world. This stance has had a tremendous impact on education in that it empowers teachers/students by entitling them to a voice. But, on the other hand, there is in Freire's work a feeling of 'homelessness', as Giroux calls it, both in the sense of modernist 'universalism', that is, a commitment to universal human rights, and 'in the postmodern sense that suggests there is little possibility of ideological and hegemonic closure' (Giroux, 1994a: 144).

Although Freire's work has been widely applied throughout Third World countries, it resulted both from his European and non-European experiences and from his intellectual sources. A political exile and an educational expert, he came into contact with different schools of thought and with different pedagogical experiments throughout the world. Not surprisingly, in Freire's works we can find a sense of belonging and, at the same time, a sense of detachment. Both are essential to being critically aware of one's own reality as he argues himself that 'the "distancing" from the object is epistemologically "coming closer" to it' (Freire, 1998: 93). Freire moved, physically and intellectually, across class, cultural and national borders which made his theories very contemporary, flexible, and usable in any educational setting. However, this process does not occur peacefully since his educational thought is unsettling and aims at change. It is not only progressive in the modern sense or 'progressive in a postmoderm sort of way' as he describes it (Freire, 1993: 81, translation mine), but also 'transgressive' (Giroux, 1997b: xi). His educational theories are not rebellious but they are revolutionary since they threaten the status quo by revealing and appealing to freedom of mind and to action. Besides his genuine and unequivocal struggle for establishing justice and democracy in the name of the least powerful inhabitants of his country, he displayed a bipolar way of approaching culture, politics, and education by combining belonging with detachment, closeness with distancing, reflection with action, experience with utopia, critique with possibility. These complementary orientations were inscribed in the essence of CP.

Critical Pedagogy: A Language of Critique and Possibility

CP aims at blending a 'language of critique' with a 'language of possibility' in education, according to Giroux's terminology (Giroux, 1989, 1992, 1997b). This means that it recognises the importance for education of the various steps that go from the addition of information, through the interpretation and critique of knowledge and society, to the transformation of reality, in a process of knowledge appropriation and application. However, critical pedagogues do not accept it as a chronological evolution throughout the school system or life and require that these steps should be interwoven. Therefore, besides acknowledging the significance of interpreting reality, critical pedagogues reinforce the schools' potential for critique and democratic intervention.

A language of critique entails a critical understanding of society as it is, with different layers of meaning and with several forces in interaction. In sum, it involves a deconstructive view of reality and a challenge to fixed interpretative frames. Furthermore, not only does it call for teachers/students to construe their own cultural identities critically and recognise the Others', it also demands that they question their role in the surrounding community, as citizens of their own country and as citizens of larger social and political communities. On the other hand, critical awareness of a situation nurtures the desire for change and enables the 'language of possibility that admits utopia as a possible dream' (Freire, 1993: 90, translation mine). A language of possibility results then from the urge to explore new alternatives, to envision a revitalisation of democratic ideals and to engage in social change. In Giroux's words, a language of possibility 'points to the horizon of the "not yet"' and involves a utopian project of education implying 'the creation of new cultural spaces that deepen and extend the possibility of democratic public life' (Giroux, 1997b: 223, 252). The combination of a language of critique with a language of possibility turns education into a form of cultural politics, for it will explore the potential for the improvement of our societies and for the development of a new ethics that suits the fabric of our multicultural and transnational communities.

A pedagogy of reflection

Reflection is an indispensable and delicate tool for CP. Indeed it is a complex aspect because it is the battleground where critical pedagogues are urged to combine modernist with postmodernist notions of the Subject as well as an Habermasian with a Derridean concept of rationality.[6] The stress on reflection, proposed by critical pedagogues, is also the subject of some controversy probably due to the fact that educators were taken by surprise after a continued emphasis on the technical training of skills both for learners and teachers. Despite both Dewey's and Freire's compelling focus on the role of reflective thinking in education, it was greatly ignored or misunderstood by education technicians eager to turn their theories into methods.

CP does not define reflection as the solipsistic activity of a stable and unified self, or as a train of thought framed within a previously established pattern, or even as an exclusive higher-order intellectual aptitude. We can recognise here the influence of a poststructuralist/postmodernist view of a fragmented self. Since Critical Pedagogy focuses on the multi- and intercultural nature of contemporary societies, the acknowledgement of the plural and contextualised construction of the self is most helpful in achieving its purpose. Although critical pedagogues are aware of the importance of reason as a historical legacy of the Enlightenment, more particularly for education, they subscribe to a position which occupies a middle ground between the intercommunicative kind of rationality proposed by Habermas and the decentred/deconstructed postmodern notion of subject. Even Habermas, whose effort to reaffirm reflectiveness as an irrevocable conquest of modernity is well known,[7] admits that there is, alternatively, a pressing need for its conversion:

> The reciprocal interpersonal relations that are established through the speaker–hearer perspectives make possible a relation-to-self that by no means presupposes the lonely reflection of the knowing and acting subject upon itself as an antecedent consciousness. Rather, the self-relation arises out of an *interactive* context. (Habermas, 1992: 24, his emphasis)

Reflectiveness has then had to widen its focus, from a fragmented analysis of a fixed and compartmentalised reality to a more holistic approach to interrelational sets of discourses. It has also had to switch from the set goal of achieving generalisations based on verified facts to the identification of hidden meanings or speculation over uncontested truths. Reflective thinking here is closely connected with critical thinking defined as 'the ability to step beyond common sense assumptions and to be able to evaluate them in terms of their genesis, development and purpose' (Giroux, 1997b: 26). Dewey had already given us a hint of this link:

> There may, however, be a state of perplexity and also previous experience out of which suggestions emerge, and yet thinking need not be reflective. For the person may not be sufficiently critical about the ideas that occur to him. (Dewey, 1933: 16)

Dewey recognises the existence of several stages of consciousness which are recurrent in research made on the role of critical reflection in CP. Throughout his work, Freire also refers to his own early distinction between 'naïve transitivity' and 'critical transitivity' (Freire, 1974, 1991). While the first is regarded as a simple interpretation of facts, the latter consists of a deeper understanding of problems which should correspond to a more interrogative and dialogic stance.

This conceptual ladder of reflection inspired several studies applied to CP either put into practice in learning contexts (Ada, 1988; Wink, 1997: 125) or focusing on teacher development (Silva, 1993). Ada's Creative Reading Model distinguishes four interrelated levels of communication, which are: (a) the descriptive; (b) the interpretive; (c) the critical; and (d) the creative. While the first two levels entail a passive understanding of facts or situations, the critical and the creative levels aim at questioning and transforming principles and values. As for Silva's research study on the role of critical reflection in professional development programmes for practising educators, the author identified three elements of reflection, namely: (a) the cognitive element 'which attempts to describe how teachers process information and make pedagogical decisions'; (b) the critical element 'which focuses on the substance that drives the thinking, values, goals and experiences of educators'; and (c) the interpretative element through 'which educators reflect and describe their own interpretation of the events that constitute and occur during their reflective process' (Silva, 1993: 21). The integration of these three elements is designed to eventually encourage teachers to connect their work to the wider context of their schools both in an interpretative and transformative manner. By also promoting critical reflection among teachers, this will engage them into the process of being 'transformative intellectuals', as defined by Giroux. These projects and studies prove that critical reflection is indeed teachable/learnable. Freire is adamant that critical awareness, whose development culminates in *'conscientização'*, will not emerge except through a 'critical educational effort' (Freire,

1974: 19). The recognition that critical reflection is teachable/learnable brings profound changes to the concept of education.

With this in mind, there are several definitions of critical reflection that help clarify the concept. To start with, Dewey's definition of what he thought constituted reflective thought may be helpful here:

> Active, persistent, and careful consideration of any belief or supposed form of knowledge in the light of the grounds that support it and the further conclusions to which it tends. (Dewey, 1933: 9)

In other words, reflective thought consists of continuous pondering over the justifications and consequences of convictions or statements. The importance of justification in critical thinking is repeatedly pointed out in Habermas' works too in terms of 'validity claims', as we shall see (Habermas, 1972, 1979, 1984, 1992, 1993). In the above definition, Dewey still refers to the 'active' nature of the reflective act. For both philosophers, Dewey and Habermas, and for Freire as well, reflection interweaves with action. According to Freire, 'action and reflexion constantly and mutually illuminate each other' (Freire, 1974: 151). This articulation between reflection and action provides for the nullification of the dichotomy between theory and practice, thus changing the educational practice, which has strongly relied on this division, into a praxis, as recommended by CP.

Another relevant aspect of the action–reflection interdependence is the relationship between the conscious and the unconscious that has been emphasised by critical theorists under the influence of Freud. The concepts we rely on in everyday interactions, language-in-action (rules, words), or routine responses, remain largely unconscious. The recognition of this fact is a particularly useful contribution made by the Frankfurt School and adds to the important role critical reflection plays in CP (Giroux, 1997b: 51–65). Also related to this issue is the interconnection between critical thinking and emotion which was introduced by postmodern feminists and acutely captured by critical pedagogues (Giroux, 1992; Kincheloe & Steinberg, 1993). Being a critical thinker involves more than being rational and emotion is not viewed as an inferior cognitive stage. Emotion is given a key role in CP in that it is considered as a fundamental stimulus for cognitive, interpretive, critical and creative reflection-in-action.

However, several issues must also be raised when putting critical reflection into practice. The first question is whether it has a general dimension or a specific one. This has been the motive of discussion between authors with, on one side, the assumption that 'critical thinking is linked conceptually with particular activities and special fields of knowledge' (McPeck,

1981: 56) and, on the other side, the counterstatement that it is possible to 'develop reasoning skills which are general in that they can be applied to many diverse situations and subject matters' (Siegel, 1988: 20). The next issue to be questioned is whether critical reflection/thinking is a skill, a capacity, a habit, a disposition, a trait of character, the possession of a rich collection of arguments, something else or a mixture of all these. Again, authors diverge on this point and critical thinking is often characterised as an expression of being intelligent, appropriate, fair, impartial, or correct. In this instance, it is useful to resort to Dewey's identification of the attitudes he considers as prerequisites for a 'good thinker'. They are: (a) *Open-mindedness*, which is 'an active desire to listen to more sides than one'; (b) *Whole-heartedness*, in the sense that one is 'thoroughly interested in some object and cause'; and (c) *Responsibility*, which involves careful consideration of the consequences of one's actions (Dewey, 1933: 30–3). Dewey concedes that these attitudes are usually considered as traits of character rather than intellectual resources and that they are associated with other attitudes that he acknowledges as being 'moral'.

More recently, Barnett has explored the role of critical reflection in higher education. He emphasises the importance of reflection as 'metacritique' that consists of a critical stance towards one's own knowledge, the self and one's social context(s) as well as the existence of external reflection that involves 'the capacity to become an *other* to inhabit if only briefly, a cognitive perspective that is unfamiliar' (Barnett, 1997: 19, his emphasis). Both processes, according to Barnett, inevitably lead to critical action.

Not surprisingly, when it comes to clarifying the actual practice of critical reflection/thinking in education it is inevitable that ethical and political issues appear. What has been said so far indicates that critical awareness is achieved through education, that it will not occur automatically by means of the mechanical training of skills or through information input alone and that it cannot exist independently of specific traits of personality or particular modes of conduct that have to be cultivated (Dewey, 1933; Freire, 1974, 1998; Passmore, 1967; Siegel, 1988). This poses the need for a dialogic praxis of education which will necessarily result in a reconsideration of ethical principles, so that a new ethics develops that is not imposed but intercommunicatively negotiated. This procedure should articulate a radicalisation of democratic behaviour that then constitutes the political component of the whole process.

With regard to the political implications of critical reflection in education, it is necessary to focus on the relationship between critical thinking and ideology (Giroux, 1997b; Siegel, 1988). The concept of ideology, as it is understood by critical pedagogues, should be considered in both its negative and positive aspects. On the one hand, it is oppressive in that it determines the way one interprets and responds to one's context. On the other hand, it is useful because it provides a framework for doing so, and, if illuminated by critical reflection, it can indeed be emancipatory since the latter discloses the underlying meanings and interests embodied in the ideological discourses and practices at work in our societies. This explains the importance of metacritique as emphasised by Barnett (1997). Giroux provides an insightful explanation of the emancipatory potential of the critique of ideology:

> The ideological dimension that underlies all critical reflection is what lays bare the historically and socially sedimented values at work in the construction of knowledge, social relations, and material practices. (Giroux, 1997b: 84–5)

As Giroux points out, critical reflection undermines any asphyxiating tendencies of ideology because it challenges straightforward authoritarianism, enforced imposition and intellectual obscurity. A critique of ideology in the form of critical reflection is self-emancipatory because it enables one to be critical about one's own critical thinking. Likewise, critical reflection is socially emancipatory since it makes possible 'an increasingly critical perception of the concrete conditions of reality' which, in Freire's words, coincides with 'nascent hope', that is, 'society now reveals itself as something unfinished, not as something inexorably given' (Freire, 1974: 13).

Critical reflection is, therefore, a vital element for the development of critical cultural awareness both in educational and intercultural contexts. It is important to develop metacritical capacities, in Barnett's terms, in educational settings so that they can then be applied to experiential learning. Phipps illustrates well how to carry out metacritique in foreign language/culture classes by leading her students to reflect critically upon their own learning experiences and the feelings they experience when confronting 'the new' (keywords are: 'surprise', 'excitement', 'passion', 'you are a voice'). Her students feel that reflecting critically 'is not simply some kind of intellectual abstraction' since 'it makes you recognise what you are doing' and it 'gives you a sort of different way to look and see'. They eventually come to the conclusion that 'society was there, it was what [they] lived, but [they] didn't really have a view of why it was like that' (Phipps, 2001a: 129–48). In experiential learning situations, the notion of a multilayered, intersecting and permeable cultural Subject is determinant both for the understanding of her/his own identity and for the relation of Self with Other. Likewise, reflecting critically on the differences between cultural patterns will facilitate the justification of beliefs and actions of Self and Other and the evaluation of consequences of one's actions as they might appear in the framework of presuppositions of the Other. From this perspective, reflection-in-action allows for the coming into consciousness of factors that interact in a cross-cultural event such as the unconscious concepts and rules or routine responses that are taken for granted by each side as well as the emotional impetus that drives the cultural encounter. Critical awareness of the interrelated levels of communication that may occur in discourse, of the attitudes that must be cultivated or of the skills, general or subject specific, that need to be exercised, contributes greatly to the improvement of intercultural communication. As extensively discussed in previous sections, culture, ethics, and politics form a tight web. Therefore, critical cultural awareness demands reflection upon the whole network of values, principles and power games. Viewed in this light, critical cultural awareness, partly achieved through critical reflection, constitutes a source for emancipation, which is, in Habermas' words, 'the viewpoint central to the formation of identity' (Habermas, 1987b: 114). Emancipation here is considered not only as self-sufficiency but also as the capacity to reach a more comprehensive and enlightened stage of communication.

A pedagogy of dissent

Either difference is recognised but not entitled to a voice or, if it is legitimised and given an equivalent status, it may generate opposition, contestation and even confrontation. Therefore, a politics of difference involves what Mohanty calls a 'public culture of dissent' (Mohanty, 1994: 162). Paradoxically, the pursuit of equality in modern societies has developed into an emphasis on consensus and hegemony. Consequently, the social and cultural systems have become more exclusive since this pursuit marginalises the particular, while the validation of difference attempts to be more inclusive. However, a culture of dissent does not necessarily lead to a simple celebration of relativism, to the presentation of irreconcilable subjectivities, or to the irreversible and permanent confrontation of opponents (Giroux, 1981: 125). Nevertheless, contradiction, contestation or opposition should be given legitimacy, voice, space and time. These should not be looked down upon as something unnatural or bad, to be kept private, or to be quickly controlled. The lack of consideration awarded to conflict itself has given rise to long and violent confrontations of all kinds and to rupture itself. Furthermore, dissent does not lose a sense of wholeness because it looks at separate parts in terms of their interrelationships, nor does it prevent a politics of solidarity.

CP aims at preparing young people for a politics of difference and considers that this is not happening yet. The social reality that is expressed in subject content and materials is hegemonic, if not homogeneous. At the most it includes some controversial perspectives, but it does not deal with conflict in depth (Giroux, 1997b: 22). This reality collides with that outside the classroom which is impregnated with crude and fictitious violence. Because lived or media-provided realities are much more impressive than the one supplied by the teacher, the latter loses meaning and vitality. As far as foreign culture teaching/learning is concerned, it is nothing new to say that most representations conveyed in the classroom seem to belong to rather different worlds than the ones students experience through media input or in actual encounters with natives from the target cultures, wherever this may happen, which may end up in conflict, stereotyping, or even rejection.

The postmodern endorsement of dissent may, therefore, play an essential role in pluralistic democracies, and by extension in CP, although this view contradicts the modernist quest for consensus achieved through rational argumentation, persuasion, economic progress and finally consent (Mouffe, 1996a: 7–8). Postmodern deconstruction emphasises the contradictory nature of identities, relies on the partiality of meanings, interrogates the legitimacy of dominant ideas and the voicelessness of those who have been silenced. This entails transforming what has been established, unlearning what has been learnt, renouncing what has been taken for granted. A process such as this does not develop without turbulence.

Dissent is organically linked to *critical* thinking and, if solidly grounded, stems from *critical* reflection. If Horkheimer's distinction between traditional and critical theory, to be described later, is taken into account, the separation made within a traditional framework between theory and practice, knowledge and experience, thought and action provided the intellectual with an aseptic environment that protected her/him from social tensions, while the critical theorist is caught in the web of relations and tensions existent in society (Horkheimer, 1972). Moreover, critical dissent, as a procedure of critical thinking and as one possible result of critical reflection, connects with social and political intervention since it questions the status of what Foucault called 'regimes of truth' which determine what is true and what is false and the implications this has for structures of power. Foucault captured the never-ending interaction between power and resistance thus:

> ... there are no relations of power without resistances; the latter are all the more real and effective because they are formed right at the point where relations of power are exercised; resistance to power does not have to come from elsewhere to be real, nor is it inexorably frustrated through being the compatriot of power. It exists all the more by being in the same place as power; hence, like power, resistance is multiple and can be integrated in global strategies. (Foucault, 1980: 142)

The creative tension that flows from the association, on equal terms, between traditionally opposing and hierarchically placed poles such as power and resistance, theory and practice, knowledge and experience, thought and action allows for the search for truth that goes beyond apparent consensual harmony. This notion of power that is dynamic in that it operates in constant negotiation with resistance, also responds to Williams' understanding of hegemony as a 'lived process', a 'culture' that 'is also continually resisted, limited, altered, challenged by pressures not at all its own' through processes of 'counter-hegemony and alternative hegemony, which are real and persistent elements of practice' (Williams, 1977: 112).

Therefore, in a politics of difference and dissent, processes of 'resistance' and 'counterhegemony' are understood as having a dialogic nature since they depend on negotiation, can be looked at from different perspectives, and rely on transitory stages. Walsh makes a useful distinction between traditional oppositions, which the author describes as 'essential, static, inevitable, and outside human control', and dialogic oppositions characterised as 'ongoing and continuous' and that 'are recognized as socially, historically and temporally situated, and can be impacted by people's actions' (Walsh, 1991: 34). In other words, the dialogic character of a culture of dissent imbues opposing movements with a sense of possibility, project, or even utopia that complements the driving force of critique that is rooted in the combination of critical reflection with a dissenting attitude.

Cultivating the art of dissent in a dialogical manner contributes greatly to the unfolding and to the deepening of critical cultural awareness. To be critically aware of any native or foreign cultural framework requires the acknowledgement of contradictions and oppositions, of the partiality of meanings, and of the interrelational character of convictions and practices. It involves the recognition of the ongoing, unstable, socially and historically contextualised, but, nonetheless, creative tensions between power and resistance, hegemony and counterhegemony, consensus and dissent. In sum, it means understanding cultural identity, as we shall see, as a process including multiplicity, dissonance and change. In a cross-cultural encounter, being critically aware will also provoke dissent in that a discourse of dissent, within the scope of critical cultural awareness, should also promote the critique of the relation between culture and power as a moral/ethical issue involving the denunciation of injustices suffered by subjugated, neglected, or outcast groups (Giroux, 1988: 97). However, a culture of dissent does not rule out a discourse of solidarity, but goes further in that it requires emancipatory action aiming at the assertion of everyone's cultural and political rights. It does not neglect 'a hypothetical, argumentative stance' (Habermas, 1993: 12), but adds the legitimacy of a more vigorous type of argumentation. As discussed in the next chapter, both consensus and dissent are useful tools for the development of critical cultural awareness since they turn the We-versus-They dichotomy into an interdependent relationship. From this perspective, both consensus and dissent remain as transitory and procedural elements in intra- or intercultural communication.

A pedagogy of difference

The postmodern notion of difference inspired the idea of a 'border pedagogy', introduced and expanded by Giroux, which constitutes a pedagogical response to the postnational, postcolonial and multicultural contexts we live in nowadays (Aronowitz & Giroux, 1991; Giroux, 1992). The independence of the remaining colonies coincided with a worldwide movement of ethnic revival that has also echoed throughout Europe and, therefore, the superiority and legitimacy of a Eurocentric perspective which had imposed epistemological, ethical, political models on the whole world was called into question. Border pedagogy, as a framework for developing critical cultural awareness, rejects a predisposition to essentialist Eurocentrism towards any culture, either within or outside Western societies, and favours the inclusion, in their own terms, of non-European cultures in curriculum content. This disposition accounts for global awareness and interest in exploring the concept of border pedagogy as a legitimate element of the study of language and culture.

Border pedagogy endorses the 'decentring' discourse of postmodernism and highlights the cultures that were once marginal or inferior. It also 'deconstructs' the idea of a monolithic cultural subject and perceives her/him as multifaceted, ever-changing, in relation to a complex, also evolving society. Although, in the 1960s and 1970s, a new and serious interest in forgotten and neglected identities emerged, these remained as monolithic categories of gender, race, ethnicity, age, and social class. Later, intersections between these categories started to be considered mainly by postmodern theorists.[8] Border pedagogy opposes the traditional view of difference as deviance and refuses the individualistic, depoliticised, and ahistorical celebration of diversity characteristic of the liberal discourse (Darder, 1991).

Nonetheless, still revealing great influence from the postmodern mindset, border pedagogy blurs any epistemological, cultural, and social boundaries. It transcends traditional borders and creates seamless borderlands because it is not hindered by limitations of any specific discipline knowledge or of high culture. Furthermore, it annihilates established social constructs and originates new contexts which fully accommodate new identities and generate new meanings. Aronowitz and Giroux provide a brief description of this process:

> In this case, students cross over into realms of meaning – maps of knowledge, social relations, and values that are increasingly being negotiated and rewritten as the codes and regulations that organize them become destabilized and reshaped. Border pedagogy decenters as it remaps. The terrain of learning becomes inextricably linked to the shifting parameters of place, identity, history, and power. (Aronowitz & Giroux, 1991: 119)

This notion of border pedagogy focuses on physical, political and cultural borders. The development of modernity created physical boundaries based on gender, race, age, nationality and ethnicity. These borders were 'materialised' in terms of socio-economic classes, political rights and, cultural status, and these, in turn into divisions of space.[9] Postmodern concepts of identity, as we shall see, attempt to respond to post-national, multicultural societies, racial and ethnic hybridity, improved longevity, and social movements that enhance the legitimacy of beliefs of each possibility. As far as knowledge is concerned, the traditional Western canon has been expanded and displaced by other perspectives and narrations.

A pedagogy of difference represents an attempt to respond to the reality just described. It aims at legitimising students' identities and expanding the range of possible options by promoting their critical experience of different cultural codes, in sum, at enabling them to make full use of their capabilities. It focuses on presenting alternatives to the students' frames of mind and widening their horizons critically since 'such borderlands should be seen as sites for both critical analysis and as a potential source of experimentation, creativity, and possibility' (Giroux, 1992: 34). Such a philosophical and educational framework is very enlightening and challenging for critical educators who are concerned with increasing their students' cultural awareness, since it suggests profound changes in both curriculum content and an approach to teaching/learning that keeps in mind the education of a citizenry able to participate fully in a pluralistic society. Therefore, not only are topics introduced that were previously ignored, but they are also considered in their own terms, from multiple points of view and enriched by integrating interdisciplinary perspectives. However, such undervalued margins of cultures, generally identified with popular and minority cultures, should not merely be 'added' to the curriculum just as motivators to get the students to study 'more serious' topics, as curiosities aimed at complementing the prevailing view of a culture, or as a 'tourist trip' into the exotic or the different. Such cultures, whether foreign or not, coincide with legitimate aspects of the students' everyday lives which should be given careful consideration as important components of their identity and as affirmation of their beliefs and attitudes. Moreover, all cultural representations should be considered critically with regard to their contribution to the whole cultural milieu and their strategies for integrating it. Giroux is clear on this issue:

> The knowledge of the 'other' is engaged not simply to celebrate its presence, but also because it must be interrogated critically with respect to the ideologies it contains, the means of representation it utilizes, and the underlying social practices it confirms. (Giroux, 1988: 106)

The study of a culture does not only involve the acknowledgement of facts, that is, the input of geographical, historical, social or political data. It should focus on the complexity of hidden meanings, of underlying values, and how these articulate with the micro- and macrocontexts they integrate. Therefore, 'students must engage knowledge as bordercrossers' (Aronowitz & Giroux, 1991: 118), that is, they must locate different cultural codes, look beyond the obvious, and identify the deep structure of traditions. In other words, a pedagogy of difference does not mean the simple expansion of topics and it is important that the approach echoes the philosophy that underlies the change of content. This difficulty shows in teaching practices which integrate new cultural content but whose per- spective/approach to it is traditional in every sense. That is, the lesson proceeds according to the same structure and the same perspective, except that a new topic is introduced. Briefly, apparent change distracts the teacher from real change. Giroux, again, gives some direction in this matter:

> The pedagogical goal here is not to have students exercise rigorous analytical skills in order to arrive at the right answer, but to better exercise reasoned choice through a critical understanding of what the codes are that organize different meanings and interests into particular configurations of knowledge and power. (Giroux, 1989: 149–50)

By understanding the organisation of meaning and interest in particular cultural codes and how those reflect particular configurations of knowledge and power, students, although studying a foreign culture, should be able to 'translate' them into their own context. Hence, they should recognise some of the issues, desires, successes, and challenges they face in their everyday lives. The meanings and interests of the Other will echo their own thoughts and feelings and, by becoming critically aware of them, students will identify and clarify their own struggles, points of view, predispositions, which are likely to help them make more enlightened choices. Furthermore, McLaren makes a distinction, which is useful for foreign culture teachers/learners, between 'the *concrete other*' and 'the *generalized other*'. Without neglecting the significance of the postmodern emphasis on the specific, McLaren points out the need to focus also on the general, 'without which it is impossible to speak of a radical ethics at all' (McLaren, 1995: 140). A pedagogy of difference is, therefore, concerned with the particulars but finds their meaningfulness in the way they articulate with each other and how their achievements and struggles can be translated into the language of a *'generalized other'*. In sum, it does not lose sight of totality and actively incorporates a plan for citizenship education within a larger project of radical democracy for multicultural societies where difference and dissent do not hinder co-operation but rather encourage affirmation, negotiation and dialogue.

A pedagogy of dialogue

Dialogue was connected with the very beginnings of formal education in ancient Greek and Roman societies, but, with the modernisation of schooling it was replaced by a monological type of communicative interaction based mostly on preplanned one-way presentations from the teacher to the students and vice versa or by directed dialogue. Freire described this pattern of communication, usual in what is today called traditional education, as 'narrative' and 'prescriptive' since it avoided the actual exchange of ideas (Freire, 1970). Claims for the re-establishment of dialogue in classrooms were a leitmotiv in Dewey's and Freire's pedagogical theories and constitute a common ground for all critical pedagogues.

Besides the fact that 'the pedagogy of dialogue is a historical pedagogy' (Gadotti, 1996: 2), the concept of dialogue in pedagogy has changed depending on the political and social thinking of the times and on the educational trends of the moment. So, the pedagogy of dialogue may range from a deep concern for humanising the pedagogical relations, and from an effort to stimulate learning, to one that validates dissent and expects ideological discourse. However, besides the historicity of the notion of pedagogical dialogue, a pedagogy of dialogue can always be distorted, as Gadotti points out:

> Pedagogical theories suffer, together with practice, from certain distortions which can completely disfigure them. Thus, the word dialogue can hide elements such as complacency and complicity, in which the demands and the compromise with teaching content and education completely disappear. The word dialogue can also be used as a pretext for absenteeism or a negative form of domination, allurement, and seduction, with the aim of reaching a false conclusion, a unity without tensions, or a dialogue without opposition. (Gadotti, 1996: 4–5)

Therefore, there is always a danger of transforming classroom dialogue into a chat or informal conversation, into a futile operation of glamour on the part of the teacher in order to catch students' attention, or even, under (un)conscious false pretences of neutrality, into an indoctrinating transmission of the 'truth'. However, CP views dialogue as both attitude and process. In order to embark on knowledge as 'border-crossers', according to Giroux's definition, to engage in critical reflection, and to articulate consensus and dissent in a constructive way, teachers/students must engage in a dialogic relationship. Moreover, preparing students to become active and responsible citizens involves fostering an interactive, dialogic attitude. For this purpose, it is necessary to provide pupils with the conditions which will enable them to actively discuss the complexities of producing meaning and take advantage of the possibilities available to link knowledge and experience. Students need the classroom to be what Giroux calls a 'safe space', where they can 'cross ideological and political borders to clarify their own moral visions' (Giroux, 1997b: 262) and also move beyond cultural borders in order to approach other cultural patterns, interpret them critically and eventually challenge their own common-sensical assumptions. Such 'space' must be felt to be 'safe' by both teachers and students in order to make productive interaction possible, for the dialogical and critical search for knowledge bears a sense of uncertainty, of apparent lack of accuracy, and of incompleteness that must be accepted by everyone in the process as a potentiality and not as an impediment. The first step for this to happen should be to encourage 'both subjective and collective awareness of this very condition' (Walsh, 1991: 139).

The critical notion of a pedagogy of dialogue, one that relies on ongoing, reflective and dialectical dialogue, makes it clear that this approach is not about adding a few novel aspects to classroom interaction, but instead is about questioning the very nature of teaching/learning. It is also not a question of depriving teachers/students of their most cherished assets such as truth, certainty, accuracy and completeness, but more of instilling ideals and principles, showing directions and possibilities, providing means and tools to make this approach viable in the learning context.

A pedagogy of dialogue is nurtured by a pedagogy of difference and dissent, establishes a bridge between reflection and action, advocates empowerment, and relies on critical hope. Consequently, critical dialogue is not exactly trivial conversation, teacher-directed talk, or debate where rhetorical achievement is more important than meaning discussion, but involves meaning interrogation, investigation and production. A pedagogy of dialogue is thus a case of change and action, as Wink argues:

> Dialogue is change-agent chatter. Dialogue is talk that changes us or our context. Dialogue is profound, wise, insightful conversation. Dialogue is two-way, interactive visiting. Dialogue involves periods of lots of noise as people share and lots of silence as people muse. Dialogue is communication that creates and recreates multiple understandings. It moves its participants along the learning curve to that uncomfortable place of relearning and unlearning. (Wink, 1997: 36)

A pedagogy of dialogue is, therefore, an open exchange of ideas that makes a difference. It is joyous, serious, and challenging. It is galvanising and reflective and it is about communication rather than persuasion, and empowerment rather than assertion.

A pedagogy of empowerment

Power has always been linked to education either ostensibly or implicitly. However, it has always been understood as a bipolar mechanism (state/people; powerful/powerless; teacher/student), as descendent (from above), as authority (by those above) and oppressive (by those below). The interconnectedness between power and education has been disguised by a technical conception of schooling placing the focus on the efficiency of the teaching/learning situation understood as a unit of a mass production and market-oriented educational system or, according to other theorists, as economic and ideological pressures upon the school, as mentioned in the previous chapter. However, CP rejects the neutrality of the first approach and considers this latter view as a basis for developing a language of critique. Nevertheless, it has engendered a language of possibility that emerges from a critical, reflective and dialogic process. A critical notion of empowerment combines a language of critique with a language of possibility by combining the modernist legacy of emancipation with the complementary postmodern assumption of difference. Mollenhauer, who first applied Habermas' ideas to education, defined emancipation as 'the freeing of the subject – in our case those growing up in our society – from conditions that limit their rationality and the social actions connected with it' (quoted in Young, 1989: 58). Empowerment, as viewed by critical pedagogues, is multifaceted since it incorporates this notion of emancipation as the liberation from rational oppression, focuses on the need for material equality, and highlights the creative nature of the process of empowerment itself. This interpretation of power as potentially enabling relies heavily on Foucault's unorthodox understanding of power relations:

> Power must be analysed as something which circulates, or rather as something which only functions in the form of a chain. It is never localised here or there, never in anybody's hands, never appropriated as a commodity or piece of wealth. Power is employed and exercised through a net-like organisation. And not only do individuals circulate between its threads; they are always in the position of simultaneously undergoing and exercising this power. (Foucault, 1980: 98)

Foucault gives critical pedagogues the motive and the hope for a language of possibility by identifying power as pervasive, belonging to no one, and available to everyone. This is an enabling view of power in that it does not see it merely as repressive but as largely generative. This conception of power allows for an interpretation of culture that does not disregard the workings of different groups that produce their particular versions of history, knowledge, beliefs and values within unequal relations of power, therefore, one that does not limit the discussions of power to a few social and political spheres (Aronowitz & Giroux, 1991; Darder, 1991: 27). From this standpoint, critical cultural awareness entails not only an affirmation of difference but also its interrogation, that is, the perception of difference in relation to its dialogic construction. In sum, this capacity, which Kreisberg designates as 'critical cultural literacy' and defines as 'the ability to critically analyze one's social and political world on multiple levels', involves not only reading about differences, but reading them critically (Kreisberg, 1992: 19).

Empowerment is generally described as the individual or collective process of taking control over one's life and context (Delgado-Gaitan & Trueba, 1991; Kreisberg, 1992). Giroux, however, provides further clarification of this notion as 'the ability to think and act critically' and elucidates the individual and social implications of such a process by considering that 'individual powers must be linked to democracy in the sense that social betterment must be the necessary consequence of individual flourishing' (Giroux, 1992: 11). This binary notion of empowerment, as both individual and social, makes it a fundamental component of citizenship education, but in a different way from the modernist sense. Within the dominance of the nation-state, the notion of citizenship resulted from 'a constant correlation between an increasing individualization and the reinforcement of this totality', so there were two opposing poles which fortified each other through confrontation (Foucault, 1988: 162). On the contrary, the concept of empowerment, as understood by critical pedagogues, entails the development of the individual in her/his quest for the improvement of society and, therefore, implies an ethical and political perception of the exercise of citizenship.

The category of voice, which is essential to empowerment, incorporates this idea in that it is a possible representation of the self and/or the group, in fusion or interactively. More precisely, the concept of voice allows for the representation of areas of identity left uncovered by the individual/nation dichotomy and also allows for transgressive identities that may represent the intersection of national, ethnic, race, class, or gender categories. Voice may thus stand for a self carved out by its multiple social relations. Walsh is clear on this issue:

> But while voice is tied to subjectivity and identity, its ongoing shaping and formulation are part of a broader social and cultural formation. As such, voice is not an expression of individual consciousness but a reflection of and a coming to terms with the multiple and complex social relations and realities that inform consciousness and position the individual with respect to an 'other'. (Walsh, 1991: 33)

From this perspective, voice is not in essence a singular or unitary expression of a particular individual entity, be it the individual or the nation. On the contrary, it reflects the interaction between several elements in transitory positions. Informed by this notion of voice, empowerment consists of the critical awareness of the ongoing power relations and the critical capacity to challenge them, and, therefore, constitutes an indispensable element for the exercise of a critical citizenship.

Accordingly, a pedagogy of empowerment inspires intercultural education in that it 'cannot work as an intermediary of the respective national cultures' (Borrelli, 1991: 283). These are not understood as singular and monolithic voices but as reflections of multiple and complex layers of meaning that struggle for primacy within unequal relations of power. Likewise, because such asymmetrical power positionings do not happen only within nations but among nations as well, notions of voice and empowerment are also useful in cross-cultural/national encounters where individuals are critically aware that they have to negotiate relations of power relations at its 'extremities', in the sense Foucault describes this process, and that they are not invested with the power of a forged national voice, according to Anderson's view of nations as 'imagined communities' (Anderson, 1983; Foucault, 1980). Therefore, they need to confront and let their multiple and complex identities resonate at the local and everyday level without hiding behind masks. A pedagogy of empowerment also overrides the soft notion of 'tolerance' for cultural difference by entitling every community or individual to a voice and by conceiving power as something to be mediated at the grass roots level. Hence the role of a critical intercultural education framework to educate citizens who are prepared to interact with, not just adapt to, these new cultural, ethical and political configurations. They are empowered, not just educated, citizens equipped to articulate their own patterns of experience with other cultural codes and, eventually, become active citizens in their diverse social contexts.

In a pedagogy of empowerment teachers/students are obviously the main 'vehicles of power' (Foucault, 1980: 89). Although teachers cannot empower students, they can provide the conditions for them to accomplish empowerment, and nobody can empower teachers but themselves. To give teachers the power to make curriculum decisions does not empower them, hence the difference between an 'institutionally empowered teacher' and a 'culturally and critically empowered' one (Kanpol, 1994: 54). Changing topics or methodologies, having the power to make decisions, and using the latest technologies do not make a critical pedagogue. Becoming a critical pedagogue implies a change of perspective. This point was made by Giroux when he advised radical pedagogues to 'rework those aspects of the traditional curriculum in which democratic possibilities exist' (Giroux, 1997b: 107).

For a pedagogy of empowerment to take place, it is important that the teachers themselves initiate a process which may involve a paradigm shift or rebalancing of their knowledge, beliefs and attitudes. Second, they must be aware that they have just initiated a never-ending process, which they will pursue in collaboration with their students with the aim of constantly exploring its possibilities. Third, teachers must challenge and encourage their students to find their own voice by enabling them to critically decode their own experiences and by expanding their horizons. As the role of the family weakens, media cultures compete, with great advantage, against schools in the formation of cultural identities. Through the media, young people may, if they are not critical about what they are watching or listening to, be exposed to distorted visions of power, and may absorb unsuitable models. They may also be unscrupulously targeted by marketing planners, and be deprived of any social, ethical or political voice (Aronowitz & Giroux, 1991; Giroux, 1997a). Furthermore, most of the extracurricular contact young people have with the foreign cultures they learn at school happens via the media. Consequently, forming media-critical culture–literate consumers is part of the task of forming empowered citizens in contemporary democratic societies (Buckingham, 1998). This is a process that Williams describes as 'practical consciousness' in action, that, in this case, takes the form of 'a process often described as development but in practice [is] a struggle at the roots of the mind'. This struggle involves 'confronting a hegemony in the fibres of the self' as well as 'grasping the known' in order to conceive the unknown (Williams, 1977: 212). In sum, in order to become empowered producers and mediators of culture, teachers/students need to critically decode the messages they receive in their everyday lives and to creatively construct their own voices in order to fulfil their role as active citizens of the various communities to which they belong.

A pedagogy of action

CP is a pedagogy of action in that it perceives knowledge as constructed, social, open to critique, and transformative and it acknowledges the educational process as reflective, dissensual, dialogical, and empowering. From this perspective, teachers/students are active participants in cultural production and social transformation. Action, as understood by critical pedagogues, is praxis in that it articulates reflection and action, theory and practice, thinking and doing. In other words, critical action is an informed, reflective, engaged and creative practice. According to Giroux, praxis 'represents the transition from critical thought to reflective intervention in the world' (Giroux, 1981: 117). The link between action and critical/reflective thinking and their mutual dependence was also emphasised by the Frankfurt theorists who expressed their concern for the rational organisation of human activity, following the German philosophical tradition, and worked on making evident the relationship between theory and practice. As far as educational theory is concerned, Dewey himself concentrated on the interconnectedness between 'experience' and 'reflective thought' by emphasising that the material and the purpose of thinking were actions. As he saw it, the act of thinking was prompted by a problematic situation and it was during the course of their interaction that ideas emerged as 'anticipations of possible solutions' (Dewey, 1956: 188). Likewise, Freire concentrated on both the active side of learning and knowing and the reflective component of acting that account for the distinction between 'authentic praxis' and 'pure activism' (Freire, 1970: 52). According to him, 'to know is a transitive verb, a verb that expresses an action', which means that to learn is to produce and to think entails acting (Freire, 1998: 91). Nevertheless, thought and action, as well as theory and practice, while interacting do not dissolve into each other although their interplay affects the nature of each. Knowledge, in Freire's opinion, makes sense only when inspired by and applied to reality, that is, it is culturally produced, based on experience and it continually goes back to its roots, at the same time transforming and fortifying them.

A pedagogy of action, here understood as a 'pedagogy of praxis', in Gadotti's words, is not simply about 'utilitarian practice' or 'pure activism', it is practice informed by theory which leads to transformative action (Gadotti, 1996). The influential role theory plays in pedagogical practice is acknowledged by educators who apply Critical Theory to education and also by Young, who has worked on the implications of Habermas' theories for education, and draws attention to the fact that theory always underlies practice whether we are aware of it or not. He states:

> Practice is inevitably theorised, it is just a question of whether one theorises it in the taken-for-granted categories of the status quo, with their aura of naturalness and indeed, of being uncontaminated by anything so unrelated to a peaceful life as 'theory' or whether one tries to distinguish between the inevitable and the constructed aspects of reality. (Young, 1989: 168)

Most teachers are not aware of the theory that supports their practice nor do they consider it important. Moreover, the relationship between theory and practice is largely taken as subtractive, that is, by becoming more theoretical one is supposed to become less practical and vice versa. By and large, theory may be considered useful to pedagogical practice if it is presented in the form of a method which implies change by replacing old routines with new ones. However, some teachers are pleasantly surprised when they find out that what they have been doing by intuition is not so different from some theory they read about and realise that they have actually been theorising. Furthermore, their practice becomes much more effective when they become critically aware that they are actually 'building theory' (Wink, 1997: 48).

The articulation between action and theorising offers the 'possibility of disidentification' (Ball, 1995), that is, of re-evaluating and reforming prevailing practices formerly taken as natural and inevitable, and also the prospect of 'an engaged pedagogy' which means an active commitment to the teaching/learning process under way (hooks, 1994). And both aspects allow for transformative action which was previously identified as a main goal for CP. However, practice embedded in theory is not necessarily innovative, liberating, or emancipatory (Giroux 1994a: 116; hooks, 1994: 61; Peim, 1993: 6). Theory is thus foundational to transformative action but it is not liberating on its own, this is the function of critical thinking driven by a quest for self and social transformation. In order to be emancipatory and transformative, pedagogical practice needs to be explicitly political and to show ethical concerns. It is only when schools are critically aware of their role as cultural, social, and political agencies that social and educational reform will happen.

The importance of critical cultural awareness aiming at tranformative action is obvious when it deals with one's home culture but is less evident when it concerns foreign culture teaching/learning. Within the supremacy of the nation-state, national cultures tended to be understood as autonomous and self-sufficient. Accordingly, a cross-cultural convergence, at any level, would mean the encounter of two distant and self-contained unities. These would come into contact but seldom interact or, at least, little emphasis, in general, was put on the extent to which they were permeated by each other in such an encounter. This notion loses validity in our multicultural societies which tend to recognise their increased dependence on global structures and on each other. As a human being and a citizen of the world, the individual is made ethically responsible for all other living beings that share life and this planet with her/him. From a political point of view, the individual is asked to act as a committed citizen of wider international and transnational circles, such as the European Union, for example. Within her/his social circle, the individual is constantly bewildered by new images, new habits, new possibilities and is forced to make a choice. Moreover, from a philosophical perspective, the individual is expected to compose her/his identity from within the multiple and complex interrelations available.

In sum, from this perspective, the citizen of the future should know that her/his actions will make a difference and will resonate in the wider circles of her/his citizenship. Furthermore, in a cross-cultural encounter, the more critically and culturally aware the participants become, the less it is controlled by 'givens' and, therefore, cross-cultural interactions develop into culturally, socially and politically active, productive and transformative events. Education is preparation for the future and foreign culture classrooms ought to be the sources of active citizens prepared to responsibly engage the new emerging structures and to consciously intervene in the shaping of history.

A pedagogy of hope

Finally, one essential feature in the discourse of CP is a discourse of hope which Freire accentuates and which 'points to the horizon of the "not yet" ' (Freire, 1993; Giroux, 1992: 77). This central dimension allows the movement to overcome a language of critique, which is also fundamental in CP, and move towards one of possibility. The notion of hope here is not one of the nostalgic recovery of lost values, a romanticised utopianism, a refuge from apocalyptic fear or a humanistic discourse that is, at the same time, self-assertive and compassionate. It is, on the contrary, what Giroux calls 'radical hope' that entails the belief that every human being is entitled, within historical limits, to give a legitimate and meaningful contribution to the course of life within the scope of her/his various concentric social circles (Giroux, 1994a: 170).

The world has lately undergone profound changes, and Europe, in particular, has, in Williams' words, been through a 'long revolution' and has embarked on a 'journey of hope' (Williams, 1983). In his opinion, 'inevitabilities' have been challenged, that is, a discourse of critique has been used to the full and in such a way that we are now able to deconstruct what was settled and given as inevitable, so we can 'begin gathering our resources for a journey of hope'. And further, according to this author, there is ground for such an optimism because we have, at least, accomplished 'the outline of a unified alternative social theory' that involves changes of mind, of relations, of balances, and the disruption of binary divisions that were taken as fixed and unquestionable, such as emotion versus intelligence. Williams calls our attention to 'the new movements of our time – peace, ecology, feminism' which upset this separation in that they are emotional to the extent that they express 'a direct and intransigent concern with actual people' while displaying the same level of 'rational and intelligent' aptitudes in their campaigns and strategies (Williams, 1983: 243–69).

The concept of hope in CP also articulates the components of emotion and rationality by including desire, dream, courage, conscious risk, programming, reasoning, critical analysis and agency. The element of hope in pedagogy involves having a project which integrates a greater need for change in which education plays a significant role. Williams again felt this urge, as he set forth:

> The central need of the years towards 2000 is the discovery of adequate social and political agencies through which this urgent development can become generally available. Yet this is only one way of seeing the problem. What has also to be considered, and reconsidered, is the quality of the new information and intelligence, and of the kinds of connection they offer to our actual and usually crowded thinking. It is a question, that is to say, of how far any of us have got the analysis and therefore the signals right. (Williams, 1983: 19)

The rediscovery of the potentialities of the educational system, as a social and political agency, in order to make this development available is certainly one of the possibilities open to Williams. The notion of a pedagogy of hope as a form of cultural politics, as it was formulated by Freire, may well be one possible way to turn the school into one of those agencies suggested by Williams. Freire also considers hope as an 'ontological need' that is, however, 'anchored in practice' and must be 'critical' in order to avoid despair (Freire, 1993: 9–14, translation mine). His notion of 'critical hope' echoes Williams' concerns about the ways of putting such a project into practice and suggests that the discourse of critique and of possibility should be made interdependent.

A pedagogy of hope based on a critical rationale is indispensable for the teaching/ learning of foreign cultures within a global as well as a European context. In order for the struggle against discrimination and xenophobia on any grounds – class, race, gender, cultural status, linguistic particularities or other – to succeed, the discourse of critique, which has been vital for the dismantling of traditional frames of mind, has to expand into one of transformation in which the notion of critical hope is of the utmost importance. At the beginning of a new millennium, our multicultural global village and a daringly renovated world are in urgent need of citizens prepared to interact interculturally, keeping in mind the renewal of the democratic society, and foreign language/culture education should play a definitive and unequivocal role in launching this immense project. As cultural workers, foreign language/culture teachers should commit themselves to the moral and political struggle for improving the quality of intercultural communication and, therefore, of human life in general.

The Critique of Critical Pedagogy

CP has been subject to criticism from several sectors. There are arguments upon which most critics tend to agree such as its obscure language and the exaggerated burden it places on schools and teachers. Other criticisms come from different perspectives, whether of critical theorists or postmodernists, who blame CP for attempting to reconcile philosophical theories which are essentially different. On the whole, in educational circles, CP is regarded with suspicion for it connects education with critical thinking. Although critical thinking, as a general concept, is always included among educational objectives, when it comes to the consideration of its application in more specific terms, it always provokes controversy or even opposition (McPeck, 1981: 1).

Reconciling the irreconcilable

On philosophical grounds, CP took a risky path when it tried to design a philosophy of education by merging two divergent schools of thought, namely Critical Theory and Postmodernism, which have been used partially and mingled according to CP's own vision. Its construction of theory has been the target of most criticisms concerning the philosophical positions of its educational tenets. Critical theorists, such as Sultan, argue that Habermas has provided the best potential for developing a critical pedagogy (Stanley, 1992: 123), while neglecting the fact that Habermas' philosophical arguments have themselves been subject to criticism, also by American CP theorists (Giroux, 1992: 47–50). On the other hand, CP has been blamed for undertheorising the discourse of postmodernism (Usher & Edwards, 1994: 220) and continuing to depend heavily on modern ideals of reason and emancipation based on universal principles (Bowers, 1991; Ellsworth, 1989; Luke & Gore, 1992; Wardekker & Miedema, 1997), although it is recognised that critical pedagogues do 'reappropriate, redefine, and reground them' (Burbules & Rice, 1991: 397). Besides, their discourse is considered to be unsurprisingly authoritative due to its neo-Marxist and Frankfurtian roots (Gore, 1993:

114) and is accused of treating the oppressed as an indivisible mass with uniform needs and wishes (Weiler, 1993), that is, overlooking difference in the name of a common plight. Giroux acknowledges the difficulties of this delicate balance between modernist and postmodernist impulses when he states that 'at its worst, critical pedagogy as a form of educational criticism has been overly shaped by the discourse of modernism' (Aronowitz & Giroux, 1991: 117). But he explains how he intends to keep the balance while directly answering his critics:

> This is not a liberal call to harmonize and resolve differences, as critics like Elizabeth Ellsworth (1988) wrongly argue, but an attempt to understand differences in terms of the historical and social grounds on which they are organized.
> ... To detach them [differences] from the discourse of democracy and freedom is to remove the possibility of either articulating their particular interests as part of a wider struggle for power or understanding how their individual contradictory interests are developed with historically specific conjunctures. (Giroux, 1997b: 151–2)

Thus, critical pedagogues hold on to the belief that this philosophy of education may rely on opposing philosophical theories in order to incorporate different perspectives that may complement each other.

The intricacies of the cultural continuum

The emphasis of CP on cultural production rather than on cultural transmission led some voices on the conservative side to claim that educational excellence should be understood as the input and evaluation of a (de)finite body of knowledge 'needed to thrive in the modern world' (Hirsch, 1988: xiii). For Hirsch, cultural literacy means the mastery of a canon of information specific to a national homogeneous culture or to a cultural elite. However, this view of culture does not, according to Giroux, suit a critical pedagogy because it 'expresses a single durable history and vision, one at odds with a critical notion of democracy and difference' (Giroux, 1992: 94). Nevertheless, Taylor's critique of Freire focuses on the lack of a definition of literacy in his texts, which may well allow for an imposition of the educator's culture on the learner and initiate a process of de-culturation (Taylor, 1993). But Freire emphasises that 'all information holds the possibility of expanding into education if the information is critically received by the informed' (Freire, 1996: 99). The process of cultural production through dialogue based on the experience of the learner is a leitmotif in CP which, however, causes some discomfort among those who understand cultural literacy as the 'discourse of the elites' to be democratically passed on to as many as possible (Aronowitz & Giroux, 1991: 41).

The rhetorical hallmarks of Critical Pedagogy

The lack of clarity in the discourse of CP is a general comment made by its critics, Giroux's style being generally considered as excessively impenetrable. He is accused of cultivating an arrogant style which makes his work inaccessible to teachers (Apple, 1996b; Ellsworth, 1989). But, Freire's writing as well as the discourse of CP in general are also regarded as obscure and overabstracted, with too much recourse to metaphorical language and repetitions that make it, on the one hand, elitist, and, on the other hand, subversive (Bowers, 1991; Taylor, 1993). Thus, the critics say, it has little connection with the teachers' reality and its impact is limited. However, it seems interesting here to refer to the opinion of one practitioner of CP:

> The irony is that this new language helped me break out of previous ways of knowing. Another contradiction! The thing I thought was the barrier (language) was the very thing that helped me break through the barrier. The language of critical pedagogy made me crazy at first, and ironically, finally opened the door to more complex understandings for me. (Wink, 1997: 23)

CP has its own particular language. It is challenging in that it deals with concepts in a different way and offers new paths for thought. Teachers may either draw back from it or become fascinated by its intricacies. Although the discourse of CP is accused by some of conveying a vision that still is patriarchal and colonising, one that hides a male-dominated notion of public life and a patronising concept of literacy (Luke & Gore, 1992; Taylor, 1993), others, however, consider it to be a 'new' type of discourse that not only makes CP distinctive but also itself conveys a particular message.

Theory in practice

According to its critics, neither the rhetoric of CP nor its message provide clear guidance to teachers' practice, instead it remains too much at the theoretical level. Teachers are, therefore, left with the difficult task of designing practices to match the theory (Bowers, 1991; Gore, 1993). Gore identifies 'two strands of critical pedagogy', on the one hand, Freire and Shor, who articulate pedagogical practices, and Giroux and McLaren, on the other hand, who develop a 'critical *educational theory*' rather than a 'critical *pedagogy*' (Gore, 1993: 41–2, her emphasis). Despite his practical approach, Freire is, nevertheless, considered 'too psychological, too utopian' (Taylor, 1993: 2). However, Giroux confirms that it is necessary both 'to define theory as central to any viable pedagogical practice' and to 'address the meaning and purpose of critical pedagogy as a concrete practice' (Giroux, 1994a: 112), although he has certainly been more involved in the first task than the second one. Nevertheless, the venture of relocating theory at the centre of pedagogical practice has turned out to be essential for the change of both theory and practice and for teacher's development.

On the other hand, CP is blamed for being too directive (Gore, 1993) and for having disregarded the fact that teachers may not share its vision of the new society (Bowers, 1991: 248) or even that 'possible contradictions between the desires of critical pedagogy and the desires of actual learners' may occur as well (Usher & Edwards, 1994: 220). This possibility has not been ignored by CP theorists who acknowledge the fact that 'it is likely that those who choose this approach will encounter initial resistance by some students' (Aronowitz & Giroux, 1986: 52) and also that 'critical pedagogy becomes, for many students, an uncomfortable and self-contesting exercise' (McLaren, 1995: 19). In actual fact, CP is a difficult task for teachers and learners for, although it is accused of being too teacher-centred and of giving teachers too much authority (Ellsworth, 1989), it places great responsibility on teachers not only with regard to their teaching practice but also to their position in the school in relation to administrators, colleagues and parents (Cochran-Smith, 1993; Passmore, 1967). Although any process of change involves fear of the unknown, without some risk-taking, no significant change will occur (Fullan, 1993: 25). Therefore, both prospective and in-service teachers that become acquainted with CP do perceive it as 'risky business' (Kanpol, 1997: 110); however, in Freire's words 'those wanting to teach must be able to dare' (Freire, 1998: 4). Despite claims that Dewey did not see the school as the '*sole* instrument' meant to solve the social, economical and moral problems of society (Ravitch, 1978: 10–13), Giroux puts a heavier responsibility on the school:

> ... it is important to note that while schools are not the sole sites for implementing social change, they do offer an important terrain on which to provide future generations with new ways for thinking about the building of a more just society. (Giroux, 1997a: 65)

In spite of the gap that seems to exist between the ambitious goals of CP and the limited reception that it has achieved among educators and learners, and also despite the voices of those who rush to identify its demise claiming it 'to have been a stillborn child' and the 'very few remaining proponents of critical pedagogy' to be 'relics of bygone times' (Wardekker & Miedema, 1997: 46), studies and projects are being undertaken throughout the world in order to pursue the paths indicated by Freire and his followers. Moreover, critical thinking remains on the agenda of contemporary philosophical authors and of educational programmes in general. If teachers are supposed to teach their learners to be critical, they will first have to find out what this means and get used to doing it. Teachers may still refuse to dare. Nevertheless, it is important that teachers and learners know what and why they are giving up.

Conclusion

Critical Pedagogy is presented here as the educational framework for the development of critical cultural awareness in foreign language/culture education. It relies upon the combination of critical discourse with the commitment to transformative action and, therefore, claims that education should be embedded in social context and that its political nature should be explicitly recognised and endorsed. Critical Pedagogy draws from different philosophical and educational theories, namely Critical Theory, Postmodernism, Cultural Studies, Progressivism, and Reconstructionism, in order to construct its own vision of knowledge, culture, society, and education. It advocates a number of precepts, which were summarised here, namely the enhancement of critical reflection in articulation with critical dialogue and critical action, the validation of difference and dissent, and the cultivation of empowerment and critical hope. These are considered here as the main tenets for a pedagogy which aims to develop critical cultural awareness. However, these notions should be understood in the light of the different schools of thought that have constituted the theoretical background of Critical Pedagogy and, therefore, enriched by their divergent, sometimes colliding, points of view. For the purpose of this study, it was considered necessary to expand upon the understanding of the particular implications of both philosophical frameworks that Critical Pedagogy draws from, namely Critical Theory and Postmodernism, for the development of critical cultural awareness applied to contexts of intercultural communication, as follows in the next chapter.

Notes

1. Giroux helps to clarify the notion of ideology as it is used by CP. He explains that 'ideology refers to the production, consumption, and representation of ideas and behavior, all of which can either distort or illuminate the nature of reality' and that 'when linked to the notion of struggle, ideology illuminates the important relationships among power, meaning and interest' (Giroux, 1997b: 75).
2. Giroux, who is more explicit about his borrowing from Critical Theory, focuses mainly on the works of the Frankfurt School (Horkheimer & Adorno, Marcuse, Benjamin, and he takes a critical look at Habermas' communication theory).
3. Although Marcuse was more open to popular cultural and political movements in the 1960s as he experienced them in the United States and even became a mentor of youth movements there, like Horkheimer and Adorno he focuses on mass culture sameness and the alienatory effect it causes on its consumers (Marcuse, 1991).
4. Giroux and McLaren, who most predominantly discuss postmodernism applied to CP, focus their studies mainly on French poststructuralists and postmodern feminist writers.
5. Although the phenomenon is hardly new, the concept and the term 'interdisciplinary' re-emerged and was adopted in mid-twentieth century as a reaction against the fixed boundaries between disciplines established by modernity. Interdisciplinarity has been both contested and supported by academia, generating intense debates, although research on Cultural Studies has undoubtedly been implementing it widely. For further discussion of definitions of interdisciplinarity, its history, theory and practice, consult Klein (1990).
6. Habermas' version of transcultural rationality, achieved through communicative action (Habermas, 1987b: 314–15) versus Derrida's concept of rationality as 'logocentric' (Siegel, 1988: 49).
7. Habermas' insistence upon the growing need for reflection in modern society is a constant in his works. For example, he says that 'the urge to reflective understanding of society and our activities goes deeper and is more widely spread in modern society than it has ever been before ... There is no route back from reflectiveness' (Habermas, 1993: 22).
8. Categories such as 'women', 'black', 'young', 'Caribbean' started to be intersected and their boundaries were unclear. McLaren advises educators to consider Gloria Anzaldúa's *mestizage* theories 'that create new categories of identity for those left out or pushed out of existing ones'. He still adds that 'the sites of our identity within postmodernity are various' (McLaren, 1995: 228).
9. These categories, nationality, ethnicity, race, gender or age, are generally allocated to particular spaces that generated distinctions, restrictions, or even exclusion, like nation/region, official/unoffical, public/private, Welcomed/No-(coloureds, women, Irish), ghettoes, clubs, etc. On divisions of time and space in late modernity see, for example, Giddens (1984).

Chapter 2
Philosophical Foundations for Critical Cultural Awareness

In order to establish the philosophical foundations for critical cultural awareness within the scope of this study I will draw on two different philosophical frameworks, Critical Theory and Postmodernism, neither of which is monolithic in itself. My objective is to identify aspects from each philosophical framework that may be relevant for and complementary to understanding just what critical cultural awareness entails. From the early formulation of Critical Theory emanates a notion of rationality that is rooted in social processes and illuminates the understanding of cultural knowledge and communication as viewed by Horkheimer, Adorno, and Marcuse. Their original view has been expanded and radicalised by the postmodern critique with respect to the manipulative character of media-produced culture as well as radicalised by the postmodern description of culture as contingent, intricate, particular, and often impenetrable. However, I will also highlight the aspects that separate the universalist, consensual and normative vision of linguistic/cultural communication provided by Habermas, whose views are related to but different from those of Horkheimer, Adorno, and Marcuse, from the postmodern vision based on difference and discordance. Furthermore, the alternative proposals for cultural description and analysis made by both Critical Theory and Postmodernism and the respective variants within each of these frameworks are also focused upon.

Critical Theory

Critical Theory is a philosophical system of principles that has been connected with the Frankfurt School ever since Horkheimer coined this term and contrasted it with what he named Traditional Theory in his 1937 essay on *Critical Theory* (Horkheimer, 1972). Horkheimer based Traditional Theory on a positivist concept of reason that, according to him, developed with the evolution of scientism, while he viewed Critical Theory as an attempt to root rationality in social interaction. By relating knowledge to society, Critical Theory accentuates not only the social but also the political character of rationality, thus honouring the original Marxist foundations of the Frankfurt School. The critique of the Enlightenment and of instrumental reason was then expanded by Horkheimer and Adorno and by other contemporary members of the Frankfurt School like Benjamin, Marcuse, Fromm, etc.

Although also engaging in the critique of instrumental reason, Habermas, who became the leading figure of the Frankfurt School's second generation and currently the name most often associated with Critical Theory, takes a different stance from his predecessors towards modernity. He considers their critique of modernity excessive and states that Horkheimer and Adorno's *Dialectic of Enlightenment* 'does not do justice to the rational content of cultural modernity in bourgeois ideals (and also instrumentalized along with them)' (Habermas, 1987b: 113). Moreover, he explicitly compares their thesis with Nietzsche's nihilism, although he considers that the nature of their pessimism does not coincide with that of poststructuralism and therefore 'Adorno's "negative dialectics" and Derrida's "deconstruction" can be seen as different answers to the same problem' (Habermas, 1987b: 184). In spite of his own critique of the instrumentalisation of reason during the evolution of modernity, he ultimately tried to rescue modern rationality by introducing his own concept of communicative rationality. Within this position, his theories provide some valuable contributions for the development of this study, although they are restrictive in some aspects as we shall see. Before describing Habermas' theories on communication and some of the earlier Frankfurt theorists' critique of mass culture, it is useful to identify their perceptions of instrumental, critical, and intersubjective ways of reasoning.

Instrumental reason

As a result of the Enlightenment, reason was accorded an ontological status, becoming considered a superior faculty essential to Man. Its essentiality made it value-neutral, transcultural, ahistorical, and universal in the sense that it was not, or at least should not be, historically or culturally contaminated. This premise inspired the search for emancipation on the basis of equality, which ultimately occurred on an individual basis and which was restricted to those considered to be highly rational human beings excluding, for example, civilisations other than that of the West as well as women. Thus, the primacy of Reason became the overarching quality that determined every other feature in the elaboration of the modern mind.

Moreover, the nature of the enlightened type of rationality was furthered by and developed in order to suit scientific activity. Notions such as experiment, method, measurement, demonstration and evidence which have been linked with the idea of a systematic, quantitative and objective type of knowledge, played an important role in the conception of the modern scientific mind. Reality was thus objectified, reified and organised in order to favour the analysis of its functioning. This model, exemplified by the natural sciences, has since been applied to every other field of knowledge.

The application of method to reasoning was decisive in the development of science itself and to the evolution of modern society on both economic and political levels. The scientific method became a link between opposing tendencies such as capitalism and socialism, who took it for granted as well as exploited the implications it had for the development of the industrial world. Scientific reasoning developed then into instrumental reason in that it tends to isolate and control, split fact from value, and, as a consequence, treat people and environment as instruments.

The mechanisation of work and the routine of everyday life structured according to characteristic features of modernity such as the division of time and space resulted from an understanding of modern life and work that privileged its functionality (Giddens, 1984). As a consequence, organisation[1] galvanises social, economic, political and interpersonal relations in modern societies in the form of the bureaucratisation of society.

Critical reason

Members of the Frankfurt School endeavoured to undertake the critique of instrumental reason, by which they meant reason deprived of its critical possibilities, that is, its reduction to technological rationality aiming for prediction, precision and production and its subordination to industry. Horkheimer and Adorno's seminal work, *Dialectic of Enlightenment*, paved the way for a later critique of the Enlightenment drawing attention to its positivist use of reason and identifying the concept of instrumental reason:

> Positivism, which finally did not spare thought itself, the chimera in a cerebral form, has removed the very last insulating instance between

individual behavior and the social norm. The technical process, into which the subject has objectified itself after being removed from the consciousness, is free of the ambiguity of mythic thought as of all meaning altogether, because reason itself has become the mere instrument of the all-inclusive economic apparatus. (Horkheimer & Adorno, 1972: 30)[2]

The authors understand instrumental reason to be a suprasocial, utilitarian kind of knowledge used by a subject emptied of her/his self-consciousness and also, as Habermas points out, of self-reflection. This is the critique of modernity itself considered as a final stage into which the Enlightenment has fallen and eventually betrayed itself. Not even Marxism escapes blame: 'Marx reduces the process of reflection to the level of instrumental action ... *Marx conceives of reflection according to the model of production*' (Habermas, 1972: 44, his emphasis).

The tenets mentioned above – positivist thought, individualism, objectification, universalism, economicism – were explored by Horkheimer in the distinction he draws between Traditional and Critical theories (Horkheimer, 1972). Through Critical Theory, Horkheimer locates all human rational activity within a social framework.[3] Rationality emancipates human activity but not in a neutral and detached way. Critical thinking is itself unsettling and, at the same time, it is fed by social tension. It analyses the underlying relations among members of society, brings individual and collective motives into consciousness and lays bare institutional powers.

Despite their critique of instrumental reason, Frankfurt theorists do not dismiss the early postulates of the Enlightenment and their purpose is, in the end, to recover the potential of enlightened reason whilst keeping in mind the rational reorganisation of modern society.[4] As McCarthy explains in his Introduction to Habermas' *The Theory of Communicative Action*, theirs is 'an enlightened suspicion of enlightenment' (Habermas, 1984, p. v). They wanted to promote a society made critically rational and this is what makes the Frankfurt School's Critical Theory such an important source for educational refinement. According to Misgeld, the aim of establishing a critical community is what brings Habermas and Freire together (Misgeld, 1985: 108), for with the technical instrumentalisation of reason modern society has fallen short of the best possibilities of attaining enlightened reason mostly by missing the human side of it.

However, Habermas does not dismiss instrumental reason altogether and among his knowledge-constitutive interests he includes the 'technical' and the 'practical'. The first aims to describe the 'comprehension of the objectified reality' while the latter is more connected with the cultural sciences and means the 'maintenance of the intersubjectivity of mutual understanding' (Habermas, 1972: 176). On the other hand, these can only be considered as knowledge-constitutive interests when referring to the 'emancipatory cognitive interest' because the latter implies reflection.[5] All three types of knowledge-constitutive interests orient different aspects of life, 'the technical interest guides work, the practical guides interaction, and the emancipatory guides power' (Lakomski, 1999: 177). Thus, Habermas does not reject the technical or practical interests, but makes clear that they will have to aspire to an emancipatory quest that comprehends self-reflection, for knowledge-constitutive interests can only be considered as such when they intend more than the simple reproduction or self-preservation of society. Likewise, rising above basic needs was the ultimate aim of the early ideals of the Enlightenment.

Furthermore, unlike traditional thinking, by which Horkheimer means the Enlightenment way of thinking,[6] critical thought does not separate theory from practice, knowledge from action, or value from fact in order to avoid tension, to achieve absolute truth or to be totally objective. It is conscious of being partial, political, interrogative, even disturbing but also of never attaining absolute truth. Its aim is to go deep beneath the surface of things and to question established notions. In his 'Introduction' to Horkheimer's text, Aronowitz writes that 'it is the task of critical theory to see "the human bottom of nonhuman things" and to demystify the surface forms of equality' (Horkheimer, 1972: xiii). This description leads us close to Freud's travelling from unconsciousness to consciousness, and eventually approaches Derrida's 'deconstruction'[7] or Foucault's 'capillary level of power'[8] as we shall see later.

Critical Theory is thus intensely social and political since the Frankfurt School, on the whole, maintains the tenets of Marxism with respect to political emancipation and social justice. Horkheimer considers that it is Critical Theory's task to 'illuminate' the 'rational organization of human activity' and he concedes that, to some extent, he got this idea from German idealism (Horkheimer, 1972: 245). He also sees reality as the product of human activity and since the latter is a complex interweaving of desires, expectations, rhythms, goals and interests, the resulting reality is marked by tension and impermanence. The critical philosopher accepts reality as such because 'a philosophy that thinks to find peace within itself, in any kind of truth whatsoever, has therefore nothing to do with critical theory' (Horkheimer, 1972: 252).

Although Critical Theory seeks transcendence through rationalisation, it is immanent by nature because it departs from the everyday issues of an interactive society. Despite reinforcing the need for theorising, theory is embedded in practice and stems from action which is reflective. It has its *locus* in the social setting understood as a dynamic whole:

> Critical thinking is the function neither of the isolated individual nor of a sum-total of individuals. Its subject is rather a definite individual in his real relation to other individuals and groups, in his conflict with a particular class, and finally, in the resultant web of relationships with the social totality and with nature. (Horkheimer, 1972: 210–11)

Critical Theory does not deal with the individual or the collective as isolated units, but focuses instead on the interactions between individuals and groups, none of which are self-contained entities since they exist 'intersubjectively', in Habermas' terms.

Nevertheless, for Horkheimer, as well as for Habermas, the main element of the social process is still rationality and the goal is emancipation. Emancipation in this sense is achieved through critical thinking which for the early Frankfurtians had the aim of rescuing the oppressed as well as a declining culture. For Habermas, emancipation means more precisely the power of reflection and vice versa since 'the pursuit of reflection knows itself as a movement of emancipation' (Habermas, 1972: 197). In addition, Habermasian emancipation is achieved in communication free of constraints which he described as the Ideal Speech Situation (Habermas, 1970, 1979, 1984). Within this situation, emancipation entails the overcoming of domination in the form of any restriction that may inhibit free communication but is nonetheless geared towards consensus, as we shall see later. Whereas neither Horkheimer nor Adorno try to eliminate tensions in the process, Habermas seeks the more consensual and ideal aspects of human interaction. As a result, Habermas' thought tends to be situated in an intermediate position in Horkheimer's distinction between Traditional and Critical Theory. However, the use of reasoning with the purpose of social emancipation remains a legacy from the original ideals of the Enlightenment that is emphasised by the Frankfurt School. Emancipatory rationality, therefore, does not come from above. It is society which is made rational, but not in a technical manner. Instead it is a dialogical and pedagogical process which is motivated by great concern for social justice. On the other hand, Critical Theory is not deconstructive in the postmodern sense since it focuses mostly on recovering and reconstructing modernity. Despite Horkheimer and Adorno's pessimism and Habermas' utopianism, Critical Theory is essentially ambitious and vigorous.

Intersubjective reason

The Enlightenment favoured a view of the universe structured in binary oppositions, the principal of which is the dichotomy between subject and object. This was an essential division that would enable a systematic and disengaged view of reality and would foster the development of science even though it was also highly stimulated by the latter. Other dualisms, such as that of the individual/society, and the 'We/They' dichotomy, based on race or ethnicity, for example, stemmed from the general idea of a necessary division and a controlling/controlled type of relationship between subject and object where 'the distance between subject and object, a presupposition of abstraction, is grounded in the distance from the thing itself which the master achieved through the mastered' (Horkheimer & Adorno, 1972: 13). Distance, abstraction and control are key elements in the contact between subject and object.

This objectifying attitude of the subject towards the object, which was previously described as instrumental reason, justified human control over nature, which is now very much contested by radical ecologists who view animals, plants and even minerals as subjects (Ferry, 1992). Likewise, it has determined a descriptive type of knowledge about the object of research, either human or non-human. Consequently, a scientific analysis should imply a distant, disengaged, monological, objective and objectifying view of the object by the subject.

Critical Theory, on the contrary, emphasises the 'rootedness of our cognitive accomplishments' (Habermas, 1992: 7), that is, the individual does not exist independently from society, individual consciousness is interwoven with social processes and knowledge is socially produced. In sum, the subject–object type of epistemic relation is replaced by the subject–subject model (Hoy & McCarthy, 1994: 87). Critical theorists reject both the atomistic concept of the individual and the unilateral concentration of power implied in a subject–object interaction and concentrate on the creative and democratic potential of a subject–subject relationship.

Although the concept of object disappears from the equation, this is not the only alteration because there is also an essential change in the notion of subject. The concept of a solitary subject which ruled the enlightened way of thinking is definitely overcome by the notion of a social subject, and this is not an idea exclusive to the Frankfurt School but an assumption that underpins contemporary philosophical thought. Habermas identifies four 'themes' common to the philosophical movements of this century 'in spite of the boundaries between schools' which he designates as 'postmetaphysical thinking, the linguistic turn, situating reason, and overcoming logocentrism' (Habermas, 1992: 8). The change in the subject is inherent in all these themes which refer to a reconsideration of scientific rationality, to the move from the philosophy of consciousness to the philosophy of language, to the embeddedness of reason in culture and history and finally to the relocation of theory within practice. As Habermas points out, this is an evolution that has been developing throughout the twentieth century with the contributions of, among others, Nietzsche, Vygotsky, Bakhtin and Marx, to name just a few of the acknowledged founding fathers of the philosophical change in the late twentieth century. However, Habermas expanded this idea in a particular way which is, eventually, more restrictive precisely because it is normative and consensus driven.

Bearing in mind the four themes mentioned above, the notion of the 'intersubjectively recognized subject', in Habermas' terms, challenges, with regard to scientific and social research, the premises of pure, instrumental reason and, consequently, the distance maintained between theory and practice and advocates dialogical and, occasionally, even overlapping positions in subject–subject research. Likewise, as far as language is concerned, the change from the paradigm of subjectivity into the paradigm of intersubjectivity, or from the 'paradigm of consciousness' into the 'paradigm of language' as Habermas puts it, implies using language within the framework of 'communicative action'. This requires the capacity to establish 'interpersonal relations' instead of simply practising an exercise of 'subject-centred' reasoning for representational or strategic purposes, that is, aiming at descriptive knowledge or at success-oriented expression or intervention (Habermas, 1984: 86; 1987b: 314).

The intersubjectivistic orientation of the subject still differs from the subjectivistic one in that the subject draws her/his self-identification and self-representation from the ways that others identify and represent her/him while in interaction, that is, through 'intersubjectively recognized self-identification' and 'on the basis of the intersubjective recognition of reciprocal self-representations' (Habermas, 1979: 107). The fact that the process of intersubjective self-identification and self-representation takes place while in interaction is emphasised by Habermas and justifies the dynamic and impermanent nature of the intersubjective subject. Moreover, he notes, there is a 'complementary relation between ego and group identity' due precisely to the above-mentioned process that also generates the interconnectedness between the formation of self and group identities since they develop through reciprocal exchange (Habermas, 1979: 111).

Communication is thus an essential element in the formation of self and group identities because it mediates processes that constitute what Habermas calls the 'personal lifeworld' which comprehends 'all possible experiences and actions that can be attributed to the individual in his exchange with his social environment' and that enable the acquisition of knowledge and the transmission of culture within the social system (Habermas, 1979: 111). At the same time, language may set limits for a social system which itself represents the 'symbolic boundary' and 'the horizon of the actions that members reciprocally attribute to themselves internally' (Habermas, 1979: 111). Therefore, the linguistically mediated experiences which are both possible and intersubjectively recognised within a social system constitute a common core for both the lifeworld of an individual and the social system with which s/he integrates. More specifically, the scope of possible communicative interactions that are 'intersubjectively recognized' lies within the normative framework of that social system.

Habermas identifies two dimensions, the moral and the ethical, that regulate the recognition of validity claims individuals put forward in their interactions and whose recognition enables them to reach mutual understanding. Within the ethical dimension, the individual finds the validity of her/his claims in relation to her/his own identity as a member of a group, while within the moral dimension the individual appeals to a universal discourse that exceeds the boundaries of a limited group. These dimensions are complementary and provide both for unity and plurality, for transcendence and immanence in discourse. Furthermore, Habermas grounds the success of communicative action in mutually recognisable validity claims, which he identifies as comprehensibility, truth, truthfulness, and rightness, or sometimes enunciated as only the last three (Habermas, 1979: 3). Although Habermas recognises that 'they change with standards of rationality' and 'are subject in their turn to the dictate of argumentative justification' (Habermas, 1982: 273), he contextualises the definition of these validity claims within a moral–practical discourse that entails 'distancing oneself from the contexts of life with which one's identity is inextricably interwoven' and that is 'constituted only under the communicative presuppositions of a universal discourse' (Habermas, 1993: 12).

Thus, in Habermas' account, the intersubjective type of interaction does not lack normativity, which makes his theories often seem as instrumental as the ones he criticises for precisely that reason (Morrison, 1995: 24). Neither does it fragment the social reality. On the contrary, by introducing a moral–practical perspective, Habermas has been accused of imposing unity over plurality by following too closely Kant's legacy of transcendental reason, a tendency he acknowledges himself by suggesting 'the framework of a moral theory of the Kantian kind reinterpreted in intersubjective terms' (Habermas, 1993: 126). As we shall see, this is probably the main issue that separates Habermas from postmodernism in general.

This notion of a subject–subject type of interaction based on an intersubjective subject is, therefore, an important asset for the radicalisation of democracy also suggested by Critical Theory. For the critique of instrumental reason made by the Frankfurt theorists relies mostly on the concern for democracy, that is, on the fact that the technical use of reason has, by imposing a subject–object kind of interaction, prevented the practice of dialectical reasoning and the maximisation of its critical possibilities which are of utmost necessity in a radically democratic society.

The radicalisation of democracy or, at least, the regeneration of the democratic ideals of the early Enlightenment require the reinforcement of a subject–subject type of interaction. The importance of the reformulation of the legacy of Human Rights in the light of this new model should not be overlooked here. Besides comprehending a moral/universal dimension, the notion of human rights should have in mind a subject–subject model of interaction, hence, 'moral questions, like ethical questions, must be addressed from the perspective of the participants ...' (Habermas, 1993: 24). This statement shows Habermas' move towards the communicative turn in a later phase of his work. He had previously claimed that pre-given postulates, both on moral and ethical levels according to his own definitions of these terms, are validated through argumentation and justification, that is, they are 'discursively redeemable' (Habermas, 1976: 164). But he had also confirmed the existence of universal meanings either '*a priori*' which 'establish the condition of potential communication and general schemes of interpretation' or '*a posteriori*' which 'represent invariant features of contingent scopes of experience which, however, are common to all cultures' (Habermas, 1970: 363).

Habermas' conciliation between the actualities of communication and the *a priori/a posteriori* universal meanings has generated much controversy about the practicality of his notion of the ideal speech situation. This gap between the level of social theorisation and application illustrates Giddens' concept of 'double hermeneutics'[9] (Giddens, 1984: 374). However, the discourse of Human Rights and Citizenship today, considering that they emerged from the ideals of the Enlightenment and developed during modernity, should not disregard these debates or those prompted by postmodernism, described later in this chapter, on the nature of intersubjective relationships and the implications of each stance for their own theorisation and application.

In sum, an intersubjectivistic orientation implies a more dialogical way of conducting politics. The same purpose is evident in education which should adopt a pedagogy of dialogue where cultural knowledge is produced intersubjectively through the formation of the participants' identities and representations. This happens by bringing into play 'the dialectical mediation of the concrete and theoretical contexts of the word' (O'Neill, 1985: 68), that is, by making pedagogy a dialogical exercise through which teachers and learners engage in discovering the reality surrounding them as well as in discovering themselves while interrelating with it and with each other. The development of their own identities and representations as participants in their own contexts and with the contents of their study, not as mere observers, should be as much the focus of attention as the very contexts and contents themselves. The concept of intersubjectivistic dialogue may inspire and clarify the nature of dialogue in Critical Pedagogy, as described previously.

Linguistic/cultural communication

With regard to linguistic and cultural communication, Habermas provided a comprehensive Theory of Communicative Action whereby he elaborated upon the idea of communicative rationality put into practice in social settings. While designing this social theory, the author had in mind 'the rational internal structure of action oriented to reaching understanding' (Habermas, 1984: xli). In other words, he did not mean communication or action independently but the interaction of both, aiming towards mutual understanding and action co-ordination. This is the reason why his theory is worth consideration when dealing with intercultural communication. Habermas puts special emphasis on language rooted in socio-cultural processes in that 'learning to master a language or learning how expressions in a language should be understood requires socialization into a form of life' (Habermas, 1992: 63). Habermas regards language as language-in-use, as communication embedded in action. As he himself acknowledged, he drew inspiration from the concept of 'language games' introduced by Wittgenstein who explains that the term 'is meant to bring into prominence the fact that the *speaking* of language is part of an activity, or a form of life' (Wittgenstein, 1994: 11).

Habermas also borrowed Austin and Searle's distinction of 'locutionary', 'illocutionary' and 'perlocutionary' acts. In the first, the speaker simply makes statements. In the third, the speaker makes an impact on the hearer thus integrating what Habermas calls 'contexts of strategic action', that is, the speaker has a predetermined purpose which he seeks to accomplish. However, Habermas focuses his attention on 'illocutionary' acts, in which the speaker says something and acts at the same time, because they fit into the model of communicative action. Habermas confirms that he considers as communicative action 'those linguistically mediated interactions in which all participants pursue illocutionary aims' (Habermas, 1984: 295). This means that through 'illocutionary' acts the speaker, while engaging in simultaneous and co-ordinated communication with action, does not aim for individual success-oriented goals, but rather for mutual understanding and consensus.

In sum, Habermas distinguishes 'strategic' from 'communicative action'. The former is motivated by technical rationality, is more individualistic, success-oriented, and aims at influencing and directing the course of events while the latter is moved by communicative rationality, aims at establishing interpersonal relationships, reaching a common definition of the situation through mutual criticism and, ultimately, achieving consensus (Habermas, 1984). He defines 'systematic distorted communication' as that which arrives at a 'false' or 'pseudo consensus' because it hides strategic dispositions behind communicative attitudes. Moreover, communicative rationality which guides communicative action exceeds hermeneutic rationality in that communicative actors are more than observers. They establish interpersonal relationships, reach common understanding through mutual critique, and co-ordinate action (Habermas, 1984: 101).

In Habermas' account, the interactive process of communicative action relies on normativity, argumentation, justification and universalisation which take effect through the implementation of the above-mentioned validity-claims, truth, truthfulness, rightness, and comprehensibility. His concept of 'communicative rationality' is normative and universal 'for "rationality" is a limit concept with normative content, one which passes beyond the borders of every local community and moves in the direction of a universal one' (Habermas, 1992: 136). As Habermas conceived it, communicative action, although not strategic, has purpose and aims towards achieving universally applicable norms. However, since these are supposed to include critical communities, understood as reflective and active communities, they are not to be imposed or even simply interpreted and followed, but are universal principles to be reached and applied through communicative action.

It follows on from this that practical reasoning is vital in order to assure a normative framework that people do not accept passively but engage with actively and critically. By adding a reflective dimension to conforming to the norm, Habermas promotes the radicalisation of democracy, at least at the level of everyday democratic procedures. His model allows for culturally more open societies, that is, societies prepared for the continuous negotiation of assertions that may become problematic. Also, since communicative action is not strategic and its goal is thus to reach an understanding and to co-ordinate action, it is oriented towards establishing norms which, theoretically, reflect reciprocal expectations (Habermas, 1979: 118), and are rationally and intersubjectively justified and agreed upon:

> In contexts of communicative action, we call someone rational not only if he is able to put forward an assertion and, when criticized, to provide grounds for it by pointing to appropriate evidence, but also if he is following an established norm and is able, when criticized, to justify his action by explicating the given situation in the light of legitimate expectations. (Habermas, 1984: 15)

Habermas can be credited with introducing the concept of 'communicative rationality' into everyday interactions in the form of justification and argumentation. As he explains above, such a concept entails more than making statements, giving evidence, following norms or merely calling any of these into question. In fact 'communicative rationality' involves acting according to the expectations raised by existing norms and being aware of them so that one is ready to justify the resultant situation and, when necessary, to make the corrections required through discursive argumentation.

However, Habermas' vision is limited by the fact that he relies upon the ideal speech situation and his goal is consensus only and, therefore, neglects any irreconcilable disagreements. Besides, he understands justification in terms of 'intersubjectively recognized validity claims' raised for the purpose of reaching mutual recognition, mutual understanding and, eventually, an agreement in the form of intersubjectively recognised principles. As stated above, the conditions he identifies for this validation to be achieved are comprehensibility, propositional truth, subjective truthfulness, and normative rightness (Habermas, 1979, 1984). Since the aim here is that speaker and hearer reach an understanding, the basic condition is that what is said must be understandable to each of them and, second, it is vital that the statement (verbal or non-verbal) is considered to be true by both parties. It is also important that both interlocutors believe each other to be truthful and thus their interaction to be credible and capable of mutual recognition. Finally, the appropriateness of the statement to the intersubjectively recognised normative context allows for the communicative act to be perceived as legitimate. The conditions for an ideal speech situation should be fulfilled in this way, according to Habermas.

These are controversial areas in Habermas' theory because, although theoretically these norms are achieved through argumentation, understanding and agreement, in order to be valid they have to be universally recognised and so one could question, at least, the feasibility of this proposal. In Lakomksi's words the 'ideal speech situation is in principle unrealizable' (Lakomski, 1999: 182). The meaning and the scope of his notion of universal validity may also raise questions, but Habermas has no doubts in expanding it, at least partially, even across cultural borders:

> The context-dependence of the criteria by which the members of different cultures at different times judge differently the validity of expressions does not, however, mean that the ideas of truth, of normative rightness, of sincerity, and of authenticity that underlie (only intuitively, to be sure) the choice of criteria are context-dependent in the same degree ...
>
> ... Whatever language system we choose, we always start intuitively from the presupposition that truth is a universal validity claim. If a statement is true, it merits universal assent, no matter in which language it is formulated. (Habermas, 1984: 55, 58)

Habermas underestimates much of the cultural weight of the above-mentioned concepts, 'truth', 'truthfulness' or 'rightness'. He understands his validity claims as if they were untouched by the contingencies of the real world. He rejects the possibility that they are not universally valid, that they are dependent on often irreconcilable context-driven perceptions and subject to discontinuities. Therefore, his elaboration on an ideal speech situation and his request for prescriptive agreement have met with some objections. Both have been considered as idealisations that misread the complexities of contemporary societies, despite the fact that Habermas considers idealisations unavoidable, derelativising and trivial, in the sense that they are part of our everyday life (Habermas, 1993: 54–6). His ideal speech situation demands unconstrained, symmetrical communication and agreement accomplished upon validity claims that are mutually recognised. These are ideal situations which are very seldom achieved and the question is whether such idealisations are essential in order to reach universal meaning as the author argues or whether they hinder rather than promote efficient communication (Chambers,

1995).[10] Although Habermas distinguishes between minimum and maximum understanding and admits that 'typical states are in the gray areas in between' (Habermas, 1979: 3), he does explicitly link understanding and agreement:

> Reaching understanding [*Verständigung*] is considered to be a process of reaching agreement [*Einigung*] among speaking and acting subjects. (Habermas, 1984: 286–7)

With such a statement, Habermas certainly does not mean an agreement imposed on the interacting subjects, either instrumentally or strategically, or a perpetually binding one, that is, one that could not be resolved through discussion. Instead, by communicative rationality/ action, he means the arrival at a rational and intersubjective understanding of the truth or the correctness of something without being driven merely by self-interest (Hoy & McCarthy, 1994: 182). However, Habermas' notion of agreement is supposed to involve consensus, in sum, to turn diversity into unity:

> This concept of communicative rationality carries with it connotations based ultimately on the central experience of the unconstrained, unifying, consensus-bringing force of argumentative speech, in which different participants overcome their merely subjective views and owing to the mutuality of rationally motivated conviction assure themselves of both the unity of the objective world and the intersubjectivity of the lifeworld. (Habermas, 1984: 10)

Although the diversity of voices is acknowledged through the recognition of argumentation as necessary and legitimate, the function of rationality here is a unifying one, that is, once more the role reason plays is to turn dissent into consensus, not through imposition or persuasion, but through the argumentation of criticisable validity claims. The unity of reason, even though it is not one of character but one of purpose, as well as the intrinsic value of pervasive principles such as truth, truthfulness and rightness which strive towards a definite goal which is agreement in the form of consensus and the instrumental urge for the 'effectiveness of actions' are obvious remnants of the modernist heritage in Habermas' work (Habermas, 1984: 9). As Bourdieu summarises, Habermas' 'essentialist analysis of language and of "intercomprehension"... is a simple reformulation of the Kantian principle of the universalization of moral judgement' (Bourdieu, 2000: 66). Still according to Bourdieu, Habermas ignores the power relations and the 'factors of *discrimination*' that regulate the access to representation and voice in the social and political spheres and, therefore, inhibit 'a debate in which the competing particular interests, would receive the same consideration' (Bourdieu, 2000: 65, his emphasis). Although throughout his works Habermas has put progressively more emphasis on diversity, he has remained faithful to modernist ideals of harmony and universalism. For the purpose of this study, this is simultaneously a hindrance to the recognition of (inter)cultural complexities and particularities and an essential element for (inter)cultural mutual understanding, since it allows for a universal forum of commonly agreed rules achieved through discussion, argumentation and negotiation.

Unlike Habermas, Gadamer thinks it is impossible to reach agreement and he describes the process of achieving understanding as a 'fusion of horizons' (Gadamer, 1970). For Gadamer a 'horizon' is not necessarily rigid or limiting, something we cannot surpass, but a line from where we can see what lies beyond and which also moves with us. Despite using the term 'fusion', he does not consider that a 'fusion of horizons' means melting two 'horizons' into one but rather the expanding of each one in such a way that they will never be the same again. As Gadamer puts it, 'reaching an understanding in conversation presupposes that both partners are ready for it and are trying to recognise the full value of what is alien and opposed to them' (Gadamer, 1970: 348). He prioritises the process of conversation itself, because once the counterparts are willing to initiate an open conversation it takes its own path and 'no one knows what will "come out" in a conversation' (p. 345). This seems to be a more elastic comprehension of the dialogic situation which allows for the preservation of diversity, since both partners change and let themselves be carried along by the conversation which takes on an almost independent existence.

According to some authors, Gadamer's worldview provides essential explications of linguistic/cultural communication. On the one hand, Gadamer contextualises linguistic/cultural communication within a situated consciousness, that is, within its tradition, its past experiences and its present position as well as the expectations originated by them since 'for Gadamer, understanding is not only grounded in tradition, it is likewise prejudiced' (Roy & Starosta, 2001: 8). On the other hand, Gadamer opens up a new world through the dialectic of experience where 'an individual confronts the limitations of his historicity and can move beyond them ... i.e. to a new understanding of his prejudices and the possibilities or impossibilities for such prejudices' (Males, 2000: 150). Therefore, Gadamer's theory also constitutes an important resource for research on intercultural communication, as pointed out by the above-mentioned authors. Gadamer's recognition of the impact of moral, historical, social and cultural environments together with his attention to the process of *Bildung* that implies, on the one hand, the construction of 'common sense' and, on the other hand, involves change, both allow for a hermeneutics of linguistic/cultural communication that accounts for its complexities, thus offering 'extensions beyond positivistic views of intercultural communication' (Roy & Starosta, 2001: 11).

Despite the reservations described above, Habermas' theory merits consideration in terms of communicative action across cultures. In fact, Habermas provides the possibility of a universal forum for communication within and across cultures and the tools for the dialogic construction of such a space. Moreover, his concept of autonomy – emancipation – allows for the relation between the particular and the general as well as for cross-cultural relationships by questioning assumptions and habits without endangering identity since this results from the critical, and as far as possible symmetrical, discussion of established and proposed norms.

However, serious doubts should be raised about cultural misunderstandings and even fundamental irreconcilable disagreements about what is true, credible, appropriate or legitimate even on a more abstract level and about the extent to which it is possible to reach mutual understanding without trying to impose one worldview upon another. Furthermore, we might also wonder about the scope of Habermas' concept 'universal', since his theory is in many aspects ethnocentric and Eurocentric (Habermas, 1987b).

The universal character of validity-claims and, consequently, of norms of action is, nevertheless, possible, according to Habermas, because they may transcend the cultural background of the lifeworld whereas cultural values are not susceptible to universalisation because they only exist within the horizon of a particular group. Therefore, it depends on the context – system or lifeworld – as to whether the claims are universal or context-dependent, transcendent or immanent. So, Habermas explains, it is wrong to impose the rationality standards of one particular culture upon the other but it is correct to find common ground that transcends the horizon of the lifeworld. This is, in Habermas' terms, the goal of communicative action as opposed to strategic action. Furthermore, since lifeworlds are articulated linguistically they constitute forms of life/ worldviews that provide basic concepts and recurrent themes that lay the foundations for the universal dimension of communicative action (Habermas, 1984: 20–60).

Habermas associates universal discourse with moral–practical discourse, both aiming for an agreement in the context of norm-regulated action. As discussed previously, the moral employment of reason, which he distinguishes from the ethical and the pragmatic, rests on a 'higher-level intersubjectivity' where the perspectives of all participants are thrown into a crucible and through argumentation norms valid for all are agreed upon. Below this level, the ethical–existential discourse deals with unquestioned and unproblematic tenets dependent on our concrete contexts 'with which one's identity [is] inextricably interwoven' and from which we distance ourselves through moral–practical discourses (Habermas, 1993: 9–12).

In accordance with this view, argumentation, understanding and agreement exist at a higher level of intersubjectivity. Argumentation would appear to be a subversive, critical and creative element of Habermas' theory if it were not for the fact that it is coerced by inevitable consensus. Nevertheless, argumentative reason is not superseded by valid universal claims because they may be controversial and criticisable:

> We use the term *argumentation* for that type of speech in which participants thematize contested validity claims and attempt to vindicate or criticize them through arguments. An argument contains reasons or grounds that are connected in a systematic way with the *validity claim* of a problematic expression. (Habermas, 1984: 18, his emphasis)

Here Habermas' Theory of Communicative Action meets the tenets of Critical Theory by questioning the reasons underlying assertions or behaviour, by bringing into awareness that which might have been a mechanical or intuitive response and by disrupting any established practice or way of thinking. This is where Habermas' theory meets the process of ideology critique that he borrows from Marx but roots in Freudian psychoanalysis (Geuss, 1981; Larrain, 1994). According to Habermas, technocratic consciousness is depoliticising and less ideological and, therefore, hinders emancipatory communicative action because, among other reasons, it is 'less vulnerable to reflection' (Habermas, 1971: 111). In his view, ideology in the form of domination arises from 'systematically distorted communication' where strategic goals deceptively underlie communicative situations (Habermas, 1971). In other words, ideology arises because a 'partisan perspective . . . mistakes itself as universal and eternal' (Eagleton, 1994b: 4). The critique of ideology, on the other hand, results from emancipatory interest and self-reflection (Habermas, 1971). Habermas' critics, however, consider that he undermines the process of ideology critique because, on the one hand, he fragments consciousness through his overemphasis on communication and, consequently, there is no possibility for ideology nor, therefore, for ideology critique to take shape (Larrain, 1994). Furthermore, by basing ideology critique on an abstract model, the ideal speech situation, and, therefore, on 'communication free from domination, Habermas is linking rationality to the overcoming of ideology' (Larrain, 1994: 134). Nevertheless, for Habermas, 'removing restrictions on communication' which should take place at 'all levels of political and repoliticized decision-making processes' together with 'a process of generalized reflection' seem to provide the key solution for further emancipation (Habermas, 1971: 118–19). Argumentation is thus an important asset in this theory since it introduces the notion of 'discursive democracy', which is a major contribution to the radicalisation of democracy through the improvement of deliberative processes (White, 1995).

However, Habermas has been accused of hyperexploring the rational potentialities of Western civilization, of relying too much on the cognitive aspects of the self rather than on the emotional ones, and of not making room for the disclosure of other frames of mind (Warren, 1995: 181). Although he introduced an innovative discursive element while designing his Theory of Communicative Action, he did, in fact, retain the foundations of Western forms of reasoning. He accuses postmodernists such as Lyotard and Derrida, and the neopragmatist Rorty, of being radical contextualists and ethnocentric because they favour the particular rather than the universal, the conflicting rather than the compliant, since for them 'the concept of communicative reason is still accompanied by the shadow of a transcendental illusion' (Habermas, 1992: 144). Although Habermas' idea of communication relies on the diversity of voices and his concept of agreement is transitory, his goal is, nevertheless, democratic unitary thinking and he disapproves of postmodern radical contextualism. In fact, Habermas builds a *critical* defence of modernity in that he acknowledges its exaggerated and distorted use of reason but he also tries to preserve the potential of reason for the purpose of democratic emancipation.

The 'colonization of the lifeworld'

The expression which Habermas coined to identify the overinsistence upon instrumental rationality within culture was the 'colonization of the lifeworld' (Habermas, 1987a). The lifeworld, *Lebenswelt*, provides individuals with unproblematic convictions and definitions of situations that enable them to come to an understanding with others. Although these convictions and definitions result mostly from the interpretations of the surrounding world provided by the previous generations of a cultural group, the limits of each lifeworld are not very clear (Habermas, 1984: 70). Nevertheless, the maintenance of these interpretative systems allows cultural traditions to reproduce and this can occur either in a natural or in a critical manner. A cultural tradition may reproduce its interpretative systems naturally, without any previous planning, or critically, by 'release[ing] the semantic potentials of the tradition' (Habermas, 1973: 70). If, however, 'it is objectivistically prepared and strategically employed', that is, it allows itself to be regulated by technocratic consciousness, the cultural tradition loses its force (Habermas, 1973: 70). The 'colonization of the lifeworld' consists of the excessive presence of this last possibility and it is one of the 'pathologies' of advanced industrial societies, as Habermas points out in his critique of instrumental reason (Habermas, 1987: 305).

With the development of high technology and the spread of information, the lifeworld has been invaded by the structures of 'cognitive–instrumental' rationality, that create 'artificial languages' (Love, 1995: 59), to the detriment of the 'moral–practical' and the 'aesthetic-expressive' dimensions of culture. Habermas identifies these three dimensions of culture – cognitive–instrumental, moral–practical, and aesthetic–expressive – and states that there should be a balanced interaction between them, otherwise the communicative process is incomplete (Habermas, 1985: 9–11). The overemphasis on an economic–administrative form of rationality, that arises from the predominance of the cognitive–instrumental dimension, has caused an 'imbalanced rationality' which is at the root of the colonisation process (Habermas, 1984: 183). This does not mean that Habermas is discrediting the process of modernisation altogether, but he advises against the predominance of one dimension over the others. Since *'there is no administrative production of meaning'* (Habermas, 1973: 70, his emphasis), cultural resources start to wither and both the lifeworld and the social system lose vitality because there is loss of meaning and loss of freedom (Love, 1995: 55). Furthermore, they can only be revitalised through discourse within the lifeworld from where communicative rationality emanates, since the original meanings that individuals submit to communicative action and to universal validity-claims spring from their immediate context, the lifeworld. So, according to Habermas, the original communication, which he links closely with democratisation, takes place mostly at the grass roots level of the lifeworld.

According to Habermas, the lifeworld is thus the very locus of cultural reproduction and identity formation. Therefore, its colonisation represents an imposition on the lifeworld of artificial identities by the broader instrumental, bureaucratic social system, through subsystems that are regulated by money and power, as Marcuse also noted (Marcuse, 1991). Not only does this process suffocate the natural development of the lifeworld and prevent the critical reproduction/production of culture, by causing alienation and impeding reflection, but it also dissolves an area of 'nonidentity' within the broader social system that usually allows 'incomplete socialization, escape valves for implosive deviance, nonconformity' (Agger, 1985: 11). This area of 'nonidentity', as Agger calls it, that supports universal understanding is an important element in Habermas' theory since it allows some space for progressive individuation and universal intersubjectivity which are his ultimate goals. This is the reason why he runs into disagreement with postmodernist multiculturalists who, in principle, share his rejection of the colonisation of the lifeworld but discard universal intersubjectivity. Although Habermas' ultimate goal is universal consensus, he defends the integrity of the lifeworld from colonisation by technocratic consciousness because the latter hinders emancipation, unconstrained communication and, therefore, universal communicative intersubjectivity.

The notion of 'colonisation of the lifeworld' can be related to the concept of 'cultural invasion' developed by Freire for educational purposes (Freire, 1970: 150; Misgeld, 1985). These concepts carry a strong message for teachers and learners of culture since they raise awareness about cultural processes, the media, and the different arenas where cultural reproduction/production takes place, despite previously mentioned criticisms (Taylor, 1993). Furthermore, the consideration of both notions calls for the development of reasoning capacities and of communicative/cultural competences that are indispensable for participatory democracy, which for Critical Theory means the control of our lives through critical thinking and emancipatory engagement within, for Habermas, communicative symmetric relations with the ideal speech situation in mind (Habermas, 1979: 61; 1992: 138; Horkheimer, 1972: 244).

Terms such as 'colonisation' and 'invasion' are used here not in the usual sense of physical incursion but to mean a violation of identities, cultural values and symbols. They do not have necessarily to do with geographical limits nor do they apply to the Third World only. Viewed in this light, cultural colonisation also applies to literate urban individuals who are precisely the subjects Habermas means when he speaks about 'colonization'. For Habermas, the notion of 'colonization' has an ideological connotation in that it is the invasion of consciousness by technocratic consciousness which emerges out of technological progress (Habermas, 1971). However, he ignores the social asymmetries caused by economic progress and, instead, focuses on distortions in communication (Larrain, 1994). Moreover, when speaking about modernity, Habermas also increasingly concentrates this process within Europe. He acknowledges Europe's responsibility in overemphasising instrumental reason, but he considers that Europe itself has the potential to critique and redirect its own development:

> Modern Europe has created the spiritual presuppositions and the material foundations for a world in which this mentality has taken the place of reason. That is the real heart of the critique of reason since Nietzsche. Who else but Europe could draw from its own traditions the insight, the energy, the courage of vision – everything that would be necessary to strip from the (no longer metaphysical, but metabiological) premises of a blind compulsion to system maintenance and system expansion their power to shape our mentality. (Habermas, 1987: 367)

Habermas locates his theory and the notion of colonisation within the limits of the industrialised societies of the West, since he understands modernisation as a process in evolution, as yet unfinished, which the rest of the world is following at different speeds (Habermas, 1985). Despite this Eurocentric/ethnocentric perspective that is to be avoided, the habermasian notion of 'the colonization of the lifeworld' can be most useful for the development of critical cultural awareness in foreign culture education. It focuses on the threat against not only the critical reproduction/ production of culture within the lifeworlds of both the native and target cultures but also against the dynamics of the establishment of a universal ground for mutual understanding as postulated by Habermas. The latter risks being 'colonized' by technocratic consciousness, artificial identities and instrumental interests which prevent the free negotiation of norms and principles since the latter are previously determined by those very interests.

The massification of culture

The production and consumption of culture has been one of the principal preoccupations of the Frankfurt theorists. Although a comprehensive view of their theories exceeds the scope of this study, there are a few aspects, pointed out by some of its earlier members, which were considered useful at this stage. They adopted an interdisciplinary perspective on culture that enabled them to understand multidimensional aspects of cultural themes. Unlike Marxism, they took a holistic view of cultural meanings without making them dependent on particular class related interests. Furthermore, they imbued the study of culture with a political significance that surpassed any previous attempts to do so (including that of Marx), such as studies in prejudice and antidemocratic trends (Adorno *et al.*, 1950), and on mass culture in advanced industrial societies (Marcuse, 1991). Nonetheless, their rejection of the capitalist manipulation of culture for the purposes of profit and control owes much to their early Marxist background (Agger, 1992: 57).

In spite of having adopted what is often considered an elitist perspective towards popular culture, the early Frankfurt theorists, namely Horkheimer, Adorno, Benjamin, and Marcuse, dedicated much of their work to the then emerging mass culture. When Horkeimer, Adorno and Marcuse composed most of their writings on this subject they were war refugees in the United States and lived for some time in California, not far from Hollywood, so they could not avoid focusing on culture as it was being produced and consumed in the affluent American society of the time. In fact, they were very sensitive to the manipulation of culture for the purposes of domination, not only in terms of economics, which they were aware of due to their above-mentioned Marxist background, but also in terms of political control as a consequence of their experience of Nazism in Germany. In 1940s America, particularly in California, they found a much subtler manipulation of culture, especially by means of pleasure (Marcuse, 1991).

Their profound interest in the study of popular culture as well as their particular perspectives on it paved the way for the formation, later in the century, of a specific interdisciplinary area of studies to be known as Cultural Studies and also for the postmodernist approach to cultural consumption (Baudrillard, 1998a). Despite the fact that their theories can be seen as the foundations for these subsequent studies of popular culture which have focused on cultural diversity, the Frankfurt theorists took a rather monolithic view of popular culture *en masse* (Agger, 1992). To a greater or lesser extent, their approach to mass culture provided new guidelines that have been further expanded by those involved in Cultural Studies, namely postmodernist theorists on culture.

The 'culture industry'

Horkheimer and Adorno introduced the term 'culture industry' in their book *Dialectic of Enlightenment* in order to show that culture was being instrumentalised in accordance with the general mood of modern society. Advances in technology and the development of mass communications were apparently making the Enlightenment ideals of equality possible while, at the same time, betraying assumptions of critical emancipation. Masses of artifacts and images were available to a larger sector of the population, although they simultaneously deepened class and economic divides between the haves and the have-nots and intensified material greed while weakening the importance of cultural values and traditions. Hence, Horkheimer and Adorno, as well as Marcuse, focused on the torpor of the masses inebriated with images, words, and devices, made to love and to hate the same characters, to desire and to reject the same things, to agree and to disagree with the same ideas. Horkheimer and Adorno capture this sentiment well in the following comment:

> Something is provided for all so that none may escape; the distinctions are emphasized and extended. The public is catered for with a hierarchical range of mass-produced products of varying quality, thus advancing the rule of complete quantification. Everybody must behave (as if spontaneously) in accordance with his previously determined and indexed level, and choose the category of mass product turned out for his type. Consumers appear as statistics on research organization charts, and are divided by income groups into red, green, and blue areas; the technique is that used for any type of propaganda. (Horkheimer & Adorno, 1972: 123)

Here the authors emphasise the fact that uniformity is imposed from the outside, not by coercion but as if it were driven by spontaneous desires of the consumer who indeed cannot escape the powerful appeals to her/his senses. Both consumers and products are stripped of their identities and values, they become statistics representing the purchasers and the purchased. Individuals experience their needs, joys, frustrations or successes according to what is predetermined. Though these processes may be highly rational, they are not critical. This is the reason why Marcuse reminded his readers that 'freedom of thought, speech, and conscience were – just as free enterprise, which they served to promote and protect – essential *critical* ideas' (Marcuse, 1991: 1, his emphasis).

It is relevant here to relate the Frankfurt theorists' theory of culture to the concept of 'ideological hegemony' put forward by Gramsci. His theory connects with that of Horkheimer, Adorno and Marcuse in their common concern about the new methods of domination in advanced industrial societies that do not rely on coercion but on persuasion and consent. Gramsci explained that 'hegemony' is not necessarily brought about by the state alone but through the 'balance between political society and civil society', that is, with the help of organisations such as schools (Gramsci, 1975: 204). Thus, Gramsci drew our attention to the strategies of domination that underlie the everyday procedures of social and cultural institutions. Since advanced industrial societies possess sophisticated technology and democratic apparatuses these strategies tend to be more elaborate and, therefore, less obvious. In sum, 'hegemony is primarily a *strategy* for the gaining of the active consent of the masses' (Buci-Glucksmann, 1982: 119), that is, by universalising ideological assumptions it also generalises predispositions, interests and needs.

This illustrates the 'particular kind of deceptive, mystifying function' that ideology plays in society and that originates in 'false consciousness' (Eagleton, 1994b: 7–11). In this case, forces of domination, representing political, economic or other powers through illusory technologically mediated representations of society and alluring discourses generate wishes or potential needs. This scenario corresponds to the definition of ideology as 'a world-picture which stabilizes or legitimizes domination' put forward by Geuss in order to describe one of the Frankfurt School's theses on ideology (Geuss, 1981: 31). Besides, within the context of technologically advanced societies, 'false consciousness' produces not only illusions but also desires. Geuss also points out the 'analogy between ... ideologically false consciousness and individual neurosis (Geuss, 1981: 39). Technical/scientific rationality is apparently neutral, objective and, therefore, non-ideological. This is not the case, however, and Marcuse was the first to analyse 'the political content of technical reason' by emphasising the unacknowledged character of political domination in advanced capitalist societies (Habermas, 1971: 85).

Accordingly, Marcuse discloses the existence of 'false needs' in contrast with the ones he designates as 'true needs'. Those he calls 'false needs' are needs that the individual considers as her/his own but which are actually suggested by 'external powers over which the individual has no control' and which are, in fact, artificial and dictated by the interest of others (Marcuse, 1991: 5). The individual feels them as needs because s/he is influenced to do so. Ironically, s/he is made to believe that only by fulfilling those needs is it possible to achieve happiness. However, the result may be either 'euphoria in unhappiness' or a 'Happy Consciousness' that the author defines as 'the belief that the real is rational and that the system delivers the goods' and both happiness and unhappiness here mean to conform to that state of affairs (Marcuse, 1991: 5, 84). In Marcuse's view, only the individual can say which are her/his own true needs and this can only take place when s/he is free, autonomous and intellectually capable of acknowledging them:

The judgement of needs and their satisfaction, under the given conditions, involves standards of priority – standards which refer to the optimal development of the individual, of all individuals, under the optimal utilization of the material and intellectual resources available to man. (Marcuse, 1991: 6).

Here Marcuse stresses the importance of promoting the individual's autonomy through the development of her/his intellectual capacities and the best use of the material conditions available. This conforms to the point Frankfurt theorists have made which is the reinforcement of the deliberative power of the individual based on the development of her/his capacity of judgement. By stressing the ideological content of mass culture, they did not mean to disdain popular culture altogether, and indeed their approach towards it was serious and rigorous (Agger, 1992). Instead they aimed to awaken passive consumers and turn them into active consumers/producers of culture. This intention shows evidence of the deep democratic concerns that led them to reject the more or less subtle control of the citizens' ideas and social behaviour in both capitalist and socialist modern societies.

Their theory of culture also conveys a powerful message for educators, and especially for teachers and learners of culture. The young have been a vulnerable target of the culture industry and even though in the 1960s young people appeared capable of taking over the reins of this industry by imposing 'a sense of distinctiveness and vision', we can hardly say that this has been the case (Giroux, 1997: 37). Therefore, the school has a very important role to play in the formation of critically aware cultural agents by preventing 'cultural invasion', in other words, 'the suppression of capacities for cultural and social criticalness' (Misgeld, 1985: 77). This does not in the least mean the rejection of any sort of cultural production coming from outside one's own cultural group, but rather the refusal to be passive, uncritical, acculturated consumers of 'dehistoricized' culture produced by the culture industry for the purposes of profit and control (Agger, 1992: 68).

Critical Theory and critical cultural awareness

Under the assumptions of this study, Critical Theory is the basic, although not limiting, philosophical foundation for critical cultural awareness. It contributes to the clarification of the contents and modes of critical cultural awareness in that it originally rejected the perception of reason as transcultural and neutral and, therefore, roots processes of reasoning in social and cultural interaction. As a result, cultural knowledge is viewed as socially and interactively produced. Critical Theory thus acknowledges the political nature of social and cultural life of all members of a society. With respect to the modes of approaching culture, it offers an intersubjective/interactive paradigm in that it recognises a subject/subject type of interaction. For Habermas, this means that communication is founded on symmetrical positions of the subjects involved in interaction. For critical theorists in general, this means that cultural knowledge is not viewed as a distant object to be acquired but as a process of reciprocal identification and representation, accomplished mostly through interpersonal relations. Cultural knowledge relies, therefore, on experience and communication.

Furthermore, critical reflection is considered an important tool for demystifying surface cultural and social expressions and representations and, within Habermas' theory, for reaching mutual understanding through argumentation and justification. Critical Theory provides a democratic foundation for critical cultural awareness in that it conveys great concern for social justice and political emancipation through critical reflection and unconstrained communication. Despite engaging in a critique of aspects of modernity based on their critique of instrumental reason, critical theorists also provide a critical defence of the ideals of modernity, especially emancipatory rationality and free communication which are main tenets in the development of critical cultural awareness. From this standpoint, critical theorists urge the development of the individual's intellectual capacities for criticism of new methods of cultural domination in advanced industrial societies. The enhancement of the liberating power of critical rationality is, therefore, a valuable asset that the notion of critical cultural awareness borrows from Critical Theory.

Nonetheless, there are some weaknesses in Habermas' contribution to critical cultural awareness since he neglects the probabilities of irreconcilable disagreement about what is true, credible, appropriate, or legitimate, within and across cultures. However, his position also provides the possibility of a universal forum for communication and the tools for the dialogic construction of such an arena. Although his postulation of a higher level of intersubjectivity and of an area of cultural non-identity as a basis for complete comprehension are questionable, they are useful for envisaging consensual areas in (inter)cultural communication. In sum, Habermas' utopianism is as useful as the critique of it for the study of inter- and intracultural relations.

Finally, the early postulates of Critical Theory provided a theory of culture that was the basis of later approaches to culture, such as Cultural

Studies and Postmodernism, and this makes it essential for the study of critical cultural awareness. Habermas, on the other hand, elaborates a theory of communication that relies upon mutual agreement and universal consensus and, in this instance, constitutes the antithesis of Postmodernism. However, his emphasis on the universal, comprehensive, comprehensible, and consensual elements of cultures and of communication is also worth consideration by theories of intercultural communication and, moreover, within the framework of critical cultural awareness.

Postmodernism

Postmodernism is a broad term that conveys a change of perspectives in approaching life and art in the so-called age of late-, high- or postmodernity. This tendency originated after the second World War in the arts, involving mainly painting, architecture, and also literature, but it has gradually penetrated social theory and political analysis. It comprises disparate movements and authors that do, however, share some common attitudes such as a profound critique of modernity, a particular sensitiveness to otherness and difference, an attempt to comprehend the unfolding of a new era, and, directly or indirectly, the commitment to a radicalisation of democratic ideals.

A broader representation of the New York Group of postwar intellectuals is believed partly to have initiated postmodern social and cultural criticism in the 1950s (Featherstone, 1988). However, some doubts have also been cast on their postmodern stance since these intellectuals refused to consider as intellectually valid their contemporary counterculture movements, which are assumed to have been the precursors of the postmodern turn in the 1960s (Jummonville, 1991). In the mid-1970s, Ihab Hassan is recognised as having started to use the term postmodernism consistently in relation to social and cultural criticism and to theorise about it, even before Lyotard made it widely known (Bertens, 1995; Frow, 1997; Lyotard, 1986).

No conclusive definitions of postmodernism could be found in the reviewed literature since 'there is, as yet, no agreed meaning to the term postmodern' (Featherstone, 1988: 207), moreover, 'in a rapidly changing terrain it can only be provisional . . . and is likely to be replaced by a series of other terms, as the cultural projects labelled postmodernist begin to diverge' (Boyne & Rattansi, 1990a: 9), and, finally, 'the very playfulness of postmodernism(s) precludes any premature foreclosure of its own meaning' (Turner, 1993b: 5). Nevertheless, postmodernism is recognised as an 'intellectual fact (or anti-intellectual fact, as some would prefer to call it)' (Niznik & Sanders, 1996: vii), besides, 'the nature and depth of that transformation are debatable, but transformation it is' (Harvey, 1989: 39), and, furthermore, 'it is possible ... to discern the main contours of what, for better or worse, is dubbed postmodernist philosophising' (Cooper, 1998: 61). Eventually, we may adopt, for further reflection, Peters and Lankshears' suggestions for defining postmodernism:

> What has been called the 'crisis of reason' is a crisis not only of foundational approaches to knowledge and morality, but also of the foundations of our institutions. 'Postmodernism' is the general, if ambiguous, term used to refer to these cultural crises ... It has been described as a method, a philosophy, an attitude, a tonality, a style, a moment, a condition, a movement and even a theory, suggesting a unitary body of presuppositions and assumptions ... Postmodernism pits *reason* in the plural – fragmented and incommensurable against the universality of modernism and its conception of a unified human reason ... it is a questioning of the past as an ordered, linear and cumulative development which represents Western civilization as the apex of this process of cultural evolution. (Peters & Lankshear, 1996: 3–17, their emphasis)

The above excerpt singles out several aspects covered by current theorising on postmodernism namely the difficulty in describing it, its identification as a crisis or 'implosion' of modernity (Baudrillard, 1981, 1998a, b), its incursion into cultural, social and political spheres, its disruption of notions like the unitary subject and universal validity, and its questioning of the hegemony and supremacy of Western civilization with regard to knowledge legitimation and status.

Postmodernism, understood as a corpus of philosophical and ideological assumptions developed as an attempt to describe and represent life at the turn of the century, constitutes a particular response to the condition of post- or hypermodernity in late capitalist societies. When describing 'the family of terms derived from the "postmodern" ', besides 'postmodernism', Featherstone identifies 'postmodernity', 'postmodernité', and 'postmodernization', and explains that the term postmodernity suggests 'an epochal shift' whereas postmodernisation indicates 'a process with degrees of implementation' (Featherstone, 1988: 197–201). Therefore, the notion of postmodernity proposes a new era, which does not necessarily imply a rupture, as is also acknowledged by Lyotard, despite having himself identified a *Postmodern Condition*: 'I have said and repeated that, in my opinion, "postmodern" did not mean the end of modernism but a different rapport with modernity' (Lyotard, 1988a: 64, translation mine). It follows on from this that postmodernity provides the context for postmodernism while postmodernism supplies some guidelines in order to explore, hypothesise about, and interact with our contemporary postnational and postindustrial societies. As a result, postmodernism theorising, using French poststructuralist criticism as its basis, has been further developed and applied, via an attraction/suspicion relationship, by social studies, cultural studies, gender studies, globalisation and citizenship theories.

Furthermore, postmodernism has undertaken a critique of Western societies from the point of view of the Other, that may arise from within or outside them, in relation to both their own changing nature and their position in this global, postcolonial, post-European world. The abovementioned interdisciplinary fields of study have embarked on this critique from a postmodernist perspective by exploiting key ideas suggested by French philosophers like Lyotard, Derrida, Foucault and Baudrillard, as we shall see later. Derrida notes with regard to the role of Europe in the modern world:

> Europe has also misunderstood its image, its visage, its shape and placement, its taking-place, by understanding itself as a thrusting dagger, a phallus if you like, therefore, a cape for the world civilisation or human culture in general. (Derrida, 1991: 28–9, translation mine)

By re-evaluating its own position in this global, postcolonial, and post-European world, postmodern Europe has to recreate its own nature by decentring itself. This is a different perspective from Habermas', as described previously, who, by exclaiming 'who else but Europe could draw from its own traditions the insight, the energy, the courage of vision . . .' (Habermas, 1987b: 367), confirms Europe's centrality and not only negates European equality with other civilisations but also ignores the fissures made in European hegemonies by the presence and contribution of new or old ethnicities that have recently acquired legitimacy and voice within European societies. Postmodernism attempts to deal with these new developments by providing new insights, although some are apocalyptic, into the paradoxal process of simultaneous de-differentiation and hyperdifferentiation in our contemporary societies. According to Wexler 'modernity is the era of differentiation', differentiation between high and popular culture, among disciplines, scientific and social spheres, while 'postmodernity is typified by dedifferentiation, blurring of boundaries and disintegration of separate domains' (Wexler,

1993: 168). However, postmodernism is also characterised by hyper-differentiation, by the affirmation of heterogeneity, by the assertion of dissent, by the 'microanalysis of discrete institutions, discourses, or practices' (Best & Kellner, 1991: 220).

In fact, instead of postmodernism it would be more exact to speak of postmodernisms in the plural, although in this case there is a danger that the concept of the postmodern may seem lost, vague or slippery. However, it is precisely because postmodernism implies the negation of absolutes (Lyotard, 1986) that the concept of the postmodern is a non-absolute itself, that is, not only does it include a multiplicity of visions but it also negates, from the outset, the possibility of an absolute version. Foster attempted nevertheless to make a useful distinction between a 'postmodernism of resistance' that he described as a 'postmodernism which seeks to deconstruct modernism and resist the status quo' and a 'postmodernism of reaction' that 'repudiates the former to celebrate the latter' (Foster, 1985: x). Basically, Foster distinguishes between a postmodernism that longs for the past and reacts against changes which have taken place in late modern societies (of reaction), and a postmodernism that struggles against the social, cultural, and political stabilisations of modernity that have turned ideals of equality into impositions of uniformity, organisation into hegemony and bureaucracy, etc. (of resistance). This opposition clarifies the existence of two main trends among postmodernists which are basic for understanding not only postmodernism but the critique of modernity in general. The critique of modernity had already been undertaken by Critical Theory, as described previously, and to some extent also by pragmatists, as we shall see, mostly as a critique from within the modernist frame of mind. It was triggered either by disillusionment (Horkheimer & Adorno, 1972), or the acknowledgement of the need for completion of the project of modernity (Habermas, 1985), or from a pragmatic, non-programmatic perspective, that rejects foundational principles but recovers practical reason (Cherryholmes, 1994; Putnam, 1995). According to Foster, the critique of modernity, from a postmodernist angle, is undertaken either by reacting against the very process of modernisation and longing for a return to tradition understood uncritically, or by resistance 'not only to the official culture of modernism but also to the "false normativity" of a reactionary postmodernism' and by tackling a 'critical deconstruction of tradition' (Foster, 1985: x). This last version predominates among the authors examined in this study.

On the whole, postmodernism as a theory has been regarded with some reservation because of the lack of consistent self-theorising and better definition of its own borders. Some of its versions have been blamed, in general, for tending to 'throw out the very concept of social system and society' (Best & Kellner, 1991: 220), for 'failing to articulate significant mediations, or connections, between various social phenomena' (pp. 223–4), for 'splintering power and domination into an amorphous multiplicity of institutions' (p. 221), for being 'often inconsistent' (p. 267), 'overly culturalist' (p. 269), or excessively rhetoric and hyperbolic (p. 277). Despite its tendency towards cultural analysis and increasing politicisation through the disruption of hierarchies and the acknowledgement of the exercise of power games at a local level, postmodernists are still identified by their 'overemphasis on aesthetics at the expense of politics' (May, 1999b: 24). The limits of postmodernist theoretical sources are also renowned for their insistence on a language of description rather than explanation, on a language of critique rather than transformation (Aronowitz, 1987; Giroux, 1992, 1997b), although their potential for clarification of cultural, social, and political performance is considered important and has been widely probed, redefined, and refined.

In fact, postmodernism has, in general terms, provided a critique of modernity that is impossible to ignore in language and culture studies and, more precisely, the above-mentioned postmodernism of resistance has undertaken deconstructive analyses of modern institutions such as the educational system, the mass media, political organisations, social practices, etc. and provided new insights into the nature of (inter)-linguistic and (inter)cultural processes. Therefore, it seems important here to give a brief description of the critique of modernity as it has been made by postmodernism and of the key notions that have become essential for taking a postmodern perspective on (inter)cultural issues.

To put it simply, three major family trees, whose branches interweave, may be identified as influencing contemporary philosophical thought. The first one, which was decisive for modern thought and is now the basis for those philosophers who are trying to rescue modernity by accomplishing it, is rooted in Kant and develops through Hegel, Marx, and Freud to Habermas. The second one, which initiated a tentative rupture with modernity and impacts upon postmodernism begins with Nietzsche, and passes through Heidegger to French poststructuralists, especially Derrida. The third one starts with Darwin and develops through the American pragmatists such as James and Dewey to neopragmatist Rorty. Some authors like Lyotard and Rorty, however, combine aspects from several streams although revealing a stronger identification with just one.

Wittgenstein is also worth mentioning as a powerful, unaffiliated source of inspiration to both Habermas, as previously indicated, and the postmoderns. His conceptualisation of 'language games' influenced both Habermas' Theory of Communicative Action and postmodern notions of contingency and fragmentation. Wittgenstein's philosophy is of the utmost importance for postmodernist descriptions because he looks at the world 'from the point of view of *meaning*, rather than the point of view of *being* (as Plato does) or *knowing* (as Descartes does)' (Finch, 1977: 242–3). Mainly in his late work *On Certainty*, he supplies postmodernism with restrictions to the universal validity of truth through statements like 'the *truth* of certain empirical propositions belongs to our frame of reference' (Wittgenstein 1969, .83: 12) or with some nihilistic considerations on the grounds of our knowledge such as 'the difficulty is to realize the groundlessness of our believing' (.166: 24).

It is widely recognised that French poststructuralists, among whom Lyotard, Derrida, Foucault and Baudrillard are given special focus in this study, have been used as main sources by postmodern theorists of political, social and cultural studies worldwide (Best & Kellner, 1991; Boyne & Rattansi, 1990b; Kellner, 1988; Ross, 1988). These authors provided postmodern theorists with key notions such as those which will subsequently be examined – metanarratives, *différend*, deconstruction, *différance*, simulation, technologies of power/of the self – which have proved to be extemely fertile for further postmodern endeavours. In other words, 'postmodern theory appropriates the poststructuralist critique of modern theory, radicalizes it, and extends it to new theoretical fields' (Best & Kellner, 1991: 26), despite the fact that, except for Lyotard, none of the above-mentioned authors has acknowledged or theorised the postmodern as such or identified himself as postmodernist (Bertens, 1995; Hoy & McCarthy, 1994).

For the purpose of this study, postmodernism will be understood in a very broad manner and will also include neopragmatism, to be more exact Rorty's concept of solidarity. Although, as previously stated, pragmatism belongs to a different philosophical stream and therefore should strictly be included in a different category, neither Derrideans nor Deweyans reject their commonalities. Their shared rejection of foundational reason and, consequently, of universally valid principles, their fight for justice and recognition of the contingent character of cognition and morality allows us to combine both philosophical traditions to a certain extent (Mouffe, 1996a; Rorty, 1996a). However, it is not possible to put Rorty alongside Derrida, for example, for 'deconstruction is pragmatist, *but it is not pragmatist all the way down*' (Critchley, 1996: 37). Rorty explains the difference in more detail:

> Derrideans tend to think that the more questioning, problematizing and mettant-en-abîme you can squeeze into the day's work, the better. Deweyans, on the other hand, think that you should only question when you find yourself in what Dewey called a 'problematic situation' – a situation in which you are no longer sure what you are doing. (Rorty, 1996c: 44)

On the one hand, neopragmatists are blamed for not questioning or problematising enough and therefore engaging a notion of pluralism where there is no concern for the specific struggles of the various groups within the ideological and material conditions of their social contexts. At worst, neopragmatism, and Rorty in particular, 'appropriates its [postmodernism's] central assumptions as part of the defense of liberal capitalist society' (Aronowitz & Giroux, 1991: 61). On the other hand, pragmatism adds a practical, utilitarian component to the deconstructivist enterprise of postmodernism, thus establishing a bridge between modernism and postmodernism without losing sight of the contingent and transitory character of their solutions (Cherryholmes, 1994).

It follows on from this that it is possible and useful for the purpose of this study to examine the contributions of the postmodern critique of modernity and the potential of some key concepts introduced mainly by poststructuralist theory, which were extended to postmodern political, social, cultural and educational theories of identity, citizenship, or democracy, and that may finally be applied to the development of critical cultural awareness within the study of foreign languages/cultures.

Postmodernism *versus* modernism

Postmodernism/postmodernity has been described mostly in opposition to modernism/modernity. In fact, most authors – Derrida, Foucault, and even Lyotard – who have been used as sources by postmodern theorisers, have produced more descriptions of modernity than of postmodernity (Smart, 1993). Theorists of postmodernism themselves frequently base their depictions on synoptic charts and dichotomic descriptions of this opposition (Featherstone, 1988; Frow, 1997). Moreover, concepts like modernism and modernity have acquired specific meanings in postmodern discourse:

> The concept of 'modernity' has today a quite different content from the one it had before the start of the 'postmodern' discourse; there is little point in asking whether it is true or distorted, or in objecting to the way it is handled inside the 'postmodern' debate. It is situated

in that debate, it draws its meaning from it, and it makes sense only jointly with the other side of the opposition, the concept of 'postmodernity', as that negation without which the latter concept would be meaningless. (Bauman, 1988: 219)

Accordingly, the notion of the postmodern does not exist except in relation to the notion of the modern; furthermore, the fact that we employ the first concept reveals a specific rapport with the latter. Therefore, each concept necessarily refers to the other and they mutually influence each other. This leads to the controversy about whether postmodernity implies the end of modernity and, subsequently, about the exact meaning of 'end' in this context. Martins recalls Cournot in order to conclude that '"end" does not necessarily mean extinction or termination but can be variously construed as exhaustion, completion, fulfilment or consummation' (Martins, 1998: 152). This definition allows various possibilities in the relationship between modernity and postmodernity that range from a renewal of the original pledge of modernity to a nihilistic sense of exhaustion.

The feeling that there is a radicalisation of modernity or that a shift away from it may be inevitable is due to the intense evolution of technology, change in the constitution of societies, and modification of the world economic and political order that have taken place in the last decades and are, at the same time, unstoppable and problematic. Radicalising modernity means acknowledging its unfolding, wanting to cope with its excesses and accepting that it is irreversible. Giddens compares modernity to a 'juggernaut – a runaway engine of enormous power which, collectively as human beings, we can drive to some extent but which also threatens to rush out of control and which could rend itself asunder' (Giddens, 1990: 139). Nonetheless, critics of modernity want to divert its path and, in some cases, to slow its pace. However, both tendencies – a radicalisation of it or a break with it – will somehow coexist because the radicalisation of modernity is happening anyway and the need for change proceeds from it. And Giddens continues by saying that 'the juggernaut of modernity ... is not an engine made up of integrated machinery, but one in which there is a tensionful, contradictory, push and pull of different influences' (p. 139), that is, he acknowledges the fragmentation, heterogeneity and antagonism that permeate our societies. This is where 'radical modernists' and 'postmodernists' (Giddens, 1990: 150) simultaneously associate and separate. In our world, where heterogeneity is a given fact that no one can avoid, we can either try to neutralise fragmentation and antagonism, learn to live with them, or even try to benefit from them. In general terms, while radical modernists adopt universalising and globalised perspectives, postmodernists emphasise the particular and the conflicting.

The most consensual aspect of contemporary thought concerns the actual world we live in, despite the different interpretations and the divergent solutions presented. The mental, social, political and economic institutions we live with, legacies of the enlightenment tradition, are being challenged both by the formation of overarching political and economic structures emerging from globalising influences, and by international mobility and consequent acculturation and cross-culturation of citizens together with the strengthening of ethnic communities. So, while the most cherished legacy of the Enlightenment is the quest for equality, the main concern today is how to deal with difference by making sure there is equity and equivalence.

The development of the concept of equality throughout modernity and its consequences for the organisation of society have been much challenged by postmodernists. Taking as a starting point Gramsci's analysis of the functioning of democracy within the modernist framework, postmodernists have emphasised the need for differentiation. Gramsci identified a strategy in modern democracy that he called 'hegemony', aiming at 'bringing about not only a unison of economic and political aims but also intellectual and moral unity' that became an important tool for the postmodernist critique of modernity (Gramsci, 1971: 181–2). Just because hegemony presupposes uniformity and agreement, does not exclude the possibility of oppression. Although Gramsci identifies another strategy, 'consent', which in a participative democracy is supposedly 'active', this does not preclude the use of persuasion and, at worst, manipulation. Moreover, hegemony may signify that a single cultural model is imposed through the consent of the majority. The imposed cultural model and the consenting majority will then overlap and generate a centre, broad enough to be widely recognised, but nonetheless subduing whatever is dissonant or pushing to the margins, even excluding, whatever is different. Lyotard illuminates this point in his discussion of the modern versus the postmodern condition:

> I will use the term modern to designate any science that legitimates itself with reference to a metadiscourse of this kind making an explicit appeal to some grand narrative, such as the dialectics of Spirit, the hermeneutics of meaning, the emancipation of the rational or working subject, or the creation of wealth. For example, the rule of consensus between the sender and addressee of a statement with

truth-value is deemed acceptable if it is cast in terms of a possible unanimity between rational minds: this is the Enlightenment narrative ... (Lyotard, 1986: xxiii)

This is how Lyotard describes the legitimising process of what he calls the 'grand narratives' of the Enlightenment which become consensual by conforming to truth-like metadiscourses subtly imposed by/on rational minds. The postmodern critique of modernism has targeted the modern conceptualisation of reason and the way it determines the understanding and application of the notion of equality. In modernist terms, as viewed by postmoderns, the search for emancipation was based on equality translated into access to a given model. With regard to knowledge, it led to the creation of (a) unique and transcendent canon(s) of information that a more conservative tendency has tried to keep in the hands of an elite and a more socialist wing would have distributed. This canon is one example of what Lyotard refers to above as 'metadiscourse', and 'grand narrative'.

The predominance of an established canon would then be reflected in the emphasis on standardised language and knowledge which was epitomised by the spread of education and the development of the mass media. Education made available to all through a national system, which Ferry qualifies as 'exoéducatif'[11] is, in fact, an official channel used to supply a fixed selection of knowledge which becomes necessary for socio-economic integration and for the elaboration of a civic conscience, and decisive in order to make a common type of discourse accessible to the average citizen. In addition, public information grew into the mass media due to technological development, which has allowed the stabilisation and standardisation of languages/cultures, the dissemination of stereotyped cultural models and the establishment of rituals, thus enabling the formation and consolidation of national cultures understood as 'imagined communities' (Anderson, 1983).

The worship of reason entitled Man, as its only owner, to enthrone himself and therefore to promote the power of the individual based on his rational nature and thus justified the development of overarching collective identities grounded on intellectual premises, the machine of the nation-state for example. Bureaucracy tended to replace solidarity and the relationships established in between the One (individual) and the Totality (nation), namely those based on ethnic or kinship ties, weakened. The philosophical distinction between Subject and Object was also dictated by the importance and concept of modern reason and forged hierarchies based on this premise. This would, for example, provide a new explanation for women's inferiority since not only were they physically less strong but also less rational. It also generated new types of domination over nature, either the environment or human nature. In sum, historical developments aimed at progress, cultural evolution meant the progress of reason, and reason was a transcendent, universal asset.

However, moderate postmodernists do not imply a rupture with modernity and, therefore, do not reject its values or principles as a whole. As Laclau argues, 'postmodernity does not imply a *change* in the values of Enlightenment modernity but rather a particular weakening of their absolutist character' (Laclau, 1988: 67). Postmodern pragmatists, for example, do not negate reason either, as Rorty admits, 'we so-called "relativists" refuse, predictably, to admit that we are enemies of reason and common sense' (Rorty, 1996b: 32). Postmodernists are mostly against using rationality as an excuse to force universal foundations and dogmas on democratic citizens and turning rationality into the major, if not the only, element for the implementation of democracy. Not only is postmodern reason plural, but it is also fragmented according to time and space. In postmodern terms, there is no universal paradigm for rationality and the latter is subject to 'rationality games' (Carrilho, 1994). This concept was obviously borrowed, as the author himself states, from the Wittgensteinian idea of 'language games', and by analogy it means that we follow rules, go along with the contingencies of the game, reinvent the rules, face the situations and change tactics according to each particular game and the players involved. Dependent on these different conceptualisations of reason are the notions of truth and consensus. Postmoderns view both truth and consensus as contextualised and transitory and refuse their unconditional link with rationality. More radical postmodernists, like Derrida, Baudrillard, and their followers, use reasoning in a different way from modernists, radical modernists, and even pragmatists, possibly in a more aesthetic way, with a lot of questioning, interrogating, and 'problem dissolving' (Hoy & McCarthy, 1994: 163).

Within this discourse, the French and American critiques of modernity introduced certain concepts – metanarratives, *différend*, deconstruction, *différance*, technologies of power, simulation, solidarity – which were further expanded in new theoretical fields that have initiated an interdisciplinary critique of the formation, representation and expression of cultural and political identifications within democratic frameworks.[12] I will follow Williams in selecting some 'terms of reference' that I will describe 'not only to distinguish the meanings but to relate them to their sources and effects' with regard to the development of critical cultural awareness in foreign language/culture education (Williams, 1958: 18). The following 'terms of reference' reveal, again following Williams, changes in *'structures of feeling'* or in 'structures of experience' that have emerged as new 'meanings and values as they are actively lived and felt' and which 'can be defined as social experiences *in solution*' (Williams, 1977: 132–3, his emphasis). Therefore, the 'terms of reference' below act as markers of a renovated worldview and indicate new perspectives towards experience as actually lived and felt in contemporary societies, and whose meanings may influence our visions of intercultural relations.

'Meta- and micronarratives'

Lyotard's definition of the *Postmodern Condition* as 'incredulity towards metanarratives' has been widely quoted and rephrased (Lyotard, 1986: xxiv). He identifies 'the dialectics of Spirit, the hermeneutics of meaning, the emancipation of the rational or working subject, or the creation of wealth' as examples of the grand narratives in modern society (p. xxxiii). The so-called metanarratives are very powerful because they encompass paradigms of 'legitimation' and 'delegitimation' for the definition of truth and justice and, therefore, provide the criteria according to which knowledge and performance are evaluated. Lyotard names this legitimation process cultural imperialism because such grand narratives are also understood as self-evident and irrefutable and control cultural production. Lyotard's critique of modernity here is, therefore, mainly epistemological, since his question is about 'who decides what is knowledge' (Lyotard, 1986).

According to Lyotard, modernity made the specific and the particular depend on broader and more abstract objectives, that is, on totalising myths that silenced the counter- and micronarratives. In this instance, he distinguishes between idealist, utopian and humanist emancipatory narratives of legitimation which have been replaced in late capitalist societies by a narrative of power imposed either through the scientific paradigm of knowledge or the creation of wealth and by the relation of both with the nation-state. Although in Cooper's account few twentieth century philosophers have been truly 'modern' in Lyotard's sense, Lyotard identifies the postmodern condition as the process of 'delegitimation' of such metadiscourses (Cooper, 1998: 64). In his terms, the postmodern implies a more refined sensitivity towards difference and a disposition to engage with the incommensurable, all this reflected in epistemological change.

However, such an explosion, or implosion in Baudrillard's terms, of the modern *episteme* does not necessarily limit the epistemological scope since 'the sense of "representational" space within which all kinds of narratives may be inserted [has] expanded' in this simultaneously global and local world (Robertson, 1995: 32). In fact, although a postmodern perspective focuses on the particular, a postnational and global world has multiplied the number of particular social and cultural circles accessible to us. In this regard, what postmodernism should refocus on, in Giddens' opinion, is the notion of evolutionary unidirectionality since 'evolutionary theories are highly prone to merge "progression" with "progress" because of ethnocentric assumptions which, while probably not logically implied in evolutionism, are very difficult in practice to avoid' (Giddens, 1984: 232–3).

In sum, it is the totalising, unidirectional, and absolutist character of metanarratives that is called into question by the postmodern condition, since the latter entails, on the one hand, the splintering of knowledge into *'bits'* of information and, on the other hand, its validation according to the ethos of each community (Lyotard, 1988b: 203; Stephanson, 1988: 36).

'Différend'

Lyotard has also introduced the concept of the *différend* which is very useful for understanding the postmodern notion of communication. The postmoderns, in general, and Lyotard, in particular, have crusaded against the idea that consensus should be the goal of communication as postulated by Habermas. As Lyotard views it, consensus should only be a stage within a discussion, therefore, it is transitional and located (Lyotard, 1986). From this standpoint, he identifies a situation in social discourse, the *différend*, which is a kind of 'original asymmetry' which cannot be subject to 'judgement, or arbitration, or even easy negotiation' for 'lack of a common language' (Buci-Glucksmann, 1988: 35, translation mine). However, Lyotard warns, the *différend* does not entail a *litige*, only a *conflit* between two or more *règles de jugement*, originating from untranslatable *régimes de phrases*, which may be equally legitimate (Lyotard, 1983). Lyotard views the *différend* as the instant when what emerges in communication exceeds what can be phrased at that very moment and, therefore, it encompasses silence (Lyotard, 1983: 29–30). Boyne provides a succint description of what the *différend* entails:

> It is a question of linking incommensurable discourses, of doing this apparently impossible thing rather than seeking a rule which will

prescribe how it is to be done, or which will explain why it cannot be done. That there is no such rule is the first principle of *Le Différend*, and, for Lyotard is the root of politics. (Boyne, 1998: 218)

Here Boyne grasps the dynamics of postmodern communication as described in *Le Différend*. Such a dynamics is characterised by the weakening of the role of legitimating/delegitimating metanarratives existing beyond the actual act of communication and, therefore, characterised by the enhancement of the (non)communication circumstance itself. The *différend* is thus the moment where differences, the incommensurable, are acknowledged not as an impediment but as part of the process of communication and, therefore, can be articulated even if only through silence.

'Deconstruction'

Derrida's deconstruction has become one of the most popular concepts appropriated from postmodernism by cultural studies in general. In consequence, it has been redefined repeatedly and, therefore, needs some clarification. First, it has frequently been used almost as a method of analysis or at least been understood as having 'a unity of approach, method, or style' (Hoy & McCarthy, 1994: 200). However, Derrida clarifies that 'deconstruction is not a method and cannot be transformed into one' and that it is 'neither an *analysis* nor a *critique*' (Derrida, 1988: 3). He then explains that he does not view deconstruction as critique in the Kantian sense, in the sense of transcendental critique which implies judgement and decision. Hence, Derridean deconstruction is nihilist since it focuses on 'the experience of undecidability', that is, on 'the distance between the plurality of arrangements that are possible out of it [the structure to be deconstructed] and the actual arrangement' (Laclau, 1996: 54). Deconstruction thus concentrates on the diversity of possibilities available for each circumstance and takes both their non-accomplishment and accomplishment into consideration. Furthermore, it does not adopt a perspective from a distant, neutral, analytical standpoint because its perspective is assumed from inside that web, it is one that is *engagée*, highly dependent on context. Deconstruction is also described by Derrida as 'an event that does not await the deliberation, consciousness, or organization of a subject', that is, it takes the subject forwards and it is through this web of (non)possibilities that the subject moves incessantly (Derrida, 1988: 4). However, this does not mean that the subject gives up reasoning and is carried along unawares. Instead, the subject deconstructs, disrupts, displaces at the same time that s/he is her/himself deconstructed, disrupted, displaced by events.

Second, deconstruction has been understood as interpretation, more precisely as a kind of hermeneutics or, at least, 'within the tenets of hermeneutics' (Hoy & McCarthy, 1994: 189–200). However, postmodernists reject this idea because they view Gadamer's theory of hermeneutics as based on a holistic perception of tradition and culture which, according to them, are fragmented and, therefore, impossible, as wholes, to influence interpretation and give it a unitary form.

Third, deconstruction also differs from a dialectical approach because it 'is based in rereadings – the refusal of final meaning (or synthesis), even momentarily', it looks for the 'unknowable', and relies on 'breaks and discontinuities in meaning' (Edgerton, 1996: 43–4). Deconstruction is thus a nihilist, never-ending approach to truth since it takes as its starting point the belief that truth is illusory, impossible to grasp totally, because the latter does not exist in a complete form ready to be apprehended.

However, deconstruction presupposes the existence of structures and, furthermore, 'a conscious acknowledgement of the ordered structure', although it also conceals 'an attempt to subvert it' (Edgerton, 1996: 44). This is confirmed by Derrida who explains that deconstruction is both a 'structuralist gesture or in any case a gesture that assumed a certain need for the structuralist problematic' and, at the same time, 'an anti-structuralist gesture' and, moreover, that 'its fortune rests in part on this ambiguity' (Derrida, 1988: 2). Accordingly, he claims for 'the destruction, not the demolition but the de-sedimenting, the de-construction' of the structure (Derrida, 1976: 10). From the Derridean point of view, whatever is constructed can and should be deconstructed. It could also be reconstructed, although Derrida seems to neglect this stage (Hoy & McCarthy, 1994: 36). This is the reason why postmodern deconstruction is a nihilist and ironical strategy. In this regard, it differs from the pragmatist notion of deconstruction that focuses on the contingency of life and self but also on their potential for reconstruction through a constant search for solutions and accomplishment.

However, Derrida claims, deconstruction is an important tool for political critique, for example, since it 'allows, on the one hand, a reflection on the nature of the political, and on the other hand, ... a hyperpoliticization' which, he explains, 'permits us to think the political and think the democratic by granting us the space necessary in order not to be enclosed in the latter' (Derrida, 1996: 85). From this standpoint, postmodern deconstructionism disagrees with some radical modernism which emphasises that contextual diversity 'can just as well, at least in many circumstances, promote an integration of self' and, therefore, provide the theoretical basis for a mild cultural pluralism characterised by diversity within unity (Giddens, 1991: 190). On the other hand, it also disagrees with some multiculturalisms that 'aim to establish in the margins of hegemonic systems alternative sources of meaning and moral authority' through differentiation strategies (Willet, 1998: 3). In sum, postmodern deconstructionism is a useful political tool for multicultural democracies because it entails a 'deep restructuring of relations of recognition' (Fraser, 1998: 35). It does not rely on differentiation between groups but rather on hyperdifferentiation, in other words, on differentiation within and across groups.

Postmodernist deconstruction is thus nourished by difference and instability. These are the materials of which the homogenised and stabilised structures – be they the political, social, cultural institutions, conventions or the individual – are made, structures which Derrida does not reject. Therefore, Derrida notes, 'chaos is at once a risk and a chance, and it is here that the possible and the impossible cross each other' (Derrida, 1996: 84). Whatever modernity tried to discard or refine in order to confirm authority – difference, instability, dissonance, ambiguity – postmodern deconstruction takes as resources in order to interrogate, disrupt, displace hierarchical constructions.

'Différance'

Derrida also coined this term that has been widely used in cultural studies. By writing *différance* with an *a*, the author wants to include in the same word both meanings of the verb *différer* which combines to differ and to defer. The word *différance* with an *a* thus results from the combination of the noun *différence* and *différant*, the present participle of the verb *différer* (Derrida, 1972). Therefore, *différance* incorporates the notion of difference, that is, disparity, contrast, antithesis, *'espacement'*, as well as the notion of deferral, that is, suspending, withholding, temporising, *'temporisant'* (Derrida, 1972). While the concept of difference entails a static, constant, finalised and closed representation of dissimilarity, the verb form of deferring adds fluidity, discontinuity, incompleteness to it. Therefore, *différance* implies difference that is *'toujours entre ou en-train-de'*, in other words, always in process (Bennington and Derrida, 1991: 79). This associates difference with the idea of a game that never ends and cannot be enclosed by the present tense, because it depends on preconcepts that evolve and diverge constantly. In Derrida's words, '*différance*, which is neither a noun nor a concept, seems to be stragegically most appropriate to conceive, or even pattern ... what is irreducible in our times' (Derrida, 1972: 7, translation mine). Although the concept of *différance* may, on the one hand, make difference seem more abstract and intangible, on the other hand, it enriches that notion because it problematises disparity, it interrogates nonconformity, it negates the perception of difference as opposing ends that become closer together or farther apart but never cross, and it disrupts the idea that when they meet they come to final and complete decisions or, moreover, that these will be considered positive if they emerge from consensus or negative if from dissent.

'Simulation'

Simulation and simulacrum are concepts used by Baudrillard to portray the '(un)reality' of postindustrial, late-capitalist, contemporary society. Although he gives an apocalyptic view of the present age, which he describes as 'the end of the *scene of the political*, the end of the *scene of the social*, the end of the *scene of history*', he also gives an interesting account of the role images and virtual reality play in postindustrial societies (Baudrillard, 1998b: 5). As Baudrillard sees it, 'we are already beyond the end', there is no progress, history is no more progressive but retrospective, even time is often counted regressively,[13] we live through illusions which are not produced by our senses or our minds, but by computers, satellites, etc. (Baudrillard, 1998b).

The political and the social are no longer real because they are programmed, we consume them in images that emanate from the screen, in 'a state of fascination and vertigo linked to this obscene delirium of communication' (Baudrillard, 1985: 132). According to Baudrillard, even democracy is reduced to the 'democracy of the TV, the car and the stereo' which are not concrete either because they exist through images, what we see beyond the objects, and represent the 'democracy of social standing' (Baudrillard, 1998a: 50). As a result, in consumer societies the democratic principle of equality has turned into the principle of happiness understood as 'measurable in terms of objects and signs' (Baudrillard, 1998a: 49). In addition, the production of knowledge and culture as well as the 'rediscovery' of the body and of nature are no more than 'a non-rational process of consumption ... a *simulation*, a "consommé" of ... signs', that is, knowledge, culture, body, nature are 'recycled', therefore not genuine (Baudrillard, 1998a: 100). In fact, as he himself acknowledges, Baudrillard is more concerned with 'the mode of disappearance' rather than with 'the mode of production' which confirms his nihilism (Baudrillard, 1981: 232, translation mine).

Furthermore, Baudrillard affirms that we are 'beyond the critical stage' and presents the hypothesis of 'an ironic stage' where either 'the extermination by technology and virtuality of all reality – and equally of the illusion of the world' will occur or these will be perpetuated through 'an ironic destiny of all science and knowledge' (Baudrillard, 1998b: 9). Despite situating the ironical stage beyond the critical one, he undertakes an ironical critique of the postmodern society by unveiling the illusory side of our 'realities' as produced by technology for commercial purposes and by expanding on what he calls the 'implosion of meaning', that is, the collapse of inner meaning, through the media. Baudrillard thereby provides a valuable contribution towards a critical approach to culture. Although Baudrillard's critique is ironic and apparently too focused on the surface of events, which goes against both the traditional and modern concepts of critique, it captures precisely the superficiality, velocity and intensity of images we are subjected to and which have had such a powerful impact on the political, social and cultural developments of the postmodern age.

'Technologies of power'

Foucault's theory of power provided some new insights for cultural studies, more specifically for multiculturalism and gender studies. While rejecting the predominance of both liberal and Marxist theories of power, which he calls 'economism in the theory of power', since they relate domination to relations of production, Foucault undertook an *'ascending analysis of power'* by focusing on relations of power that permeate the basic levels of society (Foucault, 1980: 88–99, his emphasis). According to Foucault, 'power in the substantive sense, *"le pouvoir"* doesn't exist', instead, 'power means relations, a more-or-less organised, hierarchical, co-ordinated cluster of relations' (Foucault, 1980: 198). The author suggests that power is not some kind of property that we own or that we can pass on to anybody, rather, power is constantly generated through social relations among individuals although it results mostly from the arbitrariness of conventions imposed by institutions.

On the one hand, Foucault recognises that the 'infinitesimal mechanisms' through which power circulates in society are 'invested, colonised, utilised, involuted, transformed, displaced, extended, etc., by ever more general mechanisms and by forms of global domination' and, therefore, he recognises repressive and oppressive power (Foucault, 1980: 99). But, on the other hand, he identifies individuals as 'vehicles of power, not its point of application', that is, he underestimates power that comes from above and denies that it is an exclusive, pre-existent possession in the hands of those who were granted some (Foucault, 1980: 98). Moreover, Foucault fragments power into pieces that do not even necessarily coincide entirely with institutions, either national or global, or with individuals. In Foucault's words, such mechanisms of power 'function outside, below and alongside the State apparatuses' and operate at the 'extremities' where power becomes 'capillary' (Foucault, 1980: 60, 96).[14] Moreover, 'capillary' does not necessarily coincide with the individual either, since 'it may be sub-individual or trans-individual' (Gordon, 1980: 255). His notion of decentred power corresponds, therefore, to the decentring of the subject, that is, power is created while exercised and it comes into being through and across individuals.

This conception of power as circulating, to some extent rather independently, dispossesses both institutions and the individual but, on the other hand, it makes power more available. Foucault perceives power as plural and local, and emphasises the 'productive aspect of power' because it is something you do not only have either to submit to or struggle for but also to operate. For that purpose, Foucault identifies the 'technologies of self' which 'permit individuals to effect . . . a certain number of operations . . . in order to attain a certain state of happiness, purity, wisdom, perfection, or immortality' (Foucault, 1988: 18). Although he is sceptical about the ways power has been exercised, at the same time he perceives a constant potential for liberation and empowerment in its exercise at local and individual levels.

Foucault also uncovers the liberating potential of 'capillary' power by claiming the legitimacy of *'subjugated knowledges'* which he accomplishes by demystifying truth as 'a thing of this world' and 'produced only by virtue of multiple forms of constraint' (Foucault, 1980: 81–3, 131). By dissecting the 'circular relation' among truth, knowledge and power, he deconstructs the conventions that affirm truth and classify knowledge, both produced on the basis of hierarchical power relations and whose production reconfirms the latter. Foucault's perception of power is, therefore, fundamental for the development of critical cultural awareness since it empowers the individual as a permanent negotiator, mediator, and producer of culture and makes her/him aware of the power games at work in every interaction.

'Solidarity'

Rorty elaborates on the notion of solidarity which he presents as a main goal of pragmatism. He confesses that philosophically he has more affinity with French poststructuralists, although he has more political compatibility with Habermas (Rorty, 1989). Therefore, he rejects the idea that solidarity is a transcultural bond based on some universal attribute as, for example, the fact that we are all human, on moral principles brought about by the superior faculty of reasoning, or achieved through argumentation (Rorty 1989, 1996b). He also shares the Nietzschean scepticism about the existence of a natural predisposition for solidarity 'at the "deepest" level of the self' (Rorty, 1989: xiii–xv). As a pragmatist, he views solidarity as the cultivation of tolerance, as a feeling that is constructed through practice, and, like Habermas, he frames it within the notion of moral progress achieved, however, through 'imagination and sentiment, rather than reason' (Rorty, 1996c: 49). Therefore, for pragmatists solidarity has 'only an ethical base, not an epistemological or metaphysical one' (Rorty, 1991: 24).

It follows on from this that Rorty perceives the character of solidarity as limited by historical situation and also by the relationship with the community. He even admits that the pragmatist understanding of solidarity is 'ethnocentric' and bases the concept on the relationship between the individual and her/his community (Rorty, 1991):

> ... our sense of solidarity is strongest when those with whom solidarity is expressed are thought of as 'one of us,' where 'us' means something smaller and more local than the human race. (Rorty, 1991: 191)

Solidarity is thus relativised as a bond with those to whom we feel closest. However, this circle is not limited by, for example, ethnic affiliations, rather it is described as a circle of 'private affections' where 'self-creation' is included. Rorty's perception of solidarity is, to some extent, populated by American individualism in the form of what Putnam calls 'solipsism with a "we" instead of an "I"' (Putnam, 1990: ix).

On the other hand, Rorty is not against cosmopolitanism, he looks for similarities among differences, and tries to include 'in the range of "us"' people who are 'wildly different from ourselves' (Rorty, 1991: 192). He, therefore, shows a tendency to neglect the way differences are constructed and to devalue them by assimilating 'them' into 'us'. Rorty bases his vision of solidarity on a dream of harmony which is, in some aspects, more Habermasian than postmodern. However, pragmatists view contingency and uncertainty in their world and their dream of social justice entails some deconstructive readings although following utilitarian premises of 'relevance' (Cherryholmes, 1994). The pragmatist perception of solidarity is nevertheless worth considering within this study because it combines a pragmatic and, to some extent, a postmodern orientation, in that it is relativising and contextualised, and a broader democratic orientation. Therefore, it provides interesting material for critical discussion of the concept in relation to intercultural collaboration.

Cultural identity and difference

Postmodernism provides new philosophical foundations for the very nature of the subject, culture and society, and, in consequence, for theories of identity. It attempts to respond to contemporary societies by emphasising the contingency, fragmentation, and incompleteness of self and collective identities. Therefore, it stimulates a new approach that enriches the understanding of the process of identity formation in our multicultural, global societies. The idea of a decentred self that presides over all poststructuralist and postmodern theories animates the subject to enjoy disparate experiences without the preoccupation of achieving a self-contained, unitary, and final condition. According to Jameson, even Marx's account of capitalism can accommodate the changes in society that have led to the cohabitation of identity and difference 'which we otherwise seem ill-equipped to think' about since it concerns 'the way in which a thing can both change and remain the same' (Jameson, 1998: 171). In the context of late capitalism or postindustrialism identity formation within a postmodern frame of mind is, therefore, a complex, never complete process. The postmodern subject is fractured, multilayered, and always in transition, resulting from the intersections of several discourses that are constantly being built within networks of culture and power. Therefore, postmodernists in general prefer to use the term identifications rather than identity because the first conveys a sense of plurality and continuum that is inherent to the postmodern conceptualisation of the process. Despite the fact that the postmodern focus on cultural fragmentation seems to contradict Ingold's view that the emphasis on culture fragments prevents one from experiencing the whole continuum of self-development in successive exchanges with both human and non-human environments, postmodernist arguments in general also accentuate movement and change (Ingold, 1993).

From this perspective, all circles of identity formation are likely to create legitimate identifications that interweave. Postmodernist theories of identity have influenced theories of representation based either on separatism, claiming that different groups should be entitled to different treatment, or hybridity theories, which focus on identities that result from the intermingling of groups. In consequence, while the first have admitted different identifications within a predominant identity, hybridists have explored the differentiation of elements within hybrid identities. Despite the acknowledged fact that the postmodern self lacks 'the depth, substantiality and coherence of the modern self', postmodern theories of identification, on the other hand, capture the plurality and flexibility of the contemporary self (Good & Velody, 1998b: 5). However, Grossberg contests what he calls 'such theories of identity on broader terms' for 'they remain within the strategic forms of modern logic' (Grossberg, 1996: 93). According to Grossberg, the modern has constructed its worldview upon a differentiation process although 'the modern constitutes not identity out of difference but difference out of identity', in other words, difference emanates from the differentiation between stable and independent identities (Grossberg, 1996: 93). Swingewood also grounds his theory on the premise that modern thought has been based upon 'differentiation' but goes even further by stating that postmodernism constructs its worldview upon 'de-differentiation', that is, the erosion of boundaries (Swingewood, 1998). Grossberg, on the other hand, proposes, as a countermodernist theory, a 'politics of otherness' that relies on the concept of difference not as essential to human beings but inscribed in their minds and bodies by articulations of social power relations and that acts as transformative practice by recognising the equivalent status of the Other.

On the whole, theories of difference in contemporary societies range from hegemony, where difference should be annulled in the name of a common project, be it a nation, the European Union, or even globalisation, to an intermediate stage of diversity within unity, generally called pluralism, to more or less radical stages of differentiation and hyperdifferentiation. A postmodern stance connects more with the last stage but also includes elements from the earlier one. The assumption common to both stages, which is reinforced by postmodernist theories, is the 'de-hierarchisation' of difference. More than blurring boundaries, post-modernism deconstructs and demolishes cultural hierarchies in general, such as European/non-European, north/south, scientism/non-scientism, urban/rural, high/popular, mainstream/minority cultures.

The 'delegitimation of grand narratives', in Lyotard's terms, and, in parallel, the potential for legitimation of 'any' narrative, opens a wide field for options and combinations, and, therefore, for identifications, that destabilise old essentialisms and absolutisms with regard to identity formation. Again Swingewood has to be mentioned here as one of the discordant voices on this matter since he believes that modernity is itself 'the celebration of healthy relativism, scepticism towards authority and grand, finalising narratives ...' (Swingewood, 1998: 173). He accuses Lyotard of 'defin[ing] modernity in narrow and impoverished terms ... for wholes can coexist with difference, diversity and openness' (Swingewood, 1998: 161). Furthermore, in Swingewood's opinion, postmodernism does not provide an adequate response to the 'new forms of cultural production' and Baudrillard, in particular, simplifies the description of processes of communication in contemporary societies by reducing them to consumption while disregarding production and, consequently, creation (Swingewood, 1998: 171–2).

In fact, the new culture industries, as described by postmodernism, provide risks as well as unknown possibilities for identity formation within technologically dominated, ephemeral *mise-en-scènes* of culture. On the one hand, it is a process which, in the end, involves 'a massive acculturation to a sterilised culture' (Baudrillard, 1981: 105, translation mine). On the other hand, the mass media not only provide endless opportunities for the interpenetration of cultures but they also produce marketable difference themselves since '*it is upon the loss of differences that the cult of difference is founded*' (Baudrillard, 1998a: 89, his emphasis). In other words, difference is supplied by the mass media in marketable models through a 'gigantic enterprise of production of the artificial and the cosmetic, of pseudo-objects and pseudo-events ... , as a denaturing or falsifying of an "authentic" content' (Baudrillard, 1998a: 126). Therefore, the world of available identifications is not wholly real, if we give credit to Baudrillard's apocalyptic visions, and it follows on from this that a postmodern theory of identity must also take into account the simulations of the cultural and the social which now have such a great impact on identity formation.

Still related to the incursion of the mass media in the formation of identities, it is worth mentioning the dismantling of boundaries between the public and the private which is also endorsed by postmodern discourse. The eruption of the private into the public has had a strong impact on both the form and the content of public discourse and, inversely, on private discourse as well. The 'conversationalization' of public discourse, in Fairclough's terms, has also occurred in its contents (Fairclough, 1995:

138). Therefore, issues which were once kept private or not mentioned at all are today openly discussed in the public arena. Likewise, emotions are recognised in the public forum and, moreover, granted some space within processes of rationality (Damásio, 1994; Goleman, 1996). The process of identity formation is, therefore, deeply altered by these changes in the cultural and social atmosphere which have particularly inspired postmodern theorists.

In addition, the validation of dissent in social and cultural relations, which postmoderns value as a possibility for promoting diversity and change, not only legitimates a wider range of options in the construction of identities, but also provides a more challenging type of discourse in the whole process. From this perspective, identifications do not happen passively but are formed through struggle. Moreover, Foucauldian theories that focus on power operating at the micro levels and, more precisely, Foucauldian 'technologies of the self', corroborate a description of identity formation geared to the legitimation of the contradictions, inversions, or even ruptures that the process entails and to the search for happiness. In sum, despite discordant positions on these issues, recent theories of identity have been deeply influenced by postmodernism, especially in aspects connected with culture as we shall see later in this study.

Postmodernism and citizenship

Recent developments in citizenship theory also reflect some influences from postmodernism (Mouffe, 1992a, 1996b; Soysal, 1998). Citizenship 'was an emblem of modernity' in that it translated into practice the concept of the equality of individuals united by civil contract before the state (Wexler, 1993: 164). Since postmodernism retheorises the individual, the cultural and the social, it also provides a new perspective for the political. However, postmodernism was at first labelled as apolitical due to its aesthetic or, at the most, transpolitical approach to social and political issues, in other words, the postmodernist critique has ignored and subverted conventional political institutions and formal politics. In fact, poststructuralist writings display deconstructive, ironic, and even cynical views of formal politics, and postmodernist writings on citizenship or on related subjects like education, racism, multiculturalism, etc., have been inspired by them. But, on the other hand, postmodernist approaches to power, knowledge, discourse, communication, and social relations have not only enabled a 'hyper-politicization' (Derrida, 1996), but also a 'reconceptualization of the political' (Squires, 1998: 126).

Unlike those who tend to concentrate their visions of the world on the 'underlying commonalities' and to focus on 'the expressions of this common humanity, shaped by the same bodies and brains and the same physical world', despite acknowledging 'myriad cultural forms' (Keesing, 1994: 9–18), postmodern perspectives scrutinise the divergent, the conflicting, the intersecting and that which merges together. Nevertheless, poststructuralist/postmodern theorisers of the political do not reject original ideals of modern democracy like equality of rights, freedom, social justice or general ethical principles that guide modern societies in the search for such ideals, despite Lyotard's delegitimation of meta-narratives, Derrida's deconstruction of tradition, or Foucault's contingent micropolitics (Best & Kellner, 1991; Connor, 1989; Stephanson, 1988). However, a so-called postmodern cultural politics of difference has postulated that formal politics are based on institutions, conventions, consensuses which result from artificial stabilisations of unsettled social functions and although stability is necessary, it is provisional since instability is recurrent. And, 'it is to the extent that stability is not natural, essential or substantial, that politics exists and ethics is possible', therefore neither politics nor ethics can provide a final stage to aim at but rather both operate in the midst of stability versus instability impulses (Derrida, 1996: 84).

Postmodernism has thus inspired theorisation about radical democracy which, on the one hand, endorses the ideals of democratic tradition and, on the other hand, reformulates them 'in a way that makes them compatible with the recognition of conflict, division and antagonism' (Mouffe 1992b: 12). Accordingly, Mouffe discards the possibility of a 'final realization of democracy'. However, she distinguishes the radical democracy she advocates from 'other forms of "postmodern" politics ... for which pluralism understood as the valorization of all differences should be total' because these 'could never provide the framework for a political regime' (p. 13).

Citizenship theory and praxis are thus a forum where postmodernist theorisation of the social and the political confronts the development of democratic ideals in modern society. Although Mouffe does not reject liberal democracy altogether, she acknowledges its crisis due to the fact that 'politics has been reduced to an instrumental activity', that is, 'the limitation of democracy to a mere set of neutral procedures' and 'the transformation of citizens into political consumers' have turned the exercise of democratic citizenship into the mere give-and-take of rights and duties. Therefore, Mouffe emphasises the role played by conflict and antagonism in the workings of democracy since the recognition of these elements animates the dynamics of democracy and sanctions diversity and contingency.

A cultural politics of difference, inspired by postmodern postulates, has problematised issues of institutional access and representation in that the fragmentation of the self and of social and cultural life together with a different articulation between the global and the local require a different approach to those issues. Not only may the citizen apply for membership of and protection from a myriad of local, national and transnational organisations, but s/he may also have her/his multiple private/public identities represented in the political arena. Matters which previously belonged to the private domain have invaded politics through the implantation of various new social movements and, furthermore, postmodern approaches to culture and knowledge have also related them to power issues. The postmodern emphasis on micropolitics has consequently reinforced a more participative perception of citizenship, although some authors express a different opinion like Swingewood, for example, who blames Baudrillard for defining a 'culture of passivity' by overestimating consumption while minimising production (Swingewood, 1998: 171–2). Nevertheless, Grossberg's 'politics of otherness', for example, despite his view of the Self and Other as having no '*specific* relations' between each other, involves the 'particular (contextual) power to affect and to be affected' since their relations are unspecified from the start but they are specifiable further on in terms of social power (Grossberg, 1996: 94, his emphasis). This does not mean that the citizen of the Enlightenment was not expected to be active, on the contrary, he (who was accepted as such) was first assumed as a revolutionary citizen who demanded a 'new capacity for self-determined agency (subjectification)' (Donald, 1996: 178). However, still according to Donald, 'this citizen-subject has no identity other than that produced by the Law' and 'assigned identities are transformed and recreated as individuals negotiate the Law's play of power' (Donald, 1996: 175). Therefore, political participation is much more 'a passionate belief in the life and death importance of the role . . . in which the fulfilment of the self is linked to the longed-for development of society as a rational and non-conflictual community' (Donald, 1996: 185–6). Donald then defends the right to 'opacity' of the 'men and women about town' which means the right to reformulate and to recreate their identities as citizens and make way for the 'otherness of the self'. His rejection of submission to prescribed roles, however, does not exclude a politics of emancipation of the self, the self being understood as contingent and spaces of non-identity being allowed to cohabit with fugitive identifications, some of which remain hidden.

The demands for active citizenship, from a postmodern perspective, do not stop within the limits of instrumental citizenship, in terms of the enjoyment of political rights of representation, but they aim at a more effective exercise of citizenship. Postmodernism identifies first and foremost the existence of power circulating everywhere and being operated by everybody in everyday life (Best & Kellner, 1991; Connor, 1989). Baudrillard goes even further when he states that 'the common illusion about the media is that they are used by those in power to manipulate, seduce and alienate the masses' but instead, he writes, 'the ironic version is precisely the opposite' (Baudrillard, 1998b: 8). In fact, the dependence of politics on the media, on show business, and on opinion polls reveals the illusory power of those in control and, hence, the importance of deconstruction in the process of exercising citizenship. In addition, Derrida affirms that there is 'no deconstruction without democracy, no democracy without deconstruction' and he defines deconstruction as the 'self-deconstructive force in the very motif of democracy, the possibility and the duty for democracy to de-limit itself' (Derrida, 1997: 105).

In conclusion, despite the above-mentioned reservations on this matter, postmodernism provides a new conceptualisation of the subject, the cultural and the social, as well as mechanisms which enable a reformulation of the idea of democratic citizenship. It certainly offers a startling, 'ironist' view of democracy while deconstructing the functioning of its institutions, the workings of power games, the illusive aspects of our 'reality', discovering the potential of antagonism and conflict, and offering a new understanding of solidarity. In sum, it interrogates and activates the role of the citizen in postmodern, multicultural, postnational democracies.

Postmodernism and critical cultural awareness

Postmodernism offers an aesthetic, deconstructivist, cynical, and ironical version of cultural critique that opens new possibilities for foreign language/culture education. It is not critical in the sense that implies evaluation, judgement or decision according to pre-given models. Nor is it analytical in the sense of fragmenting a linguistic/cultural whole in order to become knowledgeable about the whole, from a distant, objective and neutral point of view, in the search for the truth that is there waiting to be discovered. On the contrary, postmodernism engages a critical approach to culture from inside the (inter)cultural webs of meanings, one that is highly dependent on context, that defers conclusions, that relies on (un)decidability, that is, on the plurality of arrangements possible and the role both their accomplishment and non-accomplishment seem to play. It does not try to fragment the whole in order to understand how it works, rather, it takes an overall look at the fragmented, evolving and uncircumscribed structures. Postmodern cultural critique interrogates, explores, even evaluates while keeping its point of view restricted, situated, and dispossessing any perspective from universal validity. It moves beyond cognitive parameters and responds to emotional and aesthetic impulses. The following statement by Wittgenstein is very inspiring for further elaboration on this aspect of postmodern cultural critique:

> People who are constantly asking 'why' are like tourists who stand in front of a building reading Baedecker and are so busy reading the history of its construction, etc., that they are prevented from seeing the building (1941). (Wittgenstein, 1980: 40)

Although postmodern cultural critique is also interrogative and exploratory, it takes a deconstructivist, disruptive, ironical, and aesthetic approach. This is best exemplified by the perspective it takes on difference which constitutes a main tenet for cultural critique. Postmodern cultural critique negates the perception of difference as composed of opposing, self-contained ends that may come closer together or farther apart but never cross. Difference is fluid, but constructed through struggle, and it results from the interaction between power and cultural truths. Cultural difference is acknowledged in the public sphere and is not limited to private spaces. It is not treated as exotic, instead, its very existence is considered commonplace because each one of us is partially the Other. Postmodern cultural critique discards any one cultural model as essentially prevalent over the others.

Postmodernism provides new theoretical tools for understanding knowledge production and consumption. It demolishes boundaries between disciplines, high and popular cultures, cultural facts and virtual cultures. It offers new insights that may empower the marginalised and subjugated cultures, it problematises cultural processes of identification, and, therefore, it may inspire a more radicalised and critical exercise of citizenship since it relates the cultural to the political.

Despite the importance of the above-mentioned contributions, postmodern versions of cultural criticism also involve taking risks. Turning difference into another totalising myth that discards any possibility of unity or restricts solidarity to circumscribed areas and predefined limits is clearly one risk. Providing one-dimensional apocalyptic, sceptical, and anti-utopian descriptions of the world may be rather negative in an educational setting and so may a permanent and invariable deconstructivist approach. Providing only loose relativistic and particularistic views of cultural issues also leaves out a holistic dimension that, while taking the multiple perspective into account, may contribute to the understanding of how they relate to each other and, therefore, to well-founded criticism.

However, postmodern versions of cultural criticism have unquestionably offered refined attempts at addressing and reassessing culture in postindustrial and postnational societies where cultural issues have overflowed, disrupted, and blurred boundaries between sexes, classes, races, ethnicities, and nation-states. Moreover, postmodern cultural descriptions have also provided new paths for understanding and exploring the interpenetration of cultures in a global world and the production and consumption of cultural (im)materiality in an electronically mediated age, and above all, revealed the need for new approaches to cultural criticism.

Conclusion

Both Critical Theory and Postmodernism offer multiperspectival and up-to-date approaches to culture critique. To a greater or lesser extent, both depart from the rejection of absolutism, dogmatism, and instrumentalism in rationality, knowledge and culture. Both ground reason and contextualise the subject in social and cultural interaction, and attempt to grasp the complexities of social and cultural contexts. Both are concerned with social justice based on equity and equivalence. Both incorporate theory and practice, take interdisciplinary approaches to culture, more or less directly politicise culture, pay serious attention to popular culture and condemn its instrumentalisation and manipulation. On the one hand, Critical Theory accentuates the emancipatory power of rationality, albeit in critical and communicative modes. It goes beyond simple emphasis on critical reflection and its critique is based on a committed, emancipatory, transformative attitude. Critical theorists, especially Habermas, take a more utopian view, despite Horkheimer and Adorno's melancholic pessimism, while postmoderns are, at times, more dystopic, even apocalyptic in Baudrillard's case. Critical theory relies on the balance between cognitive, practical, and aesthetic rationality, while postmoderns adopt an aesthetic, nihilist, and ironical stance. Critical theorists admit tensions and argumentation but they aim, especially Habermas, for agreement and consensus, whereas postmodernism is nourished by difference and dissent. Postmodernism focuses mainly on

Philosophical Foundations for Critical Cultural Awareness

de-differentiation and hybridity, as well as hyperdifferentiation, on inconclusivess and undecidability. Both philosophical frameworks will be taken into consideration, as distinct but complementary, throughout the remaining chapters, viewed against a backdrop of Critical Pedagogy and in relation to critical cultural awareness. In the next chapter, they illuminate the critique of the models and documents under appreciation for exploring the critical dimension in foreign language/culture education. The interpretations of cultural identity and citizenship also reflect the philosophical theories described above. They also inspire the elaboration of questions both in the questionnaires and in the interviews. Finally, the proposals made for teacher development also keep in mind these philosophical/educational frameworks.

Notes

1. The definition of organisation adopted here is 'the regularised control of social relations across indefinite time-space distances' (Giddens, 1991: 16).
2. The meaning of the term 'positivism' in the works of the Frankfurt theorists has always been understood as a generalisation including different schools of thought which the authors perceived as united by common trends that they connected with the use of instrumental reason in science: 'Throughout its history, "positivism" was used by the Frankfurt School in a loose way to include those philosophical currents which were nominalist, phenomenalist (that is, anti-essentialist), empirical, and wedded to the so-called scientific method. Many of their opponents, who were grouped under this rubric protested the term's applicability, as for example Karl Popper' (Jay, 1996: 47–8ff).
3. Horkheimer dismisses what he considers the 'supreme concepts of Kantian philosophy' mainly the 'ego of transcendental subjectivity' and 'consciousness-in-itself' (Horkheimer, 1972: 203).
4. In Horkheimer's words 'it would be a mistake, however, not to see the essential distinction between empiricist Enlightenment of the eighteenth century and that of today' (Horkheimer, 1972: 232–3). And in the *Dialectic of Enlightenment*, the critique of the Enlightenment *par excellence*, it is possible to read that 'we are wholly convinced – and therein lies our *petitio principii* – that social freedom is inseparable from enlightened thought' (Horkheimer & Adorno, 1972: xiii).
5. For educational purposes, Giroux distinguished three modes of rationality, the technical, the hermeneutical and the emancipatory, based on the three levels – technical, practical and emancipatory – of knowledge-constitutive interests identified by Habermas (Giroux, 1983).
6. Horkheimer refers to Traditional Theory as 'theory in the traditional sense established by Descartes and everywhere practised in the pursuit of the specialized sciences ...' (Horkheimer, 1972: 244).
7. In McCarthy's words 'deconstruction is not a matter of simply renouncing ideas of reason but of interrogating them, disrupting and displacing them,

revealing them to be illusions that are so deep-seated as to be irremovable' (Hoy & McCarthy, 1994: 34).
8. Foucault explains: 'But in thinking of the mechanisms of power, I am thinking rather of its capillary form of existing, the point where power reaches into the very grain of individuals, touches their bodies and inserts itself into their actions and attitudes, their discourses, learning processes and everyday lives' (Foucault, 1980: 39).
9. Giddens defines 'double hermeneutic' as 'the intersection of two frames of meaning as a logically necessary part of social science, the meaningful social world as constituted by lay actors and the metalanguages invented by social scientists' (Giddens, 1984: 374).
10. In his 'Introduction' to Habermas' *Postmetaphysical Thinking*, Hohengarten claims that Habermas 'uses 'ideal' in a specifically Kantian sense to designate something that has a regulative function but is unattainable in actual fact' and continues by explaining that the author uses such idealisations as *'critical* reference points' (his emphasis) because he does not impose what these idealisations should consist of for a particular group (Habermas, 1992: xi).
11. Since modern society limits the traditional method of endogenous cultural reproduction through the family and the immediate social circle, it had to create an external system that would complement it and, to a certain extent, even replace it (Ferry, 1992: 42).
12. Postmodern authors generally prefer the word 'identifications' rather than 'identity' because the first conveys a sense of transience better than the latter which implies more static and permanent links.
13. Baudrillard gives the example of the digital clock on the Beaubourg Centre (Baudrillard, 1998b: 2).
14. Foucault introduced the term 'capillary' in opposition to the notion of central power in order to illustrate the narrowest expression of local power which slips through individuals and institutions (Foucault, 1980).

Chapter 3
The Critical Dimension in Foreign Culture Education

The previous discussion of the theoretical frameworks, both educational (Critical Pedagogy) and philosophical (Critical Theory and Postmodernism), provided some guidelines which apply more specifically to the development of critical cultural awareness in foreign culture education. These principles and issues identified from theory will be the basis, in this chapter, for developing a theory of critical cultural awareness, first through the description of cultural identities and the ways that different focuses on this matter determine different approaches to foreign cultures. Second, a critique of models and documents that have been key references in foreign language/culture education is undertaken, also based on these principles. Finally, I shall argue, also guided by the principles enunciated below, for the political nature of foreign language/culture education and its relationship with citizenship education.

Principles Suggested for Foreign Culture Education

As stated above, by using the theoretical discussions in the previous chapters, we can draw up some guidelines for undertaking a critical approach to foreign cultures that I will classify into five dimensions: the interaction between Self and Other, the cultural, the educational, the political and the ethical dimensions. These postulates will structure the critique of certain models and documents in the field and support a thesis for the understanding of foreign language/culture education as cultural politics.

The interaction between Self and Other

- identities are multilayered and transitory, and develop intersubjectively;

- no one should be regarded as culturally inferior or colonisable;
- everyone is entitled to cultural legitimacy and to a voice;
- cultural narratives coincide/differ in several aspects;
- cultural narratives should be interrogated and understood critically;
- interaction between Self and Other requires critical reflection;
- it works through the negotiation between the universal and the particular;
- it includes both convergence and conflict;
- it involves 'border–crossing' in both epistemological and cultural terms;
- it is influenced by one's position in relation to the Other;
- it is driven both by cognition of facts and emotional impulses;
- it involves interreaction and interdependence between Self and Other;
- it entails power relations;
- it involves argumentation and justification;
- it may generate a productive and transformative outcome.

The cultural dimension

- each culture consists of a multiplicity and complexity of meanings;
- culture is constantly being produced and reproduced;
- culture is produced within a web of tensions;
- cultural creation involves dissonance and change;
- each culture is constantly challenged by new images, new habits and new possibilities;
- different cultures share common elements and challenges;
- increasing transgressions of cultural boundaries must be taken into account;
- traditionally marginalised cultures should be legitimised;
- cross-cultural encounters foster 'border-crossing' and the creation of 'borderlands';
- traditional division between 'high culture' and 'popular culture' is obsolete;
- an ethnocentric perspective must be avoided;
- the various cultural representations within the whole cultural framework, national or other, should be acknowledged;
- different traditions within the same cultural group should be identified;
- common-sense and taken-for-granted assumptions should be challenged;

- one's own patterns of experience should be articulated with other cultural codes;
- a sense of belonging should be combined with a sense of detachment in relation to any cultural code;
- 'reflection-in-action' should be assumed as a rule for cultural interaction;
- informed, reflective and committed cultural practice should be promoted.

The educational dimension

- teachers/students are cultural workers;
- teachers are transformative intellectuals;
- cultural knowledge crosses disciplinary borders and social arrangements;
- discussion about the complexities of producing meaning should be fostered;
- cultural affirmation, negotiation, and communication should be encouraged;
- cultural interrogation, exploration, and creation should be stimulated.

The political dimension

- the political nature of education should be made explicit;
- the interaction between macro- and microcontexts should be taken into consideration;
- the multiplicity and complexity of subject positionings that reflect particular configurations of power should be grasped;
- everyone's political rights independently of their cultural background should be asserted;
- the capability to challenge ongoing relations of power should be promoted;
- cultural realities should not only be interpreted but also transformed;
- the individualistic, ahistorical and depoliticised celebration of diversity should be avoided;
- the integration of citizens into new political configurations should be facilitated.

The ethical dimension

- choice according to principles, not just rules, should be fostered;
- the relationship between culture and power should be considered a moral/ethical issue;
- access to diverse ethical frames of reference should be facilitated;
- one's moral/ethical visions should be discussed;
- discrimination and xenophobia on any grounds should be fought;
- solidarity and co-operation among different cultural groups should be encouraged;
- human beings are ethically responsible for each other and for the planet they share.

The 'Intercultural Speaker' and the Question of Cultural Identity

The foreign language learner used to be somebody who, for various reasons, was learning a foreign linguistic code that would enable her/him, in most cases, to exchange information or to accomplish the fulfilment of basic needs while in contact with a speaker of that language. Both the native and the target languages corresponded, in this case, to different nationalities, therefore each speaker was identified with a different self-contained cultural unit and remained so even after the cross-cultural encounter. The emphasis on a communicative competence-based approach and, consequently, the attention drawn to cultural matters has led to the identification of 'Intercultural Communicative Competence'[1] as one fundamental aim in foreign language/culture education. Hence, the foreign language/culture learner is viewed as an 'intercultural speaker', someone who 'crosses frontiers, and who is to some extent a specialist in the transit of cultural property and symbolic values' (Byram & Zarate, 1997, 11). This concept raises questions about the cultural identities of intercultural actors and has profound consequences not only for the approach taken in foreign language/culture classes but first and foremost for teacher development due to the effect of such a notion on teachers' 'professional identity' (Byram & Risager, 1999: 79).

The main target for the foreign language/culture learner/teacher is no longer to imitate a circumscribed and standardised model of a native speaker (Byram, 1997b; Byram & Zarate, 1997; Kramsch, 1993a, 1998c). Instead the focus is on the interaction between cultural actors, that is, on the intercultural encounter. The notion of an intercultural speaker responds to contemporary theories about cultural identity as socially constructed, always in the process 'of "becoming" as well as of "being" ' (Hall, 1990: 225), as 'points of temporary attachment to the subject positions which discursive practices construct for us' (Hall, 1996: 6). The idea of the intercultural speaker also confirms the description of learners/ teachers as 'border-crossers' who negotiate between the universal and the particular, create transitional cultural 'borderlands', and combine a sense of belonging with a sense of detachment (Giroux, 1992). The definition of an intercultural speaker may be further clarified by a 'paradigm of intersubjectivity' as put forward by Habermas who affirms that one is responsible for the construction of one's own identity which takes place 'in the performative attitude of participants in interaction', although he views it within the scope of a quest for emancipation through consensual truth (Habermas, 1979: 107). The postmodern conception of identity as fragmented, plural, 'never definitive but always relational' (Bertens, 1995: 191), is also a useful contribution towards defining the intercultural speaker's identity.

According to the principles enunciated above, the *critical* intercultural speaker is aware of the multiple, ambivalent, resourceful, and elastic nature of cultural identities in an intercultural encounter. S/he is aware of her/his role as a 'mediator' between two, or more, cultural identifications (Byram 1997a: 56), which include the criss-crossing of identities and 'the "positions" to which they are summoned; as well as how they fashion, stylize, produce and "perform" these positions' (Hall, 1996: 13–14). S/he is aware that eventually an intercultural encounter is about 'the way each culture views the other in the mirror of itself' and about negotiating one's own cultural, social and political identifications and representations with the other's (Kramsch, 1998a: 26).

In fact, in the view of practising teachers in general, as we can confirm in the sample described in the following chapter, the image of the foreign language learner has gradually become that of a language/culture learner who is prepared to impart as much as to receive cultural knowledge. However, although most of these teachers take geographical and ethnic diversity within the target cultures into account to some degree, they are still not very much aware of the fragmentation and the interconnectedness of the cultural identities they are dealing with.

National/ethnic identities

In modern times, cultural identities have traditionally been built on the basis of a 'similarity–dissimilarity pattern' geared towards an internal homogeneity that strengthens the frontier against the external heterogeneity (Akzin, 1964: 30). This idea has applied to both nationalities and minority ethnic groups which have been perceived as cultural cocoons. Such a constructed internal homogeneity has accounted for stereotypes and prejudices formed on the basis of definitive self- and/or other's cultural representations. With respect to the study of foreign cultures this notion has translated into a 'foreign-cultural approach' and/or a 'multicultural/approach' (Risager, 1998) that, in the former case, establishes the 'national' culture as the target and, in the latter, focuses on cultural diversity within the nation while viewing the ethnic groups as 'cultural islands' in opposition to the mainstream.

Nevertheless, it is important that the intercultural speaker has an understanding of both concepts, the nation and the ethnic group. Nation-states continue to be 'authorized authors' in a postnational and an international context (Soysal, 1998: 196), nationalism goes on inspiring political developments throughout the world (Smith, 1979), and the nation is still a prevalent system of cultural representation in our days (Hall, 1992). On the other hand, minority ethnic groups have become more visible within the nations due to a reappraisal of ethnicity, to civil rights movements, and to postcolonial migrations that have turned capitals in developed countries into multicultural settings, thus demanding a group-differentiated notion of nationality (Hall, 2000; Young, 1998).

The *critical* intercultural speaker, however, has to problematise both concepts, the nation and the ethnic group, in terms of their origins and their present developments. Both the nation and the ethnic group are ethnic communities or *'ethnies'* that share among other things 'a definite sense of identity and solidarity' (Smith, 1986: 29), hence the intrinsic equivalence of both and even their overlap according to those who 'imagine' the nation as a single ethnic group (Anderson, 1983). However, in modern times the 'nation' won political recognition through processes of 'politicization of ethnicity', that validated the supremacy of one ethnic group over others, and/or, 'ethnicization of the polity' where a national identity was created out of a heterogeneous population (Grillo, 1980: 7). In either case, the national identity is, to a greater or lesser extent, a 'fictive ethnicity' (Balibar, 1991: 96) and the nation is 'an imagined political community – and imagined as both inherently limited and sovereign' (Anderson, 1983: 15). Therefore, the formation and maintenance of any national community is always the result of a long process of struggle and compromise (Banton, 2000).

The *critical* intercultural speaker must then be aware that the development of ethnic identities, national or otherwise, involves a constant negotiation between remembering and forgetting, idiosyncracies and common interests. Furthermore, s/he must be aware that the process of modernisation, on the other hand, has made societies more interdependent and populations more interactive. National and ethnic identities have become more permeable, they influence each other and, therefore, cultural identities reflect 'ruptures and discontinuities' that enrich their 'uniqueness' (Hall, 1990: 225). The *critical* intercultural speaker needs to move beyond the universe of self-contained cultural homogeneities/diversities, without ignoring them, to 'cultural difference' as a 'time of cultural uncertainty' in 'the articulation of new cultural demands, meanings, strategies in the political present' (Bhabha, 1994: 35). In sum, s/he is conscious that national/ethnic cultural identities are made of both persistent and changeable components whose articulation adopts particular forms and meanings in specific circumstances.

In fact, the general prevailing perception of target cultures, which was confirmed in the study I carried out among upper secondary school teachers of EFL, is that of national cultures, with minority cultural islands within them, as we shall see in the next chapter. Although teachers are aware that national cultures interact more and more these days, they tend to perceive this process as restricted to the media and to the growing influence of American (Hollywood) culture.

Global/local identities

The intensification of globalisation has deepened the complexity of cultural identities. Postcolonial times have brought large groups of Third World migrants into the backyards of the main developed cities while the Third World Movement[2] has attempted to make these populations more visible in Western societies. Although these minorities are starting to make a difference in Western societies, Third World cultures remain mainly the exotic construct that is successfully marketed through the media.

At the same time, the boom of information technology has developed a 'third culture' that has spread mostly from the United States to the rest of the world through television, cinema and the Internet, which exists above the control of the nations. This has generated a sudden overproduction of culture (Featherstone, 1995), and has created a transnational *'languaculture'* that accounts for the existence of the same trends, habits and even values in different points of the globe (Agar, 1994). Cultural homogenisation and cultural hybridity are frequently referred to as the most evident consequences of globalisation (Bhabha, 1990; Featherstone,

Lash & Robertson, 1995). However, homogenisation is not totally perceived as an overriding flow that sweeps national and local cultures away nor is hybridity only viewed as the 'melting pot' of cultures. On the contrary, both tendencies are also understood as potentially creative. Cultural hybridisation is described as an upsurge of new forms of life:

> Hybridity unsettles the introverted concept of culture which underlies romantic nationalism, racism, ethnicism, religious revivalism, civilizational chauvinism and culturalist essentialism . . .
>
> Hybridization is a factor in the reorganization of social places. Structural hybridization, or the emergence of new practices of social co-operation require and evoke new cultural imaginaries. Hybridization is a contribution to a sociology of the in-between, a sociology from the interstices. (Pieterse, 1995: 64)

Globalisation is thus perceived as enabling rather than suffocating. Even the market-driven culture industry that floods the mass media all over the world is understood, to some extent, as recycled locally and the clash between cultures as stimulating cultural reconstruction. Therefore, the impact of the global on the local seems to be perceived as productive since 'globalization, defined in its most general sense as the compression of the world as a whole, involves the linking of localities' as well as the ' "invention" of locality', since local cultures are profoundly disrupted by the sudden cultural explosion and implosion of a postmodern/postindustrial world (Robertson, 1995: 35). The 'glocalization', in Robertson's terms, of cultures implies a constant dialogue between them through movements both outwards and inwards that have not only intensified the production of culture but also call into question taken-for-granted assumptions and habits established locally (Featherstone, 1995; Robertson, 1995). Global movements, such as the ones concerned with ecological or women's issues, have had a great impact on local social structures and frames of mind and their local realisation has contributed to their global affirmation. Moreover, the 'glocalization' and hybridisation of cultures has made it possible to build our cultural identities out of the endless cultural combinations available or just 'to slip easily in and out' of them (Featherstone, 1995: 9).

An understanding of such developments may have a strong influence on the study of foreign cultures. A 'transcultural approach' takes into consideration the fact that cultures are constantly interweaving, that some languages act as *linguae francae* between non-native speakers and that this situation may be useful in the form of cross-cultural contacts between learners of the same foreign language (Risager, 1998). Such an approach allows for a wider range of *'languaculture'* patterns for the intercultural speaker to choose as models since it promotes contact with their worldwide realisations – world Englishes, for example – while it simultaneously 'draws attention to internal variation in geographical, social, ethnic or linguistic terms' (Byram & Risager, 1999: 158). Therefore, the cultural scope in the study of foreign cultures not only widens but also deepens, thus providing the learner/teacher with endless possibilities to be explored.

The *critical* intercultural speaker takes critical advantage of the world opened wide to her/him by appreciating the different narratives available, by reflecting upon how they articulate, how they are positioned in terms of each other and how their positions affect their perspectives. S/he tries to prevent deep-seated prejudices from influencing her/his judgements of other cultures, for example by not taking an ethnocentric evaluation of them whatever her/his personal response to them may be. S/he is suspicious of consumerist attitudes promoted by the culture industry and is critical about its role as a homogeniser. S/he recognises that it is not possible to be in control of all factors in an interaction nor possible therefore to avoid tension and misunderstanding totally but that it is possible to deal with them in a friendly manner if one is very aware that there are unknown and unreachable areas in any intercultural encounter:

> The difference between disjunctive sites and representations of social life have to be articulated without surmounting the incommensurable meanings and judgements that are produced within the process of transcultural negotiation. (Bhabha, 1994: 162)

As Bhabha claims here, differences and divisions have to be articulated in an intercultural encounter without necessarily having been solved or erased. The *critical* intercultural speaker is conscious that disjunctions, discontinuities and ruptures are an everyday reality in the complex process of making meaning out of an intercultural encounter, that most will remain so and, because of this, they may also contribute to the accomplishment of the whole exchange. S/he makes full use of the opportunities for establishing various cross-cultural contacts either professional or personal that enable her/him to accumulate a variety of experiences. However, the *critical* intercultural speaker is not a cosmopolitan being who floats over cultures, but someone committed to turning intercultural encounters into intercultural relationships whereby s/he deliberately exposes herself/himself to networks of meanings and forces and reflects critically upon them.

In teachers' views, illustrated in the next chapter, globalisation may have a double meaning. On the one hand, it represents a way out, in terms of the possibility of making contact with other cultures through the Internet, the media and increasing mobility. On the other hand, it entails the danger of cultural colonisation by either a foreign culture, e.g. American, or by media and virtual cultures. Although teachers are committed to promoting a critical approach towards foreign and media cultures they do not seem to explore more deeply the complexities of the interaction between macro- and microcontexts, the global and the local. Likewise, they are aware that conflict may be used as a source of energy in intercultural communication but they do not probe into the potential strategies to use it this way either in the students' social contexts or through student school exchanges abroad.

The 'third space'

An intercultural encounter encompasses an interaction between the multiple identifications of the social actors, the perceptions they have of each other's identities and the fact that some are more dominant in particular circumstances (Byram, 1997a: 56; Byram & Fleming, 1998: 7). The role of the *critical* intercultural speaker is to be as aware as possible of what is really going on during the interaction. However, eventually the interaction is more than the sum of its parts because the intercultural encounter stretches the cultural identities involved and the exchange takes place 'in-between' them or at their extremities. And the critical question is 'How are subjects formed "in-between", or in the excess of, the sum of the "parts" of difference (usually intoned as race/class/gender, etc.)?' (Bhabha, 1994: 2).

This idea was metaphorically elaborated by Byram and Zarate, while describing their vision of an 'intercultural speaker' in terms of the concept of frontiers that s/he is supposed to cross, by rejecting the representation of a frontier as a line between national territories 'which can equally be crossed in one direction or the other' (Byram & Zarate, 1997: 11). The notion of 'crossing frontiers' may be summarised, in practical terms, as 'the ability to make and sustain personal contact with one or more members of the foreign community' (p. 12), somewhere 'in-between' or at the elastic borders of our selves. This 'open-country' where the extensions of our selves meet is identified by Bhabha as the 'Third Space' and described as 'unrepresentable in itself', a place where 'the meaning and symbols of culture have no primordial unity or fixity' and where 'the same signs can be appropriated, translated, rehistoricized and read anew' (Bhabha, 1994: 37–8).

This notion of a third possibility in-between or beyond the Self and the Other is useful for the understanding of the complexities of an intercultural encounter and has already been explored by Kramsch. This author recommends a 'third perspective, that would enable learners to take both an insider's and an outsider's view on C1 and C2' and that it should be 'integrated into a critical pedagogy', as we shall discuss later (Kramsch, 1993a: 210, 243).

The nature of this third arena where intercultural competence should develop and which is to be explored in foreign culture education may be further elaborated through the discussion of philosophical concepts, introduced in the previous chapter, such as 'intersubjective rationality', which Habermas identified as resulting from the self- and hetero-representation of subjects in interaction, and an area of non-identity, which Habermas described as the space where we dismiss our identifications and reach universal understanding. The discussion of the notion of the 'fusion of horizons' as introduced by Gadamer, meaning the expansion of our 'horizons' in order to reach understanding, would also be pertinent to this subject. On the other hand, the discussion of the concept of *différance* as perceived by Derrida is fundamental here since it expresses the inconclusiveness of the encounter.

It is important, however, to underline that this 'open-country' where an intercultural exchange may be fulfilled, as it is comprehended in the concept of the intercultural speaker, does not reject the identifications which it builds upon, some of which were described above, but rather it relies on the dynamic negotiation between them. Nevertheless, it draws, to some extent, on 'the importance of the alienation of the self in the construction of forms of solidarity' (Bhabha, 1990: 213), in other words, it also relies on the creation of blank spaces in our identities where we can, to some extent and momentarily, 'merge' together. Some educators and students who have reflected upon issues of identity have suggested that the concept of identity, as we traditionally view it, is largely Eurocentric and too centred on the individual (Sparrow, 2000). This idea is reinforced by the vision of 'the experiential continuity of being in the world' that does not isolate human beings from their social and physical environments or from all the experiences they have had, are having and look forward to or those they avoid having (Ingold, 1993: 230). Therefore, intercultural competence depends on the combination, which does not always reach equilibrium, between allegiance and disengagement, forgetting and remembering, affirming and deferring. Critical cultural awareness of the situations provides the necessary abilities to ponder, decide and/or recognise which resources are to be or were put into action in a particular circumstance.

This view of the intercultural encounter is difficult to realise in teaching practices without a strong theoretical basis, and we shall see in the next chapter that this is missing in some professional contexts of foreign language/culture education. Such a perspective requires not only experiential activities but demands that they are both preceded and followed by theoretical input and above all by reflection.

The Critical Dimension in Models for Intercultural Communicative Competence

Intercultural communication as a field of study may be best described as an academic discipline that created 'an interdisciplinary theoretical model of intercultural interaction, relations, and communication' (Smith *et al.*, 1998: 56). It was established after the Second World War and stemmed from the works of E. T. Hall, *The Silent Language*, *The Hidden Dimension*, and *Beyond Culture*. Its first applications were not in education but in training courses aimed mainly at the Peace Corps and later at disparate audiences, namely business people, health care workers, social workers, international students, refugees, and also some educators. The first two models presented below – Brislin/Yoshida's and Bennett's – are examples of such training courses. They aim at preparing students psychologically to deal with cultural difference and, unlike the subsequent models, do not include language teaching/learning.

In one of his early works, Hall made the important statement: 'Culture is Communication' (Hall, 1959: 119–26). This could not be ignored by foreign language researchers/teachers who were concerned about developing communicative competence among their students. Therefore, this message started echoing among foreign language educators during the 1980s as shown by the Seelye, Damen and Robinson models, discussed below. Moreover, as Hall also pointed out, cultural communication implies choice since 'no culture has devised a means for talking without highlighting some things at the expense of some other things' (Hall, 1959: 120), and a conscious decision relies very much on a critical mind. Therefore, it is evident in other models discussed below – those of Kramsch, Byram and Pennycook – that during the 1990s there was a greater emphasis on the development of critical cultural awareness within foreign language/culture education.

Brislin/Yoshida model (1994)

Brislin has edited and co-authored several books containing activities that have been used for programmes, courses, and workshops on cross-cultural communication within the field of cross-cultural psychology. In these works, he and his collaborators develop a model that underlies such activities and which consists of a four-step approach: '(1) Awareness; (2) Knowledge; (3) Emotions (includes attitudes); and (4) Skills (involving visible behaviour)' (Brislin & Yoshida, 1994: 26). With the first step, the authors aim at raising consciousness of one's own and the others' cultural values and the way these affect behaviour. They also make their trainees aware that some differences are insurmountable and therefore they train them to feel comfortable with difference *per se*.

As far as knowledge (2) is concerned, the authors point out the need for some practical knowledge about legal or other matters which have to be sorted out immediately after arrival in a foreign country, and for Area-Specific Knowledge that includes information about the geography, economy, history, or other aspects of the country. Within this step, they also include Culture-General Knowledge, which deals with general issues that may occur in an intercultural experience regardless of which culture, such as anxiety, misunderstanding, or difference *per se*, and Culture-Specific Knowledge, that concerns rituals, hierarchies, organisation of time and space, etc. in the particular culture they are interacting with.

With respect to the last two steps that refer to emotions/attitudes and skills/behaviour the authors try to facilitate personal control through role-plays and simulations that raise awareness of the motives that lie behind the situations and to bring up suggestions for coping with stress and anxiety. The authors make use of other models to devise skills to be acquired and even provide a table with behaviours Americans can adopt when interacting with Germans, Japanese, etc. The activities are very much based on discussions, on prepared and scripted role-playing, and include recommendations for specific behaviours. However, most of these activities are hardly critical despite the benefits of intercultural training presented by the authors, such as the development of complex thinking with regard to intercultural relations, of 'world-mindedness' that they describe as an interest in what happens in other countries, of self-confidence, of better interpersonal relations, more cultural sophistication, etc. (Brislin & Yoshida, 1994: 165–71). Although they generate intercultural awareness through dialogue and discussion, they tend to be prescriptive, goal-oriented, based on skill training and aimed at controlling behaviour. Nevertheless, Brislin/Yoshida's model provides some suggestions that are worth taking into consideration while promoting critical intercultural competence such as the importance of raising consciousness of one's own and the other's cultural values, of feeling comfortable with difference, of knowing how to deal with general feelings generated by an intercultural experience and of facilitating personal control. Moreover, the authors provide endless examples of which a selection is worth critical discussion in teacher development workshops or even in foreign language/culture classes.

In fact, professional training on intercultural communication has, in general, remained detached from foreign language/culture education and teacher development. The teaching of foreign languages for business purposes has nevertheless tried to fill this gap. This mutual influence may be beneficial for both sides since foreign language/culture education, especially at university level, cannot lose sight of professional training and the latter could make use of research done on intercultural communication for pedagogical purposes in order to put some of the overgeneralisations they make into question. Furthermore, some management specialists on matters of intercultural communication in international business, like Hampden-Turner and Trompenaars, have been theoretically developing more refined studies about the professional and personal experiences of foreignness (Hampden-Turner & Trompenaars, 2000). They take a simultaneously theoretical and practical approach to intercultural relations from a dilemma perspective based on antithetical concepts such as Universalism versus Particularism, Individualism versus Communitarianism, etc. Although their work still relies on generalisation, their theory develops with elaborate reflections upon (inter)cultural performances in professional settings that may also be useful for the professionals of education.

Bennett's model (1993)

Bennett's model is developmental and aims at a growing 'intercultural sensitivity' which the author defines as 'the construction of reality as increasingly capable of accommodating cultural difference that constitutes development' (Bennett, 1993: 24). Bennett thus understands our relation with difference in terms of personal growth. He identifies two main stages, the 'ethnocentric' and the 'ethnorelative', and the path that links both is an increasing process of self- and cultural-awareness and an intensification of intercultural relations. Within the 'ethnocentric stage' the author distinguishes three levels, 'denial', 'defense', and 'minimization', which are themselves subdivided. At the 'denial' level, difference is made invisible through several strategies such as emphasising what is common between native and foreign cultures, establishing broad categories among different cultures, which the author calls 'benign stereotyping' (p. 31), or ignoring/disposing of intrasocietal difference. The author also points out several 'defense' strategies namely over- or devaluing judgements of other/own cultures. Within the 'minimization' level, the author calls attention to avoidance of difference on universal grounds either for biological or religious reasons, for example, because we are all human beings or we are all God's children.

Bennett also identifies three levels within the 'ethnorelative stage' which are, 'acceptance', 'adaptation', and 'integration'. At this stage, cultures are understood in relation to each other and 'one's world view as a relative cultural construct (cultural self-awareness)' (p. 50). 'Acceptance' is the lowest level of positive intercultural sensitivity and it implies acknowledgement of and respect for behavioural and value differences. At the next level, 'adaptation', one is expected to intensify the relationship with different cultural patterns while still keeping one's own cultural identity almost intact, in other words, intercultural skills are 'additive' to one's native skills (p. 51). Within this level the author distinguishes between 'empathy', which means the ability to understand/ imagine the other's perspective and even to 'give up temporarily one's world view' (p. 53), and 'pluralism', which means a situation of bi- or multiculturalism understood as 'the internalization of two or more fairly complete frames of reference' (p. 55). The author points out that the difference between his understanding of 'empathy' and of 'pluralism' is that, in the first, difference is external to the self while in the latter it is internal.

Bennett considers 'integration' as the climax of intercultural sensitivity as far as his model is concerned. However, he also distinguishes two steps within this level which are 'contextual evaluation' and 'constructive marginality'. According to the author, the former is often the last stage for many people and it involves integrating different aspects of two or more cultures into a new identity through self-reflection and the capacity to analyse and evaluate situations and to act without conforming totally to the constraints of one established cultural framework. 'Constructive marginality' means a step further in being independent from cultural constraints, residing at a transcultural level where analysis occurs systematically and there is no necessary attachment to one cultural framework.

This model is based on developmental psychology and, therefore, builds on the assumption of constant and steady personal growth. Although the author frequently posits the possibility of paralysis and regression, this model represents, to some extent, a simplification of complex situations where the cultural issues are traversed by other pressures on one's cultural identities, such as gender, race, age, status, commitments, personality, etc. However, the model is worth taking into consideration because it gives some interesting input for foreign culture education if it is examined critically and put into practice keeping its limitations and potentialities for a critical approach to intercultural relations in mind. Its interest lies in the fact that its main concern is to raise awareness of one's attitude to difference, that it addresses the disparate responses that may occur, points out motives and risks that may lie behind them, and suggests some strategies for some common situations. Furthermore, it aims at some sophistication when dealing with difference since the highest levels imply more elaborate manners of relating with the Other which require some critical understanding of these processes. Another positive aspect is that it is multidimensional, encompassing cognitive, affective and behavioural aspects. However, it lacks an account or explanation of 'difference-within-difference', for example, of the complex, non-linear process in which cultural identities relate, and of the socio-political inscriptions that cultural bodies display/hide, in other words, of the pressures that disrupt a steady progression in the development of acculturated identities into intercultural ones. In sum, Bennett's model does not problematise the formation of (inter)cultural identities sufficiently.

Nonetheless, psychology is one of the disciplines whose presence has been felt behind most of the research into intercultural communication. Academic research in this area has been a great resource for academic research in foreign language/culture education. However, with respect to practice, especially at university level and considering professional preparation in all areas, it is also worth considering practical work. Despite some oversimplification while providing useful guidelines for expatriate and frequent-flyer professionals, Marx's recent work, for example, also takes a scientific, but practical, approach to this issue that deserves attention (Marx, 2001). None of the secondary-school teachers I interviewed mentioned any theoretical or practical work in this field, although I believe that it has been increasingly taken into account in the context of foreign language/culture education for specific purposes, e.g. Business Studies, and mainly in the newly introduced subject of Intercultural Communication itself.

Seelye's model (1982, 1992)

Seelye's model was the first well-known structured framework for introducing culture into foreign language classes. It is based on 'Goal-Oriented End-of-Course Performance Objectives'. The author identifies seven goals that call for students' awareness of the ways culture conditions language and behaviour, for their capacity to make and evaluate general statements about a culture, and for their curiosity about the target culture and ability to locate and organise information about it. Several activities are provided as examples as well as some techniques that the author introduces as 'Culture Assimilators', 'Culture Capsules', and 'Culture Clusters'. This model is not explicitly critical in that it does not present a consistent preoccupation in developing critical cultural awareness about the target and native cultures with social and political implications. Since it aims at shaping behaviour, it overrelies on generalisations about the target culture especially on notions of cultural appropriateness; for example, about the appropriate table manners to use in a French home which the student has to display in one activity. However, it does show some awareness of social and regional variations and of making students aware of the role convention plays in shaping behaviour, thus allowing some space for a critical educator to select some ideas and suggestions.

Seelye's model stands half-way between foreign language/culture education that frequently relies on the acquisition of cultural content or on functional language activities and on professional training on intercultural communication that often rests on cultural generalisations and stereotypes. Seelye's attempt to relate both is praiseworthy although it displays some weaknesses, as mentioned above. However, none of the participants in the research project that will be described later, all of them foreign language educators at secondary school level, referred to his work.

Damen's model (1987)

Damen's work in the late 1980s provided another important contribution towards validating the role culture should play in foreign language classes and paved the way for the development of studies in this area. It represents a comprehensive study drawing on broad interdisciplinary literature and introducing concepts which were new in foreign language teaching/learning. In her diagram 'The Mirror of Culture' she designates the expected manifestations of intercultural communication as self-awareness, empathy, awareness and acceptance of diversity, tolerance, and lack of ethnocentrism, which look rather cautious today when compared to the demands of a critical pedagogy. She also defines cross-cultural awareness as a continuum process of acculturation into bi- or multiculturalism, which is problematic if we take into consideration theories that emphasise group differentiation or other possibilities of intercultural cohabitation. In addition, the space she allocates to intercultural communication as a fifth dimension, given equal status to listening, speaking, reading, and writing, seems today a modest position and a questionable arrangement. However, more than a decade ago, her model introduced a daring vision of foreign language classes as places where culture should be addressed, where intercultural communication should be a main goal, where teachers should have an interdisciplinary background and reassess their roles as cultural guides and pragmatic ethnographers. Damen did indeed pose some critical questions, namely: 'Consider the difficulty of discussing "American" culture. Whose culture? What culture? What rules? What patterns?' (Damen, 1987: 20). She also made some critical statements such as that 'instances of intercultural communication are more likely to result in miscommunication than in meaningful communication' (p. 23). Furthermore, citing Rohrlich, she identified a 'third level of analysis' which she called 'The Synthetic Level – The Dynamic Perspective' that results from the interaction between the 'Intrapersonal Level – The Private Perspective' and the 'The Interpersonal Level – The Public Perspective' and made it the basis of her model. In sum, Damen's work may be considered a milestone in the reinforcement of a revival of cultural content and in the introduction of a new framework in foreign language education that provided foundations for new developments such as a critical pedagogy of foreign language/culture education.

Damen's concepts were widely referred to in the national syllabus which was being followed by the participants in the research project described later although no participant, all of them secondary school teachers of EFL, mentioned her work explicitly. Nevertheless, her ideas, such as cultural self-awareness, awareness of and tolerance towards cultural diversity and rejection of ethnocentrism can be recognised in the participants' responses. The importance she granted to the cultural component, together with an interdisciplinary and critical approach to it, also resonates throughout their statements.

Robinson's model (1988)

Robinson understands the process of learning about a foreign/second culture as an expansion of the students' experiences in their native/home culture. Therefore, she does not view it as an additive process through which the student adds more objective knowledge about another culture to knowledge about her/his own. It implies instead a subjective involvement with the other culture, a synthesis of both the native and the foreign cultures where one lies deeper and the understanding of the other grows from the first. However, Robinson's aim for culture learning/teaching is ultimately 'cross-cultural understanding'. For this to be attained she envisages a stage of 'cultural versatility' where 'differences between people will be decreased' (Robinson, 1988: 101). This has become a popular vision among foreign language/culture educators who, following Robinson, focus mostly on similarities among cultures and perceive intercultural communication as empathising and feeling comfortable with a person from another culture. This entails a harmonious and consensus-driven idea of intercultural relations that is not critical. Nevertheless, this author emphasises the use of ethnography among teachers/learners of foreign languages/cultures that gives way to a deeper exploration of cultural experiences.

Robinson is another author who has been a permanent presence in foreign language/culture education bibliographies. Her proposals for a subjective involvement of the student in her/his learning of cultural content, for a greater focus on universal aspects of cultures, for the softening of people's cultural differences and for the stimulation of people's empathy towards these differences are still echoing among foreign language/culture educators. The participants in the research project I carried out were not an exception.

Kramsch's model (1993a/1998a)

Kramsch's model is based on the combination of three intellectual traditions which the author identifies as 'the critical, the pragmatic, and the hermeneutic' and that she summarises respectively as understanding others, making yourself understood and understanding yourself (Kramsch, 1993a: 183). This framework reveals first Kramsch's concern with dialogue and the production of meaning which runs through her model. Accordingly, she locates the production of meaning across cultures, as previously mentioned, in a 'third perspective' where 'meaning, i.e., culture, is dialogically created through language *in discourse*'

(Kramsch, 1998a: 27). In order to build that 'third place' which, in Kramsch's terms, corresponds to 'cross-cultural understanding', she recommends four steps:

1 *Reconstruct the context of production and reception of the text within the foreign culture (C2, C2').*
2 *Construct with the foreign learners their own context of reception, i.e. find an equivalent phenomenon in C1 and construct that C1 phenomenon with its own network of meanings (C1, C1').*
3 *Examine the way in which C1' and C2' contexts in part determine C1" and C2", i.e. the way each culture views the other.*
4 *Lay the ground for a dialogue that could lead to change.*

(Kramsch, 1993a: 210, her emphasis)

Kramsch then clarifies that steps 1 and 2 occur simultaneously (p. 221) and later she reverses the order between the two (Kramsch, 1998a). It is evident in this model how much the author values a subjective/intersubjective and intercultural approach realised in discourse. In her view, culture is produced during the dialogical exchange of ideas and emotions between particular individuals with particular stories and visions.

Therefore, Kramsch challenges some myths such as the 'native speaker' as a model for the foreign language/culture learner/teacher and the use of 'authentic materials' as sufficient tools for a critical pedagogy. According to Kramsch, the 'universal' model of the native speaker is not only fictitious but an imposition on learners/teachers preventing the full exploration of dialogic meaning-making in the classroom. With regard to the use of 'authentic materials', Kramsch expresses the view that they are the products and the tools of native speakers who are not necessarily critical individuals, and therefore, they may be either critical or uncritical cultural representations (Kramsch, 1993a).

Finally, Kramsch affirms that a 'third perspective' takes place 'if it is integrated into a critical pedagogy' that transforms both 'the transactional' and the 'interactional' discourses in the classroom, the first of which refers to the exchange of information and the latter to the discussions between teacher and students and among students (Kramsch, 1993a: 243–4). The main features of a 'critical foreign language pedagogy' as defined by Kramsch are, in sum, an awareness of the socio-cultural context of the student, of the school and the classroom cultures, and of the resourcefulness of language that may play the leading role here in changing the perceptions and visions of those individuals in the classroom.

Kramsch's model therefore concentrates largely on the production/reception of cultural meaning within the classroom through dialogue and hermeneutics. It is based on subjective/intersubjective responses, on exploration, interpretation and description. Although it aims at changing the status quo, such change occurs mostly at a personal level, despite the intersubjective character of the individual development, and it is classroom-based, despite the incidental consequences for society. Therefore, it leaves out other implications of a critical pedagogy of foreign language/culture education namely an explicit social and political commitment.

There are several aspects in Kramsch's model that represent a recent tendency in a growing number of foreign language/culture educators of more advanced levels, as also shown by the research project described later. Her challenge to the myth of a standardised native speaker and her recommendation for the use of authentic materials have inspired practising professionals in this area to attempt new approaches. Likewise, much emphasis has been given to the subjective/intersubjective reception and production of texts by official documents, as we shall see later, namely in the Standards for Foreign Language Learning (USA) as well as by the participants in the research project to be reported later. Her main concern about a critical interpretation of the target and native cultures is also a requirement in the national syllabus these teachers were following.

Byram's model (1997a/b)

Byram has designed a model for 'Teaching and Assessing Intercultural Communicative Competence' that includes five 'factors' which correspond to *'savoirs'*: (a) *savoirs*; (b) *savoir comprendre*; (c) *savoir être*; (d) *savoir apprendre/faire*; and (e) *savoir s'engager* (Byram, 1997b). The author further elaborates a diagram where he makes the reader visualise the positioning of the factors/*savoirs* in relation to each other and also a taxonomy of objectives and modes of assessment for each of the factors. The first four *savoirs* had been introduced in a previous work (Byram & Zarate, 1997), and had also been included in the Common European Framework, which we shall discuss later. Here, however, Byram not only redefines the first four *savoirs* but also adds a fifth element — *savoir s'engager* — where he includes 'political education'' and 'critical cultural awareness' and which he describes as the 'Education' factor (Byram, 1997b: 34). Byram is very clear about the importance he gives to this factor not only by placing it in the centre of his model but also by stating that 'the inclusion in Intercultural Communicative Competence of savoir s'engager/critical cultural awareness as an educational aim for foreign language teaching is crucial' (p. 113).

Byram also provides the reader with a definition of 'Critical cultural awareness/political education' as *'an ability to evaluate critically on the basis of explicit criteria perspectives, practices and products in one's own and other cultures and countries'* (p. 53, his emphasis). The author makes a first important statement by acknowledging a political dimension to education, and to foreign language/culture education in particular, and by explicitly recognising the link between critical cultural awareness and political education. Byram subsequently identifies a taxonomy of the main objectives within this factor which are: (a) 'identify and interpret explicit or implicit values in documents and events in one's own and other cultures'; (b) 'make an evaluative analysis of the documents and events which refers to an explicit perspective and criteria'; (c) 'interact and mediate in intercultural exchanges in accordance with explicit criteria, negotiating where necessary a degree of acceptance of them by drawing upon one's knowledge, skills and attitudes' (p. 53). Byram provides the teacher with many clues to reflect upon how to implement a critical dimension in her/his classes. It is evident that the author attaches great value to comparative/contrastive analysis between 'one's own and other cultures', to cultural awareness by trying to bring the unconscious to consciousness and by making the implicit explicit, to the ability of making an analytical evaluation on the basis of explicit criteria, and to the establishment of interpersonal relationships strengthened by negotiated acceptance, therefore, to experiential learning. He later gives further guidelines such as placing documents or events in context, uncovering ideologies, being aware of potential conflict while attempting negotiation and accepting difference (p. 63).

Although Byram gives priority to analytical thought by emphasising the importance of 'a rational and explicit standpoint from which to evaluate' (p. 54), he also gives some consideration to both 'a reflective and analytical challenge' (p. 35), and, moreover, to both 'analysis and deconstruction' (Byram, 1997a: 61). By describing critical cultural awareness as, as quoted above, 'an ability to evaluate critically on the basis of explicit criteria' as well as 'an ability to "decentre"' (Byram, 1997b: 34), the author makes use of a wide spectrum that combines modern and postmodern concepts of reasoning.

Byram also underlines the importance of making judgements for a critical approach to culture, but he stresses that, because 'entirely value-free interpretation' is unlikely to happen, if one is aware that s/he is making a judgement, provided s/he makes her/his criteria explicit, it 'allows a conscious control of biased interpretation' (Byram, 1997b: 35). Furthermore, 'in an educational framework which aims to develop *critical* cultural awareness' he also includes 'relativisation of one's own and valuing of others' meaning, beliefs' (p. 35, his emphasis). Byram further accounts for the relevance of critical evaluation in foreign culture education by considering the notion of empathy, which has in general been a keyword in socio-cultural competence, as uncritical precisely because 'learners are expected to accept and understand the viewpoint and experience of the other, not to take a critical, analytical stance' (Byram, 1997a: 61).

Byram's definition of foreign language teaching/learning as 'foreign language education' (Byram, 1989), his involvement in including a European dimension in foreign language education in Europe, and his identification of 'political education/critical cultural awareness' as a main factor for Intercultural Communicative Competence may indicate that he acknowledges the role of foreign culture education as one of cultural politics, without having used the phrase. In particular when referring to the inclusion of Cultural Studies in foreign language/culture education Byram claims that:

> ... learners can also be encouraged to identify the ways in which particular practices and beliefs maintain the social position and power of particular groups. The analysis can become critical. Furthermore, the analysis can be comparative, turning learners' attention back on their own practices, beliefs and social identities – and the groups to which they do or do not belong – and this analysis too can be critical. (Byram, 1997b: 20)

Here the author recognises the potential of including a critical stance in foreign language/culture classes for clarifying and problematising the learners' identifications and representations of the Self and the Other and its social and political implications. According to Byram, critical cultural awareness should be dealt with and assessed as specifically integrated in the other *savoirs*, while studying particular languages/cultures, and also be made 'generalisable' for the study of or interaction with other cultures (Byram, 1997b), precisely because it implies the development of a critical attitude that may apply to any society although it materialises within particular contexts. Likewise, being considered a strong contribution to learners' education and development, it should be included in all levels of foreign language/culture education (Byram, 1997a).

Byram's writings have, to a great extent, been responsible for the growing significance attributed to the cultural component within foreign language education in Europe and for making teachers more interested in adding a critical dimension to it. Both of these effects have had a great impact on teacher training. The participants in the research project I carried out did not mention his work directly but their ideas revealed some influence of his thought, namely the added emphasis placed on a critical approach, of his analytical and evaluative attitude towards foreign cultures and of his preoccupation in making the implicit explicit through dialogue. However, some of the more elaborate aspects of his theory, such as 'the ability to decentre' he proposes, as well as the relativisation of one's own beliefs he stimulates, are yet to be realised in teaching practices as shown in the study of which I shall give account later.

Pennycook's model (1994)

Pennycook developed a model for 'the critical pedagogy of English' within the scope of the teaching/learning of English as an International Language (Pennycook, 1994: 296). He takes a postcolonial, non-Eurocentric perspective of language/culture education in Third World countries. He starts by questioning the hierarchical arrangement of the world Englishes and aims at giving 'voice' to those who use English throughout the world, as a first, second, or foreign language, to represent themselves. He draws on Giroux, hook, and Walsh's concepts of 'voice' to consider the syllabus of English as 'something to be negotiated, challenged, appropriated' by the students (p. 299). He enhances the importance of 'localizing' the teaching/learning of a global language such as English while he claims support from Bakhtin's and Foucault's theories that language is realised socially and culturally and that it implies the negotiation of meaning in particular situations. His model indeed reflects the dynamic and 'dialogic' character of language as perceived by Bakhtin and the 'capillary' nature of the discursive relationship between power and knowledge described by Foucault.

His approach is therefore a 'bottom-up' perspective (p. 28), that implies the appropriation of a global language to 'write back' students' cultures, histories and knowledges (p. 296). It is in this aspect that he diverges from Phillipson's description of linguistic imperialism, as he himself points out. According to Pennycook, Phillipson displays a linguistic point of view, focusing more on language planning and on issues of linguistic human rights, while he himself addresses the problem from a cultural point of view by enhancing the intercultural realisation of a global language used to express localised cultures and representations. In fact, Pennycook is more concerned about the acknowledgement of the other side of the coin, that is, to validate the local appropriations and the plurality of cultural realisations in the global language. On the other hand, Phillipson takes the position of denouncing an oppressive situation but from a 'top-down' perspective, in other words, he focuses his critique on the overarching institutions that implement linguistic and cultural imperialism. Nevertheless, he recognises that 'the belief that ELT is non-political serves *to disconnect culture from structure*' and he makes use of Freire's '*concientização*' in order to appeal to 'the establishment of linguistic counter-hegemonies' (Phillipson, 1992: 67, 249).

Pennycook develops the potential for a critical pedagogy to the full since he links the concept of 'voice' to 'agency' by empowering students/speakers of English as a global language into subjects who perform their own representations and by understanding a critical pedagogy of English as cultural politics. Pennycook affirms the political nature of education in general and his students are supposed to challenge particular and historical relations of power both vertically and horizontally and to stand as cultural actors. His model makes an interesting contribution towards intercultural competence in a postcolonial global world since he considers that:

> ... the formation of counter-discursive positions in English has implications not merely for the re-presentation of the postcolonized self but also for the representation of the post-colonizing self. (Pennycook, 1994: 324)

Here the author proposes a radical change in the linguistic/cultural interaction between ex-colonisers and ex-colonised, in their roles and representations. He advocates on that account a reformulation of the positions oppressor–oppressed, that in postcolonial times have acquired mainly a linguistic/cultural format disguised as economic progress, and urges the development of an intercultural form of communication 'as new meanings, new counter-discourses come into play in our shared language' (p. 325). This change involves not only the empowerment of the 'postcolonised self' but also a decentred and redefined 'postcolonising self' who needs to find a new identity within the new type of relationship.

His non-Eurocentric approach is not yet widely popular in Europe, as is evident in the study I shall report later. It is not widespread in the United States either except for those educators who are involved in Critical Pedagogy, most of them working with minority students. In fact, as stated by the author himself, it was from the Critical Pedagogy movement that he drew his inspiration to develop his praxis in Asian contexts. However, this approach has been disseminating in non-Western countries, mainly in Asia, as is revealed, for example, in the work of

Canagarajah who has further developed a theory of EFL from a peripheral standpoint into what he calls 'a pedagogy of appropriation' in which students' actual discursive and cultural contexts are respected (Canagarajah, 1999).

The Critical Dimension in Reference Documents

Both the *Common European Framework* and the *Standards for Foreign Language Learning* were issued in 1996, and currently represent the main conceptual frameworks for foreign language/culture education in the Western world. Interestingly, they have different approaches with respect to taking a critical perspective on the foreign cultures to be learnt, as discussed below.

The *Common European Framework* (Council of Europe)

This document describes itself as a 'European framework of reference for *language* teaching, learning and assessment' whose 'general aim is to overcome *linguistic* barriers' (2.1, emphasis mine). In fact, culture is granted a minimal role throughout the document and is more visible within the 'general competences' which are presented as the background 'knowledge, skills and characteristics' the language learner is expected to possess (3.1). The document puts its main focus on 'communicative language competences', that encompass 'linguistic competences', 'sociolinguistic competence', and 'pragmatic competences' (4.7.2), and on 'language activities' within an 'action-oriented approach' (3.1). This approach is, in the end, functional, with objectives defined in terms of 'better performance', 'optimal functional operation', or 'fulfilment of tasks' (7.2.1).

The 'general competences' are considered to be: (1) 'declarative knowledge (*savoir*)'; (2) 'skills and know-how (*savoir-faire*)'; (3) 'existential competence (*savoir-être*)'; and (4) 'ability to learn (*savoir-apprendre*)' (4.7.1). The development of these competences is supposed to improve the 'ability to relate to otherness' (3.2.1). Within the first competence, 'declarative knowledge (*savoir*)', the document includes factual information about the world and the target societies and cultures, having in mind its regional and social diversity. It also comprehends awareness of the relationship between native and target cultures viewed in terms of the recognition of their similarities and differences. There are several specifications but no explanation of concepts or strategies under this item (4.7.1). Teaching/learning processes are not problematised either, such as the perspectives to be taken while dealing with factual knowledge or while recognising similarities and differences. Should it be made from a neutral or an engaged point of view, for example?

The second 'general competence' to be described is 'skills and know-how (*savoir faire*)' that entails the social skills one needs to interact with people from other cultures. However, the social skills to be acquired by the learner are namely the ability to behave 'appropriately', meaning 'in accordance with' the conventions of the 'society and culture of the community or communities in which a language is spoken'. This guideline does not presume a critical attitude from the teacher/learner since it ignores the multiplicity and diversity of positions included previously in the 'sociocultural knowledge' (4.7.1.1.2) to which it refers, and it implicitly relies on a fictitious, standardised notion of 'native speaker' (Byram & Zarate, 1997; Kramsch, 1993a, b, 1998c) and on her/his judgement of what is 'appropriate' (Fantini, 1999). In fact, the list of aims also includes the ability 'to bring the culture of origin and the foreign culture into relation with each other', 'to identify and use a variety of strategies for contact with those from other cultures' and 'to deal effectively with intercultural misunderstanding and conflict situations' (4.7.1.2.2). However, no explanations are provided under this item either.

We may gather that the notion of intercultural awareness/skills that incorporates both declarative (*savoir*) and practical knowledge (*savoir-faire*) remains vague and ambiguous, contrasting with the detail and importance given to language issues. It is noted that similarities and differences between native and target cultures should be brought to the fore, that regional and social diversity should be considered, that cultures should be placed in context, and that they should be brought into relation. However, it is not suggested that these assumptions should raise critical questions, such as 'From whose point of view?', 'From what perspective/position?', 'In which context?', 'How do parts/differences articulate?', 'What changes/challenges are they undergoing?', 'What is there that is not so evident?', 'Does this reflection help clarify any particular experiences we have had?', 'What can we do about what seems to be wrong?', 'Why does it seem to be wrong?', 'From what perspective/position are we "voicing" our judgements?', etc. There are also concepts that remain unclarified and above all unquestioned such as 'cultural sensitivity', 'cultural intermediary', and 'to deal *effectively* with intercultural misunderstanding and conflict situations' (emphasis mine). They are taken-for-granted and it is not suggested that they should be dealt with otherwise, that is, critically by submitting them to reflection and discussion.

The third 'general competence' to be identified is the 'existential competence (*savoir-être*)' that is understood as a reflection of individual identities comprehending 'attitudes, motivations, values, beliefs, cognitive styles and personality types' (4.7.1.3). In terms of attitudes the foreign language learner is expected to display openness towards other cultures and 'willingness to relativise one's own cultural viewpoint'. However, these attitudes, like the other 'existential competences', are perceived basically as individual characteristics, personality traits. They are also viewed as 'culture-related' and, therefore, understood as essential, intrinsic, restricted to the individual and determined by culture. Although susceptible to change while in use and through learning, identities are not perceived here to be always and intrinsically in process and to be socially constructed. They are viewed as static and 'therefore sensitive areas for inter-cultural perceptions and relations' (3.2.1). The possibility of the user/learner developing an 'intercultural personality' is also taken into consideration. However, this is reported to raise 'important ethical and pedagogical issues' in the sense that one should wonder whether to consider it 'an explicit educational objective'. 'Cultural relativism' is here viewed as a possible danger to 'ethical and moral integrity' (4.7.1.3). Moreover, such 'existential competences' are further described as 'openness', 'conviviality' and 'good will' to be used to 'make up for' linguistic deficiencies (7.1.3) and also as 'discretion, politeness, smiling affably, patience, etc.' (7.2.2). In sum, '*savoir-être*' is ultimately viewed as a last-resource strategy to compensate for linguistic incompetence. In other words, the agenda for intercultural competence here, if this is the case, turns out to be based on good manners. The philosophical, social and political implications that the phrase 'existential competence (*savoir-être*)' promises and that are included in the attitudes described previously as openness to what is new and different, relativising one's value-system, and distancing oneself from conventional attitudes, remained unexplored.

It follows from what has been pointed out above that the critical potential remains unexplored precisely because these competences are considered as 'general'. Despite the fact that they are indeed general, in the sense that they may be transferable from the study/experience of one culture to another, in order to be *critical* they have to be applied to one concrete culture/community/society. The lack of this aspect accounts for the possibility, raised in the document, of making them invisible in foreign language classes, by assuming that they already exist, or of delegating them to other realms, such as other subjects taught in the native language, 'special courses or textbooks dealing with area studies', or to be acquired naturally 'through direct contact with native speakers and authentic texts' (6.7.2.4). Otherwise, 'general competences' may be 'treated ad hoc as and when problems arise' and there is one possibility among the eight suggested when they may be developed 'through an intercultural component designed to raise awareness of the relevant, experiential, cognitive and socio-cultural backgrounds of learners and native speakers respectively' (6.7.2.4).

In short, it is implied in this document that the cultural component and the development of intercultural competence are part of 'general competences', a background knowledge that the language user/learner is expected to possess/acquire but that may not be materialised in the foreign language classroom. As far as the critical dimension of foreign culture education is concerned, it is neither explicitly nor implicitly included in the document, nor is it hindered or valorised.

Standards for foreign language learning: Preparing for the twenty-first century (USA)

Although this document is like the previous one examined also entitled 'Standards for Foreign *Language* Learning' (emphasis mine), language and culture are interwoven throughout. It starts with the 'Statement of Philosophy' where it affirms that 'the United States must educate students who are equipped *linguistically and culturally* to communicate successfully in a pluralistic American society and abroad' (p. 7, emphasis mine). Furthermore, it includes, implicitly and to some extent explicitly, a discourse for a critical pedagogy of foreign language/culture education.

The document identifies three major organising principles for developing the standards for foreign language learning: (a) 'the broad goals of language instruction'; (b) 'the curricular elements necessary to the attainment of the standards'; and (c) 'the framework of communicative modes' (p. 27). The main broad goals distinguished for foreign language education are 'the five C's': (1) Communication; (2) Cultures; (3) Connections; (4) Comparisons; and (5) Communities. Standards and Sample Progress Indicators are defined for each area and on the whole provide guidelines that aim to develop the students' critical perspective of other cultures, of their own culture and of the interaction among them, as will be pointed out below.

The first goal, Communication, is considered central. However, since the five areas are interlinked, students are supposed to have 'experience in the other goal areas to have content worth communicating' (p. 37). Accordingly, the 'effectiveness' of communication within this goal is a main concern, which requires that the speaker is critically aware of the factors involved in the intercultural encounter and willing to negotiate. With this in mind, the language learner is also advised to develop effective strategies for observing and analysing cultures, besides the traditional ones of reading and listening, speaking and writing. This framework for intercultural communication responds to the vision incorporated in the three modes of communication identified as the Interpersonal, the Interpretive, and the Presentational, in that it takes into consideration the interrelational as well as the productive and the receptive performances. The standards devised for this goal correspond to the communicative modes, so the students are expected to exchange information and opinions, share feelings and personal reactions, interpret and present information, concepts and ideas, in direct, mediated, productive or receptive communication using both oral and written language (pp. 35–42). In the Interpersonal Mode, students are expected to be effective communicators through active negotiation of meaning, by observing and monitoring each other, by taking into consideration the existence of different practices and different patterns of interaction that are, to some extent, culture related (pp. 32–3). Both the Interpretive and the Presentational Modes require, according to the authors, a more profound knowledge of the other culture(s), since there is no active negotiation of meaning. Therefore, these modes also demand culturally 'appropriate' strategies that facilitate the 'appropriate cultural interpretation of meanings' by the receptors at both ends (pp. 32–4). It is implicit here that the 'intercultural speaker' evaluates critically to what extent, mostly in the interpersonal mode because there is direct negotiation, strategies in use are effective, without necessarily having to meet the usual patterns of the target culture, and how, mostly in the interpretative and presentational modes, the communicative strategies have to meet more closely the patterns of the target culture in order to facilitate communication.[3]

The second main goal-area is Culture which is also granted great importance since, according to the authors, 'the true content of the foreign language course is not the grammar and the vocabulary of the language, but the cultures expressed through that language' (pp. 43–4). The first important statement made within this area is the rejection of the division between formal ('big C') and daily life ('little c') cultures which are considered 'inseparable' from each other and 'inextricably woven into the language of those who live in the culture' (p. 44). Instead, three components are identified, Perspectives, Practices and Products, which are themselves interrelated. Theoreticians in the field have welcomed this definition as an important contribution since it 'allows for enormous flexibility that honors what teachers bring to the classroom' and it also 'points directly away from culture as information toward culture as an integrated aspect of language learning' (Lange, 1999: 60–1; see also Met & Byram, 1999). This definition also encompasses a critical approach to culture due to the dynamic interrelation among philosophical perspectives, patterns of social practices and tangible and intangible products, thus entailing the perception of cultural practices and products as embodiments of concepts, ideas and values while these grow from discourse, action and transformation. The critical dimension in foreign language/culture education therefore consists of reflective and conscious participation in such cycles.

From this standpoint, the authors develop a whole approach to culture which may be considered critical because it implies that students should '*expect* differences', 'become skilled observers and analysts of other cultures', learn 'how to put them into perspective within the cultural framework of the other language', develop an 'insider's perspective', and 'explore the process of stereotyping and the role stereotypes play in forming and sustaining prejudice' (pp. 44–5). The authors also encourage experiential learning through 'many different kinds of interaction with members of other cultures', 'personal exploration in the language of the culture', and 'actual participation in the exchange of information and ideas' which is also welcomed by theoreticians in the field (Met & Byram, 1999), and which is indeed an indispensable asset for a sound critical pedagogy of foreign cultures.

However, as Met and Byram point out, the changing character of culture is not very explicit in this document perhaps because perspectives (meanings, attitudes, values, ideas) are 'reified and described as an objective reality waiting to be discovered, observed and analysed by the learner' (Met & Byram, 1999: 67). This is, nevertheless, an important aspect for a critical pedagogy of foreign cultures because the movement and instability of value and meaning in cultural 'bodies/objects' produces a constant flux that cannot be ignored by a critical intercultural speaker since that is what determines the reality of each moment. Furthermore, although the authors refer to the existence of different cultures within a single language they confine them to geographical limits representing them 'as monolithic, shared by all the speakers of the same native language in a given geographical space' which is not a critical or accurate description of our multicultural societies (Met & Byram, 1999: 67). Therefore, the document does not give sufficient account of intrasocietal cultural multiplicity, evolution, or transgression.

The three other goal-areas, Connections, Comparisons, and Communities, challenge the borders of the native culture and the foreign language/culture classroom. Within Comparisons the student establishes bridges between her/his mother tongue/native culture and the other languages/cultures with respect to the networks of perspectives, practices and products in a view across the border. There are two levels, however, to consider and which are not mentioned in the document, the culture-general and the culture-specific, which prevents the understanding of differences as absolutes and also the formation of overgeneralisations (Fantini, 1999). Engaging in critical comparison/contrast of cultural aspects involves taking good note of both levels and also of the fact that they are not enclosed or totally separate.

Another controversial aspect to keep in mind while comparing/contrasting different cultural aspects is that 'comparisons are always rooted in the perspective of the onlooker', therefore they always involve some kind of judgement (Fantini, 1999: 185). However, this entails biased interpretations and the first step in overcoming such conditioned perceptions of other cultures is becoming critically aware of our own cultural and personal standpoints, and then perhaps, as Fantini suggests, by means of *'suspending* judgement' (Fantini, 1999: 186). Without entering into such details, the authors of this document emphasise the fact that comparison/contrast of aspects of different cultures involves reflecting upon them which leads to awareness of those aspects that otherwise would remain unnoticed. In this way, learners acquire the habit of 'hypothesizing' about the ways languages/cultures work in their settings (p. 53). Hence, students develop an intercultural sensitivity to difference, which includes the cognitive, affective, and behavioural dimensions, and which enables them to make hypothetical speculations, projections, or even predictions thereby avoiding absolute judgements. All this together reveals a critical stance.

Through Connections and Communities goal-areas, students actually maximise the whole of their knowledge, skills, and experience by establishing direct or mediated connections – making use of any accessible media of communication – across disciplines and across communities, on a personal, local, or other level. The document refers, in particular, to the use of e-mail, audio and video tapes, television, newspapers, magazines, and cultural events in general and puts special emphasis on aspects of personal interest for the purpose of enjoyment. This is in fact a critical area of foreign language/culture education that needs to be addressed, since for students of many levels the implications of cross-culturalism are, on a short-term basis, linked to the entertainment/information industry rather than to career prospects, with the exception of the last levels of secondary or higher education. Unfortunately, foreign language educators have long ignored this aspect and, consequently, neglected its role in preparing critical consumers of such an industry that has recently more particularly focused on young people.

Finally, 'The "Weave" of Curricular Elements' should be mentioned because it plays an important role in establishing the grounds for a critical pedagogy. The elements identified are: (a) Language System; (b) Communication Strategies; (c) Cultural Content; (d) Learning Strategies; (e) Content from Other Subjects; (f) Critical Thinking Skills; and (g) Technology. These elements imply concepts – language, communication, culture, learning, critical thinking – which have been explored throughout the descriptions of the main areas, and contain tools – system, strategies, content, skills, and technology – whose use has also been discussed. As a result of their interweaving, the document suggests that learners should 'derive meaning from context', communicate 'effectively', 'reflect upon and evaluate the quality and success of their communication', 'maximize their use of what they know', select and incorporate new knowledge as well as knowledge from other disciplines, take greater advantage of high-tech sources, consider different perspectives to what they know, and 'arrive at informed conclusions' which lead the way to a critical use of the curricular elements (pp. 30–1).

According to Lange, there is an imbalance between the Standards objectives and progress indicators in the document, since 'the performance indicators ask for relatively uncomplicated performances, while the standards themselves project more complicated performances' (Lange, 1999: 70). Lange draws this conclusion from his study of the quality of the culture standards. He bases his study on the taxonomies of cognitive and affective objectives for education (Bloom, 1972; Krathwohl, *et al.*, 1964). In general terms, he reports that the results suggest the need for 'more complicated cognitive behaviours such as apply, analyze, synthesize, and evaluate' and the same for the affective domain, which needs more demanding indicators such as 'value, conceptualize, organize, and characterize the learner's own values' (Lange, 1999: 65). Without necessarily rejecting the need for expansion of progress indicators, it seems to me that the criteria used for the indicators suggested above should be the subject of discussion and further study which takes other evaluation criteria into consideration since, under the principles underlying a critical pedagogy, the progress to more complicated behaviour and affective indicators is not inevitably one towards a more analytical mind. Therefore, this is an issue that needs further attention.

In conclusion, this document may be considered to stand not far from the philosophical and pedagogical tenets of a critical pedagogy, although it never tries to define itself as such or explicitly admits to embracing its ideals. However, it falls short of the requirements for a critical pedagogy of foreign languages/cultures, by ignoring the political dimension of such a task which it does not endorse explicitly at any stage, and which is an important element of a critical pedagogy of foreign culture, as is pointed out in the following section. The document may nevertheless be regarded as an attractive and valuable agenda for foreign language teachers, teacher trainers and researchers who view themselves as critical educators. Moreover, there seems to be a consensus among foreign language/culture educators and scholars in the United States that, by bringing theory and practice together, by emphasising communication about contemporary cultures, by recommending the development of capacities to perform in everyday life, by suggesting that youngsters engage in community projects and by stimulating the pertinent use of technology, this document represents a paradigm shift in the field (James, 1998; Welles, 1998). The impact of this document on curricula design and on teaching practices has been recognised as significant and widespread at the grass-roots level. Several state projects which had begun to be designed before the national Standards had a great deal in common with this document as well as several of those which have subsequently been modelled upon it closely or simply referring to it, except for a dozen states (James, 1998; Sandrock, 1997; Trayer, 1997). Finally, the sweeping debate that this document has raised about its articulation within literature and grammar-based college curricula is in itself valuable (James, 1998; Welles, 1998).

The Political Dimension of Foreign Language/Culture Education

Education is always political and the disciplines dealing with language and culture even more so because they involve issues of identification and representation. Therefore, it is not critical cultural awareness *per se* that makes foreign language/culture education political since education 'is necessarily political' (Wringe, 1984: 34). However, critical cultural awareness makes the political nature of foreign language/culture education more evident by denying that it is neutral even when it intends or pretends to be so. Foreign language/culture education has a political role which, on the one hand, is particular within the curriculum, by engaging in cultural politics, and, on the other hand, adds to a broader political component, namely education for democratic citizenship. Both aspects of its political dimension are discussed below.

Foreign language/culture education as cultural politics

As some of the authors discussed above point out (Byram, 1997a, b; Canagarajah, 1999; Pennycook, 1994), learning/teaching a foreign language/culture implies taking an ideological view of the world beyond our cultural borders which reflects the way we perceive ourselves within our own culture and its position towards the Other. This insight, therefore, reflects what we are intrinsically and, in reverse, provides a mirror which, in this instance, is the other culture/cultural actor, who helps us take a look at ourselves. In sum, meeting the Other and her/his view of ourselves generates a process of (self)reflection, since 'one cannot "see" or hear the familiar until it is made strange' (Edgerton, 1996: 166). However, the process of becoming critically and culturally aware is more complex than just realising that there is a They and a We. It entails becoming aware of the web of intra- and intercultural meanings that are always struggling and evolving. The more conscious we are of the constraints, implications, and possibilities that each situation carries, the more critical we become. The role that the development of critical cultural awareness in foreign language/culture classes may play for the clarification of one's own and others' ideological perspectives on social/cultural matters is underlined by Byram:

> This 'educational' component of Intercultural Communicative Competence adds the notion of evaluation and comparison not just for purposes of improving the effectiveness of communication and interaction but especially for purposes of clarifying one's own ideological perspective and engaging with others consciously on the basis of that perspective. The consequence may include conflict in perspectives, not only harmonious communication. (Byram, 1997b: 101).

An intercultural encounter does not take place in a vacuum where two autonomous and fixed cultural identities establish a straight and direct line of communication. The open space where the interaction takes place becomes full of direct and indirect messages. Evaluation and comparison of one another does not happen in opposite-directional parallel lines, on the contrary, ideological perspectives from both sides 'collide' and the more conscious they are the less probable that they prevent communication from flowing. Despite conflicting, different cultural views may establish communication with each other if they are both conscious of the process going on and, therefore, conflict is kept under control.

Intercultural interactions, like intracultural ones, involve power relations, since 'culture and power are dialectically connected and therefore inseparable like the two sides of a coin' (Borrelli, 1991: 279), and on that account they are not symmetrical. The relations between culture and power are determined by assumptions of status that are not only the ones between culture and capital but include those that involve ethnicity, gender, age, etc. and matters of political legitimacy in general. However, in an intercultural situation, networks of culture and power in both cultural systems do not often correspond to each other since the ways in which people identify what is right/wrong and view questions of authority pass through 'ethical/political filters' deriving from culture, among other factors (Fox, 1997: 98). According to Fox, these filters account for different morally, politically and socially (un)acceptable actions which may cause misjudgements and conflict. Therefore, foreign language/ culture education should aim at producing intercultural speakers not just armed with the 'appropriate' behaviours to move within the foreign culture but also prepared for the 'unpredictable' and for 'cop[ing] cognitively and affectively with [their] new experience' (Byram *et al.*, 1991b: 10).

Power relations are not always oppressive and restrictive, they may be made enabling and generative (Foucault, 1972). Therefore, the fact that we have to confront them in intercultural encounters, moreover mostly in subtle and ambiguous terms, is not necessarily disabling because they allow for negotiation and, consequently, for creative cultural production. Meanings and values that were once held as universal become relativised, priorities are challenged, and new possibilities start to be considered. The intercultural learner starts to 'read' the surrounding world in different ways:

> Confrontation with their own culture seen from the perspective of others is an important means of bringing unconscious and 'naturalised' beliefs into consciousness so that their relativity and specificity can be acknowledged. (Byram & Morgan, 1994: 44)

Foreign language/cultural education should provide space for reflecting the ways knowledge and culture are constructed according to contingent and transitory historical constraints. By confronting two or more realities where cultural/political articulations were accomplished differently, it is possible to raise awareness of the limits of traditions on both sides and provide some grounds for critical cultural revitalisation, transgression, and creativity (Bennett, 1998).

Moreover, the range of contacts and experiences which are now accessible has widened and their intensity has also increased due to a greater mobility and advances in communication technologies which have considerably facilitated cultural exchange. This is a world where identifications and representations are in constant contact and change and foreign language/culture has an important role to play because young citizens in today's world have to consciously mediate between various competing identity loyalties and to differentiate among those available.

Besides the long-established traditional national/ethnic identities, the local/global dynamism has made other identifications visible through the emergence of massive groups of interest that range from gender, race, or age affiliations to consciousness-specific matters such as animal rights or green issues, and, at the same time, it has produced new cultural forms that often emerge from hybrid identities. Access to diversified options requires a critical mind capable of constantly making provisional or final choices. Therefore, 'opportunities must be genuine in the sense that people must know about them and be aware of their value' (Wringe, 1984: 29), and this does not only entail having access to comprehensive information and experience but being capable of being critically selective of them. More precisely, 'reflexive multiculturalisms', in Rattansi's terms, should resist the tendency to 'overglamorize' hybrid identities that often emerge as 'cultures of nihilism', or cultures of violence among marginal young people, or those that are very transitory and have no political significance or social representation (Rattansi, 1999: 106). Furthermore, foreign language/culture pedagogy that publicly acknowledges its political nature should never try 'to propose alternative media or cultural practices to replace those in which students are already invested, inventing marginal and populist counterdiscourses' (Grossberg, 1994: 20). In short, a critical pedagogy of foreign language/culture should be subversive enough to unveil dominant hegemonies and selective enough not to embark on an 'anything goes' perspective, as is argued by Crawford and McLaren:

> A critical pedagogy should speak against the notion that all cultural realities need to follow one dominant narrative or that all diverse cultural realities need to be given voice, since it is obvious that many of these realities harbor racist, classist, and sexist assumptions. The

key here is not to insist simply on cultural diversity, transforming culture into a living museum of contemporary choices, but a critical diversity. (Crawford & McLaren, 1998: 146)

It is important that intercultural speakers take a critical view of linguistic/cultural codes, perceive their limits, appreciate the fact that they are particular responses to specific circumstances and evaluate them critically. Evaluation here is not understood as the ultimate goal, at the end of the critical line, but as one operation among many in the critical cycle, as we shall see later. Therefore, critical choices are mostly provisional although based on definitive principles. At work here are simultaneously an analytical/evaluative kind of operation and the postmodern tendency for 'deferring' final meanings.

This being said, it is the task of foreign language/culture education to interrogate dominant and subordinate ideologies, to give 'voice' to those discourses that have been silenced and to the particular narratives of the students, and to make connections between different narratives both at the local and global levels; even, for example, when English-speaking students throughout the world learn Standard English as a second language (Roth & Harama, 2000). This is not only an epistemological but also a social, political and ethical enterprise, since it engages with education for self and social change. Critical intercultural learning involves more than experiencing, interpreting, and accommodating to other cultures, it entails making connections, exploring articulations, and changing representations. Therefore, it has profound implications for the way students construct their cultural identities and, consequently, for the way they respond to their everyday lives. In fact, 'democracy is necessarily about attempting to change things in cooperation with others' (Wringe, 1984: 42) and since the scope of our social circles has been widening more and more due to intense contact between the global and the local, foreign language/culture teachers/students need to learn how to co-operate at various levels and be aware that these do not work separately but actually interact.

Furthermore, the political dimension of intercultural learning is generally associated with education for ethnic minorities (Fennes & Hapgood, 1997: 56), which is very limiting in scope and discriminatory. This perception of the political is linked to the resolution of social problems at a local level while the policies of the cultural at other levels remain unexplored. The relationship between the political and the cultural stays very much at the level of the institutionalised political and cultural powers which constitute an elite that makes decisions while the population in general do not think they have a say. Disciplinary expertise and a venerated canon have contributed to the lack of political awareness among public intellectuals. Cultural studies have introduced the political and the pedagogical into culture and thereby this triangle has been installed in the foreign language/culture classes too.

Therefore, the recognition of the political dimension in foreign language/culture education implies rethinking the teacher's role. By discarding their role as ambassadors of a foreign culture, the model of a standardised native speaker, and the concept of a static, self-contained, and strange culture, as well as by acknowledging the interactive nature of culture learning and production and the social, political, and ethical implications of intercultural learning/teaching, the foreign language/ culture teacher becomes more concerned about issues of communication and solidarity. In other words, 'by striving to bring learners from ego-centricity to reciprocity, teachers are stimulating their personal growth in an international world' (Byram & Morgan, 1994: 39), that is, teachers tend to focus as much on the educational, political and social aspects of teaching/learning a foreign language/culture as on the mastery of a linguistic/cultural code.

The critical educator is described by Freire and Giroux as a 'transformative intellectual' who expands the notion of teaching from one of 'reading the word' to one of 'reading both the word and the world'. This perception of the teacher's role is very helpful for the foreign language/ culture teacher who is developing a praxis, where s/he intermingles theory and practice, reflection and action, in order to cope with the students' cognitive and emotional growth in terms of intercultural sensitivity and with rapid change at both local and global levels. As a cultural worker, the foreign language/culture teacher may transform the hermeneutic exploration of a foreign code into an act of cultural creation by investing her/his students with the power to critically share intercultural events, interrogate their own and others' histories, and commit themselves to the responsibility of building this intercultural world.

Foreign language/culture education and citizenship education

Citizenship education is now being reintroduced in some European countries as an independent subject at all levels of basic and secondary education. It is also a concern in some Asian countries such as Singapore, with its concept of National Education. It has also recently been given special attention in various disciplines, including foreign language/

culture education due to its new focus on identity issues. Although the meaning of citizenship varies from country to country according to historical legacies and cultural contexts (Council of Europe, 1998; Potter, 1999; Starkey, 2000), its modern meaning has been linked with the organisation of the nation-state and, therefore, governmental undertakings in general have been concerned mainly with national unity and common good. In the United Kingdom, for example, the Final Report of the Advisory Group on Citizenship establishes three main strands for citizenship education – social and moral responsibility, community involvement and political literacy – that are confined, to a great extent, to individual, local and national circles. Despite mentioning, in relation to the third strand, that 'preparation[s] for conflict resolution and decision making related to the main economic and social problems of the day ... are needed whether these problems occur in locally, nationally or internationally concerned organizations', the report does not refer to intercultural exchanges nor does it consider a multilayered citizenship based on multiple identities (Advisory Group on Citizenship, 1998: 13).

The *Final Report on Citizenship in the United Kingdom* also mentions among the skills and attitudes which are considered essential 'the ability to use modern media and technology *critically* to gather information' and 'a *critical* approach to evidence' (Advisory Group on Citizenship, 1998: 44, emphasis mine). However, this consideration may remain rather vague if not applied concretely to the realm of our everyday life in a global and multicultural world where 'talk about the public must be simultaneously about the discourse of an engaged plurality and critical citizenship' (Aronowitz & Giroux, 1991: 81). If citizenship education ignores this commitment, it will not fulfil its role in fostering solidly democratic behaviour. This is what is missing in the above-mentioned report which 'presents a rather limited view of multiculturalism, which sees it as being about visible minorities, rather than about all citizens in the society, including the majority white population' (Osler, 2000b). As this author points out, the report states that 'majorities must respect, understand and tolerate minorities and minorities must learn and respect the laws, codes and conventions as much as the majority' (Advisory Group on Citizenship, 1998: 17–18). This statement is pervaded by prejudices about majorities and minorities, and consequently it has a different discourse for each, since the majority is assumed to respect the laws while the minorities are not and, furthermore, the minorities are not asked to 'tolerate' the majority. Nevertheless, it seems a good example of how much the lack of critical cultural awareness can distort a sound objective, of the importance of its development for citizenship education and, therefore, it reveals the need for particular interaction between citizenship education/educators and foreign language/culture education/educators.

This document works with a traditional notion of citizenship that is based on the enjoyment of civil, political, and social rights as identified by Marshall, quoted in the document (p. 10), and inter- or transnational discussion is perceived mainly in connection with economic issues, whether for employment purposes or allocation of resources, that is, from an individual or a national perspective. Cultural rights are omitted and, therefore, the discussion about intercultural power relations both at the intra- and international levels is avoided (Osler, 2000a).

However, non-governmental institutions concerned with universal matters such as human rights, environmental issues, ethnic minorities, etc., and intergovernmental institutions, such as the Council of Europe, have called our attention to the need for widening the scope of citizenship education so that it responds to a global and multicultural world. The Council of Europe *Declaration and Programme on Education for Democratic Citizenship Based on the Rights and Responsibilities of Citizens* adopted by the Committee of Ministers in May 1999 reinforced, among other objectives, that this programme 'prepares people to live in a multicultural society and to deal with difference knowledgeably, sensibly, tolerantly and morally' (Council of Europe, 1999). Hence, the Council of Europe has also recognised the valuable contribution that foreign language/culture education/educators may make to citizenship education and launched a project 'Language learning for European citizenship' (1989–1996) aiming at enabling citizens 'to learn to use languages for the purposes of mutual understanding, personal mobility and access to information in a multilingual and multicultural Europe' (Council of Europe, 1997a: 8). This was also the motive of the conference 'Linguistic diversity for democratic citizenship in Europe' where it was stated that 'the development of language education policies must take place with full cognisance of the relationship to the development of the competences of the democratic citizen' (Byram & Ó Riagáin, 1999: 11). In sum, by drawing attention to cultural matters, especially if it includes a critical dimension, foreign language/culture education may contribute to the debate about cultural rights in intra- and international settings.

To a greater or lesser extent, citizenship education has been perceived either as moral education, dealing with universal and abstract concepts of the individual and of the good, or as political education, within a national frame of formal politics that may range from the mere transmission of information about political institutions to partisan politics and indoctrination. Because 'the notion of political education was often associated with the political indoctrination of totalitarian regimes' (Wringe, 1984: 89), in most countries, for example the United Kingdom and Portugal, the term 'political education' is avoided and the term 'citizenship education' is preferred.[4] Moreover, citizenship education is usually meant to be ruled by a ' "common sense" approach' (Advisory Group on Citizenship, 1998: 60), which is, however, just as risky of being indoctrinating since in both cases teachers may, deliberately or not, be unaware, as may their students, of the relativity of their perspectives, of their political implications, of the various options available and their constant evolution.

In fact, the idea of citizenship may be viewed and lived from different perspectives that may be simplified in two main tendencies. These are: (a) the individual/liberal point of view, generally linked with modernity, and (b) the communitarian one, deriving from pre-modern traditions (Habermas, 1994; Miller, 1995; Mouffe, 1992a; Shafir, 1998). The balance between these two tendencies, whether the individual or the collective is more important, is perceived differently by current theories on citizenship that put their focus on the relationship between the national and the individual, the global and the individual, the global and the local, or the national and the minority cultural groups (Pearce & Hallgarten, 2000). Furthermore, whether the focus is more on the individual or the collective, these relationships may be understood vertically and/or horizontally (Byram, 1996: 65). Therefore, the relationship between the individual and the state or the individual and the community(ies) – which may be cross-cultural – may be viewed as hierarchical (vertical), or the focus may be put on the collection of individuals (horizontal), and in the latter case either the individuals are considered as independent (liberal) or dependent on each other (communitarian). These tendencies are combined in each teacher/student's perception of citizenship in a very particular way according to certain factors and circumstances that are deeply related to cultural frameworks and are more and more affected by intercultural exchanges both at the intra- or international levels. Therefore, it is important that citizenship educators are critically aware of the implications of these nuances for, as Giddens points out, 'education in citizenship should above all be education of the critical spirit: a critical engagement with one's own position in society and an awareness of the wider forces to which all of us as individuals are responding' (Giddens, 2000: 25). For the same reason, critical cultural awareness – within and across cultures – is an essential element to be brought into citizenship education.

In addition, postmodern, postnational and multicultural visions and realities are having a great impact on the notion of citizenship, and citizenship education must reflect these worldviews (Ichilov, 1998). Although the nation-state continues to be the main political and institutional reference for citizenship which in modern times has regulated the relationship between the state and the individual from the legal, political, and social point of view, the boundaries of the nation-state have become more and more permeable and its content more fragmented. The postwar trend for global organisation at the political and economic levels, on the one hand, and an emphasis on ethnic roots and the visibility of subnational cultural groups, on the other hand, have changed the role of the nation-state. Once a self-contained political and cultural unit, the nation-state is now a filter between the demands made by transnational organisations and the claims made by inter- and intranational movements and communities.

There is thus an array of positions on citizenship that cover a wide spectrum of possibilities reaching from the defence of the national perspective as the main collective glue that inspires citizenship despite the acknowledgement of trans- and subnational levels (Miller, 1995, 2000), to more radical positions that assume postmodern, postnational, and multicultural scenarios that alter the character and the goals of citizenship education (Mouffe, 1992a, 1996b; Soysal, 1998; Young, 1998). While Miller acknowledges social diversity but calls for a common understanding of citizenship through dialogue within the nation (Miller, 1995, 2000), Habermas views the question of democratic citizenship in Europe from a transnational perspective and, ideally, as accomplished by intersubjectively reached consensus. This is the reason for Habermas' scepticism about the 'political mobilization' of European citizens due to the lack of mechanisms that ensure their participation in debates on political issues that affect their lives, thus preventing the required 'interplay between institutionalized processes of opinion and will formation and those informal networks of public communication' (Habermas, 1994: 32).

Although these two authors have rather different positions they do share a common ground whereas other more radical points of view, which do nonetheless confirm the mediating role of the nation-state, focus on newly emerging levels of citizenship and on its changing character. A postnational model of citizenship differs from the national model in that it relies on 'personhood' rather than on 'nationhood' (Soysal, 1998: 192). According to this author, in a postnational context, citizenship based on personhood results from the intensive interaction between the universal and the particular. In other words, the rights of individuals and of communities within the nation-state are secured by universal human rights which are themselves reinforced by transnational organisations, although the nation-states are in normal circumstances their 'authorized authors' and legitimate guarantors (Soysal, 1998).[5] This view identifies a multilevel citizenship structure and recognises an interplay among multiple memberships and identities both above and below the limits of the nation (Isin & Wood, 1999).

Likewise, a multiculturalist perspective has reacted against the modern conception of national citizenship that has relied on the principle of the equal treatment of citizens, and requires 'differentiated citizenship' for a heterogeneous public (Hall, 2000; Young, 1998). Its main focus is on cultural rights within national borders and, therefore, is against the existence of a common public sphere based on homogeneous cultural representations and general interests while cultural differences are kept to a private sphere (Figueroa, 2000). Multiculturalists argue that for real democracy to take place different needs and different visions for the same society must be incorporated in their own terms:

> ... the inclusion and participation of everyone in public discussion and decision making requires mechanisms for group representation ... and the articulation of special rights that attend to group differences in order to undermine oppression and disadvantage. (Young, 1998: 265)

The active integration of difference in the public sphere and the commitment to the principle of 'democratic equivalence' are also concerns expressed by moderate postmodern theorisers of citizenship who, although they reject extreme forms of pluralism because they 'could never provide the framework for a political regime', do call for radical democratic citizenship (Mouffe, 1992b: 13). Mouffe affirms that an individualistic and a communitarian idea of citizenship are not incompatible although the coexistence of both within a context of diversity is not without conflict. Furthermore, conflict is to be solved only partially and provisionally and the common good is an illusion that we must keep following:

> This is why the common good can never be actualized; it must remain as a kind of vanishing point to which we constantly refer, but which cannot have a real existence ... A radical pluralist approach, informed as it is by a non-essentialist view of politics, acknowledges the impossibility of a fully realized democracy and of the total elimination of antagonisms ... Its objective is the creation of a chain of

equivalence among the democratic demands found in a variety of groups. (Mouffe, 1996b: 24)

The above statement reveals a postmodern notion of citizenship in that it relies on a non-essentialist view of the individual and of society and on citizenship as an 'infinitely reconstructible "articulating principle"' (Ellison, 1997: 697). A postmodern version of citizenship also contests national homogeneity on the grounds that both the individual and society are fragmented since their nature is not unitary or stable nor are their boundaries impermeable. The postmodern focus on cultural complexities responds to a certain extent to the challenges of multiculturality and globality, mainly because it pleads for a 'de-hierarchization of culture' and it suggests 'a convergence between the idea of global human rights ... and postmodern cultural complexity, which recognizes the incommensurability of world-views' (Turner, 1994: 166). Accordingly, Mouffe holds that existent identities, cultural, political or other, must be deconstructed and new identities should constantly be (re)created which are 'constituted only through acts of *identification*' (Mouffe, 1992b: 11). This dynamic character of identities, produced out of evolving identifications, provides for a kind of citizenship 'not as a legal status but as a form of identification, a type of political identity: something to be constructed, not empirically given' (Mouffe, 1992c: 231). This conception of citizenship as an ongoing process rather than a static condition is inspired by and inspires new interpretations of notions such as identity, solidarity, rights and duties.

It is therefore evident that the discussions reported above about a reformulation of the concept of citizenship, and as a result of that of citizenship education, coincide, in most aspects, with those presented during the course of this study about the development of critical cultural awareness in foreign language/culture classes. Despite the fact that, as we have seen above, active and participatory citizenship has different meanings according to different perspectives, 'to sustain this view of citizens as integrated social and political actors in an increasingly fragmented public realm the practice of citizenship needs to be understood as a reflexive process' (Ellison, 1997: 711). In sum, an active citizen should be reflective, critical, sensitive and committed to issues of human suffering and dignity, both at local and global levels (Wringe, 1984). The need for reflective and critical citizens in our contemporary world is a consensual idea among theoreticians and in documents on citizenship.

Several factors have been suggested as reasons for the revival of citizenship education in the 1990s, namely the increase of cultural diversity in societies all over the world after the Second World War due to geographical mobility, more visibility for ethnic minorities, the impact of media industry and changes in personal lifestyles and moral values, which have created the need for dialogue and co-operation (Cullingford, 2000). Moreover, the rapid shift of decision-making to transnational institutions has developed new memberships and the need for reconceptualising citizenship. At the same time, the younger generations are understood as being alienated from political processes; rather than showing an interest in traditional politics, they are clearly more driven by issues that have to do with the environment and human rights (Osler & Starkey, 1996).[6] Both citizenship education and foreign language/culture education must thus respond to new challenges that have to do with fluid boundaries between established powers, disciplines, and cultures.

Learning a foreign language/culture implies widening one's horizons in terms of concepts, norms and values, in other words, to '"discover" otherness and develop a relationship with it' in wider terms than one does gradually in one's native society (Council of Europe, 1997a: 53). This process consists in what some authors have called 'tertiary socialization', which helps clarify the relationship between citizenship education and foreign language/culture education (Buttjes, 1990; Byram, 1993b; Doyé, 1999). Furthermore, the discussion developed in the course of this chapter, with respect to foreign culture education, about the question of cultural identity, the issues of critical intercultural communication, the political dimension of education, and the challenges of multilevel membership cannot be disregarded by citizenship education either.

The description of the 'intercultural speaker' and her/his competences such as *'savoir-être'*, *'savoir-faire'* (Byram & Zarate, 1997), and *'savoir s'engager'* (Byram, 1997b), is most helpful for the characterisation of an 'intercultural citizen'. As indicated previously, experiential learning through student exchanges is fundamental for students and teachers to identify and deal with cultural universals, cultural specifics, reciprocal images of each other's cultures, and to improve critical awareness of one's native culture (Byram, 1992, 1996). The political, economic, and social contexts our future citizens will have to come to terms with demand a notion of citizenship education that is more flexible but, at the same time, more empowering and, for this purpose, it is foreign language/culture education that helps facilitate intercultural communication among citizens in multicultural societies and in a global world.

As we have also seen, by critically understanding the organisation of meanings and interests in particular cultural codes and how those reflect particular configurations of knowledge and power, students, while studying a foreign culture, will recognise some of the preoccupations, desires, successes, and challenges, they face in their everyday lives. This process enables our students to make informed choices about their lives and, above all, it makes them aware that they are entitled to a choice. It follows on from this that by developing a critical perspective towards the Self, the Other, and the world, both the teacher and the students will feel more stimulated to cross borders, to step over epistemological, cultural and social boundaries, to expand the range of possible options in order to make full use of their capabilities. By becoming critically aware of the multiple levels of their cultural and political identities, teachers and students may develop a desire to be involved in political decisions and in ethical issues as well as a commitment to engage in transformative action. In conclusion, our multicultural societies are in great need of citizens prepared to interact across cultures with the revitalisation of the democratic society in mind, and foreign language/culture education should play a decisive role in launching such a project. Not only is Europe developing a supranational model but there is also a tendency in America, Asia and Africa for establishing transnational economic agreements. Therefore, foreign language/culture education is currently under great pressure to respond to new demands that should consider not only economic claims but also those regarding the political empowerment of multicultural expatriate citizens within democratic frameworks.

Conclusion

Both Critical Theory and Postmodernism, viewed in relation to Critical Pedagogy and, more particularly, to a critical study of foreign cultures, provide inspiration for the definition of a critical intercultural speaker and the nature of her/his identifications and relationships. Identity, a key concept in foreign language/culture education, is perceived, within a critical pedagogy of foreign languages and cultures, as comprehending several criss-crossing dimensions, namely the ethnic group, the regional, the national and the global dimensions, and finally a 'third space' where intercultural relations take place. A new perspective taken by Self and Other, towards oneself and towards each other, generates new perceptions of essential concepts such as identity, discourse and dialogue. It also brings about a new vision of culture, education, politics and ethics that originates new principles for foreign language and culture education.

A critical examination of some of the models and documents used worldwide as key references for foreign language/culture education helps to clarify the principles, processes, and aims that should lead to the implementation of a critical dimension in foreign culture education. To what extent and how these models and documents, which have been inspiring and/or regulating foreign language/culture education internationally, meet these principles and perspectives are questions that should be posed by and to professionals in this area. Since these models and documents have been influencing language and culture education on an international scale, it is useful for critical educators to examine them critically and, furthermore, take account of the aspects in which they do or do not promote a critical approach to foreign languages and cultures.

Likewise, both professional training models conceived for business purposes and theoretical models intended for use in foreign language/culture education must be taken into account in this still developing area of Intercultural Communication. Their strengths as well as their weaknesses must be considered by both fields. While the first provide practical and simple examples and guidelines from and for professional contexts, the latter focus on the pedagogical, and in some cases political, premises and aims of intercultural communication. By and large, a growing concern to introduce a critical dimension is noticeable in the models and documents examined here.

Finally, the enhancement of a critical dimension in the study of foreign cultures makes more evident the political nature of education and may provide a significant contribution towards education for critical/democratic citizenship by exploring the multiple layers of a postnational and pluralistic model of citizenship. The main tenets for developing critical cultural awareness within foreign language/culture education, as discussed above, will be explored in the remaining chapters when commenting upon research in the field of teachers' opinions about these issues (already mentioned in this chapter) and eventually in some proposals for the conceptualisation of professional developmental programmes aimed at teachers both at pre-service and in-service levels.

Notes

1. Byram introduced the term 'Intercultural Communicative Competence' which combines the concepts of Communicative Competence and Intercultural Competence and simultaneously differs from each of these. It expands the first concept which has been translated into the mere communication of messages and exchange of information to a focus on 'establishing and maintaining relationships' (Byram, 1997b: 3). It diverges from the latter since Byram understands Intercultural Competence as the 'ability to interact in their own language with people from another country and culture' (p. 70), while 'Intercultural Communicative Competence' implies that this is performed in a foreign language.

2. The Third World Movement was initiated in the 1960s in the United States and has been spreading throughout the world mainly due to the self-awareness of those who have emigrated from Third World to Western countries.
3. Smith, Paige and Steglitz provide a definition of 'effectiveness' and 'appropriateness' with respect to communication: 'Communication is *appropriate* when it meets contextual and relational standards (you did it right given the context); *effective* when it achieves desired ends or goals or provides satisfaction of both communicators' needs and concerns' (Smith, Paige & Steglitz, 1998: 71–2).
4. While in the United Kingdom 'there is an unspecified fear of political education' (Byram, 1996: 66), in Portugal the term 'political education' revives memories of recent dictatorial times when this subject and related activities were far from critical and there were clear and pervasive ideological impositions by the regime.
5. Recent events in Kosovo and East Timor are examples of such interventions.
6. This was evident recently in the mobilisation of young people in Portugal for the cause of the people of East Timor. Although most were not even born when East Timor ceased to be a Portuguese colony, and despite the fact that it had always been a distant and unimportant colony, young people in Portugal were deeply involved in this issue both for humanitarian and political reasons.

Chapter 4
Teachers' Voices: Critical Cultural Awareness in EFL Classes in Portugal

Teacher's voices will be represented here in the words of upper secondary school teachers of English in Portugal. Portugal is a particularly interesting case since teachers are now required by the national syllabus to carry out a 'critical interpretation' of the English-speaking cultures they teach. Furthermore, the fact that Portugal is a small country situated in the southwestern corner of Europe facing Spain to the east and the Atlantic to the west, has some significance. According to historians and poets, this Janus-like geographical position has determined the paradoxical features that characterise Portuguese identity(ies). Although Portugal was one of the first European nations to have its borders stabilised, since its political independence was established early in the thirteenth century, its national identity is itself not precisely circumscribed but is instead what may be called a 'border identity', in that it has always shown a predisposition to engage with different possibilities represented by the ocean to the west (Santos, 1994: 134).[1]

As a result of their travelling the Portuguese were the first to develop the notion of a global world (Modelsky, 1987). Because their country was small, far from the centre of Europe and closed in by Spain, its adventurous people crossed the Atlantic in search of the unknown, discovering rather than conquering. Their particular way of colonising, which Maxwell describes by saying that 'the Portuguese were not conquistadors, like the Spaniards who followed them, but maneuverers' (Maxwell, 1995: 8), among other factors, meant that Portugal was the last European power to withdraw from its colonies. This was due, to some extent, to the fact that the country had 'disguised the nature of her presence behind a skillful amalgam of historical mythmaking, claims of multiracialism, and good public relations' (Maxwell, 1995: 19) and also because the Portuguese were, in some cases, more immigrants than colonisers in their own colonies.[2]

The diaspora has lasted up to the present day. During the 1950s, 1960s and 1970s, the emigrants consisted mostly of waves of workers and political refugees heading mainly for France, Germany, the United States, Latin America and South Africa. This fact is important not only because in some areas the emigrant population is the majority rather than the established population but also because, in general, these emigrants tend to maintain links with their homeland or have returned home and have often had great influence in changing the face and soul of the villages where they were born. On the other hand, there has been recently a reverse emigration from the ex-colonies to Portugal, changing a racially homogeneous population to a multiracial one, mainly in the Lisbon area.

A brief description of the political evolution in Portugal during this century may also help to understand the context of this study. Portugal experienced a 50-year dictatorship under the *Estado Novo* (New State) which lasted till 1974, when it was ousted by the *Revolução dos Cravos* (Carnation Revolution). Besides political repression and economic standstill, the intellectual obscurantism imposed by Salazar's regime is probably the most relevant in the significance of this study. The existence of a reduced intellectual elite and of powerful censorship aiming mostly at consolidating conformism and ignorance ironically stimulated creative forms of oppositionist writing but, above all, it banned the habit of discussing ideas in public especially in formal education. Dictatorship and, just after the revolution, anarchy and the communist takeover, have made the Portuguese people value an education for critical and democratic citizenship.

Portugal joined the European Union in 1986 and has since become a member of the European Monetary Union. At the same time, it is striving to strengthen its links with the other Portuguese-speaking countries and communities around the world, mainly through the *Comunidade dos Países de Língua Portuguesa* (Community of Portuguese-speaking Countries). Therefore, the time has come for Portugal to redefine its identity. Portugal used to be central in relation to its colonies and peripheral to Europe. Now, it is adjusting to its new postcolonial role in the world and to its new central role in Europe, having to renegotiate its linguistic/cultural presence worldwide and its membership of an exclusive European club, in both cases, with much effort but little power. The development of critical cultural awareness within the educational system and within the foreign language/culture classes, in particular, can be most helpful in redefining new Portuguese identities.

Methodology

The general aims of this research project were to find out if, why and how teachers of foreign languages/cultures approach culture critically, how they define critical cultural awareness and what sort of development models would help them improve their professional performance in this area, although only part of the study appears in this book. The nature of this project called for the use of a combination of both quantitative and qualitative methods. The quantitative data resulted from the response of teachers to the predetermined alternatives presented in a questionnaire, which were based on a review of the literature and my previous experiences both as a teacher and a teacher trainer (Appendix 1, only sections 1, 2, 3 and 4 will be dealt with in this book). The quantitative data were then further expanded and clarified by the participants, in a more spontaneous way, in follow-up interviews in a focus-group format (Appendix 5).[3] In this way, the quantitative data based on the predetermined alternatives in the questionnaire were confronted with the teachers' flow of ideas in the focus-group interviews (Alasuutari, 1995). I considered the information collected through group interviews as particularly important for the design of the research project as a whole because it provided the opportunity for the extension, clarification, and specification of the issues raised by the questionnaire, through the direct interaction of the participants in a focused discussion (Morgan, 1998a; Stewart & Shamdasani, 1990). Moreover, the study focused on the operationalisation of a complex concept, the *critical*, therefore, it required complementary types of sources that would enable the elucidation both in breadth and in depth of its operationalisation (Cohen & Manion, 1994).

Most of the reviewed literature on this subject emphasises the potentialities of focus-group discussions in generating data due to the synergy and spontaneity of these events that provide for a 'wider range of information, insight, and ideas than will the cumulation of the responses of a number of individuals' in that 'a comment made by one individual often triggers a chain of responses from the other participants' (Stewart & Shamdasani, 1990: 19). The conversational mood generated in such circumstances, among professionals who are seldom given the opportunity to reflect upon their practices, accounts for the intense and prolific discussions that took place within this study. As Alasuutari puts it:

> The reason why group discussions provide valuable information is that the situation encourages the people involved to talk about things that would otherwise remain outside the conversation because they

are so self-evident. Where people talk about things that they normally do not talk about, we are bound to obtain interesting material. (Alasuutari, 1995: 94)

Since the concept 'critical' relies mostly on taken-for-granted notions that the participants do not usually talk about, they were surprised when confronted with alternative ideas and this meant that they were forced to reconsider and reformulate their ideas during the discussion. This is a natural process in focus-group discussions which should be encouraged (Vaughn, Shumm & Sinagub, 1996: 18). There were some examples of this process in the discussions within this study, especially when participants were asked whether they agreed with being *critical* about a foreign culture, whether they thought they had a *political* role while teaching culture, or whether they considered it *legitimate* to include any English-speaking culture in the syllabus. Furthermore, on some occasions, the participants not only evolved in their opinions but they also contradicted themselves and they were often made aware of this by other participants. Interaction between participants generates a continuous flow of ideas that intensifies the discussion. They are not expected to arrive with their opinions already formed or completely structured, which stimulates the dynamics of the discussion, nor are they supposed to reach consensus (Krueger, 1994), which accounts for the difficulty of data analysis.

This research project matched three types of triangulation used in research which are 'space triangulation', since schools selected for both quantitative and qualitative research were located in different regions of the country,[4] 'combined levels of interaction', more specifically the 'individual level' for the questionnaire and the 'interactive level' for the focus-group interviews, and also 'methodological triangulation', with both quantitative and qualitative methods of analysis (Cohen & Manion, 1994: 236). A concern with the consistency of results involved checking internal consistency within the questionnaire and within the interviews in order to confirm the findings throughout each of the research strategies, and also external consistency while matching the statistical results with the ethnographic analysis. This was a difficult process whose conclusions are restricted due to limited 'comparability of results' between two methods based on different types of analysis (Wolff, *et al.*, 1993: 134). Furthermore, since the focus of this study was on attitudes, similar questions, whether in the questionnaire or in the group discussions, may have elicited different responses due to changes in wording, context or emphasis (Oppenheim, 1992: 147). Therefore, the analysis of each collection of data was made separately and the integration of results was made with the comparative and contrastive elements between both sets of findings in mind.[5] A few individual interviews – with one of the syllabus authors, with an administrator of the Ministry of Education in charge of the Department of International Relations, and with a textbook author, were also carried out.

Teaching Culture Critically in Foreign Language Classes

Although nowadays there is a widespread interest in the teaching/learning of culture in language classes, its inclusion is often carried out with reservation and, in the worst cases, with some lack of seriousness. However, the majority of the participants in this project, both in the questionnaire and in the focus-group interviews, not only supported the idea that the cultural dimension in foreign language classes should be expanded (S1.1) (71%) but also agreed that developing a critical attitude towards both target and native cultures was the most important goal in learning them (S1.7) (70.5%).[6] Nevertheless, only about 60% were ready to dismiss the possibility that the study of culture in language classes can hinder progress in linguistic accuracy (S1.4) and even fewer questionnaire respondents thought that all the English-speaking cultures around the world are equally valid to be represented in an English syllabus (S1.3) (54.5%).[7] The latter results were not, however, entirely corroborated by the participants in focus-groups, as we shall see. Despite these reservations, this study proved as well that the majority of its participants thought that there should be a continuous concern with a critical approach towards foreign cultures at all levels of foreign language/culture education (S1.8) (73.3%). The possibility that an emphasis on the study of foreign cultures can contribute to the students' loss of cultural identity was also rejected both by the questionnaire respondents (S1.6) (77%) and by those taking part in focus-groups. The fact that most teachers who contributed to this research project strongly advocated the inclusion of culture and the development of critical cultural awareness in foreign language classes has also been triggered by a great emphasis of the national syllabus on the introduction of cultural studies in English classes. One of its authors confirmed this attempt:

> E, portanto, nós tentámos dar, de facto, um enfoque muito grande para que os professores percebessem que a aula de língua estrangeira, neste caso o Inglês, para já não é uma entidade franca. Quando estás a estudar uma língua estás a estudar uma cultura, ela transmite padrões culturais ...

(And, therefore, we actually tried to put a strong focus on the need for teachers to understand that in a foreign language class, in this case it is English which is not a lingua franca entity in itself, when you are learning a language you are studying a culture, it conveys cultural patterns . . .).

Likewise, the administrator interviewed at the Ministry of Education encouraged teachers to include culture in their teaching and to be critical about it:

> . . . *porque enquanto professor de Inglês és um mediador de várias culturas que, por acaso, se exprimem numa mesma língua mas que são diferentes, exactamente porque em termos de tempo, de espaço, de acumular civilazional também é diferente. Portanto, se eu enquanto mediadora não tiver uma reflexão crítica e não me projectar subversivamente sobre essa projecção, eu, se calhar, não estou a ajudar os meus alunos da melhor maneira . . .* (. . . because as a teacher of English you are a mediator of several cultures which, by chance, are expressed in the same language but which are different, because in terms of time, space and civilizational layers it is different. Therefore, if I, as mediator, do not reflect critically or do not project myself over that projection in a subversive way, I might not be helping my students in the best way . . .).

Although not as daring as to consider their role 'subversive', most teachers who participated in the focus-group discussions supported a critical approach to culture. Despite the administrator's more intense posture, teachers are closer to Kramsch's hermeneutic and dialogic model and to Byram's evaluative proposal towards culture than to the latter's and Pennycook's claims for a deconstructive and transformative stance. There were, of course, discordant voices such as the one who noted that s/he supported a critical approach *per se* but that it could be carried out in many ways other than through the teaching/learning about culture. In another group, a participant argued that it would not be possible to approach culture critically because s/he had not lived in any of the English-speaking countries, and therefore, such a critique would be unreliable. However, most of her/his colleagues did not endorse such arguments. PartCg6 (participant C in Group 6) counterargued that being critical was inevitable because we are ourselves *'sujeitos portadores, fazedores de cultura'* (carriers, producers of culture). To some extent, this teacher is sensitive to Pennycook's notion of 'writing back' since the native culture is understood as interfering, in one way or other, with one's interpretation of the target one(s).

The inevitability of being critical when teaching/learning about a foreign culture was also raised in another group where it was noted that such a practice takes place even when one is not aware of it, *'eu penso que é inevitável mesmo que a pessoa não tenha consciência disso'* (I think it is inevitable even though we are not aware of it) (PartAg7). Therefore, it is important that it be stated in the syllabus so that people feel urged to reflect upon its meaning, *'é importante que lá esteja, quanto mais não seja para as pessoas reflectirem sobre que objectivo é aquele'* (it is important that this objective is included in order to make people wonder about what it means) (PartDg7).

Another idea which pervaded most groups was that being critical was an interdisciplinary capability which was part of the student's general education, *'faz parte do desenvolvimento global do aluno . . . porque também é fundamental para a vida deles no futuro, porque se tornam cidadãos mais válidos'* (it is part of the student's global development . . . because it is also fundamental for their future, it makes them better citizens) (PartEg1).

The importance of critical cultural awareness for citizenship education and the formation of cultural identity also resonated among the groups and was confirmed by the statistical results. A great majority of respondents agreed with the view that 'European and global identities of the pupil/citizen should be fostered in foreign language/culture classes' (S1.2) (85.2%) and that 'learning about a foreign culture can change the pupil's attitude towards his/her own culture' (S1.5) (84.7%), although the teachers claim that the latter does not happen at the cost of the students' loss of cultural identity.

In focus-group discussions most participants revealed that they agreed that all English-speaking cultures around the world were, in principle, legitimate, but not all of them were equally relevant. Their argument was that it was not feasible to include some of them either due to geographical distance or lack of information and materials. In Group 2, on the other hand, a few teachers displayed a rather Eurocentric perspective, which was nonetheless contested by the others. Participant H argued:

> *A partir do momento em que os actuais [países] deixaram de ser colónias, eles adquiriram, embora tenham uns resquícios da cultura britânica, a sua própria cultura, uma identidade própria e agora são uma cultura completamente diferente. Até que ponto seria legítimo ou não estudar a cultura desses países, quando eles já têm uma ligação muito ténue com o país-mãe?* (When the present [countries] ceased to be colonies, although they still have some remains of the British culture, they developed their own culture, their own identity and are now totally different cultures. I wonder to

what extent it would be legitimate to study the cultures of those countries if they have only a tenuous link with their mother-country?).

This is an opinion that goes clearly against Pennycook's, Canagarajah's, Roth and Harama and others' claims for the legitimacy of Third World Englishes. It was not, however, a generalised view within this group or among the other groups. Most contributors shared the fact that they sometimes included contemporary texts about Australia, New Zealand, South Africa and India, although not often. PartGg3, for example, was even more intense in condemning a westernised perspective and criticised the excessive focus of the syllabus on the United States while disregarding South Africa, for example, when dealing with racism, *'estamos a dar voz, voz, voz, a quem já fala alto'* (we are letting speak, speak, speak those whose voices are already loud enough) s/he said.

Defining a Critical Approach to Foreign Cultures

Apart from a few exceptions, the definition of 'critical' with respect to teaching/learning a foreign culture has remained within a domain taken-for-granted among researchers, policy makers, and teachers. Similarly, we cannot find this word, nor any other with the same root, in the glossary of the national syllabus being implemented in Portugal, at secondary school level, although a 'critical interpretation' of the cultural content is listed as one of its main guidelines. I was curious as to whether teachers tended to reflect upon or to discuss its meaning among themselves. This problem was precisely the aim of the present study which attempted to identify the notions that, in the teachers' minds, were connected with the concept 'critical' when applied to teaching/learning a foreign culture. However, before we take a look at their responses, it seems useful to address, beforehand, the conceptualisation put forward by the administrator interviewed:

> *No meu ponto de vista, e foi sempre esse, e eu gostaria até de ratificar isso, um professor tem que ser um elemento subversivo. Subversivo porquê? Porque vai ter que, enquanto professor, junto dos seus alunos ou dos seus alunos/professores, porque pode ser formador, subverter aquilo que lhe vai aparecer como dogma ou como norma, e essa leitura subversiva, e é por isso que eu digo que é crítica, é, no fundo, procurar interrogar-se, utilizar um método maiêutico, interrogar-se a si e levar os seus alunos, os seus colegas ou os seus professores, a interrogar-se sobre aqueles conteúdos, sobre aqueles padrões e sobre aqueles modelos* . . . (From my point of view, and I would like to confirm that this has always been the case, a teacher must be

subversive. Why? S/he must be subversive because, as a teacher or a mentor, s/he has to, with her/his students or student teachers, subvert what is given as a dogma or as a rule, and that subversive reading intrinsically means, and this is the reason why I call it critical, a questioning of oneself, the use of a maieutic method, the encouragement of one's students, colleagues or student teachers, to question those contents, those patterns and those models . . .).

This statement reveals a political view of the foreign culture teacher's role because it grants her/him not only a political function but also a subversive one. In sum, the term 'critical' in this context is linked with questioning oneself and others by questioning dogmas, rules, patterns, and models. However, the questioning here is seen as 'subversive' having, as is confirmed later in the interview, a 'political' connotation because it aims at producing 'active citizens', otherwise, the teacher *'está a ser com certeza muito defensor de um* status quo' (will probably be very much a defender of the status quo).

Before considering the grounds upon which the teachers participating in this study base their critical approach, it also seems relevant to focus on the syllabus author's understanding of a 'critical interpretation of cultural patterns' which stands in the syllabus as a main guideline for the cultural content. In her own words, it means *'um olhar atento, distanciado, desapaixonado'* (an attentive, detached and dispassionate look), that is, *'vê-los das diferenças e das semelhanças, pura e simplesmente. Mas não em posição de positivo ou de negativo . . .'* (to purely and simply see them in terms of contrasts and comparisons without taking a positive/negative perspective . . .). In her opinion, *'interpretar criticamente é perceber'* (to interpret critically means to understand) but it also involves taking a stand, having an opinion, but only at a later stage:

> . . . *criticamente é tomar posição, evidentemente que é . . . tu podes tomar posição numa fase posterior . . . depois pode dar opinião, pode tomar partido, mas primeiro tem de perceber os fundamentos da sua posição.* (being critical involves taking a position . . . of course it does . . . you can take a position at a further stage . . . you can give your opinion, you can take sides, but first you must understand the grounds of your position . . .).

The author asks for an objective approach to be established, to start with, and only then is one allowed to let her/his subjectivity flow. This is an issue that is not easily resolved in Kramsch's or Byram's works.

Kramsch hesitated throughout her work about which came first or whether both happened simultaneously, as was seen in the previous chapter (Kramsch, 1993a, 1998a). Byram proposed that, in order to be critical, one should 'evaluate ... on the basis of explicit criteria' but, on the other hand, he stressed that 'an entirely value-free interpretation' is unlikely to happen (Byram, 1997a, b). On the contrary, Pennycook and Canagarajah are adamant that one departs from one's own social Self both objectively and subjectively (Canagarajah, 1999; Pennycook, 1994). The teachers also referred to the aspects mentioned by the author, mainly, the comparing/contrasting point of view, the positive/negative perspective, the questioning stance and the political nature of teaching/learning a foreign culture which generated much discussion. However, the articulation between these elements differed not only from the taken-for-granted notions upheld by the syllabus designer but also within and between groups, and that is also evident in the statistical results.

Both the responses to the questionnaire and the discussions in focus-groups coincide in showing that *comparison/contrast* between target and native culture is understood by the participants as an important element of a critical approach. However, some teachers view it as a mere recognition of similarities and differences while others include some value judgement, giving their opinion and pointing out positive/negative aspects. This division is statistically well defined since the majority of questionnaire respondents (85.8%) was split between those who aim at merely acknowledging similarities and differences between cultures while attempting to develop the student's critical cultural awareness (S2.9.1) (42.6%) and those who suggest that critical cultural awareness involves becoming aware of the positive/negative aspects of another culture, that is, it implies looking at the Other from your own cultural point of view and making a judgement (S2.9.4) (43.2%). The discussions in focus-groups supported this division and the following excerpt illustrates how group interviews led participants to reflect upon this issue:

> B: Mas tu quando estás a comparar imediatamente estás a estabelecer, constrastivamente ou por semelhança, pontos de aproximação ou pontos de afastamento, o que leva de imediato a dizer que **o outro é melhor ou é pior**. (But when you are comparing/contrasting you are immediately establishing, through contrast or similarity, points of comparison or points of difference, that which makes you say at once that **the other is better or worse**.).

E: *Eu penso que aqui é no sentido de compreender a cultura dos outros povos, é **entender porque é que eles são diferentes**, porque é que **comparando com a nossa cultura**, eles têm um procedimento e nós temos outro, temos outra maneira de ver a vida, portanto, é no sentido de compreender, é este o sentido crítico em relação às outras culturas.* (I think that it means understanding other peoples' cultures, **to understand why they are different**, why, in **comparison/contrast with our own culture**, they behave in one way and we in another, we see things in a different way, therefore, it means to understand, this is having a critical attitude towards other cultures.).

. . .

H: *Concordo, mas vejo mais pelo lado do compreender como agora tinham dito, o saber comparar com a própria cultura, mas não tendo necessariamente uma opinião favorável ou desfavorável, **é um saber captar tudo o que vem da cultura de outros povos** e depois pode ter-se uma opinião . . . **mas ter uma opinião não tem que ser favorável ou desfavorável**.* (I agree, but I see it more as understanding as you have just said, being able to compare/contrast it with our own culture, but without necessarily having a favourable or unfavourable opinion, it means being able **to comprehend everything that comes from the other culture** and then you can have **an opinion . . . but it does not have to be favourable or unfavourable**.).

. . .

G: *No fundo é conhecer o outro, é ter uma imagem de outra cultura, compreendê-la, aceitá-la e ser crítico no sentido em que se consegue ver duas, pelo menos neste caso é a britânica e a portuguesa, pelo menos conseguir **comparar duas posturas, duas maneiras de estar na vida completamente diferentes**, eu acho que nesse sentido já é positivo, é conseguir perceber o outro, e, enfim, **se quisermos ser críticos e se quisermos dizer a nossa é melhor ou pior**, saber dizer porquê e em que base é que nos podemos apoiar para criticar o outro. É preciso ter uma posição crítica e saber porque é que se crítica também.* (Intrinsically, it is basically to know the other, it is having an image of another culture, understanding it, accepting it and being critical in the sense that you can look at both, in this case the British and the Portuguese cultures, to at least be able to **compare/contrast two attitudes, two totally different ways of life**. I think that in this sense it is positive, it means managing to understand the other, and, in the end, **if we want to be**

critical and if we want to say that ours is better or worse, then we must know why and on what grounds we criticise the other. **We must take a critical position and also know why we criticise**).

(emphasis mine).

The sequence above is paradigmatic of what often happens in discussion groups, people agree, disagree, conciliate, reformulate what other members say and add new ideas. These are also four positions that typify and summarise the ideas generated by the other groups with respect to this element – comparing/contrasting – of a critical approach to a foreign culture.

Participant B considers that value judgement is implicit in comparing/contrasting and that the closeness/remoteness to one's own cultural patterns may influence one's value judgement, that is, one's perspective is always relative to one's own cultural standpoint.

For E, being critical is mainly to try to understand the different Other and her/his motives, that is, both native and target cultures are viewed as two separate blocks. Cultures here seem to be untouched by each other and being critical about each other means finding out about them and what motivates them. Therefore, despite the comparing/contrasting perspective between both cultures, they remain independent. However, a new component is introduced, that of 'understanding'.

H conciliates the previous positions by putting forward both elements: understanding and having an opinion, although s/he reformulates these concepts. S/he perceives understanding as grasping what comes from other cultures and, according to her/him, having an opinion does not necessarily imply a value judgement. Whereas in interventions B and E there was mostly an outward attitude, either of understanding or assessing the Other from our standpoint, having in mind how different they are from us, H shows a more inward perspective where understanding is apprehending and where giving an opinion does not necessarily mean assessing. S/he seems to open up both concepts, understanding and giving one's opinion, in that s/he is open to other cultures, both ready to receive some input from them and to renounce her own preconceptions while still having an opinion. To some extent, the last claim is supported by statistical data because, although, as mentioned previously, a substantial minority of respondents advocate that 'developing the pupil's critical cultural awareness involves helping him/her to become aware of the positive/negative aspects of another culture' (S2.9) (43.2%), only a small minority of respondents to the same section support the idea that 'a critical approach to a controversial topic means identifying what is right and what is wrong' (S2.6) (10.2%), or that 'having ethical concerns while teaching/learning about a foreign culture means being able to recognize right from wrong' (S2.11) (5.1%).

G tries to close the cycle by using all the elements already introduced, putting them in a certain order and adding new elements. From her/his point of view, the process involves being able to compare/contrast both cultures, which are different, then to understand the Other, accept it and, eventually, be critical about it. Nevertheless, being critical still implies, in her/his point of view, saying whether the Other is better or worse providing that you *justify* your judgement.

We may conclude that although the teachers who took part in the study, following Byram, valorise comparative/contrastive analysis they still remain at the middle stages of Bennett's developmental model since they do not view the contact between the native and target cultures as interactive. We can identify here Bennett's 'acceptance', 'adaptation' and 'empathy' stages, as described previously, since participants acknowledge and respect behavioural and value differences while keeping both cultures separate and intact although they attempt to understand the Other's perspective. Unlike Kramsch, they do not worry about the way the target culture views them/their culture. Like Byram they try to bring the unconscious to consciousness, in some cases they try to relativise their own meanings and value the others', and they do also mention constructing their value judgements upon explicit criteria.

While discussing what comparing/contrasting meant for them, the interventions transcribed above put forward some new elements that may be said to characterise a critical approach. These were also pointed out by other groups and had also been considered in the questionnaire. They were the following, 'understanding', 'looking for reasons', 'accepting' and 'justifying'.

Therefore, besides the comparing/contrasting element described above, which is part of a wider social component of a critical approach, participants in the study also valued a cognitive component which includes understanding, looking for reasons and motives, becoming aware of, and justifying, which may be summarised as *reflecting and analysing*.

Respondents to the questionnaire were more or less unanimous in placing great emphasis on the technique of analysis. An overwhelming majority expressed their agreement with the view that 'the pupil may be considered critical if s/he looks for the motives and causes behind attitudes and events' (S2.3) (92.6%), and that 'adopting a critical perspective towards cultural values, products and institutions means analysing the relationships between cultural values, products and institutions' (S2.8) (81.3%). Such statistical findings may suggest that teachers interpret the word *critical* with regard to pedagogy within the frame of reference of *critical thinking* which places great emphasis on analysis (Bloom, 1972), although focus-group discussions made it clear that reflection prevails over analysis. Furthermore, reflection appears predominantly within the context of opinion-making, as described below by PartEg1:

> ... *para lhes despertar o espírito crítico nós temos que os fazer reflectir sobre as várias perspectivas, o que torna os alunos mais conscientes e mais reflexivos em relação às coisas e, portanto, quando dão opiniões, são opiniões mais fundamentadas* ... (... in order to stimulate their critical mind we have to make them reflect upon various perspectives, and this makes our students more aware and more thoughtful about things and, therefore, when they give an opinion, it is better grounded ...).

Here reflection and awareness are linked with a critical mind but these cognitive skills are used for the purpose of social interaction while giving an opinion. However, this teacher makes claims for reflection upon various perspectives which is one of the tenets proposed by Critical Pedagogy. Reflection upon both one's native and the target culture leading to an *awareness of* differences was also mentioned often by others in the course of discussion. As PartFg7 pointed out, finding out about the reasons why people from different cultures behave differently and why different countries' historical evolutions followed the paths they did is among their objectives:

> *Eu concordo que nós abordemos a cultura de uma forma crítica até porque nós, ao falarmos de todos esses povos, temos de ver como eles são, o que é que eles fazem, e de levar os alunos a ver porque é que fazem, porque é que as coisas aconteceram* ... (I do agree that we should approach culture critically because when we speak about all those peoples, we must understand what they are like, what they do and to make our students understand why they do things, why things happened ...).

Teachers, therefore, see it as their task, as culture mediators, to stimulate their students to be reflective about cultural behaviour as well as about social and historical events. The target culture seems to provide a motive for cultural reflection and teachers tend to view their task as multifaceted since they have to make their students aware, '*é despertá-los, é encaminhá-los, é ajudá-los*' (to stimulate, guide and help them), according to PartBg4.

Some groups also viewed reflection as linked to the ability to take a *detached and objective look* at the Other and at oneself and viewed this as an important element of a critical approach. PartAg4, in particular, strongly underlined this aspect:

> ... *a abordagem crítica é eles conseguirem objectivamente afastar-se, eu acho que o que é importante é que eles fiquem atentos e que consigam ter uma abertura mental suficiente para conseguirem perceber ... que há formas das sociedades funcionarem, e funcionarem de maneiras diferentes, que podem ter tido X consequências ... eles terem a capacidade de poder debruçar-se e reflectir sobre isso ... é eles conseguirem afastar-se da situação e é eles relativizarem-se a si próprios, e isso é que é difícil. E isso é muito complicado.* (... a critical approach is to get our students to keep a detached and objective outlook, it is important that they are attentive and open-minded enough to understand ... that societies work in different ways which may have had X consequences ... it is being able to step back from the situation and it is also viewing their own perspective as relative and this is where the difficulty lies. This is the complicated part.).

The complexity of this strategy was also noted by other members of this group who either thought that it was hard to put into practice because it required abstract thinking or because they themselves had difficulty in realising why detachment was needed at all. This was an issue for most groups and it was evident that it was considered a leading objective by some teachers like PartDg7, '*faz parte da formação do aluno que ele desenvolva uma atitude crítica um pouco mais distanciada ...*' (it is part of the student's formation that s/he develops a critical attitude which is a bit more detached ...). However, it was not a widespread practice since some participants, like PartCg4, showed a greater concern for eliciting students' comments on positive/negative aspects, '*depois pedimos que faça um comentário em que vai referir os aspectos positivos e negativos, nesse aspecto o aluno já está a reflectir ...*' (then we ask the student to make a comment where s/he refers to positive and negative aspects and that means s/he is reflecting).

Despite some difficulty in defining the implications of using reflection as a strategy while teaching a foreign culture, it was evident both from quantitative and qualitative data that teachers put great emphasis on the cognitive component of a critical approach. However, it was also clear that they equally gave great significance to the affective component of a critical approach by constantly eliciting the students' emotional responses to both target and native culture. This concern is substantiated by the questionnaire results where a majority of respondents maintained that 'a critical attitude towards a certain aspect of culture is both an emotional and intellectual response' (S2.5) (66.9%). Participants in group discussions confirmed that it is their understanding that being critical is neither solely an intellectual nor solely an emotional process but draws upon both aspects. PartDg6 went even further and described being critical as the process of *gaining/finding pleasure* in learning about other cultures:

> *Mas nós podemos ter o tal sentido crítico e a visão crítica sem estarmos pela negativa. Eu, por exemplo, ao leccionar determinados aspectos de cultura, de valores éticos e morais, maneiras de estar na vida, nomeadamente de povos de língua inglesa, desde os ingleses, passando pelos australianos, etc. eu posso fruir com os meus alunos, estar a querer fruir, estar a entender as diversas maneiras de expressão e de estar na vida . . .* (But we can have that critical sense and a critical outlook without having a negative attitude. For example, when I teach about certain aspects of a culture, about ethical and moral principles, about ways of life, mainly those of English-speaking peoples, from the English to the Australians, etc., I may, with my students, take pleasure in understanding the various ways of expressing themselves and living their lives . . .).

Such an intellectual and emotional commitment to teaching a foreign culture was pervasive throughout the groups, either in a more optimistic or a pessimistic stance, and the same was expected from the students. Although some teachers expressed a certain disappointment with the reality of their everyday practices, they all wanted students to be actively involved in the task of learning about the target cultures. Therefore, they praised their students' involvement in discussions and in research about those issues that might provoke their interest or that might be suggested by the teacher. When given a few options about the most characteristic traits that can define a critical individual questionnaire respondents placed more value on their students' capacity for being either argumentative (38.6%) or curious (28.4%) rather than intelligent (22.2%) or dissatisfied (10.2%). Later in the discussion groups, teachers had the opportunity to put forward their definitions of these traits. With regard to being curious, PartGg6 mentioned the importance of the student's *search for knowledge* about the cultures s/he is learning about in order to attain a critical perspective, '*se houver uma pesquisa e uma procura do saber por parte do aluno ele vai conseguir chegar a essa postura crítica mesmo que não tenha ido ao país . . .*' (if the student does some research and searches for knowledge, s/he will reach such a critical perspective even though s/he has not been to the target country before).

Participants in Group 7 explained how they found it essential that their students *questioned* the knowledge they got from school material and via television, not only about the target cultures but also about their own environment:

> C: ... *eu considero que é importante para mim, que os alunos se interroguem sobre as coisas que recebem ... e, portanto, quando se dá textos, seja históricos, seja de enciclopédias, seja do que for, eu procuro que eles realmente se interroguem sobre aquilo, inclusivamente através de comparação com aquilo que eles vão vendo na televisão ...* (... I consider it very important that students question the information they get ... and, therefore, when they are given texts, either historical ones or from encyclopaedias, or whatever, I try to get them to think about them, including relating them to what they see on television ...).
>
> ...
>
> D: ... *vejo-me mais como lançadora de confusão, para espicaçar um pouco e destruir aqueles estereotipos que existem, perturbar um pouco aquelas mentes, às vezes demasiado linearizadas, porque a informação que lhes aparece de fora é, muitas vezes, demasiado linearizada.* (... I see myself more as a generator of disorder in order to provoke them, to dismantle those stereotypes that people believe, to disarrange those minds which are sometimes too clearly defined, because the information they get out there is often too linear ...).
>
> ...
>
> A: ... *nós conseguimos que eles se vão desinstalando do que está só aqui, acabou, isto é uma caneta, serve aqui, serve agora, acabou, destruiu, não interessa ...* (... we manage to unsettle them from the position that everything is only here and now, over and done with, this is only a pen, it is useful here and now, then it is finished, you throw it away, it doesn't matter ...).

These teachers, therefore, see it as their task to motivate and help their students to question the information they obtain from various sources, both inside and outside the classroom, and the preconceptions they construct out of such uncritical information. A also points out the need to make them stop and think in order to be able to see beyond the surface and the immediacy of things. All those quoted above seem to be aware that it is part of their role to counterbalance the superficial, stereotyped images of the target cultures that students get from the media, which accounts for some of the tenets put forward by Critical Pedagogy.

Furthermore, some respondents view this element – questioning – of a critical approach mostly within the context of dialogue by maintaining that 'the most characteristic trait of a critical individual is being argumentative' (S2.4) (38.6%). During group discussions participants revealed their definitions of this trait that had to do mostly with having students give their opinions and justify them, by providing arguments that support them, as PartHg2 did, *'o aluno exprimir-se, dizer as suas opiniões, fazê-las justificar, porque razão é que ele pensa de determinada maneira'* (the student expresses her/his opinions, justifies them, says why he thinks that way). This included the ability to defend their points of view to someone who is in a position of power, as argued by PartCg5:

> *Acho que é bom eles começarem a desenvolver o espírito crítico e, mais do que isso, saberem fazer valer a sua opinião, não serem aquele estilo de pessoa que, se o professor torce um bocadinho a cara, eles mudam de opinião ou não têm argumentos, ou não sabem defender aquilo em que acreditam. E isso eu tento ver sempre, tento sempre abaná-los um pouco e ver até que ponto eles estão seguros daquilo que dizem.* (I think they should develop a critical attitude and even more to be able to maintain their opinions, they shouldn't be that type of person who changes their opinion if the teacher frowns or who has no arguments to support their beliefs. I always try to check on that, to shake them and see to what extent they are sure about what they say).

It was a general belief that enabling students to give their opinions, justify and maintain them was an essential element of a critical approach. However, promoting a critical attitude towards a foreign culture seems to be perceived mainly as a rhetorical exercise. Only rarely did teachers advocate some kind of active social or political involvement as a purpose for their critical approaches, as we shall see below.

Additionally, most participants in this study expressed their belief that teachers should be impartial in their statements if they ever did voice them. In the view of a majority of the respondents to the questionnaire 'in his/her cultural approach, the teacher should listen to the pupils' views and be impartial' (S2.2) (54.5%) and very few thought that to 'offer his/her opinion and encourage discussion' (S2.2) (15.9%) would be a good alternative. Therefore, only open-ended, non-conclusive questioning appears to be important and the teacher does not seem to take risks and offer her/his own ideas for debate. These educators thus fail to recognise or implement an important aspect of the teacher's role as viewed by Critical Pedagogy, that of an active and transformative intellectual whose ideas are as much open to debate as their students' and who has to engage in the search for knowledge together with them. Group discussions confirmed this finding with participants H and F in Group 6 making statements such as respectively *'espero sempre mais deles uma postura crítica do que de mim mesma'* (I always expect a critical attitude more from them than from myself) and *'eu acho que o objectivo ideal é a pessoa ser imparcial e objectiva'* (the ideal is to be impartial and objective). However, most contributors tended to acknowledge that it was impossible to be completely impartial and some even ended up by admitting that complete impartiality might not be desirable, as PartFg6 did, *'não sei até que ponto não se perderá algo de humano se o professor for demasiado factual'* (I do not know to what extent something human might be lost if the teacher remains too factual).

Some teachers, however, went a little further in advocating a critical attitude by the teacher by exclaiming that *'eu não concebo . . . que nós sejamos acríticos'* (I cannot conceive of the idea . . . that we remain acritical), as argued by PartBg6, and by acknowledging the potentialities of their role, *'quando eu preparo as minhas aulas e quando em cada aula estou com os meus alunos, eu posso subverter aquilo, posso ir bastante longe'* (when I prepare my lessons and when I am with my students in the classroom I can subvert that [what I am teaching] and go a long way), according to PartDg7.

It was evident from the study that these educators did have ideas about the political implications of their role since approximately two thirds of respondents endorsed the option put forward in the questionnaire that 'having a political attitude towards the teaching about a foreign culture means establishing the relationship between its power structure and forms of cultural production' (S2.10) (69.9%). This was reinforced by some participants in the group discussions who clearly viewed teaching as a political act, as PartAg7 remarked that *'qualquer acto educativo é um acto político'* (any educational act is a political act) and PartGg2 who acknowledged that *'a própria educação e o próprio sistema educativo têm uma política'* (education and the educational system are themselves determined by politics). However, this seems to remain mostly in the theoretical, rhetorical domain because teachers do not view themselves or their students as politically active in any other practical way than by voting, when they are old enough, or by expressing informed opinions. The same seems to be the case with regard to ethical and social issues since questionnaire respondents express a view of ethics that concerns more the recognition of equality of rights and 'being tolerant with difference' (25%) rather than 'taking action against injustice' (14.2%). Therefore, we may gather from this that very few understand ethics as moral responsibility for those who suffer injustices or as involving judgement about what is right and wrong (5.1%) although in the same question respondents do go as far as 'accepting difference as equally valid' (55.1%). This lack of an active commitment against social injustice is a major hindrance to the realisation of a critical pedagogy. This tendency was confirmed by the group discussions where only PartEg2 identified action as a purpose for the development of critical cultural awareness:

> *Para adquirirem cada vez mais direitos e combaterem quando se sentem discriminados ou sentem que outras pessoas são discriminadas, lutarem por elas e pelos direitos que todos temos.* (In order to gain more and more rights and to fight when they feel discriminated against or when they feel that others are discriminated against so that they fight for them and for the rights we all have.).

Although participants on the whole, as we shall see throughout the study, avoid describing their role as politically active, they seemed to be conscious of the equality of rights among those whom for some reason they consider as different. They also seemed supportive of 'focusing on values and interest in the various perspectives' when approaching 'a controversial topic' critically (S2.6) (58%).

Finally, I became aware throughout the study, especially during the focus-group discussions, that teachers' understanding of the concept *critical* seemed to originate from their individual readings of the national syllabus and from their practice as well as from rather intuitive premises that, in most cases, varied according to their personality and their own approach to the native culture as was expressed well by PartCg7:

> *Penso que são coisas muito vastas e, de algum modo também, muito ligadas à perspectiva pessoal de cada um dos professores, portanto, de que maneira é que cada um vive a sua própria cultura, a cultura do seu país, de que maneira é que a história do nosso país tem a ver directamente connnosco, se nós vivemos essa história de uma maneira crítica . . .* (I think this is a vast issue and, to some extent, very much linked to the individual perspective of each teacher, therefore, to the way each one lives her/his own culture, the culture of her/his country, to the way our country's history has to do directly with us, and whether we live it critically . . .).

It is, however, not surprising that teachers rely on their individual experiences and visions of both native and target cultures and of their teaching practices in the absence of focused and widespread teacher education and professional development programmes on this matter. Moreover, several contributors expressed the need for a more thorough explanation of the term and for some theoretical input that would enable them to apply it effectively to their practice. This does not mean that teachers are not supposed to make their own individual readings and construct their individual practice, although they should not rely merely on intuitive premises but also on formal reflection, research and discussion so that their professional identity corresponds to Freire and Giroux's descriptions of the teacher as a cultural worker and an intellectual.

Educating Critical Citizens

Most participants in this study supported a critical approach to foreign culture teaching/learning and were very aware that by doing so they were contributing to education for citizenship. On the whole, teachers seemed to have a common understanding that the world, in general, and Portugal, in particular, are changing fast. PartBg5 captured this sentiment well in her/his comment:

> Portugal tem mudado. As pessoas já não se deixam levar tão facilmente, portanto, intervêm mais na sociedade, o que é muitíssimo importante. As pessoas criticam já sem medo, especialmente de ser presas, o que era totalmente impossível há uns anos, quem viveu esses tempos sabe. A pessoa sente-se mais à-vontade, mais aberta, mais liberta, eu acho que Portugal tem mudado, e ainda espero que vá continuar a mudar mais . . . (Portugal has changed. People do not let themselves be convinced so easily anymore, therefore, they take a more and more active role in society, which is very important. People criticise now without fear, especially fear of being arrested, which was impossible some years ago, those who lived through that time know what it was like. We feel more at ease, more free, I think Portugal has changed and I hope that it will change even further . . .).

Like this teacher, other colleagues were aware of change at all levels and of the need for Portugal to keep up with the evolution of Europe and the world. It was also evident that teachers were conscious of the new demands of identity formation at different levels since 'hoje em dia é impossível a pessoa viver isolada, cada vez mais se é cidadão da Europa ou do mundo do que propriamente português' (it is impossible today to live in isolation, more and more we are citizens of Europe or of the world rather than specifically Portuguese) according to PartBg3. They are, therefore, open to the concept of intercultural education as proposed by Damen, Robinson, Kramsch and Byram.

The administrator interviewed focused particularly on the importance of learning foreign languages/cultures, especially English, for enabling one to fulfil her/his membership of European and global spheres. In her/his point of view, English teaching is at a crossroads because, on the one hand, it has become a language for global communication, *'Inglês para a comunicação global'*, and global knowledge *'língua de conhecimento global'* but, on the other hand, it is not a *lingua franca* in its exact terms because it is always conveying some kind of culture. Therefore, it can be used as a means of communication among native speakers, who may be culturally very different, between native speakers and non-native speakers as well as among non-native speakers and, because language always carries culture with it, each situation implies complexity and negotiation. If you are a non-native speaker, you have to *'exprimir a tua própria cultura noutra língua'* (express your own culture in another language) and, moreover, *'com os falantes nativos tem que ser negociado'* (it has to be negotiated with the native speakers) wherever they come from, Scotland, New Zealand or South Africa, because *'vocês falantes dessa língua têm que saber aceitar esta minha interpretação da vossa língua'* (you, native speakers, will have to accept my interpretation of your language). S/he thus gives evidence of a more elaborated notion of intercultural communication than that of the teachers participating in this study and one that coincides with Kramsch's and Byram's approaches. However, this interviewee expressed her concern about teacher development and about teachers' awareness of such complexities:

> ... o meu problema é saber se se consegue fazer isso numa sala de aula, se os professores conseguem fazer isso, se têm consciência disso e se são capazes, porque não é fácil. (... I wonder whether one can do this in a classroom, if teachers can do it, if they are aware of it and if they are able to do it, because it is not easy.).

Some of those involved in the discussion groups did mention new possibilities that they envisage for their students in terms of mobility or, at least, they acknowledged wider horizons available via the Internet or the media. However, most teachers were, on the one hand, very sceptical about the use their students made of these facilities. On the other hand, it was not evident either that teachers themselves had grasped all the complexities of cross-cultural communication. Teachers proved to have limited experience of the target cultures as they themselves recognised and neither had most of them been able to share cross-cultural experiences with their students in school exchanges. According to their accounts, their teaching practice does not entail sufficient experiential learning, in Byram's terms, and misses the potential of at least two of the Standards proposed by the Standards for Foreign Language Learning discussed in the previous chapter, namely 'Connections' and 'Communities', aspects that deal with the establishment of communication channels across disciplines and cultures at home and around the world.

Nevertheless, respondents to the questionnaire acknowledged cultural diversity by emphasising the importance of 'recognis[ing] the existence of various communication levels' (S3.2B) (61.3%), of 'see[ing] cultures in perspective to each other' (S3.1D) (50.7%), and of being 'prepared to deal with cultural divergence' (S3.3D) (94.7%) as well as by finding it less important 'that we reinforce our national identities' despite the fact that 'both European integration and global economy have caused greater mobility of citizens' (S3.1B) (34.7%).

Some concern was expressed in the group discussions about students' attitude towards other cultures, PartBg7 having said that 'a atitude crítica deles é sempre uma atitude destrutiva em relação aos outros e sobrevalorizando a nossa cultura' (their critical attitude is always destructive towards other cultures and overvalues our own). This confirmed the agreement of about four out of five questionnaire respondents with assertions such as the 'misunderstanding between individuals from different cultures often originates from the fact that each one draws conclusions from one's own cultural patterns' (S3.4A) (80%) and also 'from the fact that individuals have prejudices about the value of other cultures' (S3.4C) (84%). PartDg1 expressed her/his astonishment at students' reactions to difference:

> ... para não tentarem olhar de lado pessoas de outras raças ou religiões por serem dessa forma ... pensar num muçulmano e como é que as mulheres muçulmanas vivem e num hindú, são tipos esquisitos, não existem, não vale a pena falar, tolerância para com os homosexuais também não existe, são da lua 'p'aí' ... falar de tolerância para com as outras raças a mesma coisa, pretos voltem para África. Eu oiço isto nas minhas aulas, e acho que a crítica e o distanciamento devia estar presente em alunos que têm 15 ou 16 anos e que eu pensei que tinham umas mentalidades um bocadinho mais abertas. (... so that they don't look down on people from other races and religions because they are different ... think about a Muslim and how Muslim women live or about a Hindu, they are weird, they don't exist, they are not worth talking about, tolerance of homosexuals does not exist either, maybe they come from the moon, when speaking of tolerance towards other races it is the same thing, blacks should go back to Africa. This is what I hear in my classes and

I think that critical spirit and some detachment should be present in 15 or 16 year old students who I thought would be a bit more open-minded.).

The need for insisting on respect and tolerance towards the Other among students was also voiced by other groups. Since students still display many prejudices, respect and tolerance should be insisted upon, *'o respeito, a tolerância, que tem que ser muito, muito batida, porque os preconceitos continuam a existir'* (we have to insist on respect and tolerance very much because prejudices still exist), according to PartAg5.

It was generally noted that students were acritical and unselective consumers of television and cinema and that they did not enjoy reading. It was a common understanding that *'no tempo livre não lêem um livro, se vêem televisão é para ver determinadas coisas, são capazes de se sentar em frente ao computador a jogar'* (they do not read a single book in their spare time, if they watch television they only watch certain programmes, they might sit and play with the computer), according to PartCg5. However, a few teachers expressed the feeling that when stimulated their students had a good sense of critique, *'têm o espírito crítico bem apurado'* (they have a refined sense of critique), according to PartDg5. Furthermore, PartAg4 voiced the opinion that their sense of critique was even more refined than hers/his at the same age, *'eles têm um sentido crítico até mais apurado do que quando eu fiz o liceu'* (they have a sense of critique that is more refined than mine when I was at school). According to PartFg5 students' sense of critique is only dormant:

> . . . *a sociedade em que estamos integrados não desenvolve muito essa capacidade nos nossos alunos, eles estão um bocado adormecidos, então a escola, para mim, deve exercer essa função de fazê-los pensar sobre as coisas, serem críticos e prepará-los para o futuro.* (. . . our society does not develop that capacity very much, they are a little half asleep so, in my view, the school should fulfil that task and make them think about things, be critical and prepare them for the future.).

Likewise, most members of focus-groups revealed their sense of duty towards preparing their students to become critical democratic citizens. This tendency confirmed the questionnaire results showing a strong support for the fact that school must prepare future citizens 'for intercultural cooperation and solidarity' (S3.5B) (74.7%). The teachers were shown to be sensitive to Byram's appeal for relating foreign language/culture education to citizenship education, which is also an important postulate of Critical Pedagogy.

Furthermore, respondents put a great emphasis on preparing a democratic society by unequivocally acknowledging that since 'nowadays society is characterised by more intimacy between different ethnicities, social classes, ages and gender' therefore 'it is necessary to recognize that all are entitled to have a "voice" ' (S3.2C) (78.7%). This was confirmed by PartEg1 in these terms:

> *Num estado democrático, pretende-se que os cidadãos tenham uma contribuição válida e activa na vida do seu país . . . e as pessoas demitem-se do seu papel activo como cidadãos porque não tiveram uma educação que lhes permita ter opiniões sobre as coisas, investigar o que se está a passar que é para poder tomar uma decisão sobre isto, porque isto é a vida do meu país e a minha opinião terá influência nos resultados, ou a opinião de nós todos.* (In a democratic state, the citizens are supposed to make a valid and active contribution to the way of life in their country . . . and people give up an active role as citizens because they have not been educated to have opinions, to find out what is happening in order to make a decision about it, because this is about life in my country and my opinion will influence the results, or the opinions of all of us.).

Although this teacher underlines the importance of the contributions of all citizens in a democratic state and most of her/his colleagues, as stated previously, emphasised the need for respect and tolerance towards minorities and towards those culturally or racially different, the participants in this study failed, on the whole, to recognise the continuous power struggles which exist in pluralistic societies. Neither did members of focus-groups account for imbalances of power and for their implications in social relationships nor did more than one in five respondents to the questionnaire consider it important 'to recognize the strategies used by each group to get itself a position within the social network' (S3.2A) (20%). And only a third found it necessary that 'power and culture is regarded as a moral and ethical issue' (S3.3C) (32%). This is another aspect where these educators deny some of the most important tenets of a critical pedagogy. In general, in this study the focus was on one-to-one relationships or on the images one sector might have of another, but teachers did not venture deeper into the sources of such prejudices, that is, they did not take into account wider interactions in the macro-context, social and political networks that have an impact on the interaction between power and culture in the microcontext and how it determines those images and day-to-day relationships.

However, participants in both phases of the study – the questionnaire and the focus-group interviews – were almost unanimous in recognising the positive outcomes of the development of critical cultural awareness in foreign language/culture classes. Both the questionnaire and the focus-group discussions focused on two main sets of objectives, the first with regard to the individual and the second to the society in general.

Promotion of self-esteem and self-determination was identified by all those taking part in the study as a major reason for the development of critical cultural awareness. The syllabus author noted that *'o que nós também tentámos passar no programa é um professor que contribua para o desenvolvimento global do aluno'* (the idea we tried to convey in the syllabus is that of a teacher who contributes towards the student's global development) and, accordingly, teachers seemed well aware of their mission as educators, *'eu como professora considero-me não só ser professora de língua mas professora no aspecto abstracto'* (I see myself not only as a language teacher but also a teacher in a more general sense), as PartAg4 put it. This teacher's understanding of her/his role as an educator meets the descriptions of Freire and Giroux and, in particular, of Byram who has been firm in designating foreign language/culture *teaching and learning* as foreign language/culture *education*. Teachers agree with Byram when they view their goals as comprehending rather than preparing speakers who are able to produce written and verbal chunks of language that are semantically and syntactically accurate.

With this in mind, contributors clarified that, although they find it most important to question those unquestioned principles and prejudices their students often display and to dismantle fixed images and understandings, it is not their intention to weaken their self-esteem. PartAg7 described how she views her role:

> ... *temos de os inquietar, temos que abalar um bocado aquela estrutura feita de clichés, e de mete a moeda sai o produto, isso faz parte da nossa missão, mas isso não quer dizer que nós lhes vamos tirar aquela base de segurança e de establidade ... os valores, os princípios e a sua auto-estima. O que se pretende, de facto, é fazer daquela ideia única que eles têm, ou seja, um traço contínuo, partir aquilo, fazer traços descontínuos, é lançar a dúvida mas fazendo-os ganhar método e terem armas para conseguirem, de facto de várias pontas fazerem algo que é a sua verdade, que é uma tomada de consciência.*
> (... we have to unsettle them, we have to shake a little that structure made of clichés, the idea that you put in a coin and you get a product, this is part of our mission, but it doesn't mean that we disturb their basis for security and stability ... their values, principles and their self-esteem. What we actually intend is to turn that exclusive idea they have which is a straight, uninterrupted line into broken ones,

it is to spread doubt but also to get them to achieve a method and give them tools to enable them to actually manage, from several directions, build something that is their truth and that implies their awareness of it.).

Teachers are supposed to make students reflect critically upon the images and concepts that they had taken for granted in order to achieve, on the one hand, more flexible interpretations of the surrounding world and, on the other hand, better-grounded convictions. This will not only raise their self-esteem but will also improve their capacity for making decisions, a fact which was acknowledged by the respondents to the questionnaire, four out of five of whom agreed that 'the development of critical cultural awareness stimulates the capacity for making decisions' (S5.a4) (82.7%). Group members also focused on this aspect by emphasising its contribution to the formation of free citizens in democratic societies, as PartAg7 did:

> . . . *quanto mais críticos nós conseguirmos que o nosso aluno seja, mais livre ele será, e o ideal seria mesmo, quanto a mim, educar-se assim a população, só que levam-se gerações, ter-se-ia que começar pela primária e por aí fora.* (the more critical our student is the more free s/he is and, in my view, the ideal thing would be to educate the whole population that way but it would take generations, we would have to start with primary school and go on from there)

The importance of the development of critical cultural awareness for purposes other than those confined to the English language/culture class was constantly invoked in the course of discussions. The syllabus author recognised the immense role the discipline can play with respect to students' global development since *'estás a dar uma riqueza imensa àquela gente, tu estás a abrir os universos dos alunos'* (you are providing them with an immense wealth, you are broadening their horizons). PartFg3 also reported how students noted that *'é por nós nas aulas de Inglês discutirmos determinados assuntos é que somos obrigados a falar, a pensar e a analisar os nossos próprios'* (it is because we discuss certain matters in the English class that we are forced to speak and think about and analyse our own). Therefore, English classes are not viewed as confined spaces but as open ones where knowledge and experiences converge and diverge too, albeit on an individual manner.

Despite the extensive influence that the critical study of a foreign culture may have on the way students relate to their own culture, participants did not perceive it as threatening for their cultural identity, but quite the contrary. Neither did most teachers agree with the idea that the invasion of the culture industry from abroad was threatening except with regard to their students' lack of a critical attitude towards it. Their complaints seemed to be more directed at the type of information that is conveyed and at the way it is consumed rather than at the idea of being invaded by foreign cultures. They seemed more disappointed about a generalised acritical positioning towards imported fashions or images than about the danger of their students becoming culturally uprooted. There were, however, some voices raised in concern at the progressive erosion, even in rural and suburban areas, of the traditional referents that teachers once used as the basis for their teaching, as PartAg3 put it, *'são miúdos que vêm sem as referências que nós usávamos como ponto de partida'* (they are young people who do not have those references we used to take as starting points). PartBg6 was more incisive in describing her/his fears about the fact that Portuguese culture is losing ground in favour of American culture when a colleague suggested students' development would be enriched through the comparison/contrast with other cultures:

> ... *nesse enriquecimento em que nós constatamos as diferenças ... até que ponto nós ao assimilarmos essas diferenças elas não destruirão as nossas raízes ... é verdade que a cultura portuguesa está a ser dizimada pela cultura americana e que a nossa identidade se está a perder ... até que ponto o país que está a aprender, que está a assimilar, abandona o seu perfil julgando que os outros padrões são melhores.* (... in that enrichment process, as we verify differences ... to what extent are we destroying our roots as we assimilate differences ... it is a fact that Portuguese culture is being decimated by American culture and that our identity is being lost ... to what extent does the population who is learning, who is assimilating, give up its cultural profile thinking that the other patterns are better?).

This teacher fears cultural invasion and loss of identity, but most of her/his colleagues expressed the belief that contact with other cultures does not endanger one's cultural identity. Otherwise, in the same group, E replied that *'é através do estudo de outras culturas que a pessoa se apercebe da sua própria, das suas próprias raízes, da sua própria identidade'* (it is through the study of other cultures that we become aware of our own, our own roots and our own identity). Moreover, other contributors argued that if the approach to foreign cultures is critical, *'serve para enriquecer as experiências dos alunos'* (it does optimise the students' experiences in their own culture) (PartEg5). Furthermore, *'todos estes aspectos da abordagem crítica são uma forma de defender a sua própria identidade'* (all these aspects of a critical approach are a way to secure their own cultural identity) (PartEg2). The representativeness of this position was made unequivocal by respondents to the questionnaire who almost unanimously agreed that 'the development of critical cultural awareness strengthens cultural identity' (90.7%).

Moreover, it was generally recognised in the focus-groups that a critical approach to foreign cultures may also contribute to intellectual and social advocacy, which is in agreement with my final argument in the previous chapter for understanding foreign language/culture education as cultural politics. The questionnaire findings showed a strong recognition that 'teaching/learning about culture stimulates intellectual curiosity' (S4.a7) (90.7%), and that 'the formation of a critical attitude generates social intervention' (S4.a5) (85.3%). Focus-group members confirmed that they expected their students to pursue their search for knowledge about other cultures outside the classroom:

> ... *essa interacção que eles depois terão até fora da sala de aula com outra ou outras culturas que acaba por ser enriquecedora para eles próprios, tomar iniciativas de pesquisar mais sobre o assunto* . . . (. . . that interaction with another or several other cultures outside the classroom is enriching for them, they may take the initiative to do more research on the subject . . .).

Here, PartCg6 refers to an extension of her/his work outside the classroom on an individual level, that is, the student seeks knowledge through further research or interaction with her/his own enrichment in mind. Other colleagues also mentioned their expectations about their students' contributions to society. PartCg7 was particularly clear on this matter and remarked that *'nós temos de fazer com que os nossos alunos sejam pessoas preocupadas com a sociedade em que vivem'* (we must make our students concerned about the society they live in). However, it was not evident in focus-group discussions nor in questionnaire results that this was a generalised concern if understood as 'social intervention' in practical terms, as we shall see below.

Although respondents showed no doubt about the role the development of critical cultural awareness can play in identity formation and in citizenship education, participants were divided between the conviction that this was translated into individual (S4.a1) (46.7%) or into group expression (44%). About four fifths of questionnaire respondents agreed that if critical cultural awareness is promoted at school it will not make intercultural communication more difficult in a social setting.

Accordingly, they disagreed that 'critical attitudes can make dialogue difficult' (S4.b2) (81.3%), or that it 'can accentuate conflict in intercultural relationships' (S4.b7) (76.0%), although it does not break any cultural borders either, according to two thirds of them (S4.b1) (62.7%). In the focus-group this was overwhelmingly confirmed and it was a main issue throughout the discussions. Group 4, in particular, expanded on this aspect and participant B concluded:

> *Eu penso que é uma preocupação de todos mesmo ao ter essa perspectiva cultural e crítica também ajudar a formar alunos que aceitem a diferença, que reconheçam essas diferenças mas que consigam viver em paz, tranquilamente com elas. Há sempre essa preocupação do aluno enquanto pessoa, enquanto cidadão.* (I think it is a real concern among us all that while having that cultural and critical perspective we help to form students who accept difference, who recognise differences, but who can live peacefully with them. We always view the student as a person, as a citizen.).

Preparing students for identifying, recognising and accepting differences, *'saber identificar, reconhecer e aceitar as diferenças'* as the same teacher put it, was considered by all groups as a major objective in foreign language/culture classes. Moreover, this concern should be included in the ultimate goal of forming democratic citizens, an idea which questionnaire respondents endorsed enthusiastically by agreeing with the statement that 'developing critical cultural awareness encourages commitment to democratic citizenship' (88.0%). The strong recognition of this goal in foreign language/culture education among the participants reinforces my belief that they are open to a critical pedagogy although their practice, as inferred from their descriptions, lacks some other important aspects, as we shall see below. There was much evidence that students are supposed to *'aprender a tolerar, a respeitar, a ouvir os outros'* (learn how to tolerate, to respect and to listen to others), (PartCg5), and that 'others' were not only those who were alike as PartAg4 pointed out:

> *Eu acho que cada vez se torna mais premente que os alunos se habituem a viver com outros, não só a viver com aqueles que têm a mesma história, a mesma tradição, a mesma cultura, a mesma língua, etc., que é o país deles, mas sim viverem com outros.* (I think that it is more and more urgent that our students get used to living with others, not only with those who share the same history, the same tradition, the same culture, the same language, etc., which is their country, but to live with others too.).

Despite this teacher's view of a country as culturally homogeneous, her/his understanding of what 'living with others' entails included the different levels of identity and of citizenship that most participants believe Portuguese citizens have to come to terms with. PartDg6 furthered the definition of citizenship as *'cidadania, eu entendo como cidadão português, mas cidadão para além do seu país, portanto, do mundo'* (I understand citizenship as being not only a Portuguese citizen, but also a citizen beyond her/his own country, therefore, of the world). The questionnaire results corroborate the notion that most teachers think that 'teaching/learning critically about cultures helps the formation of a supranational identity (European/global)' (S4.b6) (70.7%), although a noticeable number remained without an opinion (22.7%). These educators, therefore, express a main concern to add a European and global dimension to foreign language/culture classes, thus meeting Byram's proposals.

It seems interesting to note that, in this section (S4) of the questionnaire, some statements which appeal to more purposeful social and political action do provoke more 'No opinion' answers than in any other section. These are statements such as the previous one, that calls for the 'formation of a supranational identity' and also those that gather data about possible social and political effects of the development of critical cultural awareness in that it 'could help reduce violence' (S4.b8) (No opinion – 30.7%) and in that it 'has the potential to turn teaching/learning into a political act' (S4.b9) (No opinion – 20%).

It was therefore evident that, although a substantial majority of questionnaire respondents agreed, as previously mentioned, that 'the formation of a critical attitude generates social intervention' (S4.a5) (85.3%), with regard to possible outcomes for the individual, when it comes to effects in society of developing critical cultural awareness among our youngsters, teachers show some disbelief in its practical effectiveness. Despite the fact that this is one of the most important challenges issued by Critical Pedagogy, these results confront us with the difficulty of putting this goal into practice in the school context today. On the one hand, most teachers rejected the possibility that the development of critical cultural awareness 'could threaten democratic order' (S4.b5) (81.3%). However, they do not believe in its political implications at all since only a small minority responded positively to the statement that it 'has the potential to turn teaching/learning into a political act' (S4.b9) (21.3%). These final statements are, therefore, consistent with the findings displayed above that the development of critical cultural awareness does not put 'obedience and authority into question' either (S4.b4) (77.3%). This is illustrative of the absence of social/political action in these educators' vision of the outcomes of their critical approach to foreign cultures and in their description of an intervening citizen.

Although the syllabus author pointed out that their primary goal had been the student's global development which she defined as *'pensar, sentir e actuar'* (thinking, feeling and acting), therefore including 'acting' as a main purpose, not only do the questionnaire results convey that teachers have limited this concept, but also that only very few participants in focus-group discussions grasped the concept to the full. This was an issue in one group discussion where PartFg4 displayed a notion of active citizenship without establishing limits, although s/he did not present any possibilities either, by saying that *'podemos através desta abordagem crítica das culturas levá-los a esta noção do ser cidadão e ser activo e ser participante'* (through this critical approach to cultures we can lead them to the notion of being a citizen, being active and participative). PartAg4 then added:

> Os meus alunos sabem que uma coisa que eu acho importante é o orgulho de ser português, e acho que é uma das coisas que é engraçado eles verem e saberem que a própria cultura deles tem vantagens, tem desvantagens, tem aspectos positivos e tem aspectos negativos e que eles saibam e até que se preparem para mais tarde poder alterar aquilo que possa não estar tão bem . . . porque, no fim de contas, se estamos a preparar futuros cidadãos . . . (My students know that I find it important to be proud of being Portuguese and it is interesting for them to know that their own culture has advantages and disadvantages, positive and negative aspects, and that they are prepared to later change what is not so good . . . because in the end we are preparing future citizens . . .).

This notion of preparing citizens for the future, which was common in most contributors, seems to be responsible for the postponing of the exercise of an active citizenship, in social/political terms, that could change the nature of a critical approach to culture. Moreover, most teachers understood the concept of active citizenship as having mainly rhetorical implications. This was, to some extent, the case made by PartEg5 who pointed out that, *'vai ajudá-los a ser cidadãos muito melhores e cidadãos muito mais interventivos se eles desenvolverem esse espírito crítico e se souberem argumentar'* (if students develop a critical mind and know how to make arguments, this will help them to be better and more intervening citizens).

With Kramsch's model, discussed in the previous chapter, teachers, therefore, seem to believe that by developing critical cultural awareness among their students they will progressively change as individuals and, as a consequence, society will change too, although as part of a long-term process. In their view their students' intervention in society is not only postponed but it is also likely to be restricted to 'having a voice' but only if they are well informed and capable of making good arguments. Active citizenship in terms other than these will be dependent on later positions of power in society.

Active citizenship was also understood by most educators as being limited to the capacity of using institutional mechanisms for democratic participation in political decisions mostly in occasional established events such as elections. When asked whether s/he expected students to intervene in society and in politics, PartDg2 replied that *'se tiverem capacidades, porque não?'* (if they have the capacity, why not?) while, in the same group, participant A clarified that she was thinking about the right to vote and added that *'realmente a pessoa tem os seus direitos como cidadão e tem que os fazer valer nos momentos certos'* (actually, the individual has her/his own rights as a citizen and must claim them at the right moments). Keeping the social and political context of this study described in the beginning of this chapter in mind, we may conclude that, perhaps due to a long period of dictatorship, to an incipient democracy and to particular cultural features, this society tends to deal with issues of citizenship rather utopically and theoretically and it is not yet familiar with the rigorous application of these notions in everyday (school) life. Likewise, the lack of regular school exchanges with other European countries may be justified by the historical (and geographical) distance from central Europe together with traditional economic deprivation.

Conclusion

The participants in this study were extremely open to the idea of including cultural content in their language classes as advocated by the national syllabus and by the models presented in the previous chapter, although they did not refer to these or to any other theoretical model. Despite the fact that the national syllabus to which they refer is situated within the European context, it is more ambitious about the introduction of cultural content in the foreign language curriculum and a critical interpretation to it than that required by the Common European Framework. Nevertheless, it lacks the pragmatic guidelines about the cultural component that can be found in the Standards for Foreign Language Learning (USA) mainly with regard to three of the five Cs, namely Communication (the Communicative Modes), Connections and Communities.

The teachers who participated in this project also put more emphasis on the inclusion of cultural content and on a critical approach to it rather than considering them merely as 'general competences', as the Common

European Framework does. However, their perception of the development of Intercultural Competence among their students was based mainly on comparative/contrastive activities and on rhetorical skills. They did not seem to have had any contact with the document or the application of the Standards for Foreign Language Learning (USA). Neither did these teachers seem to be aware of models for professional training such as those designed by Brislin, Bochner and Lonner, by Bennett, by Seelye or any other. Their ideas about the teaching of foreign languages and cultures were closer to those of Damen, Robinson, Kramsch and, to some extent, Byram. They share with all these models the importance granted to the cultural component, as mentioned previously, and to the relationship established between the learner's native and the target cultures. These teachers also laid great emphasis on the subjective involvement of the learner with the target cultures and on her/his empathy with the people who belong to them, a practice recommended by Robinson. The comparative/contrastive perspective is also common to both Robinson's model and their teaching practices.

Like Kramsch and Byram, the Portuguese teachers rely strongly on dialogic and hermeneutic pedagogies. In agreement with Kramsch's model they are critically aware of the socio-cultural context of the classroom and pay close attention to the reception and production of meaning there. In other words, they take a microcontextual, subjective/intersubjective and intercultural approach to both native and target cultures, within the classroom, which is based on dialogue and interpretation. Along with Byram, they put considerable emphasis on the development of critical cultural awareness focused on native and target cultures, based on reflective (subjective) and analytical (objective) cognitive processes while also highlighting on evaluation and judgement to a significant extent. Their teaching practices, according to their descriptions, do aim at bringing the unconcious cultural paradigms to consciousness, in accordance with Byram's suggestion. They also accentuate the relevance of developing education for democratic citizenship within the European dimension, and globally as well, through the clarification of their students' identifications and identities. Therefore, they view themselves as cultural mediators, in agreement with Byram's model. However, they fall behind Byram's theory with respect to fully applying the idea that foreign language/culture education is political education, above all, due to a lack of experiential learning (by their students and themselves) and, consequently, of the establishment of intercultural relations, that, eventually, prevent the full achievement in practice of the principles advocated by this model.

It is also evident that Pennycook's and Canagarajah's perspectives have not yet been 'appropriated' by most of the participants in this study. Their non-Eurocentric, postcolonial perspective is still modest and they do not grasp fully the potential of their own peripheral standpoint in Europe and in the world. Contrary to a critical pedagogy of foreign cultures, the view they take of the English-speaking cultures is predominantly Eurocentric and they do not take a sufficiently critical look at all the implications of English as a global language. The concepts they put forward to define critical cultural awareness are not manifestly theorised or problematised and they do not reveal awareness of the deeper complexities of intercultural communication nor do they scrutinise the imbalances of power among different cultural groups or the interaction between macro- and microcontexts. Above all, this study indicates that most participants do not include critical agency in their understanding of a critical pedagogy. In other words, they do not engage into a committed transformation of their social realities, nor do they expect their students to do so in the present. Therefore, they do not fulfil their roles as transformative intellectuals nor can their pedagogy be characterised as cultural politics, in all the terms enunciated by Critical Pedagogy.

As far as a critical pedagogy of foreign cultures is concerned, in general, those who took part in this study revealed that they were positively receptive and sensitive to a large number of the tenets enunciated in the previous chapter. They call for a critical dimension to be implemented in the study of foreign cultures at all levels of schooling, they emphasise the emotional aspects of critical cultural awareness as much as the cognitive ones and they were able to identify and expand on the teaching activities they find most productive within a critical pedagogy. They theorised about their practices, more specifically about the 'operations' they identified as fundamental for a critical pedagogy of foreign languages and cultures. Furthermore, these teachers did acknowledge the need to change discriminatory and xenophobic attitudes towards cultural difference and divergence and they made a strong link between foreign language/culture education and citizenship education.

Notes

1. Santos explains the difference between the cultural concept of the American frontier and the way he uses this notion of border with regard to Portuguese identity. It is a 'border identity' not because beyond it there is empty land to be conquered but because it stands on the border, which is no man's land, and beyond it there is always something to be absorbed. In this case, he says, the Portuguese culture is open to 'immense possibilities of cultural

identification and creation' (Santos, 1994: 134, translation mine). Furthermore, he continues, the Portuguese regional and transnational cultural identities have always been stronger than the national one and this has led us to a 'universalism without universe which is made of the infinite multiplication of localisms' (p. 134, translation mine).
2. During the eighteenth century, in the northeast of Brasil, the work done by Portuguese emigrants was actually cheaper than that done by slaves (Santos, 1994: 133) and in Moçambique, up until the 1960s, most of the companies the Portuguese worked for were owned by the British.
3. Since the complete version of the questionnaire was very long, it was decided that the version to be sent to the schools should be divided into Questionnaires A and B. The questionnaires answered by the teachers were in Portuguese while for the purpose of this book the English translation will be used (Appendix 1). In the Portuguese version, Sections 1, 2 and 7 are common to both Questionnaires A and B, Sections 3 and 4 are included only in Questionnaire A (Appendix 2) while Sections 5 and 6 are part of Questionnaire B only (Appendix 3). Only Sections 1, 2, 3 and 4 are analysed in this book. A total number of 308 questionnaires, divided into Questionnaire A (151) and Questionnaire B (157), were sent out. Despite the length and the complexity of the questionnaires a total number of 176 were returned (57%), 75 for Questionnaire A (49.6%) and 101 for Questionnaire B (64.3%). Focus-group discussions were carried out in seven of the schools which had collaborated with the first phase of the research design by filling out and returning the questionnaires. The geographic and demographic situation of the schools was another criterion of selection of the schools where focus-group discussions took place. The whole process was based on voluntary collaboration.
4. This study was carried out in mainland Portugal, not including the autonomous regions of Madeira and Azores.
5. The statistical results mentioned here were reached through various functions of SPSS for Windows, such as Frequencies, Descriptive Statistics, Correlations, and Factor Analysis. The focus-group interviews were analysed 'vertically', within each group, and 'horizontally' across groups.
6. (S1.1) means Section 1, Question 1 of the English version of the questionnaire (Appendix 1). All subsequent quotations from the questionnaire will follow the same pattern. Questionnaires handed out to teachers were in Portuguese while this report on data analysis will use the translated version in English. The Portuguese version is available in Appendices 2 and 3.
7. The degree of agreement was expressed here, as in most cases in this questionnaire, through a Likert scale. However, the complexity of analysis of such rated scales requires that we keep in mind the discrepancies between the arithmetic value and the real meaning of the rating since it depends on the relation between the response and the weakness/strongness of the attitude statement put forward in the questionnaire (Foddy, 1993: 168; Hatch & Lazaraton, 1991: 57). Therefore, for the purpose of this report, ratings are shown simply according to two categories, agreement and disagreement. In addition, Appendix 4 displays all the questionnaire results, with the respective gradations on a Likert scale when this is the case.

Chapter 5
Preparing Critical Citizens and Educators for an Intercultural World

A *critical* approach to both native and foreign cultures, that is, the development of critical cultural awareness, should be, for both learners and teachers as learners, a continuum from secondary school into undergraduate and postgraduate studies. Likewise, it should remain a *perspective* to be adopted at lower levels of foreign language/culture education and by all citizens in general. However, special attention should be paid to the new demands for teacher development because this is understood as a necessary first step for the expansion of such capabilities among the population. Hargreaves is clear on this matter:

> It is plain that if teachers do not acquire and display this capacity to redefine their skills for the task of teaching, and if they do not model in their own conduct the very qualities – flexibility, networking, creativity – that are now key outcomes for students, then the challenge of schooling in the next millennium will not be met. (Hargreaves, 1999: 123)

It is, therefore, generally agreed that academic knowledge and training must prepare prospective and practising teachers for the challenges they are meeting or will meet in the short-term future. Not only have teachers to redefine their skills and remodel their qualities, but they also have to rearrange their knowledge into a new perspective. There is a pressing need for further and reformed academic preparation and professional development for prospective and practising teachers applied to this specific field, the education of *critical* intercultural speakers. The general acknowledgement of this need is a consequence of the challenges teachers/learners of foreign languages/cultures face today while attempting to complete their tasks. Furthermore, there are common new ventures teachers/learners of foreign cultures from all over the world have to embark on as learners or as teachers or as both, despite their different contexts.

A Multiple-Perspective Approach

First, we must consider that teaching/learning about foreign languages/cultures integrates broader educational frameworks such as Human Rights Education and Education for Democratic Citizenship. However, these should not be understood as incidental references for foreign language/culture education, least of all, as vague background information, as fashionable causes, or as short-lived bursts of sympathy at some tragedy. They should form an influential and consistent contribution to foreign language/culture education and should be included as major components in the corresponding teachers' development. Osler and Starkey help clarify the reason why the need to include Human Rights Education and Education for Democratic Citizenship in teacher development is pressing:

> Teachers are responsible for transmitting values. They need to be in a position to help their students be supportive of pluralist democracy and human rights, enjoy cultural diversity and be conscious of their responsibilities to the planet and to all those who live on it. This implies that they should themselves share these values. (Osler & Starkey, 1996: 105)

Teachers of foreign language/culture themselves need to be educated about human rights and democratic citizenship because, as described previously, they work with issues of identity, difference, equality, equivalence, and equity, and are responsible for the preparation of democratic global citizens/intercultural speakers.

Foreign language/culture education and corresponding teacher development programmes should, therefore, consider Human Rights Education and Education for Democratic Citizenship as permanent references (Byram & Guilherme, 2000). Although participants in the study described in Chapter 4 put great emphasis on these aspects, they did not convey a clear idea of their role in foreign language/culture education rather limiting this relationship to the contribution the latter can have for citizenship education in general. However, Education for Democratic Citizenship, within a broader framework of Human Rights, reinforces the political nature of foreign language/culture education and gives it the purpose that unifies the ideas which otherwise seem random references

(Carter & Osler, 2000). This framework is endorsed, in the first place, by Critical Pedagogy.

More specifically, Human Rights provide foreign language/culture education with culture-universals, basic principles, and values that traverse cultures. However, these should not remain as abstract notions and the study of documents produced by international organisations is fundamental (Osler & Starkey, 1996). Education for Citizenship, by acknowledging local, national, and global levels, also deals with the relationship between culture-universals and culture-specifics which is fundamental for the development of intercultural competence (Brislin & Yoshida, 1994; Guilherme, 2000a). Therefore, the study of culture-universals and culture-specifics as well as the discussion about the complexities of the interaction between both must take place in foreign language/culture education (Keesing, 1994). In addition, the development of critical cultural awareness, if illuminated by diverging

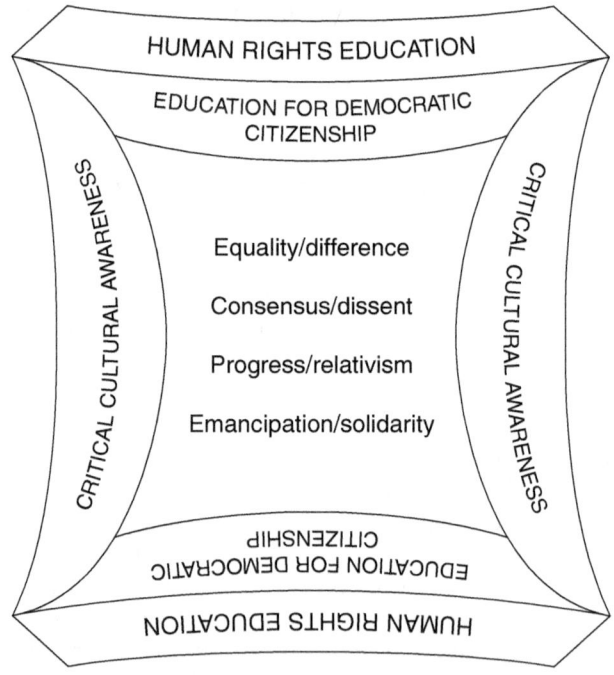

Figure 5.1 A general multiple-perspective framework for foreign culture education

philosophical perspectives as suggested by the present study, may generate a dialogic negotiation between opposing worldviews. According to the framework adopted here, equal rights should be confronted with the right to difference, the search for consensus with the inevitability of dissent, the striving after progress as a linear continuum with the potentialities of relativism that works within networks of power, and the vigour of individual emancipation with the motivating force of solidarity. This general framework for a critical approach to foreign cultures may be visualised in the Figure 5.1.

As displayed in the figure, Human Rights Education, Education for Democratic Citizenship, and, therefore, the development of critical cultural awareness should refer to philosophical worldviews that are, to some extent, contradictory. The negotiation between antithetical modes such as equality/difference, consensus/dissent, progress/relativism, emancipation/solidarity makes for a multiple perspective that enriches the comprehension of cultural complexities and allows for some flexibility in understanding intra- and intercultural interactions.

An Interdisciplinary Approach

As far as the study of foreign cultures is concerned, teachers should be mindful of its interdisciplinary nature by using different disciplinary and subdisciplinary areas, which are combined and developed according to the focus one wants to give to a particular object of study. However, Critical Pedagogy, Cultural Studies, and Intercultural Communication are viewed here as the main interdisciplinary areas upon which foreign language/culture education should rely. They should themselves be included in the subjects that deal with the teaching/learning about foreign languages/cultures both at secondary school level and in higher education and deserve special focus in teacher education and development programmes. These three main interdisciplinary areas overlap and affect each other in several aspects. This means that the borders between them are open and the development of critical cultural awareness results from their intrinsic interaction as displayed in Figure 5.2.

The figure includes main disciplinary categories, such as Sociology, Linguistics, etc., and also subcategories, all of which are fields of study that are especially relevant for each of the three interdisciplinary areas identified – Critical Pedagogy, Cultural Studies, and Intercultural Communication – and most commonly used for research in cultural studies. The disciplines or fields of study are not exclusive to one particular area since the three areas themselves interact.

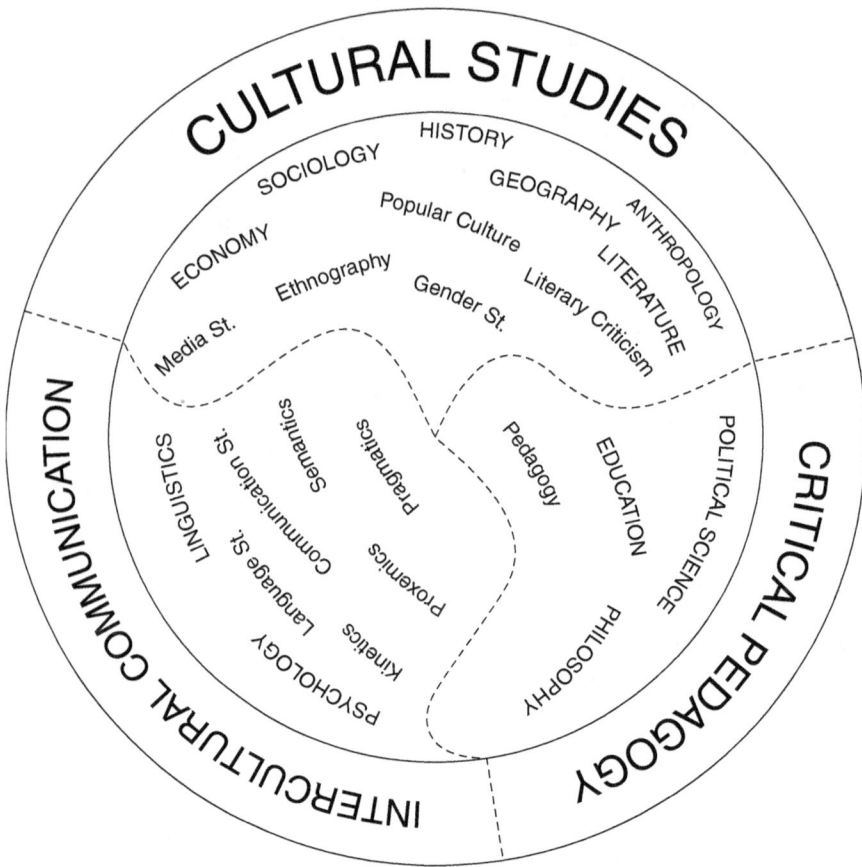

Figure 5.2 An interdisciplinary model for teaching/learning foreign cultures

However, each area – Critical Pedagogy, Cultural Studies, and Intercultural Communication – makes particular contributions, within the scope of either culture-general or culture-specific knowledge, to the development of critical cultural awareness and should receive special attention when teaching foreign languages/cultures and, therefore, in teacher development programmes. This diagram establishes the main interdisciplinary areas within which foreign language/culture education should operate and, on the other hand, it includes several options for these areas to interact and offers a variety of fields of knowledge from which to choose and to explore.

Cultural Studies

Cultural Studies (CS) is a diversified movement that has expanded all over the world, with a special boom in the United States where it has acquired specific features, although it has, in general, maintained its distinct essence. Its consistent features are, in sum, an inter-, anti- or post-disciplinary character, the abolition of the division between high and popular culture within the academy, and particular methods of inquiry and analysis. As far as the study of foreign cultures is concerned, this movement has challenged both its content and form due precisely to the above-mentioned aspects.

CS, which can be defined as 'an intellectual and political tradition, in its relations to the academic disciplines, in terms of theoretical paradigms, or by its characteristic objects of study' (Johnson, 1986/87: 41–2), cannot be ignored by undergraduate and postgraduate studies of foreign cultures. Traditional culture disciplines, which focus either on literature or on history, that do not attend to the fundamental calls of CS do not respond to the current needs of prospective and practising teachers. Despite the fact that CS cannot be considered as a methodology either due to 'its openness and theoretical versatility, its reflexive even self-conscious mood, and especially, the importance of critique' (Johnson, 1986/1987: 38), it has developed particular forms of cultural inquiry and representation such as 'ethnographic cultural description' and 'the discursive construction of situations and subjects' deriving from sociology and literary criticism respectively (Johnson, 1986/87: 50). These forms of cultural inquiry, representation, and analysis are indispensable tools in the preparation and development of foreign culture teachers, especially because of their versatile, reflective, and critical character. CS has also addressed issues of socio-political relevance such as identity, power, multiculturalism, race, and gender issues. It has also engaged in intellectually elaborate description and critique of media-cultures and everyday life topics. At the same time, it pays attention to the relationship of these studies to micro- and macrocontexts. Therefore, it works with a range of issues that is of great importance for teachers whose task is to develop critical cultural awareness and intercultural communicative competence among their students.

Critical educators of foreign languages/cultures can no longer deal with their subject matter without being familiar with interdisciplinary theoretical insights/debates about some of the above-mentioned issues and used to cultural inquiry and analysis. Giroux summarises this point:

> This is not a matter of abandoning high culture, or simply substituting it for popular culture. It is rather, an attempt to refigure the boundaries of what constitutes culture and really useful knowledge in order to study it in new and critical ways. (Giroux, 1996: 50)

Hence, defining the cultural content of the curriculum is not simply a matter of choice between either/or. It deserves careful thought because it involves many complex aspects and these should also be given attention in teacher development programmes. There has been much discussion about which disciplines should be included in the study of foreign cultures in higher education – history, political study, sociology, economics – (Kerl, 1993; Révauger, 1993). Nevertheless, several authors have preferred not to 'propose a defined body of knowledge which teachers teach and learners learn ... but rather to ensure that learners have the means of acquiring knowledge and understanding independently (*savoir-apprendre*)' (Byram, 1997e: 109). These are academic debates in which prospective and practising teachers should be involved and which should also be kept in mind when teaching foreign cultures both at secondary school and undergraduate levels.

Furthermore, there are other controversial aspects to be taken into consideration in secondary and higher education courses on foreign cultures. For example, the establishment of a 'minimal knowledge' which is considered 'representative' of a certain culture, usually a legacy of factual data that passes from generation to generation, should 'raise questions of whose values are being promoted' (Brumfit, 1997: 47). If unquestioned, such knowledge may end up 'being no more than intellectual tourism, or high-grade stereotyping' (p. 43).

In fact, the discussion about the study of British cultures by Byram and Brumfit, among others, is useful here (Bassnett, 1997). These authors raise important questions about teaching/learning about British cultures which are particularly relevant in this context as well as for teaching/learning about other cultures and for the preparation/improvement of foreign language/culture teachers. Brumfit calls our attention to the fact that 'British Studies are being promoted when the concept of "Britishness" is much disputed' (Brumfit, 1997: 42). Precisely because the concept of 'Britishness' is being questioned, as happens with most national/regional/group identities, teachers/students must not place the concept of 'representativeness' beyond doubt either. Consequently, Brumfit continues by prompting teachers to also notice 'the epistemologies that learners take for granted (knowledge as authoritative fact *versus* knowledge as best available hypothesis *versus* knowledge as vested interest of the powerful, to stereotype some contemporary positions)' (Brumfit, 1997: 50).

Finally, this author differentiates between the 'outsider' and the 'insider' perspective into British cultures, since the first looks at them as 'in some sense a "given" culture which needs describing' while the latter is 'engaged in the sometimes painful process of creating Britain through struggle' (Brumfit, 1997: 48). Kramsch adds a third element which is 'the divergence between the myths that the target culture likes to disseminate about itself through its public documents, and its reality as lived through its individual citizens' (Kramsch, 1993b: 356).[1] And Byram complicates the process even further by adding the 'mother culture' element:

> When Cultural Studies presents learners with interpretations of reality, and options for social action, that are different or even contradictory to those which learners take for granted as given and natural, then the Cultural Studies teacher should be aware of the nature of the challenge to learners' understanding of their culture and identity. (Byram, 1997a: 62)

Thus, teaching/learning critically about a foreign culture implies taking a critical look at one's native culture too. Byram therefore calls for a close collaboration between CS and Foreign Language Teaching. As a matter of fact, foreign language/culture teaching has lacked both the interdisciplinary frame of reference on cultural matters and the experience of cultural inquiry and analysis that could have deepened its critical overview but which has remained rather superficial. CS, on the other hand, should, according to Byram, widen its focus and include an intercultural perspective. Furthermore, the study of language and the study of culture are interconnected and complementary. With this in mind, teacher education should therefore consolidate this link in foreign language and culture education:

> A form of Cultural Studies which is based on a theoretically sustained integration of linguistic learning and critical cultural analysis and which includes a comparative, reflexive dimension in its methodology would be a substantial contributory discipline to the education of professional linguists. It would provide them with an in-depth understanding of the framework within which cross-cultural communication takes place, and, just as importantly, the means to extend the framework in new communication. (Byram, 1997a: 63)

The 'comparative, reflexive dimension' that Byram recommends as well as the 'integration of linguistic learning and critical cultural analysis' suggest an integrated approach whereby the growth of linguistic and cultural knowledge stimulate each other, where the 'intercultural speaker' interacts with several cultural perspectives, and where both an analytical and experiential perspective intertwine. These needs were, to some extent, also noted by participants in the study described in the previous chapter. Therefore, projects including 'home ethnography' previous to 'residence abroad' and 'ethnographic fieldwork', like those implemented in the United Kingdom, are useful models for such an integrated approach (Roberts et al., 2001). Material exchange projects carried out by students at lower levels may also provide a good example of cultural studies from a dialogical and critical perspective (Morgan & Cain, 2000). In sum, the preparation of critical intercultural mediators/educators and ultimately critical intercultural citizens requires close collaboration between foreign language/culture education and CS, from secondary school to undergraduate and postgraduate levels.

Intercultural Communication

The concept of Intercultural Communication (IC) supposedly implies both linguistic and cultural knowledge of a foreign language/culture in the form of Intercultural Communicative Competence (Byram, 1997b), that is, the ability to communicate and interact with people from different linguistic/cultural backgrounds. Interacting effectively across cultures, as I have argued elsewhere, means accomplishing negotiation between people based on both culture-specific and culture-general features that is on the whole respectful of and favourable to each and teachers must therefore acknowledge the interactive nature of teaching/learning about culture (Guilherme, 2000a). Nevertheless, the review of the literature and the analysis of data lead me to conclude that intercultural training in general has often been invisible in foreign language/culture classes at all levels and also in teacher development programmes. On the other hand, professional courses providing intercultural training often underestimate linguistic knowledge.

There is, however, a growing interest in the inclusion of intercultural communication courses in higher education mainly within the teaching/ learning of a foreign language for specific purposes, e.g. in Business or Management Studies, and in some programmes aimed particularly at prospective teachers of foreign languages/cultures. Consequently, surveys have been carried out on the 'course goals and objectives' and 'curriculum design' of 'Intercultural Communication Courses' (Fantini & Smith, 1997), on 'intercultural communication and related courses in TESOL Master's programs' (Nelson, 1998), and on the 'effects of alternative instructional approaches on cross-cultural training outcomes' (Gannon & Poon, 1997). These surveys have come to the conclusion that these programmes are still scarce, mostly for lack of trained staff (Nelson, 1998), but are increasing and gaining recognition through becoming 'credit-bearing courses' and being 'required in academic programmes offering degrees in this or related areas, ranging from undergraduate to postgraduate and doctoral levels' (Fantini & Smith, 1997: 125–6).

Most of the courses surveyed in Fantini and Smith's study, taught at universities from 11 countries, tend to 'use combinations of lecture, discussion, and experiential activities' (Fantini & Smith, 1997: 139). From the reported goals, objectives, content and implementation, we may gather that these are wide in scope, applying descriptive, prescriptive and exploratory strategies, including both linguistic and cultural knowledge – culture-general as well as culture-specific – and supplementary skills such as carrying out research. Additionally, Gannon and Poon argue that 'both didactic and experiential approaches can be useful for promoting cultural awareness', each with different relevant aspects. They concluded that 'participants in the experiential training group ... had more favorable reactions towards the training' whereas 'participants in the integrative and video training [didactic] group perceived themselves to be more able to interact with people from different cultural backgrounds' (Gannon & Poon, 1997: 441–2).[2] It follows on from this that, despite prompting different cognitive, affective and behavioural outcomes, both university-based and experiential learning are important and complementary.

In sum, the IC element at all levels of foreign language/culture education and in teacher development programmes, just like the Critical Pedagogy and Culture Studies elements, should always consist of a praxis – theory and practice – performed in an interpretative, reflective, exploratory and pragmatic mood in order to generate critical cultural awareness. On the one hand, theoretical scrutiny and speculation adds depth and credibility to the process, and on the other, without the pragmatic fulfilment Critical Pedagogy risks being merely rhetorical, Cultural Studies simply descriptive and Intercultural Communication misleadingly prescriptive.

In fact, there is an increase in academic research about intercultural communication applied to professional environments, business in particular (Geoffrois, 2001; Heydenfelt, 2000; Van Oudenhoven, 2001). However, it emerges from this study – both from the review of the literature and from the empirical data – that the *Intercultural* Communication element is not really present in foreign language/culture courses or in respective teacher education programmes yet. Nor is formal and substantial experiential learning required for prospective and practising teachers of foreign language/cultures at least in some countries such as Portugal, as confirmed by the empirical study described earlier, and Denmark (Byram & Risager, 1999). Besides, even when experiential learning is 'an obligatory element of virtually all modern languages degree programmes', such as in Great Britain, 'it is assumed that such learning [the cultural learning element] will take place by osmosis' (Roberts, 1993: 11). In general, students/teachers are not offered consistent preparation or follow-up to their experiential learning. There is, however, a growing number of exceptions, such as the Ealing ethnography research project by students of modern languages. These were introduced to ethnographic methods before carrying out an ethnographic study while abroad, they wrote up and discussed the project after returning and, finally, their projects were integrated into the curriculum and assessed as part of their final degree grade (Roberts *et al.*, 2001). Unfortunately most ERASMUS students and most practising teachers who are awarded LINGUA grants for short stays abroad, within the European Union, lack this kind of preparation. This is the reason why most teachers do not dare to develop intercultural competence among their students since they do not receive formal intercultural training themselves. In addition, as far as courses abroad intended for foreign language/culture teachers are concerned, in general there is little information/evaluation about courses available, their goals/objectives, contents, implementation, let alone about their intercultural communication purposes. This makes a description by Cain and Zarate of diverse types of stay- or visit-abroad aimed at developing openness to otherness particularly useful (Cain & Zarate, 1996).

In conclusion, an integrated approach – both intellectual and experiential – to IC should be included in both teacher development programmes and, consequently, in foreign language/culture courses and should aim at preparing effective intercultural communicators. This does not mean that teachers or students of foreign languages/cultures should be acculturated into the target culture, instead they should develop a critical spirit towards foreign culture teaching/learning, target and native cultures, intercultural interaction and exchange itself. A critical approach to intercultural communication is a major contribution to this field of research as well as to foreign language/culture education (Davis *et al.*, 2000). Moreover, foreign language/culture teachers can play an important role in this area, complementary to that of experts in intercultural management and psychosociologists working with expatriates or frequent-flyers, since, as Geoffrois argues, 'we have linguistic knowledge, we are knowledgeable about *civilisation*, about literature and culture, and these are privileged tools for cultural anthropology, and we are also aware of the importance of the sociocultural dimension in communication' (Geoffrois, 2001: 375, translation mine).

Critical Pedagogy

Critical Pedagogy (CP), as described previously, is not a method for teaching/learning culture or a methodology, if we consider the latter to be a particular combination of methods. As far as foreign language/culture education is concerned, CP provides principles that enable teachers to create a different approach that stems from a new perspective into (inter)cultural knowledge, its relation to life, and how it is positioned towards and exchanged by teachers and students of foreign languages/cultures (Hones, 1999). Therefore, CP is intrinsically related to culture, power, and communication.

As discussed previously, critical educators are: (a) reflective practitioners; (b) dialogue facilitators; and (c) 'transformative intellectuals', in Giroux's terminology, who 'treat students as critical agents, question how knowledge is produced and distributed, utilize dialogue, and make knowledge meaningful, critical, and ultimately emancipatory' (Giroux, 1988: 175). Critical knowledge is knowledge that is appropriated and made meaningful by teachers and learners alike. A critical pedagogy adopts both a questioning and a proactive stance by combining description, reflection, and interpretation with exploration, creation, and intervention.

Therefore, the main elements identified by CP, namely reflection, dialogue, action, difference, dissent, empowerment, and hope, as discussed in Chapter 1, are also relevant strategies to be used in foreign language/culture education and, initially, in professional development programmes (Silva, 1993). Teacher development programmes designed to prepare prospective and practising teachers for critical intercultural competence also need to make room for student/teachers to reflect on and discuss their (inter)cultural knowledge (what they know, how they know, and what they need to know), their (inter)cultural experiences (and the possibilities of having them), and their practices (as teachers, as learners, and as human beings and democratic citizens). Teacher trainer B argued:[3]

> ... the more time I allow for thinking/reflecting (even when it takes us from the planned curriculum), the more we learn, and the more they learn, the greater the chance that students will take meaningful action in their own context.

The need for opportunities for reflection and discussion are fundamental in the preparation or development of critical educators. The importance of self-awareness and dialogue was also mentioned by teacher trainer F:

> I use the concept of dialogue (Freire, 1970) to introduce the two most important assignments in the class. One is the Personal Narrative assignment, in which the student gets to begin an internal dialogue with the self in order to examine her own 'isms'. The other one is a dialogue with the family, in which the student creates a Family Tree going back to the family's arrival to this nation ... I make sure to have them look for 'generative themes' and explain how Freire incorporated dialogue and themes in his work.

These seem to be useful activities that help theorise, problematise, and clarify concepts and issues that intertwine human rights, democratic citizenship and intercultural competence. Furthermore, these activities also help the teacher to reflect upon her/his personal stories and assume her/his own identity and, therefore, to better define her/his role in the teaching/learning process both of her/his students and her/his own. The value of dialogue and co-operative work was also emphasised by teacher trainer C:

> ... students share their experiences and creative means of developing new ways of thinking about curriculum and pedagogy ... They are not accustomed to learn through interaction with other students, challenging the content and ideas of some of the texts that are being used in the public schools ... Students work in cooperative groups and create their own solutions. We have a lot of discussion in a variety of topics ... They learn to question their own roles and ways of thinking ... Empowering prospective teachers allows them to think differently about themselves and their abilities and to realize that they can make a difference in their lives as well as in the lives of their students.

These are some examples that illustrate how CP can be implemented among prospective and practising teachers as a 'pedagogy of reflection', of 'dialogue', of 'empowerment', of 'action', and of 'hope'. In addition, CP is a 'border pedagogy' and a 'pedagogy of dissent'. Therefore, teacher development programmes should urge teachers to locate different cultural codes, especially those which have been voiceless, to acknowledge contradictions and oppositions, to explore how they articulate with the micro- and macrocontexts they integrate, to identify the deep structures of traditions.

Furthermore, these changes should not merely consist of adding new topics to the curriculum, but of taking a new perspective towards knowledge and life. Teacher trainer D confirmed that one of the positive outcomes of including a CP dimension to her/his teacher training courses had been that her student/teachers had become better prepared 'to deal with diversity in the second language classroom'. Teacher trainer C pointed out that the texts she selects for her courses 'are chosen for the way they address not only the content of the course but also their reference to the basic premises of Critical Pedagogy, ...'. In addition, teacher trainer F emphasised that the primary factor that motivated her to strive to incorporate CP in teacher preparation was her 'commitment to social justice and equity'.

The attempt to engage students and teachers in a critical pedagogy of foreign languages and cultures aims at bringing about their commitment to critical learning and the fulfilment of their roles as individuals and citizens. As teacher trainer E put it: 'I think the most successful strategies for including CP is involving people in compelling issues and topics of mutual concern.' Some of these teacher trainers also expressed the feeling that there were not many successful models or specific strategies that motivate teachers to adopt a CP approach. This corroborates the findings of this study, that is, the great need for teacher development programmes that encourage prospective and practising teachers into a CP philosophy applied to specific subjects, such as foreign language/culture education. This attempt has already been made, however, and is becoming notorious in TESOL programmes (Brutt-Griffler & Samimy, 1999; Cox & Assis-Peterson, 1999; Pennycook, 1999).

A Critical Approach

From the theoretical discussions and the empirical findings, we may conclude that critical cultural awareness entails *a philosophical, pedagogical, and political attitude towards culture*. It may be defined as *a reflective, exploratory, dialogical and active stance towards cultural knowledge and life that allows for dissonance, contradiction, and conflict as well as for consensus, concurrence, and transformation*. It is *a cognitive and emotional endeavour that aims at individual and collective emancipation, social justice, and political commitment*. Furthermore, a critical approach to native and foreign

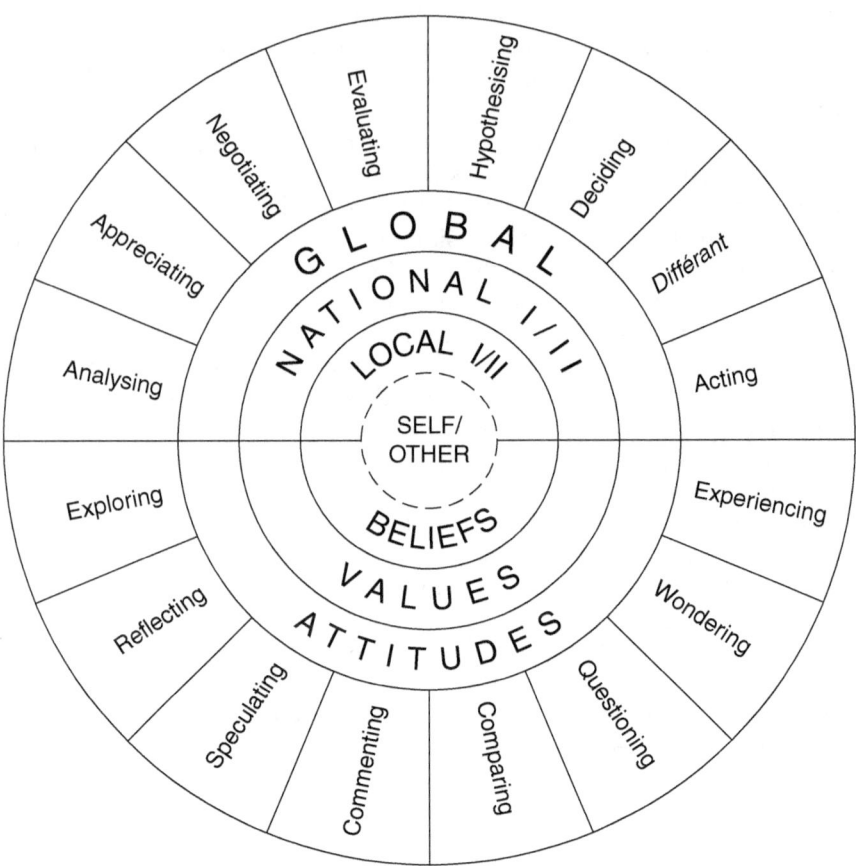

Figure 5.3 The critical cycle in foreign culture education

cultures is not a linear process that progresses gradually and steadily from less critical to more critical, but a *cyclical process* as represented by Figure 5.3.

The critical cycle comprises a series of *operations* that may range from 'experiencing' and 'wondering' to 'deciding', '*différant*', and 'acting'. Those operations more connected with an interrogative stance are gathered in the lower half of the circle while those that demand more of a proactive attitude lie at the upper half. They include a *cognitive* component such as 'comparing', 'analysing' and 'evaluating', an *affective* component which is explicit in 'appreciating' and may be implicit in some other operations like 'commenting' and 'experiencing', either in a positive or negative sense, and a *pragmatic* component such as 'experiencing' and 'acting'. These 'operations' relate to two main areas comprising different levels at and across which the above-mentioned operations work. One area includes geographical and political divisions, which may be considered as 'geo-political' – local, national, and global – and another – containing beliefs, values, and attitudes – as 'existential'. Therefore, critical operations work through the exchange between global, national I/II (native and target), and local I/II cultures and within the corresponding individual and collective beliefs, values, and attitudes, which meet in intercultural encounters.

Operations do not necessarily follow the order represented in Figure 5.3 and the critical cycle does not inevitably include all the operations mentioned here. However, they may be gathered in three main moments: (a) when one approaches and responds to culture(s) – experiencing, exploring, wondering, and speculating; (b) when one engages with and embarks on (inter)cultural observation, research and interpretation – appreciating, commenting, comparing, reflecting, analysing, and questioning; and (c) when one performs (inter)cultural acts and transforms cultural life – hypothesising, evaluating, negotiating, deciding, *différant*, and acting. These are not, however, closed compartments and their implementation in practice depends very much on the dynamics established among teachers, students, knowledge and experience.

These operations require, as shown by the figure, that they are performed according to attitudes, values and beliefs that themselves entail having a worldview that is determined by one's perspective towards difference, by one's approach towards knowledge and experience, and by one's capacity for agency. Having a critical perception of and interaction with one's own and the Other's attitudes, beliefs and values, across local, national and global levels, demands that one goes through most of the 'operations' represented in the figure having explored the philosophical and pedagogical theories enunciated in previous chapters. A critical awareness of (inter)cultural attitudes, values and beliefs towards difference, reasoning, critique, narrative, culture, dialogue, dissent, power, action, and hope does make a difference in intercultural communication and interaction.

To be more specific, both the conceptualisation and implementation of the operations above should be clarified and problematised by the discussion of leading strategies and concepts theorised in previous chapters. The connection between the operation '*différant*' and the Derridean concept of *différance* is obvious here. Situated between operations 'deciding' and 'acting', *'différant'* gives the foreign culture teacher/learner the 'right' to differ, that is, to dissonance and even dissent, and to defer her/his conclusions/decisions, at least partly, without preventing her/him from 'acting'. Notions of critical dialogue, empowerment, action, and hope should illuminate operations like 'negotiating', 'deciding', and 'acting'. The notion of *différend* should also elucidate operations like 'negotiating', 'evaluating', and 'hypothesising', for example. The discussion of 'deconstruction' helps define operations like 'wondering', 'questioning', 'exploring', and 'analysing'. Likewise, 'simulation' has special significance for understanding and enriching operations such as 'experiencing', 'speculating', 'appreciating', and 'hypothesising'. All operations entail an intersubjective, critical, and emancipatory form of reasoning.

In sum, these operations are not critical *per se*. Whether or not they promote critical cultural awareness depends on their definition and on their application and this is the reason why their conceptualisation and implementation incorporate the moment where theory and practice mingle and, therefore, the critical cycle embodies critical praxis. There are a thousand ways in which one can 'experience', 'speculate', 'appreciate', 'compare', 'hypothesise', or 'act', not all of them in a *critical* mode. Being *critical* while studying and experiencing a foreign culture involves an intellectual and pragmatic endeavour that, as previously defined, is neither totally particular nor completely general. The definition and discussion of these 'operations', based on the theoretical educational and philosophical foundations described previously, is fundamental for foreign language and culture teachers, if they are to apply them critically.

From the whole study, both in its theoretical and practical aspects, it has become obvious that these operations, if they are discussed and defined, are vital for the development of critical intercultural competence. Some of these operations were singled out by the participants in the empirical study described in the previous chapter, while they tried to describe how they approached foreign cultures *critically*. However, they did not reveal having subjected them before to theoretical or practical reflection or discussion nor did they show a comprehensive understanding of the possible interaction between them either, or of their singular function in a leading structure for the teaching/learning process. This may be explained by the lack of a general framework that gives meaning and purpose to the various elements and the way they interact (as illustrated by Figure 5.1 – within Human Rights Education and Education for Democratic Citizenship).

Finally, some operations identified in the figure, such as 'questioning', 'reflecting', 'exploring', 'evaluating', and 'hypothesising', may be considered as more explicitly critical than others and, therefore, determine the critical character of the whole process and, consequently, of the other operations as well. On the other hand, some 'operations' may be undertaken more critically by some but not necessarily in the same way by all. Their realisation also depends on the moment and on the context and, therefore, their conceptualisation and application are never definitive. The representation of these operations as cyclical shows that a critical approach is an ongoing, endless process, although teachers/learners do not necessarily follow this sequence of operations and may skip some, add others or go back and forth. This cycle of operations, with the reservations expressed above in mind, may be applied at full stretch to any topic of research on culture at upper secondary or undergraduate levels, provided it is given different emphases and approaches, and it should be discussed and applied in teacher education and professional development programmes. Its application to lower levels should be submitted to reflection, discussion and adaptation.

Several practical accounts have provided examples of the critical and intercultural application of the 'operations' identified above, such as those described in the first book in this series (*Languages for Intercultural Communication and Education*) where a number of teachers report back on projects carried out with basic, secondary and higher education students throughout Europe and in the United States and Japan. These narratives discuss, for example, *experiencing, exploring* and *commenting about* a foreign culture through ethnographic research, the media or e-mail, about *comparing/contrasting* Christmas cards, about *analysing, reflecting upon* and *appreciating* materials produced or gathered and exchanged by the students themselves, about *wondering about, questioning, negotiating* and, at times, *evaluating* underlying beliefs and values (Byram *et al.*, 2001).

Higher education is, nevertheless, crucial for promoting what Barnett calls a 'critical disposition' among present and future professionals in the area of education and beyond (Barnett, 1997). There have also been some interesting interdisciplinary attempts at developing a 'critical professionalism' in university teaching starting at undergraduate level (Walker, 2001). Phipps, for example, gives a lively and reflexive account of the process of being a 'critical professional' by *'reflecting on* practice, *refining* approaches, *collecting* stories and *discovering* a creed of values and principles' together with her students of Popular German Culture while they engage in a metacritique, in Barnett's terms, of their own roles as critical teacher/students of a foreign culture (Barnett, 1997: 71; Phipps, 2001a: 135, emphasis mine).

In order to help learners perform these operations *critically*, mindful of the different areas and levels involved, prospective or practising teachers have to experience the process themselves in the position of teachers as learners. This means that they have to be critically aware of the whole process and, moreover, reflect upon their own performance as critical learners/teachers, since being critically aware of being critical should be the first step in becoming a critical educator. This is indeed a complex process that requires programmes and projects aimed at and created by foreign language/culture teachers to provide for divergent theoretical input on issues such as identity, multi- and interculturalism, modernity/postmodernity, nationalism/postnationalism, globalism/localism, etc., and for practical opportunities where they can apply contradictory arguments and the above-mentioned operations to their own study of foreign languages/cultures. We may thus conclude that both theoretical discussion about those issues and a practical component are essential for students and prospective and practising teachers at all levels in order to promote reflective, critical, and creative praxis.

The Agenda for Foreign Language/Culture Education

From the reviewed literature, the empirical research and the reflection upon both undertaken throughout this book, it is possible to infer that the agenda, for at least the near future, as far as foreign language/culture education is concerned, has already been set both in the theorisers' and in the practitioners' minds. And its aims are: critical citizenry, critical professionalism, critical cultural awareness and critical intercultural competence. This is the ambitious challenge that university departments and schools, and consequently educators and students of foreign languages and cultures, are facing. Furthermore, these are not only audacious goals we have established for ourselves but also the requirements that our societies are forcing upon us. Educators are aware that not only education in general, but also foreign language/culture education in particular, are currently going through the process of a crisis of identity and that new strategies need to be found (Phipps, 2001b). This being said, the pedagogical and philosophical framework I have developed throughout this book is one possible formulation of a theoretical–practical model that may generate a myriad of responses when applied.

What I have been arguing for is a critical perspective towards both native and foreign cultures that rejects cultural ethnocentrism and dogmatism but does not deny the preservation of basic universal and particular principles and values. I have also called for the combination of a critical discourse with the commitment to transformative action, for a concern with social justice based on equity and equivalence as well as for the explicit recognition and endorsement of the political nature of our profession. I see it as our objective to grasp, as far as possible, the complexities of social and cultural contexts through divergent, sometimes colliding, points of view, by engaging with a vision that is both utopian and pragmatic and, therefore, transformative. Our endeavour entails a committed and emancipatory stance, albeit ironical and cynical at times. Hence, a critical approach to foreign languages and cultures involves personal and professional growth through (inter)cultural critique in a communicative mode.

Three main components for the preparation of critical citizens and educators in foreign languages and cultures were identified in this concluding chapter. First, the need for a general framework that gives meaning and purpose to the perspective taken towards the cultural contents taught/learnt and the pedagogical strategies employed. This was met by placing the promotion of critical cultural awareness in foreign language/culture education within the scope of Human Rights Education and Education for Democratic Citizenship. These fields are looked at through opposing philosophical lenses, namely modernism and postmodernism viewed as two related poles. Hence, this framework grounds a multiple-perspective approach.

Second, the need for research was acknowledged by the suggestion of an interdisciplinary approach to foreign language/culture education. Not only were various disciplinary and subdisciplinary fields found relevant to the study of culture(s), but also three main interdisciplinary areas were identified as fundamental, namely Cultural Studies, Intercultural Communication, and Critical Pedagogy.

Finally, the need for the specification of pedagogical strategies aimed at the critical study of foreign cultures was responded to by the identification of a number of 'operations' whose definitions may be provided and problematised by the theoretical reflections and discussions included in previous chapters. These operations function in relation to 'geopolitical' levels, namely local and national with respect to native and target cultures as well as global, and to 'existential' references, namely beliefs, values, and attitudes.

In sum, Human Rights Education and Education for Democratic Citizenship, all three components – Cultural Studies, Intercultural Communication and Critical Pedagogy – and more particularly the conceptualisation and application of the 'operations' identified above comprehend both a theoretical and a practical dimension that makes for an understanding of a critical approach to foreign language/culture education and respective teacher education as praxis which involves the search for (inter)cultural knowledge via committed and insightful experience, investigation, reflection and dialogue.

Notes

1. Therefore, Kramsch (1993b) recommends discussions among 'native' and 'foreign' teachers who teach the same or different foreign cultures. Unfortunately, these seldom happen among prospective and practising teachers and, when they do, 'representative knowledge' is rarely put into question and the focus of such meetings resides in common topics and/or general methodologies.
2. The authors suggest that the experiential approach may have generated less self-confidence than the didactic approach due to difficulties experienced in real interactions, which the participants who were submitted to a non-experiential programme did not experience.
3. These interviews were carried out in the United States and were mostly based on a questionnaire sent via e-mail and, in some cases, complemented with direct or phone conversations or further e-mail messages. The participants are professors/teacher trainers of foreign/second language prospective teachers. They are from Stanford University, California State University in Los Angeles, in Sacramento, in San Marcos, and in Stanislaus, and Arizona State University West in Phoenix (see interview guide in Appendix 6).

Bibliography

Ada, A.F. (1988) The Pájaro valley experience: Working with Spanish-speaking parents to develop children's reading and writing skills in the home through the use of children's literature. In T. Skutnabb-Kangas and J. Cummins (eds) *Minority Education: From Shame to Struggle* (pp. 223–38). Clevedon: Multilingual Matters.

Adorno, T.W., Frenkel-Brunswik, E., Levinson, D.J. and Sanford, R.N. (1950) *The Authoritarian Personality*. New York: Harper and Brothers.

Advisory Group on Citizenship (1998) *Education for Citizenship and the Teaching of Democracy in Schools*. London: Qualifications and Curriculum Authority.

Agar, M. (1991) The biculture in bilingual. *Language in Society* 20, 167–81.

Agar, M. (1994) The intercultural frame. *International Journal of Intercultural Relations* 18 (2), 221–37.

Agger, B. (1985) The dialectic of deindustrialization: An essay on advanced capitalism. In J. Forester (ed.) (pp. 4–21).

Agger, B. (1992) *Cultural Studies as Critical Theory*. London: The Falmer Press.

Akzin, B. (1964) *State and Nation*. London: Hutchinson University Library.

Alasuutari, P. (1995) *Researching Culture: Qualitative Method and Cultural Studies*. London: Sage.

Alexander, J. (1988) Introduction: Durkheimian sociology and cultural studies today. In J. Alexander (ed.) *Durkheimian Sociology: Cultural Studies* (pp. 1–21). Cambridge: Cambridge University Press.

Anderson, B. (1983) *Imagined Communities: Reflections on the Origin and Spread of Nationalism*. London: Verso.

Apple, M. (1993) *Official Knowledge: Democratic Education in a Conservative Age*. New York: Routledge.

Apple, M.W. (1979) *Ideology and Curriculum*. London: Routledge.

Apple, M.W. (1996a) *Cultural Politics and Education*. Buckingham: Open University Press.

Apple, M.W. (1996b) Power, meaning and identity: Critical sociology of education in the United States. *British Journal of Sociology of Education* 17 (2), 125–44.

Aronowitz, S. (1987) Postmodernism and politics. *Social Text* 18, 99–115.

Aronowitz, S. (1997) Between nationality and class. *Harvard Educational Review* 67 (2), 188–207.

Aronowitz, S. and Giroux, H. (1986) *Education under Siege*. London: Routledge.

Aronowitz, S. and Giroux, H. (1991) *Postmodern Education: Politics, Culture and Social Criticism*. Minneapolis: University of Minnesota Press.

Arthur, J. and Davison, J. (2000) Social literacy and citizenship education in the school curriculum. *The Curriculum Journal* 11 (1), 9–23.

Assman J. (1995) Collective memory and cultural identity. *New German Critique* 65 (Spring-Summer), 125–33.

Axtman, R. (ed.) (1998) *Globalization and Europe: Theoretical and Empirical Investigations*. London: Cassell.

Baker, C. (1988) *Key Issues in Bilingualism and Bilingual Education*. Clevedon: Multilingual Matters.

Bakhtin, M.M. (1977) *Le Marxisme et la Philosophie du Langage* [*Marksizm i Filosofija Jazyka*]. Paris: Les Éditions de Minuit (1st edn, 1929).

Bakhtin, M.M. (1981) Discourse in the novel. In M. Holquist (ed.) *The Dialogic Imagination* [*Voprosy Literatury i Estetiki*] (pp. 259–442). Austin: University of Texas Press (1st edn, 1975).

Balibar, E. (1991) The nation form: History and ideologie. In E. Balibar and I. Wallerstein (eds) (pp. 86–106).

Balibar, E. and Wallerstein, I. (1991) *Race, Nation, Class: Ambiguous Identities*. London: Verso.

Ball, S.J. (1995) Intellectuals or technicians? The urgent role of theory in educational studies. *Journal of Educational Studies* 43 (3), 255–71

Banks, J.A. (1979) Shaping the future of multicultural education. *Journal of Negro Education* 48 (3), 237–52.

Banks, J.A. (1986) Multicultural education: Development, paradigms and goals. J.A. Banks and J. Lynch (eds) *Multicultural Education in Western Societies* (pp. 2–26). London: Holt, Rinehart and Winston.

Banks, J.A. (1987) *Teaching Strategies for Ethnic Studies*. Boston: Allyn and Bacon.

Banks, J.A. (1989) Education for survival in a multicultural world. *Social Studies and the Young Learner* 1 (4), 3–5.

Banks, O. (1982) The sociology of education, 1952–1982. *British Journal of Educational Studies* 30 (1), 13–31.

Banton, M. (2000) Debate: The idiom of ethnicity. *Journal of Ethnic and Migration Studies* 26 (3), 535–42.

Barnett, R. (1997) *Higher Education: A Critical Business*. Buckinghamshire: Open University Press.

Barro, A., Jordan, S. and Roberts, C. (1998) Cultural practice in everyday life: The language learner as ethnographer. In M. Byram and M. Fleming (eds) (pp. 76–97).

Bar-Tal, D. (1997) Formation and change of ethnic and national stereotypes: An integrative model. *International Journal of Intercultural Relations* 21 (4), 491–523.

Bartolome, L. (1994) Beyond the methods fetish: Toward a humanizing pedagogy. *Harvard Educational Review* 64 (2), 173–94.

Bassnett, S. (ed.) (1997) *Studying British Cultures: An Introduction*. London: Routledge.

Bassnett, S. (2001) The fuzzy boundaries of translation. In R. Di Napoli, L. Polezzi and A. King (eds) (pp. 67–77).

Bates, R. (1980). New developments in the new sociology of education. *British Journal of Sociology of Education* 1 (1), 67–8.

Baudrillard, J. (1981) *Simulacres et Simulations*. Paris: Éditions Galilée.
Baudrillard, J. (1985) The ecstasy of communication. In H. Forster (ed.) (pp. 126–34).
Baudrillard, J. (1998a) *The Consumer Society: Myths and Structures*. London: Sage (1st edn, 1970).
Baudrillard, J. (1998b) The end of the millennium or the countdown. *Theory, Culture and Society* 15 (1), 1–9.
Bauman, Z. (1988) Is there a postmodern sociology? *Theory, Culture and Society* 5 (2–3), 217–37.
Baumgratz, G. (1993) Editorial. *European Journal of Education* 28 (3), 249–52.
Becher, U. (1996) European citizenship and historical learning. *Evaluation and Research in Education* 10 (2–3), 79–87.
Beck, J. (1996) Citizenship education: Problems and possibilities. *Curriculum Studies* 4 (3), 349–66.
Bennett, D. (ed.) (1998) *Multicultural States: Rethinking Difference and Identity*. London: Routledge.
Bennett, M. (1993) Towards ethnorelativism: A developmental model of intercultural sensitivity. In R.M. Paige (ed.) (pp. 21–71).
Bennington, G. and Derrida, J. (1991) La différance. In G. Bennington and J. Derrida, *Jacques Derrida* (pp. 71–82). Paris: Éditions du Seuil.
Bernstein, B. (1971) On the classification and framing of educational knowledge. In M. Young (ed.) (pp. 47–67).
Bernstein, J.M. (1995) *Recovering Ethical Life: Jürgen Habermas and the Future of Critical Theory*. London: Routledge.
Bertens, H. (1995) *The Idea of the Postmodern: A History*. London: Routledge.
Bertrand, J.T., Brown, J.E. and Ward, V. (1992) Techniques for analyzing focus group data. *Evaluation Review* 16 (2), 198–209.
Best, S. and Kellner, D. (1991) *Postmodern Theory: Critical Interrogations*. Basingstoke: Macmillan.
Bhabha, H. (1990) The Third Space: Interview with Homi Bhabha. In J. Rutherford (ed.) (pp. 207–21).
Bhabha, H. (1994) *The Location of Culture*. London: Routledge.
Biesta, G.J.J. and Miedema, S. (1996) Dewey in Europe: A case study on international dimensions of the turn-of-the-century educational reform. *American Journal of Education* 105, 1–26.
Blake, N. (1996) Between postmodernism and anti-modernism: The predicament of educational studies. *British Journal of Educational Studies* 44 (1), 42–65.
Blake, N. (1997) A postmodernism worth bothering about: A rejoinder to Cole, Hill and Rikowski. *British Journal of Educational Studies* 45 (3), 293–305.
Bloom, B. (ed.) (1972) *Taxonomy of Educational Objectives: Cognitive Domains*. London: Longman (1st edn, 1956).
Bochner, S. (ed.) (1982) *Cultures in Contact: Studies in Cross-cultural Interaction*. Oxford: Pergamon.
Borrelli, M. (1991) Intercultural pedagogy: Foundations and principles. In D. Buttjes and M. Byram (eds) (pp. 275–86).
Bourdieu, P. (1979) *La Distinction: Critique Sociale du Jugement*. Paris: Les Éditions de Minuit.

Bourdieu, P. (1992) *Réponses: Pour une Anthropologie Réflexive*. Paris: Éditions du Seuil.
Bourdieu, P. (2000) *Pascalian Meditations*. Cambridge: Polity.
Bourdieu, P. and Passeron, J.C. (1977) *Reproduction in Education, Society and Culture*. London: Sage
Bousted, M. and Davies, I. (1996) Teachers' perceptions of models of political learning. *Curriculum* 17 (1), 12–23.
Bowers, C.A. (1991) Some questions about the anachronistic elements in the Giroux-McLaren theory of a critical pedagogy. *Curriculum Inquiry* 21 (2), 239–52.
Bowles, S. and Gintis, H. (1976) *Schooling in Capitalist America: Educational Reform and the Contradictions of Economic Life*. London: Routledge and Kegan Paul.
Boyd, D. (1996) Dominance concealed through diversity: Implications of inadequate perspectives on cultural pluralism. *Harvard Educational Review* 66 (3), 609–30.
Boyne, R. (1998) Postmodernism, the sublime and ethics. In J. Good and I. Velody (eds) (pp. 210–26).
Boyne, R. and Rattansi, A. (eds) (1990a) *Postmodernism and Society*. Basingstoke: MacMillan.
Boyne, R. and Rattansi, A. (1990b) The theory and politics of postmodernism: By way of an introduction. In R. Boyne and A. Rattansi (eds) (pp. 1–45).
Bragaw, D.H. (1991) Priority: Curriculum. The global imperative and its metalanguage. *Foreign Language Annals* 24 (2), 115–24.
Breckner, R. (1998) Just single cases? Procedures and methodological arguments for hermeneutic case-analysis. Paper presented at the conference Biographical Methods in the Social Sciences. London, Tavistock Clinic, 18–19 Sept.
Breen, P. (1993) New cultural studies at Warwick University. *Language, Culture and Curriculum* 6 (1), 53–7.
Brislin, R.W. (ed.) (1977) *Culture Learning: Concepts, Application and Research*. Honolulu: University Press of Hawaii.
Brislin, R.W., Bochner, S. and Lonner, W.J. (eds) (1975) *Cross-Cultural Perspectives on Learning*. New York: John Wiley and Sons.
Brislin, R. and Yoshida, T. (1994) *Intercultural Communication Training: An Introduction*. Thousand Oaks: Sage.
Brosio, R.A. (2000) *Philosophical Scaffolding for the Construction of Critical Democratic Education*. New York: Peter Lang.
Brumfit, C. (1997) British studies: An educational perspective. In S. Bassnett (ed.) (pp. 53–64).
Brutt-Griffler, J. and Samimy, K.K. (1999) Revisiting the colonial in the postcolonial: Critical praxis for nonnative-English-speaking teachers in a TESOL program. *TESOL Quarterly* 33 (3), 413–31.
Buci-Glucksmann, C. (1975) *Gramsci et l'État: Pour une Theórie Matérialiste de la Philosophie*. Paris: Librairie Arthème Fayard.
Buci-Gluksmann, C. (1982) Hegemony and consent: A political strategy. In A.S. Sasson (ed.) *Approaches to Gramsci* (pp. 116–26). London: Writers and Readers Cooperative Society.
Buci-Glucksmann, C. (1988) À propos du *Différend:* Entretien avec Jean-François Lyotard: Introduction. *Les cahiers de philosophie* 5, 35–60

Buckingham, D. (ed.) (1998) *Teaching Popular Culture: Beyond Radical Pedagogy*. London: UCL Press.
Burbules, N.C. and Rice, S. (1991) Dialogue across differences: Continuing the conversation. *Harvard Educational Review* 61 (4), 393–416.
Buttjes, D. (1990) Teaching foreign language and culture: Social impact and political significance. *Language Learning Journal* 2, 53–7.
Buttjes, D. and Byram, M. (eds) (1991) *Mediating Languages and Cultures: Towards an Intercultural Theory of Foreign Language Education*. Clevedon: Multilingual Matters.
Byram, M. (1989) *Cultural Studies in Foreign Language Education*. Clevedon: Multilingual Matters.
Byram, M. (1992) Language and culture learning for European citizenship. In M.C. Beveridge and G. Reddiford (eds) *Language and Education* 6 (2) Special issue, 165–76.
Byram, M. (1993a) Introduction. *Language, Culture and Curriculum* 6 (1), 1–3.
Byram, M. (1993b) Language and culture learning: The need for integration. In M. Byram (ed.) *Germany: Its Representation in Texbooks for Teaching German in Great Britain* (pp. 13–18). Frankfurt, Maine: Moritz Diesterweg.
Byram, M. (1993c) Culture and language learning in higher education. *Language, Culture and Curriculum* 6 (1) Special issue.
Byram, M. (1994) Comment: Authorities and people. *International Journal of Sociology of Language* 110, 131–6.
Byram, M. (1996) Introduction: Education for European citizenship. *Evaluation and Research in Education* 10 (2–3), 61–7.
Byram, M. (1997a) Cultural studies and foreign language teaching. In S. Bassnett (ed.) (pp. 53–64). London: Routledge.
Byram, M. (1997b) *Teaching and Assessing Intercultural Communicative Competence*. Clevedon: Multilingual Matters.
Byram, M. (1997c) 'Cultural awareness' as vocabulary learning. *Language Learning Journal* 16, 51–7.
Byram, M. (1997d) Summary. In M. Byram and G. Zarate (eds) (pp. 109–12).
Byram, M. (ed.) (1997e) *Face to Face: Learning 'Language and Culture' through Visits and Exchanges*. London: CILT.
Byram, M. (ed.) (2000) *Routledge Encyclopaedia of Language Teaching and Learning*. London: Routledge.
Byram, M. and Esarte-Sarries, V. (1991a) *Investigating Cultural Studies in Foreign Language Teaching*. Clevedon: Multilingual Matters.
Byram, M., Esarte-Sarries, V. and Taylor, S. (1991b) *Cultural Studies and Language Learning*. Clevedon: Multilingual Matters.
Byram, M. and Fleming, M. (eds) (1998) *Language Learning in Intercultural Perspective*. Cambridge: Cambridge University Press.
Byram, M. and Guilherme, M. (2000) Human Rights, culture and language teaching. In A. Osler (ed.) (pp. 63–78).
Byram, M., Lloyd, K. and Schneider, R. (1995) Defining and describing 'cultural awareness'. *Language Learning Journal* 12 (Sept.), 5–7.
Byram, M., Morgan, C. et al. (1994) *Teaching-and-Learning Language-and-Culture*. Clevedon: Multilingual Matters.

Byram, M. and Ó Riagáin, P. (1999) Towards a framework for language education policies in Europe. Paper presented at the conference Linguistic Diversity for Democratic Citizenship in Europe. Innsbruck, Austria: Council of Europe.

Byram, M., Nichols, A. and Stevens, D. (eds) (2001) *Developing Intercultural Competence in Practice*. Clevedon: Multilingual Matters.

Byram, M. and Risager, K. (1999) *Language Teachers, Politics and Cultures*. Clevedon: Multilingual Matters.

Byram, M. and Zarate, G. (1995) *Young People Facing Difference*. Strasbourg: Council of Europe.

Byram, M. and Zarate, G. (eds) (1997) *The Sociocultural and Intercultural Dimension of Language Learning and Teaching*. Strasbourg: Council of Europe.

Byram, M., Zarate, G. and Neuner, G. (1997) *Sociocultural Competence in Language Learning and Teaching: Studies towards a Common European Framework of Reference for Language Learning and Teaching*. Strasbourg: Council of Europe.

California Association for Bilingual Education (CABE) (1992) *Readings for the 1992 Institute. Reclaiming our Voices: Transforming Education for Cultural and Linguistic Democracy, Part 2*. Sacramento: California Association for Bilingual Education.

Cabrera, N.J. (1995) Personal beliefs, critical thinking skills, and reasoning errors-how illogical are we?: A literature review. *Educational Research Quarterly* 19 (2), 2–24.

Cadd, M. (1994) An attempt to reduce ethnocentrism in the foreign language classroom. *Foreign Language Annals* 27 (2), 143–60.

Cain, A. and Zarate, G. (1996) The role of training courses in developing openness to otherness: From tourism to ethnography. In *Language, Culture and Curriculum* 9 (1), 66–83.

Canagarajah, A.S. (1999) *Resisting Linguistic Imperialism in English Teaching*. Oxford: Oxford University Press.

Carleheden, M. and Gabriëls, R. (1996) An interview with Jürgen Habermas. *Theory, Culture and Society* 13 (3), 1–17.

Carrilho, M.M. (1994) *Jogos de Racionalidade*. Porto: Asa.

Carter, C. and Osler, A. (2000) Human rights, identities and conflict management: A study of school culture as experienced through classroom relationships. *Cambridge Journal of Education* 30 (3), 335–56.

Carter, J. (1997) Post-Fordism and the theorisation of educational change: What's in a name? *British Journal of Sociology of Education* 18 (1), 45–61.

Casnir, F.L. (1999) Foundations for the study of intercultural communication based on a third-culture building model. *International Journal of Intercultural Relations* 23 (1), 91–116.

Chaika, E. (1982) *Language: The Social Mirror*. Rowley: Newbury House.

Chambers, S. (1995) Discourse and democratic practices. In S.K. White (ed.) (pp. 233–59).

Chatterjee, P. (1998) Beyond the nation? Or within? *Social Text* 16 (3), 57–69.

Cherryholmes, C. (1992) Knowledge, power, and discourse in social studies education. In K. Weiler and C. Mitchell (eds) *What Schools Can Do: Critical Pedagogy and Practice* (pp. 95–115). Albany: State University of New York Press.

Cherryholmes, C. (1994) Pragmatism, poststructuralism, and socially useful theorizing. *Curriculum Inquiry* 24 (2), 193–213.

Choi, J.D. (1995) Critical pedagogy: Theory and practice of a pedagogy of hope. PhD thesis, University of Missouri, Columbia.

Clarke, M. (1994) The disfunction of the theory/practice discourse. *TESOL Quarterly* 28 (1), 9–25.

Cochran-Smith, M. (1993) Learning to teach against the grain. In K. Geismar and G. Nicoleau (eds) (pp. 191–223).

Cogan, J. and Derricott, R. (eds) (1998) *Citizenship for the 21st century: An International Perspective on Education.* London: Kogan Page.

Cohen, L. and Manion, L. (1994) *Research Methods in Education.* London: Routledge (1st edn, 1980).

Cole, M. and Rikowski, G. (1997) Between postmodernism and nowhere: The predicament of the postmodernist. *British Journal of Educational Studies* 45 (2), 187–200.

Coleman, J. (1968) The concept of equality of educational opportunity. *Harvard Educational Review* 38 (1), 7–22.

Connor, S. (1989) *Postmodernist Culture: An Introduction to Theories of the Contemporary.* Oxford: Blackwell

Cooks, L.M. (1993) Critical pedagogy as communication education: Researching the possibilities. PhD thesis, Ohio University.

Cooper, D.E. (1998) Postmodernism and 'the end of philosophy'. In J. Good and I. Velody (eds) (pp. 61–72).

Corson, D. (1989) Foreign language policy at school level: FLT and cultural studies across the curriculum. *Foreign Language Annals* 22 (4), 323–38.

Corson, D. (1997) Reclaiming reality: Laying the ideology of cultural compatibility. *International Journal of Intercultural Relations* 21 (1), 105–11.

Coste, D. (1997) Multilingual and multicultural competence and the role of school. *Language Teaching* 30 (2), 90–3.

Coste, D., Moore, D. and Zarate, G. (1997) *Compétence Plurilingue et Pluriculturelle.* Strasbourg: Council of Europe.

Coste, D., North, B., Sheils, J. and Trim, J.L.M. (1998) Languages: Learning, teaching, assessment. A common European framework of reference. *Language Teaching* 31 (3), 136–51.

Council of Europe (1996) *Modern Languages: Learning, Teaching, Assessment. A Common European Framework of Reference.* Strasbourg: Council of Europe.

Council of Europe (1997a) *Language Learning for European Citizenship: Final Report (1989–96).* Strasbourg: Council of Europe.

Council of Europe (1997b) *Final Declaration of Heads of State and Governments of the Member States.* Strasbourg: Council of Europe.

Council of Europe (1998) *Project 'Education for Democratic Citizenship': Basic Concepts and Core Competences of Education for Democratic Citizenship.* Strasbourg: Council of Europe.

Council of Europe (1999) *Declaration and Programme on Education for Democratic Citizenship, Based on the Rights and Responsibilities of Citizens.* Strasbourg: Committee of Ministers, 104th Session.

Cox, M.I.P. and Assis-Peterson, M.A. (1999) Critical pedagogy in ELT: Images of Brazilian teachers of English. *TESOL Quarterly* 33 (3), 433–52.

Crawford, J. (1979) *The Creation of States in International Law.* Oxford: Clarendon Press.

Crawford, L.M. and McLaren, P. (1998) A critical perspective on culture in the second language classroom. In D.L. Lange, C.A. Klee, R.M. Paige and Y.A. Yershova (eds) (pp. 125–55).
Critchley, S. (1996) Deconstruction and pragmatism: Is Derrida a private ironist or a public liberal? In C. Mouffe (ed.) (pp. 19–40).
Crumpton, R. (1992) Policy analysis of state multicultural education programs. In C.A. Grant. *Research and Multicultural Education: From the Margins to the Mainstream* (pp. 240–9). London: The Falmer Press.
Crystal, D. (1997) *English as a Global Language*. Cambridge: Cambridge University Press.
Cullingford, C. (2000) *Prejudice: From Individual Identity to Nationalism in Young People*. London: Kogan Page.
Cummins, J. (1989) *Empowering Minority Students*. Sacramento: California Association for Bilingual Education.
Cummins, J. (1996) *Negotiating Identities: Education for Empowerment in a Diverse Society*. Ontario, CA: California Association for Bilingual Education.
Cushner, K. and Brislin, R.W. (eds) (1997) *Improving Intercultural Interactions: Modules for Cross-Cultural Training Programs*. Thousand Oaks: Sage.
Cyphert, D. (1996) Taking the helm in critical pedagogy: The basic speech curriculum as an operationalization of the paradigm. Paper presented at the 82nd Annual Meeting of the Speech Communication Association, San Diego, CA, 23–6 November.
Czaplicka, J., Huyssen, A. and Rabinbach, A. (1995) Introduction: Cultural history and cultural studies – reflections on a symposium. *New German Critique*, 65 (Spring/Summer), 3–17.
Damásio, A. (1994) *O Erro de Descartes: Emoção, Razão e Cérebro Humano*. Mem Martins: Europa-América.
Damen, L. (1987) *Culture Learning: The Fifth Dimension in the Language Classroom*. Reading: Addison Wesley.
Darder, A. (1991) *Culture and Power in the Classroom: A Critical Foundation for Bicultural Education*. New York: Bergin and Garvey.
Davis, O.I., Nakayama, T.K. and Martin, J.N. (2000) Current and future directions in ethnicity methodology. *International Journal of Intercultural Relations* 24, 525–39.
Delgado-Gaitan, C. and Trueba, H. (1991) *Crossing Cultural Borders: Education for Immigrant Families in America*. London: The Falmer Press.
Derrida, J. (1967) *L'Écriture et la Différence*. Paris: Editions du Seuil.
Derrida, J. (1972) La différance. In J. Derrida *Marges de la Philosophie* (pp. 1–29). Paris: Les Éditions de Minuit.
Derrida, J. (1976) *Of Grammatology*. Baltimore: Johns Hopkins University Press.
Derrida, J. (1988) Letter to a Japanese friend. In D. Wood and R. Bernasconi (eds) *Derrida and Différance* (pp. 2–4). Evanston, IL: Northwestern University Press.
Derrida, J. (1991) *L'Autre Cap*. Paris: Les Éditions de Minuit.
Derrida, J. (1996) Remarks on deconstruction and pragmatism. In C. Mouffe (ed.) (pp. 77–88).
Derrida, J. (1997) *Politics of Friendship*. London: Verso.
Dewey, J. (1933) *How we Think*. Boston: D.C. Heath and Company.
Dewey, J. (1956) *Democracy and Education*. New York: Macmillan (1st edn, 1916).

Dewey, J. (1977) *The Middle Works, 1899–1924, 3: 1903–1924*. Carbondale: Southern Illinois University Press

Dey, I. (1993) *Qualitative Data Analysis*. London: Routledge.

Di Napoli, R., Polezzi, L. and King, A. (eds) (2001) *Fuzzy Boundaries? Reflections on Modern Languages and the Humanities*. London: CILT.

Diaz-Greenberg, R. (1995) The emergence of voice in Latino high school students. PhD thesis, University of San Francisco.

Diaz-Greenberg, R. (1998) Towards a pedagogy of transformation: Pre-service teachers as critical intellectuals in secondary schools. In *Teaching Education* 9 (2), 420–32.

Diekhoff, G. (1992) *Statistics for the Social and Behavioral Sciences: Univariate, Bivariate, Multivariate*. Dubuque, IA: Wm. C. Brown.

Dockrell. W.B. and Hamilton, D. (1980) *Rethinking Educational Research*. London: Hodder and Stoughton.

Doll Jr, W.E. (1993) *A Post-Modern Perspective on Curriculum*. New York: Teachers College, Columbia University.

Donald, J. (1996) The citizen and the man about town. In S. Hall and P. du Gay (eds) (pp. 170–90).

Doyé, P. (1993) Neuere Konzepte der Fremdsprachenerziehung und ihre Bedeutung für die Schulbuchkritik. In M. Byram (ed.) *Germany: Its Representation in Textbooks for Teaching German in Great Britain* (pp. 19–29). Frankfurt: Moritz Diesterweg.

Doyé, P. (1996) Foreign language teaching and education for intercultural and international understanding. *Evaluation and Research in Education* 10 (2–3), 104–12.

Doyé, P. (1999) *The Intercultural Dimension: Foreign Language Education in the Primary School*. Berlin: Cornelsen.

Eagleton, T. (ed.) (1994a) *Ideology*. London: Longman.

Eagleton, T. (1994b) Introduction. In T. Eagleton (ed.) (pp. 1–20).

Eagleton, T. (2000) *The Idea of Culture*. Oxford: Blackwell.

Early, G. (1993) American education and the postmodernist impulse. *American Quarterly* 45 (2), 220–9.

Edelsky, C. (1991) *With Literacy and Justice for All: Rethinking the Social in Language and Education*. London: The Falmer Press.

Edgerton, S.H. (1996) *Translating the Curriculum: Multiculturalism into Cultural Studies*. New York: Routledge.

Elliot, J. (1991) *Action Research for Educational Exchange*. Milton Keynes: Open University Press.

Ellison, N. (1997) Towards a new social politics: Citizenship and reflexivity in late modernity. *Sociology* 31 (4), 697–717.

Ellsworth, E. (1989) Why doesn't this feel empowering? Working through the repressive myths of critical pedagogy. *Harvard Educational Review* 59 (3), 297–325.

Fairclough, N. (1995) *Critical Discourse Analysis*. London: Longman.

Fairclough, N. (1999) Global capitalism and critical awareness of language. *Language Awareness* 8 (2), 71–83.

Fantini, A.E. (ed.) (1997) *New Ways in Teaching Culture*. Alexandria, VA: TESOL.

Fantini. A.E. (1999) Comparisons: Towards the development of intercultural competence. In J.K. Phillips and R.M. Terry (eds) (pp. 165–218).

Fantini, A.E., and Smith, E.M. (1997) A survey of intercultural communication. *International Journal of Intercultural Communication* 21 (1), 125–48.
Featherstone, M. (1988) In pursuit of the postmodern: An introduction. *Theory, Culture and Society* 5 (2–3), 195–215.
Featherstone, M. (1995) *Undoing Culture: Globalization, Postmodernism and Identity*. London: Sage.
Featherstone, M., Lash, S. and Robertson, R. (eds) (1995) *Global Modernities*. London: Sage.
Fennes, H. and Hapgood, K. (1997) *Intercultural Learning in the Classroom*. London: Cassell.
Fernandes, J.V. (1988) From the theories of social and cultural reproduction to the theory of resistance. *British Journal of Sociology of Education* 9 (2), 169–80.
Ferry, L. (1992) *Le Nouvel Ordre Écologique*. Paris: Bernard Grasset.
Fetterman, D.M. (1984) *Ethnography in Educational Evaluation*. Beverly Hills: Sage.
Fetterman, D.M. (1989) *Ethnography: Step by Step*. Newbury Park: Sage.
Figueroa, P. (2000) Citizenship education for a plural society. In A. Osler (ed.) (pp. 47–62).
Finch, H.L.R. (1977) *Wittgenstein: The Latter Philosophy*. Atlantic Highlands, NJ: Humanities Press.
Fischer, G. (1996) Tourist or explorer? Reflection in the foreign language classroom. *Foreign Language Annals* 29 (1), 73–81.
Fishman, J.A. (1972) *Language and Nationalism: Two Integrative Essays*. Rowley, Massachusetts: Newbury House.
Foddy, W. (1993) *Constructing Questions for Interviews and Questionnaires: Theory and Practice in Social Research*. Cambridge: Cambridge University Press.
Forester, J. (1985) *Critical Theory and Public Life*. Cambridge, MA: MIT Press
Foster, H. (ed.) (1985) *Postmodern Culture*. London: Pluto.
Foucault, M. (1969) *L'Archéologie du Savoir*. Paris: Éditions Gallimard.
Foucault, M. (1971) *L'Ordre du Discours*. Paris: Éditions Gallimard.
Foucault, M. (1980) *Power/Knowledge*. New York: Pantheon Books.
Foucault, M. (1988a) Technologies of the self. In L.H. Martin, H. Gutman and P. H. Hutton (eds) *Technologies of the Self* (pp. 16–49). Amherst: University of Massachusetts Press.
Foucault, M. (1988b) The political technology of individuals. In L.H. Martin, H. Gutman and P.H. Hutton (eds) *Technologies of the Self* (pp. 145–62). Amherst: University of Massachusetts Press.
Fox, C. (1997) The authenticity of intercultural communication. *International Journal of Intercultural Communication* 21 (1), 85–103.
Fraser, N. (1998) From redistribution to recognition? Dilemmas of justice in a 'post-socialist' age. In C. Willet (ed.) (pp. 19–49).
Freire, P. (1970) *Pedagogy of the Oppressed* [*A pedagogia dos oprimidos*] New York: The Continuum.
Freire, P. (1974) *Education for Critical Consciousness*. London: Sheed and Ward.
Freire, P. (1987) Letter to North-American teachers. In I. Shor (ed.) *Freire for the Classroom* (pp. 211–14). Portsmouth, NH: Boynton/Cook.
Freire, P. (1991) *Educação como Prática da Liberdade*. Rio de Janeiro: Paz e Terra.
Freire, P. (1993) *Pedagogia da Esperança: Um Reencontro com a Pedagogia do Oprimido*. Rio de Janeiro: Paz e Terra.

Freire, P. (1996) *Letters to Cristina*. New York: Routledge.
Freire, P. (1998) *Teachers as Cultural Workers*. Boulder, CO: Westview Press.
Frow, J. (1997) *Time and Commodity Culture: Essays in Cultural Theory and Postmodernity*. Oxford: Clarendon Press.
Fullan, M. (1991) *The New Meaning of Educational Change*. London: Cassell.
Fullan, M. (1993) *Change Forces: Probing the Depths of Educational Reform*. London: The Falmer Press
Gadamer, H.G. (1970) *Truth and Method*. London: Sheed and Ward (1st edn, 1960).
Gadotti, M. (1996) *Pedagogy of Praxis*. Albany, NY: State University of New York Press.
Gannon, M.J. and Poon, J.M.L. (1997) Effects of alternative instructional approaches on cross-cultural training outcomes. *International Journal of Intercultural Relations* 21 (4), 429–46.
Gardner, H. (1983) *Frames of Mind: The Theory of Multiple Intelligences*. New York: Basic Books.
Gardner, R.C. and Macintyre, P.D. (1992) A student's contributions to second language learning. Part I: Cognitive variables. *Language Teaching* 25 (Oct.), 211–20.
Gardner, R.C. and Macintyre, P.D. (1993) A student's contributions to second language learning. Part II: Affective variables. *Language Teaching* 26 (Jan.), 1–11.
Geismar, K. and Nicoleau, G. (eds) (1993) *Teaching for Change: Addressing Issues of Difference in the College Classroom*. Cambridge, MA: Harvard Educational Review.
Gellner. E. (1987) *Culture, Identity and Politics*. Cambridge: Cambridge University Press.
Geoffrois, C. (2001) *La Mésentente Cordiale: Voyage au Coeur de l'Espace Interculturel Franco-Anglais*. Paris: Éditions Bernard Grasset/ Le Monde de l'Éducation.
Geuss, R. (1981) *The Idea of a Critical Theory: Habermas and the Frankfurt School*. Cambridge: Cambridge University Press.
Gibson, R. (1986) *Critical Theory and Education*. London: Hodder & Stoughton.
Giddens, A. (1984) *The Constitution of Society*. Berkeley: University of California Press.
Giddens, A. (1990) *The Consequences of Modernity*. Stanford: Stanford University Press.
Giddens, A. (1991) *Modernity and Self-Identity: Self and Society in the Late Modern Age*. Stanford: Stanford University Press.
Giddens, A. (2000) Citizenship education in the global era. In N. Pearce and J. Hallgarten (eds) (pp. 19–25).
Giroux, H.A. (1981) *Ideology, Culture and the Process of Schooling*. Philadelphia: Temple University Press.
Giroux, H.A. (1983) *Theory and Resistance in Education: A Pedagogy for the Opposition*. South Hadley, MA: Bergin & Garvey.
Giroux, H.A. (1988) *Teachers as Intellectuals*. New York: Bergin & Garvey.
Giroux, H.A. (1989) *Schooling for Democracy*. London: Routledge.
Giroux, H.A. (1992) *Border Crossings: Cultural Workers and the Politics of Education*. New York: Routledge.
Giroux, H.A. (1994a) *Disturbing Pleasures*. New York: Routledge.

Giroux, H.A. (1994b) Doing cultural studies: Youth and the challenge of pedagogy. *Harvard Educational Review* 64 (3), 278–308.
Giroux, H.A. (1996) Is there a place for cultural studies in colleges of education. In H.A. Giroux, C. Lankshear, P. McLaren and M. Peters (eds) (pp. 41–58).
Giroux, H.A. (1997a) *Channel Surfing: Race Talk and the Destruction of Today's Youth*. London: MacMillan.
Giroux, H.A. (1997b) *Pedagogy and the Politics of Hope: Theory, Culture, and Schooling*. Boulder, CO: Westview Press.
Giroux, H. (2000) Public pedagogy as cultural politics: Stuart Hall and the 'crisis' of culture. *Cultural Studies* 14 (2), 341–60.
Giroux, H.A. and McLaren, P. (1989) *Critical Pedagogy, the State, and Cultural Struggle*. Albany, New York: State University of New York Press.
Giroux, H.A. and McLaren, P. (eds) (1994) *Between Borders: Pedagogy and the Politics of Cultural Studies*. New York: Routledge.
Giroux, H., Lankshear, C., McLaren, P. and Peters, M. (eds) (1996) *Counternarratives: Cultural Studies and Critical Pedagogies in Postmodern Spaces*. New York: Routledge.
Gitlin, A. and Margonis, F. (1995) The political aspect of reform: Teacher resistance as good sense. *Journal of Education* 103 (4), 377–405.
Glaser, B.G. and Strauss, A.L. (1967) *The Discovery of Grounded Theory: Strategies for Qualitative Research*. New York: Aldine de Gruyter.
Goleman, D. (1996) *Emotional Intelligence: Why it Can Matter More than IQ*. London: Bloomsbury.
Good, J. and Velody, I. (eds) (1998a) *The Politics of Postmodernity*. Cambridge: Cambridge University Press.
Good, J. and Velody, I. (1998b) Introduction. In J. Good and I. Velody (eds) (pp. 1–18).
Gordon, C. (1980) Afterword. In M. Foucault (pp. 229–59).
Gore, J. (1993) *The Struggle for Pedagogies*. New York: Routledge.
Gramsci, A. (1971) *Selections from the Prison Notebooks of Antonio Gramsci* [*Lettere dal Carcere*]. New York: International (1st edn, 1947).
Gramsci, A. (1974) *Obras Escolhidas*. Lisboa: Editorial Estampa.
Gramsci, A. (1975) *Letters from Prison* [*Lettere dal carcere*]. London: Jonathan Cape (1st edn, 1947).
Grandy, R. (1997) Constructivisms and objectivity: Disentangling metaphysics from pedagogy. *Science and Education* 6, 43–53.
Greene, M. (1986) In search of a critical pedagogy. *Harvard Educational Review* 56 (4), 427–41.
Grillo, R.D. (ed.) (1980) *'Nation' and 'State' in Europe*. London: Academic Press.
Grosjean, F. (1982) *Life with Two Languages*. Cambridge: Harvard University Press.
Grossberg, L. (1994) Introduction: Bringin' it all back home. Pedagogy and cultural studies. In H.A. Giroux and P. McLaren (eds) (pp. 1–25).
Grossberg. L. (1996) Identity and cultural studies: Is that all there is? In S. Hall and P. du Gay (eds) (pp. 87–107).
Grossberg, L. , Nelson, C. and Treichler, P.A. (eds) (1992) *Cultural Studies*. New York: Routledge.
Guilherme, M. (1994) A outra fronteira: Nacionalidade/etnicidade e educação bilíngue nos Estados Unidos da América. MA thesis, Faculdade de Ciências Sociais e Humanas at Universidade Nova, Lisboa.

Guilherme, M. (1996) A aprendizagem de uma língua/cultura estrangeira e a sua relação com o desenvolvimento na língua/cultura materna. In M.L. Pires (ed.) *Novas Metodologias no Ensino do Inglês* (pp. 54–65). Lisboa: Universidade Aberta.
Guilherme, M. (1998) The political challenge of teaching a foreign culture. In D. Killick and M. Parry (eds) (pp. 123–8).
Guilherme, M. (2000) Intercultural competence. In M. Byram (ed.) (pp. 297–300)
Guilherme, M. (2001) The critical study of a foreign culture and citizenship education. *Anglo-Saxonica* 2, 14–15.
Guilherme, M. (forthcoming) Desafios para o ensino/aprendizagem de línguas e culturas estrangeiras em Portugal. *Revista Educação, Sociedade & Culturas*, Porto.
Habermas, J. (1970) Towards a theory of communicative competence. *Inquiry* 13, 360–75.
Habermas, J. (1971) *Toward a Rational Society*. London: Heinemann.
Habermas, J. (1972) *Knowledge and Human Interests*. London: Heinemann (1st edn, 1968).
Habermas, J. (1973) *Legitimation Crisis*. Boston: Beacon.
Habermas, J. (1976) Some distinctions in universal pragmatics. *Theory and Society* 3 (2), 155–67.
Habermas, J. (1979) *Communication and the Evolution of Society*. London: Heinemann (1st edn, 1976).
Habermas, J. (1982) A reply to my critics. In J.B. Thompson and D. Held (eds) *Habermas: Critical Debates* (pp. 219–83). London: Basingstoke.
Habermas, J. (1984) *The Theory of Communicative Action: Reason and the Rationalization of Society*, Vol. 1. Boston; Beacon Press (1st edn, 1981).
Habermas, J. (1985) Modernity: An incomplete project. In H. Foster (ed.) (pp. 3–15).
Habermas, J. (1987a) *The Theory of Communicative Action. Lifeworld and System: A Critique of Functionalist Reason* Vol. 2. Boston: Beacon Press.
Habermas, J. (1987b) *The Philosophical Discourse of Modernity*. Cambridge, MA: The MIT Press (1st edn, 1985).
Habermas, J. (1990) *Moral Consciousness and Communicative Action*. Cambridge: Polity Press.
Habermas, J. (1992) *Postmetaphysical Thinking*. Cambridge, UK: Polity Press.
Habermas, J. (1993) *Justification and Application*. Cambridge, MA: The MIT Press (1st edn, 1991).
Habermas, J. (1994) Citizenship and national identity. In B. van Steenberg (ed.) *The Condition of Citizenship* (pp. 20–35). London: Sage.
Hall, E.T. (1959) *The Silent Language*. New York: Doubleday.
Hall, E.T. (1977) *Beyond Culture*. New York: Anchor Press/Doubleday.
Hall, S. (1986) On postmodernism and articulation. *The Journal of Communication Inquiry* 10 (2), 45–60.
Hall, S. (1989) Unstated features of the cultural context of learning. *The Educational Forum* 54 (1), 23–34.
Hall, S. (1990) Cultural identity and diaspora. In J. Rutherford (ed.) (pp. 222–37).
Hall, S. (1992) The question of cultural identity. In S. Hall, D. Held and T. McGrew (eds) *Modernity and its Futures* (pp. 273–325). Cambridge: Polity, Blackwell and the Open University Press.
Hall, S. (1996) Introduction: Who needs 'identity'? In S. Hall and P. du Gay (eds) (pp. 1–17).

Hall, S. (2000) Multicultural citizens, monocultural citizenship? In N. Pearce and J. Hallgarten (eds) (pp. 43–51).
Hall, S. and Jacques, M. (1989) *New Times*. London: Lawrence and Wishart.
Hall, S. and du Gay, P. (eds) (1996) *Questions of Cultural Identity*. London: Sage.
Halse, C.M. and Baumgart, N.L. (2000) Cross cultural perspectives of teachers: A study in three countries. *International Journal of Intercultural Relations* 24, 455–75.
Hammersley, M. (1996) Post mortem or post modern? Some reflections on British sociology of education. *British Journal of Educational Studies* 44 (4), 395–407.
Hampden-Turner, C. and Trompenaars, F. (2000) *Building Cross-Cultural Competence: How to Create Wealth from Conflicting Values*. Chichester: John Wiley & Sons.
Hannerz, U. (1992) *Cultural Complexity: Studies in the Social Organization of Meaning*. New York: Columbia University Press.
Hargreaves, D. (1999) The knowledge-creating school. *British Journal of Educational Studies* 47 (2), 122–44.
Hart, T. (2001) *From Information to Transformation: Education for the Evolution of Consciousness*. New York: Peter Lang.
Harvey, D. (1989) *The Condition of Postmodernity*. Cambridge, MA: Basil Blackwell.
Hatch, E. and Lazaraton, A. (1991) *The Research Manual: Design and Statistics for Applied Linguistics*. New York: Newbury House Publishers.
Henerson, M., Morris, L. and Fitz-Gibbon, C. (1987) *How to Measure Attitudes*. Newbury Park, CA: Sage.
Hernández, H. (1989) *Multicultural Education: A Teacher's Guide to Content and Process*. New York: Macmillan.
Heusinkveld, P.R. (1985) The foreign language classroom: A forum for understanding cultural stereotypes. *Foreign Language Annals* 18 (4), 321–32.
Hewitt, N. (1993) A response to John Higham. *American Quarterly* 45 (2), 23–42.
Heydenfeldt, J.A. (2000) The influence of individualism/collectivism on Mexican and US business negotiation. *International Journal of Intercultural Relations* 24, 383–407.
Higham, J. (1993) Multiculturalism and universalism: A history and critique. *American Quarterly* 45 (2), 195–219.
Hirsch Jr, E.D. (1988) *Cultural Literacy*. New York: Vintage Books.
Hitchcock, G. and Hughes, D. (1995) *Research and the Teacher: A Qualitative Introduction to School-Based Research*. London: Routledge (1st edn, 1985).
Hobsbawm, E.J. (1990) *Nations and Nationalism since 1780: Programme, Myth, Reality*. Cambridge: Cambridge University Press.
Hobsbawm, E. (1996) Language, culture, and national identity. *Social Research* 63 (4), 1065–80.
Hodkinson, P. (1994) Empowerment as an entitlement in the post-16 curriculum. *Journal of Curriculum Studies* 26 (5), 491–508.
Hodysh, H. (1996) Theory and practice in historical research. *Educational Practice and Theory* 18 (1), 87–94.
Hones, D.F. (1999) US justice? Critical pedagogy and the case of Mumia Abu-Jamal. *TESOL Journal* (Winter), 27–33.
hooks, b. (1994) *Teaching to Transgress: Education as the Practice of Freedom*. New York: Routledge.

Horkheimer, M. (1972) *Critical Theory: Selected Essays*. New York: Herder and Herder (1st edn, 1968).
Horkheimer, M. and Adorno, T. (1972) *Dialectic of Enlightenment*. New York: Herder and Herder (1st edn, 1944).
Hoy, D.C. and McCarthy, T. (1994) *Critical Theory*. Cambridge, MA: Blackwell.
Ichilov, O. (ed.) (1998) *Citizenship and Citizenship Education in a Changing World*. London: The Woburn Press.
Ingold, T. (1993) The art of translation in a continuous world. In G. Pálsson (ed.) *Beyond Boundaries: Understanding, Translation and Anthropological Discourse* (pp. 211–30). Oxford: Berg.
Isajiw, W.W. (2000) Approaches to ethnic conflict resolution: Paradigms and principles. *International Journal of Intercultural Relations* 24, 105–24.
Isin, E.F. and Wood, P.K. (1999) *Citizenship and Identity*. London: Sage.
Jackson, P. (1968) *Life in Classrooms*. New York: Holt, Rinehart and Winston.
James, D. (1998) The impact on higher education of standards for foreign language learning: Preparing for the 21st century. *ACTFL Newsletter* (Fall), 11–14.
Jameson, F. (1998) *The Cultural Turn: Selected Writings on the Postmodern, 1983–1998*. London: Verso.
Jay, M. (1996) *The Dialectical Imagination*. Berkeley: University of California Press (1st edn, 1973).
Johnson, R. (1986/1987) What is cultural studies anyway? *Social Text: Theory/Culture/Ideology* 16 (Winter), 38–80.
Jumonville, N. (1991) *Critical Crossings: The New York Intellectuals in Postwar America*. Berkeley: University of California Press.
Kanpol, B. (1994) *Critical Pedagogy: An Introduction*. Westport, CO: Bergin and Garvey.
Kanpol, B. (1997) *Issues and Trends in Critical Pedagogy*. Cresskill: New Jersey.
Kanpol, B. and McLaren (eds) (1995) *Critical Multiculturalism: Uncommon Voices in a Common Struggle*. Westport, CO: Bergin and Gravey.
Keesing, R.M. (1994) Radical cultural difference: Anthropology's myth? In M. Pütz (ed.) *Language Contact and Language Conflict* (pp. 3–23). Amsterdam/Philadelpia: John Benjamins.
Kellner, D. (1988) Postmodernism as social theory: Some challenges and problems. *Theory, Culture and Society* 5 (2–3), 239–69.
Kellner, D. (1989) *Critical Theory, Marxism and Modernity*. Oxford: Blackwell.
Kellner, D. (1992) Popular culture and the construction of postmodern identities. In S. Lash and J. Friedman (eds) *Modernity and Identity* (pp. 141–77). Oxford: Blackwell.
Kerl, D. (1993) The case of *Landeskunde*: A vicious circle? *Language, Culture and Curriculum* 6 (1) Special issue, 5–9.
Killick, D. and Parry, M. (eds) (1997) Cross-cultural capability. The why, the ways and the means: New theories and methodologies in language education. Proceedings of the conference at Leeds Metropolitan University, 15–16 December.
Killick, D. and Parry, M. (eds) (1998) Languages for cross-cultural capability. Promoting the discipline: Making boundaries and crossing borders. Proceedings of the conference at Leeds Metropolitan University, 12–14 December.

Kincheloe, J.L. and Steinberg, S.R. (1993) A tentative description of post-formal thinking: The critical confrontation with cognitive theory. *Harvard Educational Review* 63 (3), 296–320.

King, C. (1990) A linguistic and a cultural competence: Can they live happily together? *Foreign Language Annals* 23 (1), 65–70.

Klein, J.T. (1990) *Interdisciplinarity: History, Theory, and Practice*. Detroit: Wayne State University Press.

Kleven, T. (1988) Cultural bias and the issue of bilingual education. *Social Policy* 19 (1), 9–12.

Klippel, F. (1994) Cultural aspects in foreign language teaching. *Journal for the Study of British Cultures* 1 (1), 49–61.

Kramer, J. (1990) Teaching the cultural, historical and intercultural to advanced language learners. *Language Learning Journal* 2, 58–61.

Kramer, J. (1993) Cultural studies in English studies: A German perspective. *Language, Culture and Curriculum* 6 (1), 27–43

Kramsch, C. (1983) Culture and constructs: Communicating attitudes and values in the foreign language classroom. *Foreign Language Annals* 16 (6), 437–48.

Kramsch, C. (1993a) *Context and Culture in Language Teaching*. Oxford: Oxford University Press.

Kramsch, C. (1993b) Language study as border study: Experiencing difference. *European Journal of Education* 28 (3), 349–58.

Kramsch, C. (1995) The cultural component of language teaching. *Language, Culture and Curriculum* 8 (2), 83–92.

Kramsch, C. (1998a) Teaching language along the cultural faultline. In D.L. Lange, C.A. Klee, M. Paige and Y.A. Yershova (eds) (pp. 15–31).

Kramsch, C. (1998b) *Language and Culture*. Oxford: Oxford University Press.

Kramsch, C. (1998c) The privilege of the intercultural speaker. In M. Byram and M. Fleming (eds) (pp. 16–31).

Kramsch, C. (2000) Second language acquisition, applied linguistics, and the teaching of foreign languages. *The Modern Language Journal* 84 (3), 311–26.

Kramsch, C., Cain, A. and Murphy-Lejeune, E. (1996). Why should language teachers teach culture?. *Language, Culture and Curriculum* 9 (1), 99–107.

Krashen, S. (1991) Bilingual education: A focus on current research. *Occasional Papers in Bilingual Education* 3. Washington, DC: National Clearinghouse for Bilingual Education.

Krashen, S. and Biber, D. (1988) *On Course: Bilingual Education's Success in California*. Sacramento: California Association for Bilingual Education.

Krathwohl, D.R., Bloom, B.S. and Masia, B.B. (1964) *Taxonomy of Educational Objectives: The Classification of Educational Goals*. New York: Longman.

Kreisberg, S. (1992) *Transforming Power*. Albany: State University of New York Press.

Kroeber, A.L. and Kluckhohn, C. (1952) *Culture: A Critical Review of Concepts and Definitions*. New York: Vintage Books.

Kron, F. (1996) Cultural and ideological dimensions of language awareness. *Curriculum and Teaching* 11 (2), 63–8.

Krueger, R.A. (1994) *Focus Groups: A Practical Guide for Applied Research*. Thousand Oaks: Sage.

Krueger, R.A. (1998a) *Developing Questions for Focus Groups*. Thousand Oaks: Sage

Krueger, R.A. (1998b) *Moderating Focus Groups*. Thousand Oaks: Sage.
Krueger, R.A. (1998c) *Analyzing and Reporting Focus Group Results*. Thousand Oaks: Sage.
Kumaravadivelu, B. (1994) The postmethod condition: Emerging strategies for second/foreign language teaching. *TESOL Quarterly* 28 (1), 27–47.
Kumaravadivelu, B. (1999) Critical classroom discourse analysis. *TESOL Quarterly* 33 (3), 453–84.
Kymlica, W. (1998) Multicultural citizenship. In G. Shafir (ed.) (pp. 167–88).
Laclau, E. (1988) Politics and the limits of modernity. In A. Ross (ed.) (pp. 63–82).
Laclau, E. (1996) Deconstruction, pragmatism, hegemony. In Mouffe, C. (ed.) (pp. 47–67).
Ladson-Billings, G. (1997) I know why this doesn't feel empowering: A critical race analysis of critical pedagogy. In P. Freire (ed.) *Mentoring the Mentor: A Critical Dialogue with Paulo Freire* (pp. 127–41). New York: Peter Lang.
Lakomski, G. (1999) Critical theory and education. In J.P. Keeves and G. Lakomski (eds) *Issues in Educational Research* (pp. 174–83). Oxford: Pergamon.
Lange, D.L. (1999) Planning for and using the new national culture standards. In J.K. Phillips and R.M. Terry (eds) (pp. 57–135).
Lange, D.L., Klee, C.A., Paige, R.M., and Yershova, Y.A. (eds) (1998) *Culture as the Core: Interdisciplinary Perspectives on Culture Teaching and Learning in the Language Curriculum*. Center for Advanced Research on Language Acquisition (CARLA), Working Paper Series: University of Minnesota.
Larrain, J. (1994) *Ideology and Cultural Identity*. Cambridge: Polity.
Larson, B.E. (1997) Social studies teachers'conceptions of discussion: A grounded theory study. *Theory and Research in Social Education* 25, (2), 113–36.
Leaver, B.L. and Stryker, S.B. (1989) Content-based instruction for foreign language classrooms. *Foreign Language Annals* 22 (3), 269–75.
Lederman, L.C. (1990) Assessing educational effectiveness: The focus group interview as a technique for data collection. *Communication Education* 38 (April), 117–27.
Lenoble, J. and Dewandre, N. (eds) (1992) *L`Europe au Soir du Siècle: Identité et Démocratie*. Paris: Éditions Esprit.
Levine, R. and Adelman, M.B. (1982) *Beyond Language: Intercultural Communication for English as a Second Language*. Englewood Cliffs, NJ: Prentice-Hall.
Lewis, J. and Jhally, S. (1994) The politics of cultural studies: Racism, hegemony, and resistance. *American Quarterly* 46 (1), 114–17.
Love, N. (1995) What's left of Marx? In S. White (ed.) (pp. 46–66).
Luke, C. and Gore, J. (eds) (1992) *Feminisms and Critical Pedagogy*. New York: Routledge.
Lyotard, J.F. (1983) *Le Différend*. Paris: Les Éditions de Minuit.
Lyotard, J.F. (1986) *The Postmodern Condition: A Report on Knowledge*. Manchester: Manchester University Press. (1st edn, 1979).
Lyotard, J.F. (1988a) Les lumiéres, le sublime. *Les Cahiers de Philosophie* 5, 63–98.
Lyotard, J.F. (1988b) Réécrire la modernité. *Les Cahiers de Philosophie* 5, 193–204.
Mak, A.S., Westwood, M.J., Ishiyama, F.I., and Barker, M.C. (1999) Optimising conditions for learning sociocultural competencies for success. *International Journal of Intercultural Relations* 23 (1), 77–90.

Males, T. (2000) What is critical in critical language awareness? *Language Awareness* 9 (3), 147–59.
Marcuse, H. (1991) *One Dimensional Man*. London: Routledge (1st edn, 1964).
Marshall, C. and Rossman, G. (1995) *Designing Qualitative Research*. Thousand Oaks: Sage.
Martin, R. (1988) Truth, power, self: An interview with Michel Foucault. In L. Martin, H. Gutman and P. Hutton (eds) *Technologies of the Self* (pp. 9–15). Amherst: University of Massachusetts Press.
Martins, H. (1998) Technology, modernity, politics. In J. Good and I. Velody (eds) (pp. 150–81).
Marx, E. (2001) *Breaking Through Culture Shock: What you Need to Succeed in International Business*. London: Nicholas Brealey.
Maxwell, J.A. (1992) Understanding and validity in qualitative research. *Harvard Educational Review* 62 (3), 279–300.
Maxwell, K. (1995) *The Making of Portuguese Democracy*. Cambridge: Cambridge University Press.
May, S. (ed.) (1999a) *Critical Multiculturalism*. London: The Falmer Press.
May, S. (1999b) Critical multiculturalism and cultural difference: Avoiding essentialism. In S. May (ed.) (pp. 11–41).
McCarthy, C. (1998) *The Uses of Culture: Education and the Limits of Ethnic Affiliation*. New York: Routledge.
McCarthy, M. and Carter, R. (1994) *Language as Discourse: Perspectives for Language Teaching*. Londres: Longman.
McLaren, P. (1995) *Critical Pedagogy and Predatory Culture*. London: Routledge.
McPeck, J.E. (1981) *Critical Thinking and Education*. Oxford: Martin Robertson.
Mehan, H. (1978) Structuring the school structure. *Harvard Educational Review*, 48 (1), 32–64.
Mehan, H. (1980) The competent student. *Anthropology and Education Quarterly* 11 (3), 131–52.
Melde, W. (1987) *Zur Integration von Landeskunde und Kommunikation im Fremdsprachenunterrricht*. Tübingen: Gunter Narr Verlag.
Met, M. and Byram, M. (1999) Standards for foreign language learning and the teaching of culture. *Language Learning Journal* 19 (June), 61–8.
Miles, M.B. and Huberman, A.M. (1984) *Qualitative Data Analysis: A Sourcebook of New Methods*. Newbury Park: Sage.
Miller, D. (1995) Citizenship and pluralism. *Political Studies* 63, 432–50.
Miller, D. (2000) Citizenship: What does it mean and why is it important? In N. Pearce and J. Hallgarten (eds) (pp. 26–35).
Ministério da Educação – DGEBS (1991) *Organização curricular e programas 1, 3º ciclo*. Lisboa: Imprensa Nacional, Casa da Moeda.
Ministério da Educação (1995) *Programa de Inglês, Secundário, Nível de continuação da LE1*. Departamento do Ensino Secundário.
Ministério da Educação (1996) *Desenvolvimento da Educação: Relatório Nacional de Portugal*. Genebra: UNESCO.
Misgeld, D. (1985) Education and cultural invasion: Critical social theory, education as instruction, and the 'Pedagogy of the oppressed'. In J. Forester (ed.) (pp. 77–118).

Modelski, G. (ed.) (1987) *Exploring Long Cycles*. London: Frances Pinter.
Mohanty, C.T. (1994) On race and voice: Challenges for liberal education in the 1990s. In H.A. Giroux and P. McLaren (eds) (pp. 145–66).
Montgomery, M. (1998) What is British cultural studies anyway and why are people saying such terrible things about it? In *British Studies Now* 10, 3–6.
Moore, R. and Muller, J. (1999) The discourse of 'voice' and the problem of knowledge and identity in the sociology of education. *British Journal of Sociology of Education* 20 (2), 189–206.
Morgan, C. (1995) Cultural awareness and the National Curriculum. *Language Learning Journal* 12, 9–84.
Morgan, C. and Cain, A. (2000) *Foreign Language and Culture from a Dialogic Perspective*. Clevedon: Multilingual Matters.
Morgan, D. (ed.) (1993) *Successful Focus Groups: Advancing the State of the Art*. Newbury Park: Sage.
Morgan, D.L. (1997) *Focus Groups as Qualitative Research*. Thousand Oaks: Sage.
Morgan, D. (1998a) *The Focus Group Guidebook*. Thousand Oaks: Sage
Morgan, D. (1998b) *Planning Focus Groups*. Thousand Oaks: Sage.
Morrison, K. (1995) Habermas and the school curriculum: An evaluation and case study. PhD thesis, University of Durham, England.
Morrison, K. (1996) Structuralism, postmodernity and discourses of control. *Curriculum* 17 (3), 164–77.
Mouffe, C. (ed.) (1992a) *Dimensions of Radical Democracy: Pluralism, Citizenship, Community*. London: Verso.
Mouffe, C. (1992b) Democratic politics today. In C. Mouffe (ed.) (pp. 1–14).
Mouffe, C. (1992c) Democratic citizenship and the political community. In C. Mouffe (ed.) (pp. 225–39).
Mouffe, C. (ed.) (1996a) *Deconstruction and Pragmatism*. London: Routledge.
Mouffe, C. (1996b) Radical democracy or liberal democracy? In D. Trend (ed.) *Radical democracy: Identity, Citizenship, and the State* (pp. 19–26). London: Routledge.
Mulhern, F. (2000) *Culture/Metaculture*. London: Routledge.
Murphy-Lejeune, E., Cain, A. and Kramsch, C. (1996) Analysing representations of Otherness using different text-types. *Language, Culture and Curriculum* 9 (1), 51–65.
National Standards in Foreign Language Education Project (1996) *Standards for Foreign Language Learning: Preparing for the 21st Century*. Lawrence, KS: Allen Press.
Nelson, G.L. (1998) Intercultural communication and related courses taught in TESOL masters' degree programs. *International Journal of Intercultural Communication* 22 (1), 17–33.
Niznik, J. and Sanders, J. (ed.) (1996) *Debating the State of Philosophy: Habermas, Rorty, and Kolakowsky*. Wesport, CO: Praeger.
Olshtain, E. and Kupferberg, I. (1998) Reflective-narrative discourse of FL teachers exhibits professional knowledge. *Language Teaching Research* 2 (3), 185–202.
O'Neill, J. (1985) Decolonization and the ideal speech community: Some issues in the theory and practice of communicative competence. In J. Forester (ed.) (pp. 57–76).

Oppenheim, A.N. (1992) *Questionnaire Design, Interviewing and Attitude Measurement.* London: Pinter.
Osler, A. (ed.) (2000a) *Citizenship and Democracy in Schools: Diversity, Identity, Equality.* Stoke on Trent: Trentham Books.
Osler, A. (2000b) The Crick report: Difference, equality and racial justice. *Curriculum Journal* 11 (1), 25–37.
Osler, A., Rathenow, H. and Starkey, H. (eds) (1995) *Teaching for Citizenship in Europe.* Stoke-on-Trent: Trentham Books.
Osler, A. and Starkey, H. (1996) *Teacher Education and Human Rights.* London: David Fulton.
Outram, D. (1995) *The Enlightenment.* Cambridge, UK: Cambridge University Press
Paige, R.M. (ed.) (1993) *Education for the Intercultural Experience.* Yarmouth, Maine: Intercultural Press.
Park, P. (1988) Breaking out of culture: Critical education for the silent minority. In Okihiro *et al.* (eds) *Reflections on Shattered Windows: Promises and Prospects for Asian American Studies* (pp. 94–100). Pullman, Washington: Washington State University Press.
Parker, W.C. (1997) Democracy and difference. *Theory and Research in Social Education* 25 (2), 220–34.
Passmore, J. (1967) On teaching to be critical. In R.S. Peters (ed.) *The Concept of Education,* (pp. 192–211). London: Routledge and Kegan Paul.
Payne, P. and Hickey, C. (1997) Teacher theorising, intellectual resources and praxis intentionality. *Teachers and Teaching: Theory and Practice* 3 (1), 101–17.
Pearce, N. and Hallgarten, J. (2000) *Tomorrow's Citizens: Critical Debates in Citizenship and Education.* London: Institute for Public Policy Research.
Peim, N. (1993) *Critical Theory and the English Teacher.* London: Routledge.
Pennycook, A. (1994) *English as an International Language.* London: Longman.
Pennycook, A. (1999) Introduction: Critical approaches. *TESOL Quarterly* 33 (3), 329–48.
Perotti, A. (1994) *The Case for Intercultural Education.* Strasbourg: Council of Europe.
Peters, M. (1996) *Poststructuralism, Politics and Education.* Wesport, CO: Bergin and Garvey.
Peters, M. and Lankshear, C. (1996) Postmodern counternarratives. In H.A. Giroux, C. Lankshear, P. McLaren and M. Peters (eds) (pp. 1–39).
Phillips, J.K. and Terry, R.M. (eds) (1999) *Foreign Language Standards: Linking Research, Theories, and Practices.* Lincoln, IL: National Textbook Company.
Phillipson, R. (1992) *Linguistic Imperialism.* Oxford: Oxford University Press.
Phipps, A. (2001a) Measuring performance: Some alternative indicators. In M. Walker (ed.) (pp. 129–48).
Phipps, A. (2001b) Busy foundries in modern languages and the humanities. In R. Di Napoli, L. Polezzi and A. King (eds) (pp. 185–92).
Pieterse, J.N. (1995) Globalization as hybridization. In M. Featherstone, S. Lash and R. Robertson (eds) (pp. 45–68).
Potter, J. (1999) *Education for Life, Work and Citizenship.* London: CSV, Education for Citizenship.
Prabhu, N.S. (1992) The dynamics of the language lesson. *TESOL Quarterly* 26 (2), 225–41.

Preston, P.W. (1997) *Political/Cultural Identity: Citizens and Nations in a Global Era*. London: Sage.
Putnam, H. (1990) *Realism with a Human Face*. Cambridge, MA: Harvard University Press
Putnam, H. (1995) *Pragmatism*. Oxford, UK: Blackwell
Putnam, H. (1996) The meaning of 'meaning'. In A. Pessin and S. Goldberg (eds) *The Twin Earth Chronicles: Twenty Years of Reflection on Hilary Putnam's 'The Meaning of "Meaning"'* (pp. 3–52). New York: M.E. Sharpe (1st edn, 1975).
Qualifications and Curriculum Authority (QCA) (1998) *Education for Citizenship and the Teaching of Democracy in Schools*. London: QCA.
Rassekh, S. and Vaideanu, G. (1987) *Les Contenus de l'Éducation: Perspectives Mondiales d'ici à l'An 2000*. Paris: UNESCO.
Rattansi, A. (1999) Racism, 'postmodernism' and reflexive multiculturalism. In S. May (ed.) (pp. 77–112).
Ravitch, D. (1978) *The Revisionists Revised: A Critique of the Radical Attack on the Schools*. New York: Basic Books.
Redmond, M.V. (2000) Cultural distance as a mediating factor between stress and intercultural communication competence. *International Journal of Intercultural Relations* 24, 151–9.
Révauger, J.P. (1993) Civilisation/Cultural Studies in Grenoble. In M. Byram (ed.) *Language, Culture and Curriculum* 6 (1) Special issue, 19–25.
Risager, K. (1998). Language teaching and the process of European integration. In M. Byram and M. Fleming (eds) (pp. 242–54).
Roberts, C. (1993) Cultural studies and student exchange: Living the ethnographic life. *Language, Culture and Curriculum* 6 (1), 11–17.
Roberts, C. (1994) Ethnographic approaches to cultural learning. *British Studies Now* 3 (Jan.), 2–3.
Roberts, C., Byram, M., Barro, A., Jordan, S. and Street, B. (2001) *Language Learners as Ethnographers*. Clevedon: Multilingual Matters.
Robertson, R. (1995) Glocalization: Time-space and homogeneity-heterogeneity. In M. Featherstone, S. Lash and R. Robertson (eds) (pp. 25–44).
Robinson, G.L.N. (1988) *Crosscultural Undersanding*. New York: Prentice Hall.
Rorty, R. (1982) *Consequences of Pragmatism (Essays: 1972–1980)*. Brighton, UK: The Harvester Press
Rorty, R. (1989) *Contingency, Irony and Solidarity*. Cambridge, UK: Cambridge University Press.
Rorty, R. (1991) *Objectivity, Relativism, and Truth*. Cambridge, UK: Cambridge University Press.
Rorty, R. (1996a) Emancipating our culture. In J. Niznik and J. Sanders (eds) (pp. 24–9).
Rorty, R. (1996b) Relativism: Finding and making. In J. Niznik and J. Sanders (eds) (pp. 31–47).
Rorty, R. (1996c) On moral obligation, truth, and common sense. In J. Niznik and J. Sanders (eds) (pp. 48–52).
Rorty, R. (1996d) Response to Simon Critchley. In C. Mouffe (ed.) (pp. 41–6).
Ross, A. (ed.) (1988) *Universal Abandon? The Politics of Postmodernism*. Minneapolis: University of Minnesota.
Roth, W-M. and Harama, H. (2000) (Standard) English as second language: Tribulation of self. *Journal of Curriculum Studies* 32 (6), 757–75.

Roy, A. and W.J. Starosta (2001) Hans-Georg Gadamer, Language, and Intercultural Communication. *Language and Intercultural Communication* 1 (1), 6–20.

Ruiz, V. (1993) 'It's the people who drive the book': A view from the west. *American Quarterly* 45 (2), 243–8.

Rutherford, J. (ed.) (1990) *Identity: Community, Culture, Difference*. London: Lawrence and Wishart.

Sandrock, P. (1997) State Standards: Connecting a national vision to local implementation. *ACTFL Newsletter* (Winter), 7–13.

Santos, B.S. (1994) *Pela Mão de Alice: O Social e o Político na Pós-Modernidade*. Porto: Edições Afrontamento.

Scercu, L. (ed.) (1995) *Intercultural Competence: A New Challenge for Language Teachers and Trainers in Europe 1: The Secondary School*. Aalborg: Aalborg University Press.

Scheu-Lottgen, U.D. and Hernández-Campoy, J.M. (1998) An analysis of sociocultural communication: English, Spanish and German. *International Journal of Intercultural Relations* 22 (4), 375–94.

Scholfield, P. (1995) *Quantifying Language*. Clevedon: Multilingual Matters.

Schultz, R. (2000) Foreign language teacher development: MLJ perspectives – 1916–1999. *The Modern Language Journal* 84 (4), 495–519.

Sears, A. (1996) 'Something different to everyone': Conceptions of citizenship and citizenship education. *Canadian and International Education* 25 (2), 1–16.

Seelye, H.N. (1982) *Teaching Culture: Strategies for Foreign Language Educators*. Stokie, IL: National Textboook Company.

Seelye, H.N. (1992) *Teaching Culture: Strategies for Intercultural Communication*. Lincolnhood, IL: National Textbook Company (1st edn, 1984).

Seelye, H.N. and Wasilewski, J.H. (1996) *Between Cultures: Developing Self-Identity in a World of Diversity*. Lincolnhood, IL: NTC Publishing Group.

Seelye, N. (1995) *Culture Clash*. Lincolnhood, IL: NTC Business Books.

Seelye, N. (ed.) (1996) *Experiential Activities for Intercultural Learning*. Yarmouth, Maine: Intercultural Press.

Seigworth, G.J. (2000) Banality for cultural studies. *Cultural Studies* 14 (2), 227–68.

Shafir, G. (ed.) (1998) *The Citizenship Debates*. Minneapolis: University of Minnesota Press.

Shapiro, M.J. (2000) National times and other times: Re-thinking citizenship. *Cultural Studies* 14 (1), 79–98.

Sheils, J. (1996) The Council of Europe and language learning for European citizenship. *Evaluation and Research Education* 10 (2–3), 88–103.

Siegel, H. (1988) *Educating Reason*. New York: Routledge.

Silva, D. (1993) Critical reflection: Its role in professional development programs for practising educators: A participatory research study with language teachers. PhD thesis, University of San Francisco.

Simões, A. (1992) Critical pedagogy in bilingual education: Language proficiency and bilingualism. In R.V. Padilla and A.H. Benavides (eds) *Critical Perspectives on Bilingual Education Research* (pp. 110–24). Tempe, AZ: Bilingual Press/Editorial Bilingue.

Singh, R., Lele, J. and Martohardjono, G. (1988) Communication in a multilingual society: Some missed opportunities. *Language in Society* 17, 43–59.

Sirkin, R.M. (1995) *Statistics for Social Sciences*. Thousand Oaks, CA: Sage.
Skutnabb-Kangas, T. and Cummins, J. (1988) *Minority Education: From Shame to Struggle*. Clevedon: Multilingual Matters.
Sleeter, C.E. (1991) *Empowerment through Multicultural Education*. Albany: State University of New York Press.
Smart, B. (1993). *A Pós-Modernidade*. Mem Martins: Publicações Europa-América.
Smith, A.D. (1976) Introduction: The formation of nationalist movements. In A.D. Smith (ed.) *Nationalist Movements* (pp. 1–30). London: Macmillan.
Smith, A.D. (1979) *Nationalism in the Twentieth Century*. New York: New York University Press.
Smith, A.D. (1986) *The Ethnic Origins of Nations*. Oxford: Basil Blackwell.
Smith, S.L., Paige, R.M., and Steglitz, I. (1998) Theoretical foundations of intercultural training and applications to the teaching of culture. In D.L. Lange, C.A. Klee, R.M. Paige and Y.A. Yershova (eds) (pp. 53–91).
Smolicz, J.J. (1996) Education for a global society. *Education and Society* 14 (2), 83–7.
Smyth, J. (ed.) (1989a) *Critical Perspectives on Educational Leadership*. London: Falmer.
Smyth, J. (1989b) A critical pedagogy of classroom practice. *Journal of Curriculum Studies* 21 (6), 483–502.
Smyth, J. (1989c) Developing and sustaining critical reflection in teacher education. *Journal of Teacher Education* 40 (2), 2–9.
Smyth, J. (1991) *Teachers as Collaborative Learners*. Milton Keynes: Open University Press.
Smyth, J. (ed.) (1995). *Critical Discourses on Teacher Development*. London: Cassell.
Snow, M.A., Met, M. and Genesee, F. (1989) A conceptual framework for the integration of language and content in second/foreign language instruction. *TESOL Quarterly* 23 (2), 201–17.
Soysal, Y. (1998) Toward a postnational model of membership. In G. Shafir (ed.) (pp. 189–217).
Sparrow, L.M. (2000) Beyond multicultural man: Complexities of identity. *International Journal of Intercultural Relations* 24, 173–201.
Speicher, B.L. and Bielanski, J.R. (2000) Critical thoughts on teaching standard English. *Curriculum Inquiry* 30 (2), 147–69.
Spindler, G. (ed.) (1974) *Education and Cultural Process: Toward an Anthropology of Education*. New York: Holt, Rinehart & Winston.
Spindler, G. (1982) General introduction. In G. Spindler (ed.) *Doing the Ethnography of Schooling* (pp. 1–13). New York: Holt, Rinehart & Winston.
Spolsky, B. (1989) *Conditions for Second Language Learning*. Oxford: Oxford University Press.
Squires, J. (1998) In different voices: Deliberative democracy and aestheticist politics. In J. Good and I. Velody (eds) (pp. 126–46).
Stanley, W. (1992) *Curriculum for Utopia: Social Reconstructionism and Critical Pedagogy in the Postmodern Era*. Albany: State University of New York Press.
Stake, R.E. (1995) *The Art of Case Study Research*. Thousand Oaks: Sage.
Starkey, H. (ed.) (1991) *The Challenge of Human Rights Education*. London: Cassell.
Starkey, H. (2000) Citizenship education in France and Britain: Evolving theories and practices. *The Curriculum Journal* 11 (1), 39–54.
Stephanson, A. (1988) Regarding postmodernism: A conversation with Frederic Jameson. In A. Ross (ed.) (pp. 3–30).

Stewart, D.W. and Shamdasani, P.N. (1990) Focus groups: Theory and practice. *Applied Social Research Methods Series* 20. Newbury Park: Sage.

Stuen, C. (1995) Citizenship and community service: Teaching democracy through participation. *Education Practice and Theory* 17 (1), 71–6.

Sudman, S. and Bradburn, N. (1982) *Asking Questions: A Practical Guide to Questionnaire Design*. San Francisco: Jossey-Bass.

Sutton, A. (1988) L.S. Vygotskii: The cultural-historical theory, national minorities and the zone of next development. In R. Gupta and P. Coxhead (eds) *Cultural Diversity and Learning Efficiency: Recent Developments in Assessment* (pp. 89–117). London: Macmillan.

Swingewood, A. (1998) *Cultural Theory and the Problem of Modernity*. London: Macmillan.

Taylor, P.V. (1993) *The Texts of Paulo Freire*. Buckingham: Open University Press.

The New London Group (1996) A pedagogy of multiliteracies: Designing social futures. *Harvard Educational Review* 66 (1), 60–92.

Therborn, G. (1995) *European Modernity and Beyond*. London: Sage.

Thomas, G. (1997) What's the use of theory? *Harvard Educational Review* 67 (1), 75–103.

Tilley, J. J. (2000) Cultural relativism. *Human Rights Quarterly* 22, 501–47.

Tomalin, B. and Stempleski, S. (1993) *Cultural Awareness*. Oxford: Oxford University Press.

Tomlinson, J. (1995) Teachers and values. *The British Journal of Educational Studies* 43 (3), 305–17.

Trayer, M. (1997) Foreign language standards: The Nebraska story. *ACTFL Newsletter* (Spring), 7–11.

Tremmel, R. (1993) Zen and the art of reflective practice in teacher education. *Harvard Educational Review* 63 (4), 434–58.

Trueba, H. (1990) The role of culture in literacy acquisition: An interdisciplinary approach to qualitative research. *Qualitative Studies in Education* 3 (1), 1–13.

Trueba, H. (1991) The role of culture in bilingual instruction: Linking linguistic and cognitive development to cultural knowledge. In O. Garcia (ed.) *Bilingual Education: Focusschrift in Honor of Joshua A. Fishman* (pp. 43–55). Amsterdam: John Benjamins.

Turner, B. (ed.) (1993a) *Theories of Modernity and Postmodernity*. London: Sage.

Turner, B. (1993b) Periodization and politics in the postmodern. In B. Turner (ed.) (pp. 1–13).

Turner, B. (1994) Postmodern culture/modern citizens. In B. van Steenbergen (ed.) *The Condition of Citizenship* (pp. 153–68). London: Sage.

Tye, B.B. and Tye, K. (1992) *Global Education: A Study of School Change*. Albany, NY: State University of New York Press.

Urbanski, A. and Nickolaou, M. (1997) Reflections on teachers as leaders. *Educational Policy* 11 (2), 243–54.

Usher, R. and Edwards, R. (1994) *Postmodernism and Education*. London: Routledge.

Vaca, N.C. (1981) The comparative study of values in five cultures project and the theory of value. *Aztlan* 12 (1), 89–120.

Valdes, J.M. (ed.) (1986) *Culture Bound: Bridging the Cultural Gap in Language Teaching*. Cambridge: Cambridge University Press.

Van Oudenhoven, J.P. (2001) Do organizations reflect national cultures? A 10-nation study. *International Journal of Intercultural Relations* 25, 89–107.
Vaughn, S., Shumm, J.S. and Sinagub, J. (1996) *Focus Group Interviews in Education and Psychology*. Thousand Oaks: Sage.
Veerman, D. (1988) Développer l'honneur de penser. *Les Cahiers de Philosophie* 5, 11–34.
Venn, C. (1997) Beyond Enlightenment: After the subject of Foucault, who comes? *Theory, Culture and Society* 14 (3), 1–28.
Vygotsky, L. (1978) *Mind in Society: The Development of Higher Psychological Processes*. M. Cole, V. John-Steiner, S. Scribner and E. Souberman (eds). Cambridge: Harvard University Press.
Vygotsky, L. (1986) *Thought and Language* [*Myshlenie i rech*]. Cambridge: The MIT Press (1st edn, 1939).
Walker, M. (ed.) (2001) *Reconstructing Professionalism in University Teaching: Teachers and Learners in Action*. Buckinghamshire: Open University Press.
Walsh, C. (1991) *Pedagogy and the Struggle for Voice*. New York: Bergin and Garvey.
Wardekker, W.L. and Miedema, S. (1997) Critical pedagogy: An evaluation and a direction for reformulation. *Curriculum Inquiry* 27 (1), 45–61.
Warren, M. (1995) The self in discursive democracy. In S. White (ed.) (pp. 167–200).
Wax, M. and Wax, R. (1971) Great tradition, little tradition, and formal education. In M. Wax, S. Diamond and F. Gearing (eds) *Anthropological Perspectives on Education* (pp. 3–18). New York: Basic Books.
Weiler, K. (1993) Freire and a feminist pedagogy of difference. In K. Geismar and G. Nicoleau (eds) (pp. 71–97).
Weinreich, U. (1968) *Languages in Contact*. The Hague: Mouton Publishers.
Welles, E. (1998) Standards for foreign language learning: Implications and perceptions. *ACTFL Newsletter* (Fall), 7–9.
Wellmer, A. (1988) Dialectique de la modernité et de la postmodernité. *Les Cahiers de Philosophie* 5, 99–161.
Wexler, P. (1982) Structure, text, and subject: A critical sociology of school knowledge. In M. Apple (ed.) *Cultural and Economic Reproduction in Education: Essays on Class, Ideology and the State* (pp. 275–303). London: Routledge and Kegan Paul.
Wexler, P. (1993) Citizenship in the semiotic society. In B. Turner (ed.) (pp. 164–75).
White, S. K. (ed.) (1995) *The Cambridge Companion to Habermas*. Cambridge: Cambridge University Press.
Whorf, B. (1956) *Language, Thought and Reality*. Cambridge: The MIT Press.
Willet, C. (ed.) (1998) *Theorizing Multiculturalism: A Guide to Current Debate*. Malden, MA: Blackwell.
Williams, R. (1958) *Culture and Society: 1780–1950*. Middlesex: Penguin.
Williams, R. (1961) The analysis of culture. In R. Williams. *The Long Revolution* (pp. 57–88). Harmondsworth: Penguin.
Williams, R. (1977) *Marxism and Literature*. Oxford: Oxford University Press.
Williams, R. (1983) *Towards 2000*. London: Chatto and Windus, The Hogarth Press.
Wink, J. (1997) *Critical Pedagogy: Notes from the Real World*. New York: Longman.
Wittgenstein, L. (1969) *On Certainty*. Oxford: Basil Blackwell.

Wittgenstein, L. (1980). *Culture and Value.* Oxford: Basil Blackwell (1st edn, 1977).
Wittgenstein, L. (1994) *Philosophical Investigations.* Oxford, UK: Blackwell (1st edn, 1953).
Wolcott, H.F. (1991) Propriospect and the acquisition of culture. *Anthropology and Education Quarterly* 22 (3), 251–73.
Wolff, B., Knodel, J. and Sittitrai, W. (1993) *Successful Focus Groups: Advancing the State of the Art.* In D. Morgan (ed.) (pp. 118–34).
Wringe, C. (1984) *Democracy, Schooling and Political Education.* London: Allen and Unwin.
Wringe, C. (1992) The ambiguities of education for active citizenship. *Journal of Philosophy of Education* 26 (1), 29–38.
Wringe, C. (1995) Formation autonome . . .: The first year. *Language Learning Journal* 12, 16–19.
Wringe, C. (1996) The role of foreign language learning in education for European citizenship. *Evaluation and Research in Education* 10 (2–3), 68–78.
Yin, R.K. (1994). *Case Study Research: Design and Methods.*Thousand Oaks: Sage.
Young, I. (1998) Polity and group difference: A critique of the ideal of universal citizenship. In G. Shafir (ed.) (pp. 263–90).
Young, M. (ed.) (1971) *Knowledge and Control.* London: Collier-Macmillan.
Young, R.E. (1989) *A Critical Theory of Education: Habermas and our Children's Future.* New York: Harvester Wheatsheaf.
Young, R.E. (1992) *Critical Theory and Classroom Talk.* Clevedon: Multilingual Matters.
Youngman, M.B. (1978) *Designing and Analysing Questionnaires.* Nottingham: University School of Education.
Zamel, V. (1997) Toward a model of transculturation. *TESOL Quarterly* 31 (2), 341–52.
Zarate, G. (1995) Cultural awareness and the classification of documents for the description of foreign culture. *Language Learning Journal,* 11 (March), 24–5.
Zeichner, K. (1983) Alternative paradigms of teacher education. *Journal of Teacher Education* 34 (3), 3–9.
Zeichner, K.M. (1993) *A Formação Reflexiva de Professores: Ideias e Práticas.* Lisboa: Educa.

Appendix 1
Questionnaire

SECTION 1
THE TEACHING/LEARNING OF CULTURE
IN FOREIGN LANGUAGE CLASSES

Indicate to what extent you agree/disagree with the following statements. Circle the letter which corresponds to your choice.

| A. Agree strongly | B. Agree to some extent | C. Undecided | D. Disagree to some extent | E. Disagree strongly |

1. The cultural dimension in foreign language classes should be expanded.
   A.   B.   C.   D.   E.

2. European and global identities of the pupil/citizen should be fostered in foreign language/culture classes.
   A.   B.   C.   D.   E.

3. All the English-speaking cultures around the world are equally valid to be represented in an English syllabus.
   A.   B.   C.   D.   E.

4. The study of culture in language classes can hinder progress in linguistic accuracy.
   A.   B.   C.   D.   E.

5. Learning about a foreign culture can change the pupil's attitude towards her/his own culture.
   A.   B.   C.   D.   E.

6. An emphasis on the study of foreign cultures can contribute to the pupil's loss of cultural identity.

   A.   B.   C.   D.   E.

7. The most important goal in learning about a foreign culture is to develop a critical attitude towards both target and native cultures.

   A.   B.   C.   D.   E.

8. The development of critical cultural awareness should be kept only for the most advanced levels.

   A.   B.   C.   D.   E.

SECTION 2
THE CRITICAL DIMENSION IN FOREIGN CULTURE EDUCATION

The aim of this Section is to clarify what the critical dimension in foreign culture education is about.
Choose ONE of the options. Choose the one which is closest to your own opinion.
Circle the letter that precedes your choice.

1. Every culture represents a conceptual framework that

   A. constitutes a particular way of interpreting the world

   B. is the product of a national history

   C. is the result of the cohabitation of different groups (minorities, social classes, etc.)

   D. consists of a temporary balance of ever-changing forces and ideas

2. In her/his cultural approach, the teacher should

   A. be politically neutral

   B. offer her/his opinion and encourage discussion

   C. listen to the pupils' views and be impartial

   D. guide pupils' ideas

3. The pupil may be considered to be critical if s/he

   A. is always ready to participate in debates

   B. often disagrees with her/his teacher and colleagues

   C. is sceptical about new perspectives and values

   D. looks for the motives and causes behind attitudes and events

Appendix 1: Questionnaire

4. The most characteristic trait of a critical individual is being

   A. intelligent
   B. argumentative
   C. dissatisfied
   D. curious

5. A critical attitude towards a certain aspect of culture

   A. is both an emotional and an intellectual response
   B. consists of overcoming an emotional response
   C. is an emotional response
   D. is an intellectual response

6. A critical approach to a controversial topic means

   A. identifying what is right and wrong
   B. encouraging an exchange of individual views
   C. focusing on values and interests involved in the various perspectives
   D. coming to a consensus

7. Having a critical view of a country implies

   A. recognising its positive and negative aspects
   B. being pessimistic about its future
   B. not liking the kind of society it has become
   D. knowing about the factors that explain its historical evolution

8. Adopting a critical perspective towards cultural values, products, and institutions means

   A. presenting alternatives
   B. identifying their errors
   C. questioning authority
   D. analysing the relationships between cultural values, products, and institutions

9. Developing the pupils' critical cultural awareness involves helping her/him to

   A. become aware of the positive/negative aspects of another culture
   B. question the way 'common sense' rules our routines
   C. step back from both cultures in order to have more choice
   D. acknowledge similarities and differences between cultures

10. Having a political attitude towards the teaching about a foreign culture means

   A. sharing information on the political system of the country(ies) under discussion
   B. establishing the relationship between its power structure and forms of cultural production
   C. sharing information about democratic models in more developed countries
   D. initiating a discussion about its political parties

11. Having ethical concerns while teaching/learning about a foreign culture means

   A. accepting difference as equally valid
   B. being tolerant of difference
   C. being able to recognise right from wrong
   D. taking action against injustice

SECTION 3
REASONS FOR ADOPTING A CRITICAL APPROACH

This section aims at identifying the reasons that may justify a critical approach while teaching/learning about a foreign culture.

Choose 2 (TWO) options which you find most important in each set. Alternatively, choose 1 (ONE) choice and write one of your own. Circle the letter which precedes your choice.

1. Both European integration and global economy have caused greater mobility of citizens. For this reason, it is urgent that we

   A. feel ethically responsible for each other and for the planet we share

   B. reinforce our national identities

   C. are prepared to co-operate with our partners independently of their ethnicity

   D. see cultures in perspective to each other

   E. ....

2. Nowadays society is characterised by more intimacy between different ethnicities, social classes, ages and gender. So, it is necessary to recognise

   A. the strategies used by each group to get itself a position within the social network
   B. the existence of various communication levels
   C. that all are entitled to have a 'voice'
   D. that each social group has its own place
   E. ....

3. Interaction among different cultures is more frequent now. So, it is necessary that

   A. consensus can be reached
   B. conflict is avoided
   C. the relationship between power and culture is regarded as a moral and ethical issue
   D. the individual is prepared to deal with cultural divergence
   E. ....

4. Misunderstanding between individuals from different cultures often originates from the fact that

   A. each one draws conclusions from one's own cultural patterns
   B. each individual has contradictory and unexpected responses independent from the culture s/he belongs to
   C. individuals have prejudices about the value of other cultures
   D. cultural meanings and social norms that rule our daily activity are mostly unconscious
   E. ....

5. Since school promotes contact with other cultures, it has the mission to prepare future citizens for

   A. the confrontation of ideas and values
   B. intercultural co-operation and solidarity
   C. expressing their own individuality
   D. tolerating difference
   E. ....

SECTION 4
OUTCOMES OF A CRITICAL APPROACH

This section aims at finding out possible outcomes of a critical approach on the teaching/learning about foreign culture. The first section is about the individual and the second one is about the society. Show your opinion of each of the following statements. Circle the letter which signals your choice:

A. YES   B. NO   C. NO OPINION

4. a. for the individual

1. Being critical stimulates more individual rather than group expression .... A. B. C.
2. The development of critical cultural awareness strengthens cultural identity .... A. B. C.
3. The development of critical cultural awareness favours cultural uprootedness .... A. B. C.
4. The development of critical cultural awareness stimulates the capacity for making decisions .... A. B. C.
5. The formation of a critical attitude generates social intervention .... A. B. C.
6. The development of critical cultural awareness may weaken self-esteem .... A. B. C.
7. Teaching/learning critically about culture stimulates intellectual curiosity .... A. B. C.

4. b. for the society

1. Critical cultural awareness breaks down cultural borders .... A. B. C.
2. Critical attitudes can make dialogue difficult .... A. B. C.
3. Developing critical cultural awareness encourages commitment to democratic citizenship .... A. B. C.
4. The development of a critical attitude puts obedience and authority into question .... A. B. C.
5. The emphasis on critical perspectives could threaten democratic order .... A. B. C.

6. Teaching/learning critically about cultures helps the formation of a supranational identity (European/global) .... A. B. C.

7. Taking on critical attitudes can accentuate conflict in intercultural relationships .... A. B. C.

8. The development of critical cultural awareness could help reduce violence .... A. B. C.

9. The development of critical cultural awareness has the potential to turn teaching/learning into a political act ...... A. B. C.

SECTION 5
PROCEDURES FOR A CRITICAL APPROACH

This section aims at identifying the procedures which can most promote the critical teaching/learning about a foreign culture. Circle the number corresponding its order of importance (no 5 will be the most important) in each of the following statements:

1. General principles for a critical approach to a cultural topic:

    A. Communication aims at achieving consensus 5 4 3 2 1

    B. Culture is always changing 5 4 3 2 1

    C. The division between high and popular cultures is outdated 5 4 3 2 1

    D. Cultural identities are contradictory 5 4 3 2 1

    E. Reflexion is as important as dialogue 5 4 3 2 1

2. In order to promote a critical view of the culture I teach, it seems important to:

    A. provide updated information 5 4 3 2 1

    B. identify/discuss prejudices in the materials used 5 4 3 2 1

    C. raise feelings and emotions about that culture... 5 4 3 2 1

    D. identify relationships between cultural practices, products, and ideas 5 4 3 2 1

    E. give representation of various groups within the culture 5 4 3 2 1

3. The development of a critical attitude depends mostly on:
   A. the choice of instructional materials 5 4 3 2 1
   B. the types of instructional activities 5 4 3 2 1
   C. the approach featured in the textbook 5 4 3 2 1
   D. the contents of the syllabus 5 4 3 2 1
   E. the approach suggested by the teacher 5 4 3 2 1

4. How important are these activities for the development of critical cultural awareness?
   A. Compare/constrast 5 4 3 2 1
   B. Imagine 5 4 3 2 1
   C. Comment 5 4 3 2 1
   D. True/false 5 4 3 2 1
   E. Justify 5 4 3 2 1

5. Which of the following 'operationalization procedures' (*Programa de Inglês, Secundário, Nível de Continuação da LE1*, translation mine) may best facilitate a critical teaching/learning about a foreign culture?
   A. Gathers data 5 4 3 2 1
   B. Describes 5 4 3 2 1
   C. Evaluates 5 4 3 2 1
   D. Formulates hypothesis 5 4 3 2 1
   E. Questions 5 4 3 2 1

6. What does it mean 'Interprets critically cultural patterns specific to different spheres – yours, the other(s)' and the target culture(s)' ones' (*Programa de Inglês, Secundário, Nível de Comunicação da LE1*, p. 54, emphasis mine)?
   A. Identifies cause/effect relationships 5 4 3 2 1
   B. Describes facts 5 4 3 2 1
   C. Recognises positive and negative aspects 5 4 3 2 1
   D. Analyses similarities and differences 5 4 3 2 1
   E. Collects information 5 4 3 2 1

Appendix 1: Questionnaire 261

SECTION 6
PROFESSIONAL DEVELOPMENT MODELS

It is the aim of this Section to find out the needs for professional development that teachers may have in order to implement a critical dimension in the teaching/learning about a foreign culture. Show how far you agree/disagree with the following statements. Circle the letter which corresponds to your choice:

| A. Yes, very much | B. Yes, to some extent | C. No, not particularly | D. No, not at all |

1. My academic training prepared me for incorporating a critical approach towards culture in my teaching.

    A.   B.   C.   D.

2. I usually discuss ways of developing the pupils' critical cultural awareness with colleagues who teach other foreign languages.

    A.   B.   C.   D.

3. My main concern in my teaching is to follow the syllabus faithfully.

    A.   B.   C.   D.

4. I need some training in how to address critically culture in the materials I use.

    A.   B.   C.   D.

5. I need some training in how to use critically my own personal experiences of the culture(s) I teach for pedagogical purposes.

    A.   B.   C.   D.

6. Foreign culture teachers should be given some preparation in interdisciplinary areas relevant to their teaching activities.

    A.   B.   C.   D.

7. Reflecting about the principles and values that underlie my approach to the cultures I teach is frequently part of my lesson planning.

    A.   B.   C.   D.

8. Critical teaching of culture demands of the teacher a higher level of oral proficiency.

    A.   B.   C.   D.

9. The kind of training I need most is in the methods of teaching the foreign language.

    A.   B.   C.   D.

10. Critical teaching of culture makes lesson planning more difficult.

    A.   B.   C.   D.

11. I have relied mostly on my intuition and common sense while teaching about a foreign culture.

    A.   B.   C.   D.

12. The factor that most influences my way of teaching about foreign culture(s) is the textbooks I am currently using.

    A.   B.   C.   D.

13. I need to acquire more knowledge about English-speaking countries other than the United Kingdom and the United States in order to teach about them.

    A.   B.   C.   D.

14. When teaching about English-speaking cultures it is important to place them in an international and global context.

    A.   B.   C.   D.

15. If teacher training courses are not followed by well-co-ordinated projects at schools there will be no long-term effects.

    A.   B.   C.   D.

16. Significant changes in teaching practices will only happen when teachers are aware of the theories that underlie their practices.

    A.   B.   C.   D.

17. Teachers are the most important agents of innovation in education.

    A.   B.   C.   D.

SECTION 7
GENERAL INFORMATION

This Section aims to find out biographical and demographic data which will facilitate the classification of your answers. Circle the letter that corresponds to your case:

I. <u>Biographical data</u>

1. Age:
   A. 20–29   B. 30–39   C. 40–49   D. 50–59   E. 60–69

2. Academic background:
   A. *Bacharelato*   B. *Licenciatura*
   C. *Mestrado*   D. *Doutoramento*

3. Professional status:
   A. No academic degree   B. With academic degree
   C. No teacher training   D. With teacher training

II. <u>Contacts with English-speaking countries</u>

1. Which English-speaking countries have you visited?
   ....

2. Which kind of visit/residence has it mainly been?
   (circle as many options as necessary)
   A. Tourist visits   F. Attendance on a course
   B. Grown up in the country   G. Teacher exchange
   C. Visits to close relatives   H. Pupil exchange
   D. Visits to friends   I. Other work in the country
   E. Stay with strangers   J. Other (specify) ....

3. How frequently do you usually visit countries where English is spoken:
   A. more than twice a year   E. once every five years
   B. twice a year   F. less frequently
   C. once per year   G. never
   D. once every two years

4. Where do you get information about the English-speaking countries? (circle as many options as necessary)

    A. Portuguese radio or television
    B. Foreign radio or television
    C. Portuguese newpapers/magazines
    D. Foreign newpapers/magazines
    E. Cultural institutes
    F. Courses and conferences
    G. Professional associations
    H. Visits from teachers/pupils from the country
    I. Contact with native speakers living here
    J. Own contacts abroad
    L. Other (specify) [[dots]]

5. Do you think that teachers have sufficient opportunities, *in this country*, for keeping in touch with the countries whose language(s) they teach?

    A. yes, very much
    B. yes, to a certain extent
    C. no, not particularly
    D. no, not at all
    E. don't know

III. Data about the school

1. My school is located in the

    A. north   B. centre   C. south

2. The area my school is situated is

    A. urban   B. suburban   C. rural   D. mixed

3. Describe the social background of your pupils in 2–6 keywords:

    ....
    ....

IV. Topics for further discussion

Please indicate one question in each Section you would like to discuss:

Section 1: ....   Section 2: ....
Section 3: ....   Section 4: ....
Section 5: ....   Section 6: ....

Please accept my gratitude for the time and attention that you have dedicated to this questionnaire. Thank you!

NOTE: The results of the questionnaire, in percentages, are displayed in Appendix 4.

Appendix 2
Questionário A

SECÇÃO 1
O ENSINO/APRENDIZAGEM DE CULTURA
NA AULA DE LÍNGUA ESTRANGEIRA

Mostre o grau do seu acordo/desacordo em relação a cada uma das afirmações seguintes. Assinale com um círculo a letra que corresponde à sua opção:

A. Concordo inteiramente   B. Concordo em parte   C. Estou indeciso(a)   D. Discordo em parte   E. Discordo inteiramente

1. Deveria ser dada maior relevância à dimensão cultural nas aulas de língua estrangeira

    A.   B.   C.   D.   E.

2. As identidades europeias e global devem ser fomentadas nas aulas de língua/cultura estrangeira.

    A.   B.   C.   D.   E.

3. Todas as culturas de língua inglesa espalhadas pelo mundo têm a mesma legitimidade num programa de língua inglesa.

    A.   B.   C.   D.   E.

4. O estudo de cultura nas aulas de língua tem prejudicado o aperfeiçoamento da correcção linguística.

    A.   B.   C.   D.   E.

5. A aprendizagem de uma cultura estrangeira pode mudar a atitude do aluno em relação à sua própria cultura.

    A.   B.   C.   D.   E.

6. A ênfase no estudo das culturas estrangeiras contribui para o enfraquecimento da identidade cultural dos alunos.

   A.   B.   C.   D.   E.

7. O objectivo mais importante na aprendizagem das culturas estrangeiras é o de desenvolver uma atitude crítica em relação às culturas alvo e materna.

   A.   B.   C.   D.   E.

8. O desenvolvimento de uma consciência cultural crítica só deveria ser fomentado no ensino secundário.

   A.   B.   C.   D.   E.

SECÇÃO 2
A DIMENSÃO CRÍTICA DO ENSINO/APRENDIZAGEM
DE UMA CULTURA ESTRANGEIRA

Nesta Secção procurar-se-á clarificar em que consiste a dimensão crítica do ensino/aprendizagem de uma língua estrangeira.
Escolha apenas UMA das hipóteses. Opte por aquela que mais se aproxima da sua opinião. Assinale com um círculo a letra que corresponde à sua opção.

1. Cada cultura representa um esquema de pensamento que

   A. consiste num modo particular de interpretar a realidade
   B. é o produto de uma história nacional
   C. resulta da convivência de grupos diferentes
   D. constitui um equilíbrio temporário de forças e ideias em evolução

2. Na sua abordagem cultural, o professor deve

   A. ser politicamente neutro
   B. apresentar a sua opinião e pô-la discussão
   C. ouvir a opinião dos alunos e ser imparcial
   D. orientar a opinião dos alunos

3. Pode considerar-se que o aluno tem espírito crítico quando

   A. está sempre pronto para participar num debate
   B. discorda frequentemente do que o professor e os colegas dizem
   C. é céptico em relação a novas perspectivas e valores
   D. procura os motivos e as causas das atitudes e dos acontecimentos

4. O traço mais característico de um indivíduo crítico é ser

   A. inteligente   B. argumentativo
   C. insatisfeito   D. curioso

5. Uma atitude crítica perante um aspecto cultural

   A. é tanto uma reacção emocional   B. consiste em ultrapassar uma
      como intellectual   reacção emocional
   C. é uma reacção emocional   D. é uma reacção intelectual

6. Fazer uma abordagem crítica a um tema controverso significa

   A. identificar o que é certo   B. dinamizar uma troca de opiniões
      e o que é errado   individuais sobre esse tema
   C. focar os valores e interesses que D. chegar a um consenso
      dominam as várias perspectivas

7. Ter uma visão crítica de um país implica

   A. reconhecer os aspectos positivos   B. ser pessimista em relação
      negativos desse país   ao seu futuro
   C. exprimir desagrado sobre   D. conhecer os factores que
      a sua sociedade   explicam a sua evolução
                                            histórica

8. Assumir uma perspectiva crítica perante valores, produtos, e instituições culturais é

   A. apresentar alternatives   B. identificar os seus erros
   C. questionar os que estão   D. analisar as relações entre
      em posição de autoridade   os valores, produtos, e as
                                            instituições culturais

9. Desenvolver a consciência cultural crítica do aluno consiste em ajudá-lo a

   A. tornar-se consciente dos aspectos B. questionar as normas de 'senso
      positivos e negativos de cada   comum' que regem as nossas
      cultura   rotinas
   C. distanciar-se das culturas alvo e D. reconhecer as semelhanças e
      materna para ter mais opções   diferenças entre culturas

10. Assumir uma atitude política em relação ao ensino/aprendizagem de uma cultura estrangeira consiste em

   A. informar sobre a organização política desse(s) países
   B. estabelecer a relação entre as suas formas de poder e de produção cultural
   C. informar sobre os modelos democráticos dos países mais desenvolvidos
   D. iniciar a discussão sobre as tendências dos seus partidos políticos

11. Demonstrar preocupações éticas no processo de ensino/aprendizagem de uma cultura estrangeira é

   A. aceitar a diferença como sendo igualmente válida
   B. ser tolerante para com a diferença
   C. reconhecer o que é certo e o que é errado
   D. actuar contra a injustiça e a discriminação

SECÇÃO 3
RAZÕES PARA SE ADOPTAR UMA ABORDAGEM CRÍTICA

Nesta Secção procurar-se-á identificar as razões que justificariam uma abordagem crítica no ensino/aprendizagem da cultura estrangeira.
Escolha as 2 (DUAS) opções que lhe parecerem mais importantes de cada conjunto. <u>Em alternativa</u>, escolha apenas 1(UMA) opção e apresente outra da sua autoria. Assinale com um círculo cada letra que corresponde à(s) sua(s) opção/opções.

1. A integração europeia e a economia global têm causado maior mobilidade dos cidadãos. Por este motivo, torna-se indispensável

   A. ser eticamente responsáveis uns pelos outros e pelo planeta que partilhamos
   B. reforçar a nossa identidade nacional
   C. estar preparados para colaborar com o Outro independentemente da sua etnicidade
   D. saber perspectivar cada cultura em relação às outras
   E. ....

2. A sociedade actual caracteriza-se por uma maior convivência entre etnias, classes sociais, culturas, idades e sexos diferentes. Assim, é necessário reconhecer

   A. as estratégias de cada grupo para se posicionar dentro do tecido social

   B. a existência de diversos níveis e padrões de comunicação

   C. que todos têm o mesmo direito a ter 'voz'

   D. que cada grupo social tem um lugar próprio

   E. ....

3. A interacção de culturas diferentes tornou-se mais frequente e exige que

   A. se consiga atingir o consenso

   B. se evite o conflito

   C. se olhem as relações entre a cultura e o poder como uma questão moral e ética

   D. se forme o indivíduo para conviver com a divergência cultural

   E. ....

4. Os malentendidos entre indivíduos de culturas diferentes decorrem, muitas vezes, do facto de

   A. cada indivíduo tirar conclusões com base nos seus próprios padrões .... culturais

   B. cada indivíduo ter reacções contraditórias e inesperadas .... independentemente da cultura em que se insere

   C. os indivíduos terem preconceitos em relação ao estatuto das outras .... culturas

   D. os significados culturais e as normas sociais que condicionam a .... actividade diária serem, na sua maior parte, inconscientes

   E. ....

5. Dado que a escola promove o contacto com culturas diferentes, constitui tarefa sua preparar futuros cidadãos para

   A. o confronto de ideias e valores

   B. a colaboração e a solidariedade intercultural

   C. saber expressar a sua individualidade

   D. ser tolerante para com a diferença

   E. ....

SECÇÃO 4
CONSEQUÊNCIAS DE UMA ABORDAGEM CRÍTICA

Nesta Secção procurar-se-á identificar as possíveis implicações de uma abordagem crítica no ensino/aprendizagem da cultura estrangeira. A primeira parte é dedicada ao indivíduo e a segunda à sociedade.
Exprima a sua opinião sobre cada uma das afirmações seguintes. Assinale com um círculo a letra da sua opção:

A. SIM   B. NÃO   C. SEM OPINIÃO

4. a. para com o indivíduo

1. O exercício do espírito crítico incentiva mais a expressão da individualidade do que do grupo social .... A. B. C.
2. O desenvolvimento de uma consciência cultural crítica fortalece a identidade cultural .... A. B. C.
3. O desenvolvimento de uma consciência cultural crítica favorece o desenraízamento cultural .... A. B. C.
4. O desenvolvimento da consciência cultural crítica estimula a capacidade de decisão .... A. B. C.
5. A formação de uma atitude crítica fomenta a intervenção social .... A. B. C.
6. O desenvolvimento da consciência cultural crítica pode diminuir a auto-estima .... A. B. C.
7. O ensino/aprendizagem crítico de cultura estimula a curiosidade intelectual .... A. B. C.

4. b. para com a sociedade

1. A consciência cultural crítica acaba com as fronteiras culturais .... A. B. C.
2. Atitudes críticas dificultam o diálogo .... A. B. C.
3. O desenvolvimento de uma consciência cultural crítica encoraja o exercício empenhado da cidadania democrática .... A. B. C.
4. O desenvolvimento do espírito crítico poria em causa a obediência e a autoridade .... A. B. C.
5. A valorização de atitudes críticas poderia minar a ordem democráticas .... A. B. C.

6. O ensino/aprendizagem crítico de cultura ajuda à formação
   de uma identidade supra-nacional (europeia, global) .... A. B. C.
7. A adopção de atitudes críticas acentua o conflito nas
   relações interculturais .... A. B. C.
8. O desenvolvimento de uma consciência cultural crítica faria
   diminuir a violência .... A. B. C.
9. O ensino/aprendizagem crítico de cultura estrangeira seria
   um acto político .... A. B. C.

SECÇÃO 5
INFORMAÇÃO GERAL

Nesta Secção procurar-se-á indagar sobre alguns dados biográficos e demográficos que permitirão classificar as respostas. Assinale com um círculo as letras que correspondem ao seu caso:

I. <u>Dados biográficos</u>

1. A minha idade situa-se entre:

   A. 20–29   B. 30–39   C. 40–49   D. 50–59   E. 60–69

2. A minha formação académica é:

   A. Bacharelato   B. Licenciatura

   C. Mestrado   D. Doutoramento

3. A minha situação profissional é:

   A. Sem habilitação própria   B. Com habilitação própria

   C. Sem profissionalização   D. Com profissionalização

II. <u>Contactos com os países de língua inglesa</u>

1. Quais os países de língua inglesa que já visitou?
   ....

2. Que tipos de visita/residência foram?
   (escolha todas as hipóteses que se verificaram)

   A. Visita turística   F. Frequentei um curso

   B. Cresci no país   G. Intercâmbio de professores

   C. Visitei familiares próximos   H. Intercâmbio de alunos

   D. Visitei amigos   I. Outro trabalho no país

   E. Fiquei com desconhecidos   J. Outro (especifique) ....

3. Frequência de visitas a países de língua inglesa:
   A. mais do que duas vezes por ano
   B. duas vezes por ano
   C. uma vez por ano
   D. uma vez de dois em dois anos
   E. uma vez de cinco em cinco anos
   F. menos frequentemente
   G. nunca

4. Como obtem informação sobre os países de língua inglesa?
   (assinale todas as hipóteses que se verificam habitualmente)
   A. Rádio ou televisão portuguesas
   B. Outras rádios ou televisões estrangeiras
   C. Jornais/revistas portuguesas
   D. Jornais/revistas estrangeiras
   E. Institutos
   F. Cursos e conferências
   G. Associações profissionais
   H. Hisitas de professores/alunos desses países
   I. Contactos com falantes nativos que vivem nesses países
   J. Os meus próprios contactos no estrangeiro
   K. Outros (especifique) ....

5. Acha que, *neste país,* os professores têm oportunidades suficientes para se manterem em contacto com os países cujas língua(s) ensinam?
   A. Sim, bastante
   B. Sim, até certo ponto
   C. Não, nem por isso
   D. Não, de maneira nenhuma
   E. Não sei

III. Dados acerca da escola

1. A minha escola situa-se no
   A. norte do país   B. centro do país   C. sul do país

2. A minha escola situa-se em zona
   A. urbana   B. suburbana   C. rural   D. mista

3. Descreva com 2–6 palavras-chave o extracto social dos seus alunos:
   ....
   ....

IV. Tópicos para discussão posterior

Indique uma pergunta de cada Secção que gostaria de discutir com mais detalhe:

Secção 1: ....

Secção 2: ....

Secção 3: ....

Secção 4: ....

V. Comentário

Se o desejar, escreva um breve comentário sobre este questionário e o seu tema.

....

....

....

Estou-lhe muito grata pelo tempo e atenção que dedicou ao preenchimento deste Questionário. Obrigada!

Appendix 3
Questionário B

SECÇÃO 1
O ENSINO/APRENDIZAGEM DE CULTURA
NA AULA DE LÍNGUA ESTRANGEIRA

Mostre o grau do seu acordo/desacordo em relação a cada uma das afirmações seguintes. Assinale com um círculo a letra que corresponde à sua opção:

A. Concordo inteiramente   B. Concordo em parte   C. Estou indeciso(a)   D. Discordo em parte   E. Discordo inteiramente

1. Deveria ser dada maior relevância à dimensão cultural nas aulas de língua estrangeira

    A.   B.   C.   D.   E.

2. As identidades europeias e global devem ser fomentadas nas aulas de língua/cultura estrangeira.

    A.   B.   C.   D.   E.

3. Todas as culturas de língua inglesa espalhadas pelo mundo têm a mesma legitimidade num programa de língua inglesa.

    A.   B.   C.   D.   E.

4. O estudo de cultura nas aulas de língua tem prejudicado o aperfeiçoamento da correcção linguística.

    A.   B.   C.   D.   E.

5. A aprendizagem de uma cultura estrangeira pode mudar a atitude do aluno em relação à sua própria cultura.

    A.   B.   C.   D.   E.

Appendix 3: Questionário B 275

6. A ênfase no estudo das culturas estrangeiras contribui para o enfraquecimento da identidade cultural dos alunos.

   A.   B.   C.   D.   E.

7. O objectivo mais importante na aprendizagem das culturas estrangeiras é o de desenvolver uma atitude crítica em relação às culturas alvo e materna.

   A.   B.   C.   D.   E.

8. O desenvolvimento de uma consciência cultural crítica só deveria ser fomentado no ensino secundário.

   A.   B.   C.   D.   E.

SECÇÃO 2
A DIMENSÃO CRÍTICA DO ENSINO/APRENDIZAGEM
DE UMA CULTURA ESTRANGEIRA

Nesta Secção procurar-se-á clarificar em que consiste a dimensão crítica do ensino/aprendizagem de uma língua estrangeira.
Escolha apenas UMA das hipóteses. Opte por aquela que mais se aproxima da sua opinião. Assinale com um círculo a letra que corresponde à sua opção.

1. Cada cultura representa um esquema de pensamento que

   A. consiste num modo particular de interpretar a realidade

   B. é o produto de uma história nacional

   C. resulta da convivência de grupos diferentes

   D. constitui um equilíbrio temporário de forças e ideias em evolução

2. Na sua abordagem cultural, o professor deve

   A. ser politicamente neutro

   B. apresentar a sua opinião e pô-la discussão

   C. ouvir a opinião dos alunos e ser imparcial

   D. orientar a opinião dos alunos

3. Pode considerar-se que o aluno tem espírito crítico quando

   A. está sempre pronto para participar num debate

   B. discorda frequentemente do que o professor e os colegas dizem

   C. é céptico em relação a novas perspectivas e valores

   D. procura os motivos e as causas das atitudes e dos acontecimentos

4. O traço mais característico de um indivíduo crítico é ser
   A. inteligente
   B. argumentativo
   C. insatisfeito
   D. curioso

5. Uma atitude crítica perante um aspecto cultural
   A. é tanto uma reacção emocional como intellectual
   B. consiste em ultrapassar uma reacção emocional
   C. é uma reacção emocional
   D. é uma reacção intelectual

6. Fazer uma abordagem crítica a um tema controverso significa
   A. identificar o que é certo e o que é errado
   B. dinamizar uma troca de opiniões individuais sobre esse tema
   C. focar os valores e interesses que dominam as várias perspectivas
   D. chegar a um consenso

7. Ter uma visão crítica de um país implica
   A. reconhecer os aspectos positivos negativos desse país
   B. ser pessimista em relação ao seu futuro
   C. exprimir desagrado sobre a sua sociedade
   D. conhecer os factores que explicam a sua evolução histórica

8. Assumir uma perspectiva crítica perante valores, produtos, e instituições culturais é
   A. apresentar alternatives
   B. identificar os seus erros
   C. questionar os que estão em posição de autoridade
   D. analisar as relações entre os valores, produtos, e as instituições culturais

9. Desenvolver a consciência cultural crítica do aluno consiste em ajudá-lo a
   A. tornar-se consciente dos aspectos positivos e negativos de cada cultura
   B. questionar as normas de 'senso comum' que regem as nossas rotinas
   C. distanciar-se das culturas alvo e materna para ter mais opções
   D. reconhecer as semelhanças e diferenças entre culturas

10. Assumir uma atitude política em relação ao ensino/aprendizagem de uma cultura estrangeira consiste em
    A. informar sobre a organização política desse(s) países
    B. estabelecer a relação entre as suas formas de poder e de produção cultural

C. informar sobre os modelos democráticos dos países mais desenvolvidos

D. iniciar a discussão sobre as tendências dos seus partidos políticos

11. Demonstrar preocupações éticas no processo de ensino/aprendizagem de uma cultura estrangeira é

   A. aceitar a diferença como sendo igualmente válida

   B. ser tolerante para com a diferença

   C. reconhecer o que é certo e o que é errado

   D. actuar contra a injustiça e a discriminação

SECÇÃO 3
PROCESSOS PARA UMA ABORDAGEM CRÍTICA

Nesta Secção procurar-se-á identificar quais os processos que mais podem promover um ensino/aprendizagem crítico da cultura estrangeira.

Assinale com um círculo o número que indica a ordem de importância que atribui a cada princípio/elemento actividade na realização de uma abordagem cultural crítica (o nº 5 identificará o grau mais elevado de importância):

1. Princípios gerais da abordagem crítica a um tema cultural:

	5	4	3	2	1
A. a comunicação cultural visa atingir o consenso	5	4	3	2	1
B. a cultura está sempre em mudança	5	4	3	2	1
C. a divisão entre 'alta' cultura e cultura 'popular' está ultrapassada	5	4	3	2	1
D. as identidades culturais são contraditórias	5	4	3	2	1
E. a reflexão é um aspecto tão essencial quanto o diálogo	5	4	3	2	1

2. Para promover uma visão crítica da cultura que ensino parece-me mais importante:

A. dar informação actualizada	5	4	3	2	1
B. identificar/discutir os preconceitos presentes nos materiais	5	4	3	2	1
C. despertar a curiosidade em relação a essa cultura	5	4	3	2	1
D. identificar as relações entre as práticas, os produtos e as ideias	5	4	3	2	1
E. representar os vários grupos existentes nessa cultura	5	4	3	2	1

3. O exercício do espírito crítico depende:

A. da escolha dos materiais pedagógicos	5	4	3	2	1
B. do tipo de actividades pedagógicas	5	4	3	2	1
C. da abordagem no livro de textos	5	4	3	2	1
D. dos conteúdos do programa	5	4	3	2	1
E. da abordagem sugerida pelo professor	5	4	3	2	1

4. Qual a importância destas actividades para o desenvolvimento de uma consciência cultural crítica?

A. *Compare/contrast*	5	4	3	2	1
B. *Imagine*	5	4	3	2	1
C. *Comment*	5	4	3	2	1
D. *True/false*	5	4	3	2	1
E. *Justify*	5	4	3	2	1

5. Qual a importância destes 'processos de operacionalização' (*Programa de Inglês, Secundário, Nível de Comunicação da LE1*) na promoção de um ensino/aprendizagem crítico da cultura estrangeira?

A. colige dados	5	4	3	2	1
B. descreve	5	4	3	2	1
C. avalia	5	4	3	2	1
D. formula hipóteses	5	4	3	2	1
E. questiona	5	4	3	2	1

6. 'Interpreta criticamente padrões culturais próprios de universos diferenciados – o seu, o de outro(s), o da(s) cultura(s)-alvo' (*Programa de Inglês, Secundário, Nível de Continuação da LE1*, p. 54, sublinhado meu). Qual a importância dos seguintes processos na definição de 'Interpreta criticamente'?

A. Identifica relações de causa e efeito	5	4	3	2	1
B. Descreve factos	5	4	3	2	1
C. Reconhece aspectos negativos e positivos	5	4	3	2	1
D. Analisa semelhanças e diferenças	5	4	3	2	1
E. Colige informação	5	4	3	2	1

SECÇÃO 4
MODELOS DE FORMAÇÃO PROFISSIONAL

Nesta Secção procurar-se-à indagar sobre as necessidades de formação dos professores para a aplicação de uma abordagem crítica no ensino/aprendizagem de uma cultura estrangeira.
Mostre o grau do seu acordo/desacordo em relação a cada uma das afirmações seguintes. Assinale com um círculo a letra que corresponde à sua opção:

| A. Sim, muito | B. Sim, até certo ponto | C. Não, nem por isso | D. Não, de maneira nenhuma |

1. A minha formação académica preparou-me para fazer uma abordagem crítica da cultura.

    A.   B.   C.   D.

2. Costumo discutir o modo de desenvolver uma consciência cultural crítica nos alunos com os colegas que ensinam outras línguas estrangeiras.

    A.   B.   C.   D.

3. Na minha prática lectiva, a minha maior preocupação é executar fielmente o programa.

    A.   B.   C.   D.

4. Necessito de formação sobre o tratamento crítico da cultura nos materiais que uso.

    A.   B.   C.   D.

5. Necessito de formação sobre o modo como usar criticamente as minhas experiências pessoais da(s) culturas que ensino, para fins pedagógicos.

    A.   B.   C.   D.

6. Deveria ser dada aos professores de cultura estrangeira preparação em areas interdisciplinares relevantes para a sua actividade pedagógica.

    A.   B.   C.   D.

7. Faz parte da preparação das minhas aulas reflectir sobre quais os princípios e valores que estão subjacentes ao meu tratamento das culturas.

    A.   B.   C.   D.

8. O ensino crítico da cultura exige uma maior competência oral.

    A.   B.   C.   D.

9. O tipo de formação de que mais necessito é sobre metodologias de ensino da língua.

   A.   B.   C.   D.

10. O ensino crítico da cultura dificulta a planificação das aulas.

    A.   B.   C.   D.

11. Tenho-me orientado mais pela intuição e pelo bom-senso ao ensinar a cultura estrangeira.

    A.   B.   C.   D.

12. O factor que mais influencia o meu modo de ensinar a(s) cultura(s) estrangeira(s) são os livros de textos que estou a usar.

    A.   B.   C.   D.

13. Necessito de adquirir mais conhecimentos sobre outros países de língua inglesa para além do Reino Unido e dos Estados Unidos, para os incluir nas minhas actividades pedagógicas.

    A.   B.   C.   D.

14. Quando ensino sobre as culturas de língua inglesa, devo situá-las num contexto internacional e global.

    A.   B.   C.   D.

15. Se os cursos de formação de professores não forem seguidos de projectos bem coordenados nas escolas, não se verificarão resultados a longo prazo.

    A.   B.   C.   D.

16. Só existirão grandes mudanças na prática pedagógica quando os professors tomarem consciência das teorias que estão implícitas nas suas práticas.

    A.   B.   C.   D.

17. O professor é o agente de inovação mais importante no sistema educativo.

    A.   B.   C.   D.

SECÇÃO 5
INFORMAÇÃO GERAL

Nesta Secção procurar-se-á indagar sobre alguns dados biográficos e demográficos que permitirão classificar as respostas. Assinale com um círculo as letras que correspondem ao seu caso:

I. Dados biográficos

1. A minha idade situa-se entre:

    A. 20–29   B. 30–39   C. 40–49   D. 50–59   E. 60–69

2. A minha formação académica é:

    A. Bacharelato   B. Licenciatura
    C. Mestrado   D. Doutoramento

3. A minha situação profissional é:

    A. Sem habilitação própria B. Com habilitação própria
    C. Sem profissionalização   D. Com profissionalização

II. Contactos com os países de língua inglesa

1. Quais os países de língua inglesa que já visitou?
    ....

2. Que tipos de visita/residência foram?
    (escolha todas as hipóteses que se verificaram)

    A. Visita turística   F. Frequentei um curso
    B. Cresci no país   G. Intercâmbio de professores
    C. Visitei familiares próximos   H. Intercâmbio de alunos
    D. Visitei amigos   I. Outro trabalho no país
    E. Fiquei com desconhecidos   J. Outro (especifique) ....

3. Frequência de visitas a países de língua inglesa:

    A. mais do que duas vezes por ano   E. uma vez de cinco em cinco anos
    B. duas vezes por ano   F. menos frequentemente
    C. uma vez por ano   G. nunca
    D. uma vez de dois em dois anos

4. Como obtem informação sobre os países de língua inglesa?
   (assinale todas as hipóteses que se verificam habitualmente)

   A. Rádio ou televisão portuguesas
   B. Outras rádios ou televisões estrangeiras
   C. Jornais/revistas portuguesas
   D. Jornais/revistas estrangeiras
   E. Institutos
   F. Cursos e conferências
   G. Associações profissionais
   H. Visitas de professores/alunos desses países
   I. Contactos com falantes nativos que vivem nesses países
   J. Os meus próprios contactos no estrangeiro
   K. Outros (especifique) ....

5. Acha que, *neste país*, os professores têm oportunidades suficientes para se manterem em contacto com os países cujas língua(s) ensinam?

   A. Sim, bastante
   B. Sim, até certo ponto
   C. Não, nem por isso
   D. Não, de maneira nenhuma
   E. Não sei

III. Dados acerca da escola

1. A minha escola situa-se no

   A. norte do país   B. centro do país   C. sul do país

2. A minha escola situa-se em zona

   A. urbana   B. suburbana   C. rural   D. mista

3. Descreva com 2–6 palavras-chave o extracto social dos seus alunos:
   ....
   ....

IV. Tópicos para discussão posterior

Indique uma pergunta de cada Secção que gostaria de discutir com mais detalhe:

Secção 1: ....
Secção 2: ....
Secção 3: ....
Secção 4: ....

V. Comentário

Se o desejar, escreva um breve comentário sobre este questionário e o seu tema.

....
....
....

Estou-lhe muito grata pelo tempo e atenção que dedicou ao preenchimento deste Questionário. Obrigada!

Appendix 4
Statistical Results of Questionnaires A and B

Frequencies (percentages)

Section 1

(Questionários A and B)

	Agree strongly	Agree to some extent	Un-decided	Disagree to some extent	Disagree strongly	Total	Missing
1	27.3	43.8	6.3	16.5	4.0	97.7	2.3
2	44.9	40.3	8.0	3.4	1.1	97.7	2.3
3	21.0	33.5	8.0	23.9	12.5	98.9	1.1
4	6.8	26.1	4.5	19.9	42.0	99.4	0.6
5	43.8	40.9	3.4	5.1	6.3	99.4	0.6
6	0.6	6.8	5.7	9.1	77.3	99.4	0.6
7	35.8	34.7	6.3	12.5	10.2	99.4	0.6
8	10.2	10.2	5.7	23.9	49.4	99.4	0.6

Section 2

(Questionários A and B)

	A	B	C	D	Total	Missing
1	23.9	34.7	22.2	18.8	99.4	0.6
2	14.2	15.9	54.5	15.3	100.0	0.0
3	5.7	0.6	1.1	92.6	100.0	0.0
4	22.2	38.6	10.2	28.4	99.4	0.6
5	66.5	17.0	0.6	15.3	99.4	0.6
6	10.2	29.5	58.0	2.3	100.0	0.0
7	77.8	0.6	0.0	21.6	100.0	0.0
8	11.9	5.7	1.1	81.3	100.0	0.0
9	43.2	12.5	1.1	42.6	99.4	0.6
10	19.3	69.9	4.0	3.4	96.6	3.4
11	55.1	25.0	5.1	14.2	99.4	0.6

Section 3

(Questionário A)

	More important	Less important
1. A	32.0	68.0
1. B	34.7	65.3
1. C	50.7	49.3
1. D	50.7	49.3
2. A	20.0	80.0
2. B	61.3	38.7
2. C	78.7	21.3
2. D	22.7	77.3
3. A	20.0	80.0
3. B	30.7	69.3
3. C	32.0	68.0
3. D	94.7	5.3
4. A	80.0	20.0
4. B	5.3	94.7
4. C	84.0	16.0
4. D	14.7	85.3
5. A	29.3	70.7
5. B	74.7	24.0
5. C	25.3	74.7
5. D	58.7	41.3

Section 4

(Questionário A)

	YES	NO	No opinion	Total	Missing
4.a. 1	46.7	44.0	6.7	97.3	2.7
4.a. 2	90.7	1.3	5.3	97.3	2.7
4.a. 3	0.0	1.3	5.3	97.3	2.7
4.a. 4	82.7	2.7	12.0	97.3	2.7
4.a. 5	85.3	2.7	8.0	96.0	4.0
4.a. 6	2.7	84.0	9.3	96.0	4.0
4.a. 7	90.7	1.3	4.0	96.0	4.0
4.b. 1	17.3	62.7	16.0	96.0	4.0
4.b. 2	6.7	81.3	9.3	97.3	2.7
4.b. 3	88.0	2.7	6.7	97.3	2.7
4.b. 4	12.0	77.3	6.7	97.3	2.7
4.b. 5	2.7	81.3	12.0	96.0	4.0
4.b. 6	70.7	4.0	22.7	97.3	2.7
4.b. 7	12.0	76.0	9.3	97.3	2.7
4.b. 8	57.3	9.3	30.7	97.3	2.7
4.b. 9	21.3	53.3	20.0	94.7	5.3

SECTION 5

(Secção 3 in Questionário B)

	1	2	3	4	5	T	M
1. A.	16.8	25.7	30.7	12.9	6.9	93.1	6.9
1. B.	3.0	4.0	22.8	27.7	35.6	93.1	6.9
1. C.	15.8	24.8	23.8	11.9	16.8	93.1	6.9
1. D.	19.8	25.7	26.7	11.9	5.9	90.1	9.9
1. E.	0	0	5.9	22.8	65.3	94.1	5.9
2. A.	0	2.0	14.9	27.7	50.5	95.0	5.0
2. B.	8.9	5.9	25.7	24.8	28.7	94.1	5.9
2. C.	2.0	3.0	6.9	18.8	66.3	97.0	3.0
2. D.	8.9	11.9	16.8	24.8	29.7	92.1	7.9
2. E.	9.9	16.8	17.8	26.7	21.8	93.1	6.9
3. A.	6.9	8.9	23.8	36.6	17.8	94.1	5.9
3. B.	0	11.9	14.9	31.7	36.6	95.0	5.0
3. C.	10.9	20.8	27.7	23.8	10.9	94.1	5.9
3. D.	10.9	8.9	32.7	29.7	12.9	95.0	5.0
3. E.	2.0	3.0	12.9	23.8	54.5	96.0	4.0
4. A.	0	1.0	5.9	17.8	72.3	97.0	3.0
4. B.	6.9	22.8	25.7	26.7	11.9	94.1	5.9
4. C.	0	1.0	8.9	32.7	51.5	94.1	5.9
4. D.	25.7	22.8	33.7	9.9	3.0	95.0	5.0
4. E.	3.0	6.9	21.8	39.6	23.8	95.0	5.0
5. A.	7.9	11.9	29.7	29.7	14.9	94.1	5.9
5. B.	9.9	22.8	32.7	23.8	5.0	94.1	5.9
5. C.	6.9	4.0	10.9	27.7	43.6	93.1	6.9
5. D.	3.0	5.0	18.8	42.6	23.8	93.1	6.9
5. E.	2.0	2.0	6.9	19.8	64.4	95.0	5.0
6. A.	3.0	4.0	20.8	35.6	32.7	96.0	4.0
6. B.	21.8	21.8	26.7	20.8	5.0	96.0	4.0
6. C.	2.0	5.9	16.8	35.6	35.6	96.0	4.0
6. D.	0	3.0	7.9	31.7	54.5	97.0	3.0
6. E.	14.9	13.9	28.7	28.7	8.9	95.0	5.0

1 – Less important   5 – More important   T – Total   M – Missing

Section 6

(Secção 4 in Questionário B)

	Yes, very much	Yes, to some extent	No, not particularly	No, not at all	Total	Missing
1	6.9	56.4	31.7	5.0	100.0	0.0
2	5.0	32.7	54.5	7.9	100.0	0.0
3	0	54.5	36.6	8.9	100.0	0.0
4	11.9	64.4	18.8	3.0	98.0	2.0
5	13.9	53.5	27.7	5.0	100.0	0.0
6	47.5	50.5	0.0	2.0	100.0	0.0
7	45.5	42.6	10.9	1.0	100.0	0.0
8	35.6	40.6	16.8	6.9	100.0	0.0
9	5.0	30.7	49.5	14.9	100.0	0.0
10	1.0	28.7	40.6	29.7	100.0	0.0
11	18.8	49.5	25.7	5.9	100.0	0.0
12	3.0	30.7	47.5	18.8	100.0	0.0
13	36.6	43.6	15.8	4.0	100.0	0.0
14	50.5	43.6	4.0	1.0	99.0	1.0
15	45.5	43.6	5.9	5.0	100.0	0.0
16	28.7	44.6	21.8	4.0	99.0	1.0
17	62.4	32.7	4.0	1.0	100.0	0.0

Section 7

(Questionários A and B)

I. 1.	60–69	50–59	40–49	30–39	20–29			Total	Missing
	4.0	21.0	41.5	20.5	13.1			100.0	0.0
I. 2.	M. A.	Licenciat	B. A.						
	6.8	92.0	1.1					100.0	0.0
I. 3.	Prof.	Habil.							
	98.3	1.7						100.0	0.0
II. 3.	A.	B.	C.	D.	E.	F.	G.		
	1.1	1.7	12.5	19.9	12.5	36.9	6.3	90.9	9.1
III. 1	North	Centre	South						
	26.7	50.0	22.2						

Total number of valid respondents:

- Questionnaire A = 75
- Questionnaire B = 101

Appendix 5
Interview Guide for Focus-Groups

1. The English syllabus for secondary school education – Language 1 – includes a critical dimension in the teaching/learning of culture among its objectives and guidelines. Do you think it is important to develop a critical perspective in relation to foreign cultures?

2. Why is it important to develop critical cultural awareness among our students?
   - to reinforce our national identities?
   - to prepare our students for cultural diversity?
   - to eradicate prejudices about other cultures?

3. What makes up a culture?
   - is it the product of a national history?
   - is it a temporary balance in the social interaction of different groups?

4. What does a critical vision of a country imply?
   - the evaluation of its positive and negative aspects?
   - the analysis of the relationships between its values, products and institutions?

5. Do you think all English-speaking cultures are equally valid within an English language syllabus?

6. What is the most important element to determine a critical approach? the syllabus?
   - the textbook?
   - the teacher's/student's approach?

7. What makes an approach to culture critical?
   - it deals with/discusses the materials from multiple perspectives?
   - it encourages a balanced representation of the various cultural groups?

8. The development of critical cultural awareness
   - seems to stimulate individual expression or social intervention more?
   - can it be considered a political act?
   - can it put authority in danger?

9. Does a critical perspective towards culture make dialogue between cultures more difficult?

10. What kind of development programmes do you need in order to approach critically the foreign cultures you teach?

11. What (inter)disciplinary areas do you consider most relevant for your teaching practice?

Appendix 6
Questions for American Teacher Trainers

1. To what degree do you integrate Critical Pedagogy in your teacher preparation courses?

2. What are the challenges that you face in incorporating these concepts into your course syllabi?

3. What conflicts have you found in your attempts to add a Critical Pedagogy dimension to teaching language and culture?

4. What have been your most successful strategies for including Critical Pedagogy into your teacher education programme?

5. What have been the major outcomes (positive and negative) in terms of student–teacher attitudes and performance when you added a Critical Pedagogy dimension to your teacher preparation courses?

6. Do you have any evidence that past teachers in your programme have integrated Critical Pedagogy concepts in their teaching with their own students?

7. What are the primary factors that motivate you to strive to incorporate Critical Pedagogy in teacher preparation?

8. What role do you envision (a greater or lesser role) Critical Pedagogy to play in the future as far as teacher preparation programmes are concerned?

Index

Adorno, T.W. 3, 14-15, 24, 26, 62-66, 68-69, 93, 118-119
Agency 8-9, 12-13, 56, 115, 145, 204, 221
Apple, M. 9-12, 17, 59
Appropriation 34, 144, 146
Aronowitz, S. 4, 6, 9-11, 25, 28, 43-45, 49, 52, 58-60, 67, 94, 96, 160
Awareness 5, 14-17, 34, 36, 38-40, 42-43, 45, 48-49, 51, 54, 61, 63, 80, 83-85, 88-90, 96, 101, 108, 116, 119, 121, 132-133, 134-138, 140-143, 146-147, 149, 152, 154-155, 157, 159-160, 162, 165-166, 168, 170-172, 174, 176, 179, 181, 183, 189, 191, 195-196, 198-201, 203-204, 206, 208-211, 215, 218-219, 221-222, 224-225

Baudrillard, J. 85, 91-92, 95, 100, 102, 106-107, 112, 115-116, 118, 120
Bennett, M. 132, 134-136, 157, 182, 203
Best, S. 93-95, 114, 116
Bhabha, H. 127, 129-131
Brislin, R. 132-133, 203, 208
Byram, M. 14-15, 124-125, 129-130, 132, 141-143, 147, 151, 155-156, 159, 161-162, 166, 168-169, 175, 178-179, 182, 190-193, 195, 200, 203, 207, 212-214, 216, 223

Canagarajah, A. S. 146, 155, 177, 179, 204
Cherryholmes, C. 93, 96, 110
Conflict 12, 24, 32, 40-41, 81, 98, 114-116, 122, 130, 142, 147, 155-156, 160, 164, 199, 219
Consensus 24, 40-43, 47, 68, 70, 74-75, 77, 80, 83, 90, 98, 100, 102, 106, 114, 118, 139, 154, 163, 173, 208, 209, 219
Critical cultural awareness 14-17, 39-40, 42-43, 49, 54, 61, 63, 84, 88-90, 108, 119, 121, 132, 141-143, 154, 160, 162, 168, 172, 174, 176, 181, 189, 195-196, 198-201, 203-204, 206, 209-211, 219, 222, 224, 225
Critical intercultural speaker 126-127, 129-130, 151, 167, 206
Critical reflection 27-29, 35-42, 47, 53, 61, 89, 118, 122, 196
Cultural politics 17-18, 20-22, 24, 26-27, 31, 34, 56, 114-115, 117, 145, 155-159, 188, 198, 204
Cultural Studies
– and agency 188-189, 201-202
– and critical theory 84-85
– and interdisciplinarity 26-27, 92, 208-214
– and postmodernism 25-26, 94-95, 103, 107, 117
Culture industry 3, 15, 24, 85, 88, 128, 197

Derrida, J. 62, 64, 67, 81, 92, 94-96, 100, 103-106, 113-114, 116, 131
Dewey, J. 4, 14, 22, 27-31, 35-38, 46, 53, 60, 94-96
Difference 2, 14, 17, 21, 25-26, 31, 40-46, 48-51, 55, 58, 61, 63, 90, 95, 101, 103, 105-106, 109, 110-112, 114-115, 117-118, 127, 129-130, 132-136, 139, 142, 146-147, 151-152, 161, 164, 179, 182-183, 189, 192, 197, 199, 204, 207-209, 217-218, 221
Differentiation 92-93, 98, 105, 111, 119, 138
Dissent 14, 17, 40-43, 46-48, 61, 77, 93, 106, 113, 118, 208-209, 217-218, 221-222

Eagleton, T. 80, 87

Index

Education for democratic citizenship 19, 29-31, 34, 45-47, 50-51, 55, 72, 113-116, 159-167, 198-201, 207-208
Emancipation 5, 23-24, 28, 31, 40, 49, 57, 64, 67-68, 79, 81, 83, 86, 89, 98-99, 101, 115, 125, 208-209, 219
Emotion 37, 39-40, 55-56, 81, 109, 113, 117, 122, 133, 140, 159, 184-185, 204, 219
Empowerment 1, 14, 17, 20, 32, 48, 49-51, 61, 108, 145, 167, 217-218, 222
Ethics 10, 18-19, 30, 34, 38, 40, 46, 114, 167, 188
Ethnicity 8, 16, 19, 25-26, 43-44, 50, 62, 69, 92, 98-99, 109, 118, 125-129, 156-158, 161, 163, 166-167, 194
Ethnocentrism 138, 224
Ethnography 139, 210, 214
Experiential learning 27-31, 39, 53, 131, 141-144, 149, 151, 166, 191-192, 203, 214-216, 226
Eurocentrism 6, 23, 43, 79, 84, 131, 145, 176, 204

Fairclough, N. 112
Fantini, A.E. 147, 152, 215
Featherstone, M. 90-91, 96, 127-128
Foreign language/culture education
– and eurocentrism 176-177, 204
– and popular culture 27, 45, 88
– and value judgement 178-184, 187, 192
Foucault, M. 41-42, 49-51, 67, 92, 95-96, 107-108, 114, 120, 144, 156
Freire, P. 4, 8, 14, 19-23, 28-29, 31-39, 46, 53, 55-61, 66-67, 83-84, 145, 159, 190, 195, 218
Fullan, M. 2-3, 60

Gadotti, M. 4, 47, 53
Giddens, A. 62, 65, 72, 97, 102, 105, 119-120, 162
Giroux, H. 2, 4, 6-11, 14, 18-21, 24-31, 33-34, 36-41, 43-47, 49-52, 54-55, 57-60, 62, 88, 94, 96, 119, 125, 144, 159-160, 190, 195, 212, 217
Globalisation 1, 3, 16, 23, 42-43, 54, 56, 92, 98, 102, 107-108, 110-111, 115, 127-128, 130, 144-145, 157-163, 165-167, 170, 176, 191-192, 195-196, 200-201, 203-204, 207-208, 221, 224-225
Global education 34, 43-46, 54-57, 118, 127-130, 176, 200
Gramsci, A. 10, 24, 33, 86-87, 98
Grossberg, L. 26-27, 111, 115, 157
Guilherme, M. 12, 207-208, 214

Habermas, J. 14, 24, 35, 37, 40, 43, 49, 53, 57, 62-64, 66-85, 87, 89, 90, 92-95, 102, 109, 118-120, 125, 131, 162, 163
Hall, E.T. 132
Hall, S. 16, 125-127, 164
Hampden-Turner, C. 134
Hegemony 10, 40, 42, 52, 86-87, 91, 93, 98, 111
Hidden curriculum 9-10
Horkheimer, M. 3, 14-15, 24, 41, 62-69, 83, 85-86, 93, 118-119
Human Rights 19, 22-23, 33, 72, 161, 165-166, 207-209, 218, 222, 225
Human Rights education 22, 43, 72, 188-189, 199, 207-208
Humanitarianism 8, 20, 47, 169
Hybridity 44, 111, 119, 127-128

Identity 25, 39-40, 43-45, 50, 62, 70-71, 79, 80, 82-83, 86, 89, 96, 110-113, 115, 119-120, 124-126, 131-132, 135, 145, 157, 160, 165-167, 170-171, 174, 176, 190, 192, 196-198, 200, 204, 207, 211, 213, 218, 224
Ideology 38-39, 62, 80-81, 87, 155
Indoctrination 21, 33, 162
(In)equality 10, 19, 23, 40, 49, 64, 67, 86, 92-93, 98-99, 106, 113-114, 188-189, 207-209
Interdisciplinarity 16, 26-27, 62, 84-85, 92, 118, 132, 137-138, 176, 208-211, 223, 225
(Inter)subjectivity(ies) 25, 50, 67, 70, 80, 83, 89, 119, 125, 178

Kanpol, B. 4, 6-7, 25, 28-29, 31, 51, 60
Kellner, D. 93-95, 114, 116
Kramsch, C. 15, 124-125, 131-132, 139-141, 147, 175, 178-179, 182, 190-191, 201, 203, 213, 226

Lange, D. 151-153
Lyotard, J. F. 81, 90-96, 98-99, 101-103, 112, 114

Mass media 25, 41, 51-52, 63, 83, 87, 94, 99, 107, 112, 116, 118, 127-128, 130, 152, 160, 166, 186, 191, 210-211, 223
McLaren, P. 3-4, 6-7, 10, 17-19, 25, 46, 60, 62, 157-158
Mouffe, C. 41, 95, 113-114, 162-165

Nationality 44, 62, 126

Pennycook, A. 15, 17, 132, 144-145, 155, 175, 177, 179, 204, 219
Phillipson, R. 144-145
Phipps, A. 39, 223-224
Popular culture 18, 24-26, 85, 88, 92, 117-118, 122, 211-212
Postcolonialism 25-26, 43, 92, 126-127, 144-145, 171, 204
Postindustrialism 1, 25, 92, 106, 110, 118, 128
Praxis 22, 27, 32, 37-38, 52-53, 114, 145, 159, 215, 222, 224, 226
Prejudice 78, 85, 126, 129, 151, 160, 192-195
Putnam, H. 93, 109

Race 11, 25, 26, 32, 44, 50, 56, 62, 69, 109, 130, 136, 157, 211
Racism 113, 128, 157, 177
Risager, K. 124, 126, 128-129, 216
Roberts, C. 214, 216
Robertson, R. 102, 128

Rorty, R. 30, 81, 94-96, 100, 109

Seelye, H.N. 132, 137, 203
Self-esteem 195-196, 258
Solidarity 15, 19, 26, 41, 43, 95, 99-100, 109-110, 116-117, 124, 126, 131, 159, 165, 193, 208-209
Soysal, Y. 113, 126, 163-164
Stereotype 99, 126, 137, 151, 186, 213

Teacher education 144, 189, 209, 212-217, 219, 223, 226, 262-263
Teachers' roles 2-3, 22, 26-27, 30, 32-33, 36, 45, 47-48, 51-52, 60, 159, 175, 178, 186-188, 190-191, 195-196, 206-207
Technology 4, 82, 85, 87, 107, 127, 153-154, 160
Theory and Practice 21, 24, 27, 28, 32, 37, 41-42, 52-55, 59-60, 62, 68, 70, 73, 118, 154, 159, 215, 222
Trompenaars, F. 134
Truth 6, 8, 28, 35, 41-42, 47-48, 67, 71, 74-77, 95, 99-101, 104, 108, 116-117, 125, 196

(Un)consciousness 29, 35-37, 40, 50, 52, 66-67, 69-70, 78, 80, 82-84, 87, 103, 133-134, 142, 155-157, 182, 203

Voice 1, 22, 25, 32-33, 39-41, 50-52, 58, 61, 77-78, 81, 112, 122, 144, 145, 157-158, 170, 175, 187, 193-194, 197, 202, 219

Wink, J. 6, 19-20, 36, 48, 54, 59
Wittgenstein, L. 73, 94-95, 100, 117

For Product Safety Concerns and Information please contact our EU Authorised Representative:

Easy Access System Europe

Mustamäe tee 50

10621 Tallinn

Estonia

gpsr.requests@easproject.com

www.ingramcontent.com/pod-product-compliance
Lightning Source LLC
Chambersburg PA
CBHW050323020526
44117CB00031B/1604